# Contents at a Glance

# Table of Contents

# Introduction

I t is interesting that for over 150 years, in times of controversy, public discourse has always turned to the Civil War. Everyone, it seems, is compelled to return to the war to highlight some aspect of an argument. This should not be surprising because the Civil War created the modern United States and defined the people who called themselves Americans. The war was a fundamental watershed in our history — marked by a staggering cost of 620,000 Union and Confederate casualties and 50,000 civilian deaths — defining both who we are as a nation and who we are as Americans. It is therefore natural that we continue to return to the war as a starting point for any discussion today about what America is and what America means.

The Civil War is still very much with us for a number of reasons. America's Civil War has epic dimensions, equal to Homer's *Iliad* or Virgil's *Aeneid*. Like any great epic, it has all the elements of tragedy and pathos; it has immortal heroes who control the destinies of nations. There are great battles on land and sea that stir deep emotions. The experiences of Army of the Potomac, the Army of Northern Virginia, the Army of the Cumberland, and the Army of the Tennessee marching across a vast landscape, each composed of free and self-reliant Americans joined together to strive in a common cause, surpasses Xenophon's account of the Greek army in *Anabasis*.

This was a war that consumed the vital energies of an entire continent. We are still very much aware of the human dimension of the war: The passions, the sorrows, the hopes, joys, and despair are ingrained in the American collective memory and are still relived as we venture back in time. The political dimension drove every aspect of the war and served as the ultimate arbiter of victory or defeat. It was highly complex, forcing political leaders to make exceptionally difficult decisions and to take extraordinary risks. Like all political enterprises, it had its knaves and fools as well as its more noble proponents. The military dimension included supplying the armies, providing the manpower to fill the ranks, and identifying a strategy that would ensure victory. The economic dimension involved retooling existing industries to support war production, inventing new methods, and applying innovative solutions. The diplomatic dimension was a critical battleground in itself as both the Union and the Confederacy sought to engage the European powers, with the Confederacy seeking recognition and military intervention that would assure independence, while the Union sought to deter and dissuade the temptations of any European power to intervene.

Many books have been written about each of these dimensions, but it is the whole story that continues to attract us and continues to fascinate us. Once you enter into the subject, you are suddenly surrounded with all of its various aspects, all of its emotional power, and all of its often opaque meaning. Trying to sort the story out — to make it meaningful and worthwhile in answering important questions in our own time — is the purpose of this book. By telling the story as completely and succinctly as possible, while keeping everything in perspective, will help you, the reader, to gain a fuller understanding of this critical event in our history and attain a more complete perspective on the larger meaning of past events that continue to shape our destinies as Americans.

# About This Book

The average person with more than a passing interest in the war has no place to go to gain a broad, general understanding of this crucial period in our history.

This book is intended to meet the needs of the average reader who wants to be informed without being overwhelmed with details. This book is directed toward several types of readers:

>> **First,** the person who desires accurate, easily accessible information about the major events and issues of the Civil War without encountering intimidating historical narrative or ponderous military interpretation

>> **Second,** the person who may want a refresher on the major events of the war, but who does not want to struggle through the tomes of scholars or arcane minutiae of Civil War fanatics

>> **Third,** those who are looking for a fun, how-to approach to exploring Civil War battlefields to learn more about the events directly by visiting these sites in order to enhance their appreciation and understanding of the events that took place there

The past appears remote and inaccessible to most people. The main message of this book is that history is most emphatically neither remote nor inaccessible! Politics, passions, and conflict (both armed and ideological) have always marked U.S. history. You will find similarities to the current day in the events of the past. In this way, history in the proper context can connect you to the past.

History doesn't have to be boring or intimidating. Everyone who hates history books will say that they are nothing more than dry lists of names and places and dates and jargon. That's true enough, in most cases, if you only look that far. Although this is a different kind of history book, it does follow certain conventions found in most history books. This one, like most, is arranged chronologically. Like most history books, too, it tells a story, which has a beginning, a middle, and an end. What is *different* about this book is that you can start wherever you like. You don't need to slog through the whole thing from beginning to end to understand what is going on. It is organized so that you, the reader, have maximum flexibility to pick and choose what you want to know. You can jump in at any point and still keep up with the story or select a topic to read in a chapter that interests you. Wherever necessary, terms will be defined for you, or referenced elsewhere for a detailed explanation. Obviously, names, dates, and places are here too, but they are located where you can refer to them if you need to or find them easily if you want.

## What Not to Read

Throughout the book you will find text in shaded boxes. These are the nice-to-know, gee whiz!, how about that? bits of information that many Civil War enthusiasts know. These offerings will help make you knowledgeable in conversation and mark you as someone who is not a complete novice.

## Foolish Assumptions

What is assumed about this book is that it is easy to read and will hold your interest enough to generate some thinking on your own.

# Icons Used in this Book

You will find five icons scattered throughout the chapters. These little pictures next to the text get your attention and point you to useful information:

**KEY PLAYERS**

>> **Key Players:** Seems obvious, but to help you along, some individuals will be highlighted for their actions or decisions. It will work both ways: Some individuals will be singled out for good reasons, others for not so good reasons.

**REMEMBER**

>> **Remember:** A key fact that is worth paying attention to for better understanding or some additional interesting details.

**TECHNICAL STUFF**

>> **Technical Stuff:** These are military terms you may not be familiar with.

**TIP**

>> **Tip:** This relates to battlefield visits and points out a good idea or the best way to do something to make your visit more enjoyable and useful.

**TURNING POINT**

>> **Turning Point:** A turning point is a particularly important action that creates significant changes in the outcome of an event. Watch how the cumulative effects of these turning points shape the outcome of the Civil War.

# Beyond the Book

You will have free access to the Cheat Sheet by going to the website Dummies.com and typing in "American Civil War Cheat Sheet" in the search box. It will have loads of facts and general information to help you prepare for travel to a battlefield or, because everyone has an opinion or point of view about the Civil War, it will give you a quick checklist to engage in a discussion about various aspects of the war.

# Where to Go from Here

The book itself covers a span of about 15 years, from 1850 to 1865. That time span may seem short, especially for a history book, but these 15 years were as important as any in American history. To help you understand *why*, the book is organized into seven parts, each dealing with a major theme of the war. The chapters within the parts are organized to take you through the major events of the Civil War, highlighting important facts and points of interest. Each chapter will acquaint you with words and ideas that are important to the entire story. At the end of each section, you'll find a summary of major points (just to make sure you didn't miss anything important, or if you skipped through a few chapters) to help you along. There is so much to learn — enjoy the journey!

# 1

# The War and Its Causes

# Chapter **1**

# How Did the War Happen?

Since the founding of the United States, different sections of the country had interests and priorities that competed with the interests and priorities of other sections. These conflicts had always been resolved through politics (usually some form of congressional dealmaking).

However, beginning in the 1850s, the political process for resolving these disputes became less and less effective. The differences between sections of the country were so great at that time that the survival of the union of states was in danger. Peace depended upon compromise and conciliation between congressional leaders representing each section. This chapter examines the sectional differences between the North and South that led to such a dangerous situation and provides some background to the controversies that led to the Civil War.

## The Big Picture: War and Politics

Wars have many causes. No one should ever forget that wars are fought for political reasons and objectives. Essentially, people or nations go to war to protect a vital interest, to defend territory from an aggressor, or to achieve a moral purpose (such as defending the innocent and punishing an evil). The Civil War included all of these rationales. Each side used all three justifications for fighting the other during the four years of war. And, interestingly enough, each side had a strong, valid, substantial reason for doing so.

## What's a civil war?

**TECHNICAL STUFF**

You hear the word *civil* in such terms as *civil rights, civilian,* and *civil liberty.* All are related to the concept of a common citizen, a member of society, and a state. So, a *civil war* is a war between citizens representing different groups or sections of the same country. Civil wars are unique in the history of war and usually are quite difficult to start. People have to be pretty angry and threatened to take this kind of drastic step. But when issues of survival are at stake between the opposing groups, violence can escalate quickly. After it does start, though, a civil war is quite bloody, often extreme, and very hard to end.

## The setting: 1850–1860

To understand the causes of the Civil War, you must be aware of some important events in American history — from roughly 1850 (the Missouri Compromise) to 1860 (the election of Abraham Lincoln) — that culminated in the secession of seven Southern states. These are milestones that will illustrate how specific events during this decade raised fears and created perceptions that made Americans so angry at their countrymen that they were willing to kill each other as a result.

### WHAT DO I MEAN BY NORTH AND SOUTH?

To keep things clear, here is what this book means when speaking of North and South in regional or sectional terms:

- The North consists of the Midwest states of Minnesota, Iowa, Wisconsin, Illinois, Indiana, Ohio, and Michigan. The Middle States were Pennsylvania, New Jersey, and New York. The New England states were Maine, New Hampshire, Vermont, Massachusetts, Rhode Island, and Connecticut. In 1860 the population of the North was a little over 18 million people.

- The South consists of the six states of the upper South: North Carolina, Virginia, Tennessee, Kentucky, Maryland, and Delaware, and the eight states of the lower South (Alabama, Georgia, South Carolina, Florida, Louisiana, Missouri, Texas, and Arkansas). In 1860 the total white population was slightly over 8 million, with over 3.9 million slaves.

# The North and South: Two Different Worlds

Until the expansion of the population into the rich lands of the lower South, in the first decade of the 19th century, slavery had been a dying institution. The North had slaves but freed most of them (except New Jersey) because the institution was too expensive and too inefficient to maintain. In the South, too, slavery was viewed as an institution that had no future. But this all changed with the industrial revolution that swept Europe and the states of the North. Textiles were the dominant product of new factories, which depended on enormous quantities of a raw material — cotton. As the demand for cotton rose on the world market, Americans began to look for opportunities to profit by getting in at the entry level. This meant putting as much land into cotton production as possible. The expansion of the frontier into the lower South and across the Mississippi River where the soil was rich and the weather ideal for growing cotton led many Americans to settle in this vast open region to stake their fortunes and achieve the American dream of independence and wealth. Mississippi, Alabama, Louisiana, and Arkansas rapidly became states between 1812 and 1836, even as the states of Ohio, Indiana, Illinois, and Michigan in the Midwest were added to the Union. Great fortunes were made and the U.S. economy thrived with the export of cotton to European (and Northern) factories between 1820 and 1860.

In theory, making a profit from cotton was easy to do, and the more land you put into production, the more profit you made. The invention of the cotton gin, a ridiculously simple machine that easily separated seeds from the cotton boll, allowed raw cotton to be processed in unlimited quantities. The growing and harvesting of cotton, however, required the labor of many people. From the time the seed is put into the ground until the time the cotton boll is picked, run through a gin, and baled, the crop required almost constant attention. To produce any sizable cotton crop, a large pool of labor available year-round was essential. Slaves, once seen as an unnecessary burden, now became the essential source of labor in the rapidly expanding cotton economy. Slaves, who had largely populated the coastal states of the South, were now imported into the interior to work in the cotton fields. Competition for acquiring labor made slaves more and more valuable. As prices rose, fewer and fewer people could afford to own them.

By the 1850s, cotton was the raw material that powered the world economy and slavery was the engine. Whoever could put the most land into production, plowing the profits into more land and more slaves, would reap enormous profits. Slave owning became the road to status and success for all ambitious Southerners, including free Blacks and Indians. A small farmer, if he was so inclined (and many were not), could make enough money from a small cotton farm to buy one or two slaves. With this extra manpower, he could put more land into production, make more profit in the booming cotton market, and buy more slaves. With 20 slaves, he could become a planter, and rise to social and political influence. The father of Jefferson Davis, the future president of the Confederacy, began this way and became one of the richest and most powerful men in Mississippi.

TECHNICAL
STUFF

Of the 1.4 million white families in the South in 1860, there were only 383,000 slaveholders. Only 46,000 planters owned 20 slaves, fewer than 3,000 owned 100 or more slaves, and only 12 Southerners owned 500 or more slaves. One individual owned 1,000 slaves. He was the richest man on the planet. Thus, only a tiny minority of people owned slaves in the South.

The rarified air of highly sophisticated historical minds harbors many intricate pet theories to account for the South's connection with slavery, but let's keep it simple. Wealthy slave owners were men of high social status and held political power. They were the ones who ran the state legislatures and elected men of their kind to Congress. Not surprisingly, they enjoyed great influence over Southern society and their attachment to, and defense of, slavery represented a broad consensus. Although Southern society was highly stratified, there was — in the often rough and violent Southern frontier, regardless of social position or wealth — a sense of rough equality where a white man demanded equal treatment and respect from other white men. Because it was an integral part of the landscape of the South, the institution of slavery bound slaveholders and non-slaveholders together politically, culturally, and economically. When questions arose about the future direction of the country after the Mexican-American War, slaveholders and non-slaveholders, sharing the same outlook and interests, united to defend the institution to prevent any limitation.

The North, during this same time period, was setting the stage for the industrial revolution that would transform the nation in the next hundred years. Technology harnessed to both agriculture and industry, plus a huge influx of immigrants to serve as a ready labor force, created a new dynamic economy. Textile mills (run on Southern cotton), steam engines, railroads and canals, and iron and steel factories came to dominate the landscape of New England, Pennsylvania, and Ohio. In 1860, the North held about 140,000 factories, which employed nearly a million and a half workers, who produced almost $2 billion worth of goods. New cities in the northwest such as Pittsburgh, Cincinnati, Chicago, Buffalo, Cleveland, Detroit, and Milwaukee became the engines of change in the national economy. St. Louis and New Orleans became the centers of a dynamic interregional trade. Within this atmosphere of economic change and readjustment between 1850 and 1860, the North and South were becoming more disparate, confidently moving, it seemed, in two different directions.

# The Opposing Sides

The North and the South agreed on one thing: that the future of America lay in the vast open territory of the West. The troubling question was which section of the country would determine the nation's destiny? Most of this territory had been won from Mexico after the Mexican-American War in 1846, and Northerners and Southerners disagreed over the future organization of this territory into states. The road to war began with a political struggle between the North and the South over how the western territories would be organized into states and enter the Union. This political struggle had its origins in the extensive social changes influencing the North after 1830. A religious revival known as the Second Great Awakening swept from New England into the new states of the Midwest with a message of moral revival and striving for individual perfection. Adherents believed that not only should men and women seek spiritual and personal purity through hard work and personal rectitude, but the whole of society must also be purged of unwholesome elements. Two of the most prominent threats to achieving this perfection in society were the moral evils of liquor and of slavery. Prohibition movements sprang up throughout the North, as did a movement to abolish slavery. Although these movements were not entirely popular in the North, they gained wider and deeper influence in the realm of politics.

Another powerful idea that shaped attitudes of Northerners was the notion of free labor. The future of America was a land of free white men who would move west and build happy and prosperous lives from their own efforts. This powerful vision also gained influence within Northern political circles, even to the extent of creating a new sectional political party, the Free Soil Party. Increasingly, the South was perceived as being a barrier to the limitless potential that a morally perfect country of free individuals could enjoy. Many in the North perceived Southerners as morally unfit, tainted by slavery, an institution that degraded small farmer and planter alike, making them listless, dull-witted, cruel, and violent. For Southerners, the writing was on the wall. In their vision of the future of America, the prosperity of the cotton economy would naturally expand westward. Cotton depleted the soil, requiring expansion westward to put more land into production. Without this expansion, the Southern economy would be condemned to a slow death. Of course, the westward expansion of the cotton economy meant that Southerners expected to bring slaves into the new territories.

**TECHNICAL STUFF**

*Free labor* became the catchphrase that heightened political divisions in the country. Only free (not slave) men could ensure a golden future for America. By extension, this meant that slave labor was neither legitimate nor welcome in the great West. Slavery, therefore, had to be limited and eventually destroyed if America was to fulfill its destiny. This concept had nothing to do with the status of Black men — free or otherwise — they had no place in this vision of the future. Southerners, hearing this message, and sensing that it was gaining political momentum, quickly recognized the threat to their own future in America, a place where the free labor advocates said they had no part to play.

## WILMOT'S PROVISO

The Wilmot Proviso was a resolution made by an obscure Pennsylvania Congressman, David Wilmot, who, in 1846, attached the *proviso* (a conditional clause inserted into legislation or a contract) to an appropriations bill. Wilmot's proviso stated that any territory acquired in the war with Mexico would not be open to slavery. The bill passed the House of Representatives, where the North had a majority, but it died in the Senate, where the South held the balance of power. The controversy over the Wilmot Proviso illustrated to both sections how important political control in Congress was to furthering their interests. The proviso became the basis of the increasingly bitter political struggle throughout the 1850s.

The political battle lines were drawn in 1846 with the Wilmot Proviso, which reflected the increasingly dominant opinions of Northerners who desired to bring about their vision of the future. It declared that any territory obtained from Mexico would be closed to slavery. The voices of an increasingly vocal and influential group of New England and Midwest *abolitionists* demanded a final reckoning with the South. The abolitionists felt that containing slavery only to where it currently existed (so that it would eventually die out) was a step in the right direction, but the only solution was destroying the institution altogether. As long as slavery existed, they believed, the future health of the republic was in danger. Allowing slavery to expand into the new territories would only lengthen the life of the institution, and in the end it would destroy the democratic base upon which the nation had been founded. Abolitionists and their supporters spoke darkly of the "slave power," a tyrannical, satanic entity in the South that sought to undermine and overwhelm the North. Southerners responded by loudly defending slavery as a positive good, benefitting both masters and slaves alike.

# Playing a Part in the Controversy: The Constitution

Since the founding of the United States, the South had maintained a strong hold on political power of the country. This situation often insulated the South and kept the slavery question out of the national dialogue, while also allowing Southern leaders to shape the national agenda. Over time, however, the growing population (nearly half of which lived across the Appalachian Mountains in 1860) gave Northern states proportionately more representatives in the House of Representatives. In addition, between 1846 and 1855, three million immigrants came to America; nearly 90 percent of them settled in states that did not have slaves. By this time, the balance of power had slipped away permanently from the South in the House of Representatives.

TECHNICAL STUFF

As stated in the Constitution, seats in the House of Representatives are apportioned by population. Prior to the Civil War, slaves were considered three-fifths of a person in determining total population of a state. Why three-fifths of a person? In the 1780s, the total white and Black population of the South outnumbered Northern whites, which meant that the South would essentially always have a permanent majority in the House of Representatives. To prevent this, Northerners claimed that Blacks should not be counted. Southerners would not accept this idea because, without the Black population being counted in some way, *they* would become the permanent minority in the House of Representatives. Eventually, the North and South compromised by deciding to count Blacks as three-fifths of a person for determining representation in the House (Article I, Section 2, of the Constitution — later amended after the war). This early effort at balancing power only highlighted the essential and fatal dichotomy of the institution of slavery. Slaves were considered both property *and* people in this section of the Constitution, but in reality, they could only be one or the other.

# Struggling for Power

Southerners sought to preserve the political status quo. By the 1850s the Senate became the only legislative body on which the South could rely to maintain a balance of power. Because every state had two senators, regardless of population (so says Article II, Section 3, of the Constitution), Southern senators could block anti-slavery legislation coming from the Northern majority in the House of Representatives. Increasingly, bills were introduced into the House proposing all sorts of measures to end slavery or limit its expansion any further. So, for the ten years between 1850 and 1860, the North and the South waged a political struggle to gain an advantage or maintain the current balance of power by bringing in new states allied with one region or the other.

## Amassing states: The political stakes involved

The political stakes were high for both sides (something like the end of a Monopoly game): Whoever had the most states at the end of the contest would have a majority of representatives in the House of Representatives *and* the Senate. Whichever side could do this could dictate the agenda for the country and determine the nation's future. For the South, political power meant ironclad protection for slavery and the agrarian way of life. For the North, gaining control of the country meant securing progress and prosperity through an urban-industrial-agricultural alliance based on free labor. As the differences between the sections sharpened, neither side believed it could afford to give up power or control.

As long as the number of states in the Union remained the same, there would always be a relative balance between slave and non-slave (free) states. As the population of the United States moved westward and unsettled territories filled with people, however, new states were being created and admitted into the Union. The existence of these new states raised the political stakes. The focus of sectional conflict soon rested on determining which new states would be admitted as either a slave or a free state, while also maintaining the equal balance between slave and free states. It was a daunting political problem.

## Entering the Union: The politics of compromise, 1850

As new settlers poured into California seeking gold in 1849, the debate began in Congress over how the new state should enter the Union. At this time, Congress was equally balanced in representation between slave and non-slave states. Thirty years earlier, Congress had avoided a crisis by admitting two states, one allowing slavery (Missouri) and one without slavery (Maine). However, in this instance, California's admission as a new state would tip the balance of power in favor of one region or another, most likely for the North, adding more members in the House and further building the Northern majority there, while also adding two senators, which would likely give the North control of the Senate.

# California: The Compromise of 1850

The original outline of the compromise surrounding California's admission was the product of three political giants of their time — Daniel Webster of Massachusetts, Henry Clay of Kentucky, and John C. Calhoun of South Carolina.

Under the compromise, California entered the Union as a free state (no slavery allowed). This pleased Northerners, but they were shocked to find that California's elected representatives supported the South. The compromise also allowed the territories of Utah and New Mexico to be organized as states in the future with or without slavery, depending on what the state constitution said. The South, initially pleased, soon discovered that very few people, let alone slaves, were entering into these territories, certainly not enough to organize either one as a state for some time. Eventually, both territories did allow slavery to exist, but did so on the brink of war in 1860.

# The Fugitive Slave Law

For Southerners to accept California as a free state with its potential shift of power to the North, the Congress took action to involve more Americans in sustaining the institution of slavery. The Fugitive Slave Law mandated that states return fugitive slaves to their owners. The law gave federal officers the power to capture suspected fugitive slaves and provided severe penalties for those who harbored or protected a fugitive slave. At the time, the Fugitive Slave Law was seen as a throwaway concession to the South, but it was extremely unpopular in the North because many citizens viewed the arbitrary seizure of an individual by federal law enforcement as a violation of basic individual rights and a threatening symbol of the slave power's evil influence on freedom in America. Federal officers attempting to arrest or transfer suspected fugitive slaves (this meant virtually any Black person — there was no way to determine who was legally free and who was not) were often met with violent resistance from citizens. The law simply could not be enforced, leading Southerners to decry the lawlessness of mob rule in the North.

# D.C. is free

The last part of the compromise was largely symbolic, a throwaway concession to Northerners who were offended that slavery existed within the District of Columbia, an area under federal control. A new law mandated that slaves could not be brought into the District of Columbia to be bought or sold. On the surface, this appeared to be a clear moral victory for antislavery activists. The fine print, however, revealed that slaves already within the District of Columbia could continue to be bought and sold.

# What did the compromise do?

The compromise gave each section what appeared to be a temporary advantage, and provided the nation with a politically acceptable, if temporary, solution to the dangerously divisive issue of slavery in the new territories of the West. In the long run, however, the Compromise of 1850 really accomplished very little, except to frustrate everyone and whet appetites for another confrontation — with the intention to settle old political scores and win a decisive victory to settle the question of the future of the United States once and for all.

Chapter **2**

# The Five Steps to War: 1850–1860

Throughout the 1850s, the North and South continued to diverge along economic, political, and social lines. They knew less and less about each other, and each came to believe the worst about the other side. In fact, by this time, many Northerners and Southerners viewed each other as a separate people. National consensus and compromise became impossible to achieve.

The differences between the North and South became more pronounced in this decade because neither the Congress, nor the Supreme Court, nor the president could deal effectively with the divisive issue of slavery. Events pulled both the sections, the North and South, closer to the belief that only drastic action would resolve the nation's problems.

## Setting the Stage: Five Events Leading to War

When you examine the nature of the political struggle between 1850 and 1860, you can identify five separate events, each having a distinct effect on the nation. When viewed separately, they don't seem to amount to much, but in the climate of the times, each event had a cumulative effect on the other, building a sense of nearly unbearable crisis and tension within the population that could not find release. The threat of open conflict, unthinkable in the country in 1850, became almost a predetermined conclusion by 1860.

One of the good and useful things about history is that it grants people the ability to look at events in the past, separated by time from the passions and confusion of the day-to-day events, and see how events connect in the long term. In doing this, certain events serve as guideposts to understanding how such a dramatic event as a civil war occurred. For your enjoyment and edification, the decade from 1850 to 1860 can be evaluated in terms of five steps that led to war:

>> The struggle for Kansas

>> The rise of the Republican Party

>> The Dred Scott decision

>> John Brown's raid

>> The election of Abraham Lincoln

This chapter examines each one of these points in detail, then puts them all together to provide a backdrop for the growing sense of crisis that finally led to war.

# Struggling for Kansas

As settlers continued to move into new territory, Congress was forced to deal with maintaining a balance of power between the Northern and Southern states. One approach had worked fairly well since 1820 — drawing a geographical boundary line (no slaves north of 36 degrees, 30 minutes latitude — basically the border between Missouri and Arkansas) that extended to the Pacific. This was known as the Missouri Compromise line. It worked because states could enter the Union in pairs: one above and one below the line (Maine-Missouri; Arkansas-Michigan; Florida and Texas-Iowa and Wisconsin). Most of these new Northern states (except Iowa) came from territory that had outlawed slavery in 1787. Because the rich lands of the new Southern states were ideal for growing cotton and other profitable crops, slavery followed the opening of these new states, allowing for an acceptable balance of power in the Congress.

Slavery, as an issue, did not move to the forefront of the national consciousness until after the Mexican-American War. By 1850, everything had changed (see Chapter 1). Faced now with a major crisis over the balance of power, Congress made an exception to the 1820 geographical boundary by admitting California as a free state, but remained faithful to the boundary line with the disposition of New Mexico territory as a way to mollify Southern fears. Yet shortly thereafter, the future of the Kansas-Nebraska territory posed another threat. All of that territory was above the 1820 geographical boundary, and therefore, technically, non-slave territory. The South couldn't allow that to happen unless two new slave states could also be added to balance power, which didn't look likely to happen in the near future. The territory north of the Missouri Compromise line was attractive farmland; in contrast, the arid high desert territory south and west of Texas below the compromise line reserved for slavery had little attraction for farmers, whether they owned slaves or not. Another crisis over the political control of the future of America, far more serious than the one in 1850, was brewing.

## THE "LITTLE GIANT"

Stephen A. Douglas (1813–1861), a Democrat, came to Washington as congressman from Illinois in 1843 and was elected to the Senate in 1847. He became chairman of the Committee on Territories, a position that was highly influential in dealing with the increasingly rancorous debate over the expansion of slavery into the new territories. Douglas gained influence by engineering the portion of the legislation that made up the Compromise of 1850 allowing New Mexico and Utah territories to determine their futures as slave or free states. Seeing an opportunity to solve the slavery question once and for all and unite the Democratic Party under his leadership (which would assure his reelection to the Senate in 1858 and open the door to the presidency in 1860), Douglas enunciated his doctrine of popular sovereignty. The deceptively simple formula of letting the people decide became the basis of the 1854 Kansas-Nebraska Act. In the turmoil that followed in Kansas, Douglas had to defend his policy in his campaign for the Senate against challenger Abraham Lincoln. Douglas, who stood at five feet four inches, was known as the "Little Giant." He was a formidable orator and astute politician who carefully avoided the traps Lincoln set for him in the debates and won reelection. He would find himself the leader of a fractured Democratic Party in 1860, one presidential candidate among three others, including Lincoln. Garnering only 12 electoral votes in defeat, Douglas fully supported the new Republican president, but died of typhoid fever a month before the bombardment of Fort Sumter.

# The Kansas-Nebraska Act

Senator Stephen A. Douglas of Illinois introduced the Kansas-Nebraska Act in 1854. Essentially, Douglas wanted to bypass the issue of slavery altogether in favor of westward expansion. Never believing slavery would expand into the Great Plains anyway, he proposed legislation that would allow the people who entered the territory to decide whether their future state would allow slavery or not. This idea, called *popular sovereignty*, would take Congress off the hook and give the power to individual citizens to decide the issue for themselves. While it seemed the perfect solution for a democracy, the act threw everything out of balance. Under the logic of the Kansas-Nebraska Act, all territory could legally be opened to slavery, and the compromise boundary line of 1820 no longer held.

This outraged Northerners who were willing to take action to ensure that slavery would be restricted in new territories at all costs. With the rest of the unorganized territory legally open to slavery as a result of the Kansas-Nebraska Act, the South believed the time was now or never to assert its rights and ensure that its future power base in the West would be secure. By doing so, it would stave off what appeared to be the increasingly real threat of the North eventually overwhelming the South. Without a balance between free and slave states, the North would gain a permanent majority in both houses of Congress, leaving the South to the mercy of hostile Northern politicians and abolitionists, who would dictate the future direction of the nation. The stage was set for conflict in Kansas. Whichever section won political control of Kansas — by fair means or foul — had a good chance of controlling other territories and the political power in Congress when those territories became states. The political stakes for each section now became very high.

# The violence begins

Between 1855 and 1856, Kansas experienced the horror of irregular warfare, serving as the first battleground of pro-slavery and antislavery forces. Northern abolitionist supporters sponsored settlers to move to Kansas and establish a non-slaveholding voting majority that would ban slavery in the new state. Pro-slavery groups from Missouri, called Border Ruffians, entered the state to stuff ballot boxes and intimidate non-slave owners. Soon violence became commonplace as each faction used open force and intimidation to gain an advantage. New Englanders sent rifles to Kansas (in containers labeled "Bibles") to arm antislavery paramilitary groups. Pro-slavery raiders completely destroyed the town of Lawrence, Kansas. Amazingly, only two people were killed. But acts of retaliation followed, including the murder of five suspected pro-slave settlers at Pottawatomie Creek. A radical antislavery activist named John Brown (see the upcoming section "John Brown's Raid") led the band of six murderers.

A congressional committee investigating the incident took no action. Pro-Northern newspapers played down the murders, and Brown was never prosecuted. This outraged Southerners, who claimed justice was being ignored in favor of a political agenda (this may sound familiar to you). As lawlessness took control, the country stood by as Kansas tumbled into anarchy, bleeding from a thousand wounds.

# Rising from the Collapse: The Republican Party

The struggle for political power was reflected in the birth and death of a number of political parties between 1850 and 1860. To understand the rise of the Republican Party, one must first understand the collapse of the national party system, which occurred between 1854 and 1858. For over a decade, two political parties, the Whigs and the Democrats, dominated American politics.

## Disappearing Whigs and Southern Democrats

The *Democrats* supported *states' rights,* the belief that dominant power should be held by the states rather than by the central, or federal, government. The Democrats supported the traditional view that there were limits to federal power. The *Whigs* believed in progress and modernization, supporting a strong central government and the expansion of federal power to support internal improvements to strengthen the national economy. The Whigs were strongest among prosperous farmers, manufacturers, and city dwellers, both North and South. The Democrats had strong support among frontiersmen and small farmers, many of whom desired America to expand into western lands not yet owned by the United States. Clearly, the Democratic Party favored the South's vision of what America should be. Up until 1850, the Whigs and the Democrats maintained balanced constituencies in both the North and South. This balance was essential to the political health of the nation. As long as both parties could rely on both Northern and Southern voters, the system of representative government worked. Once the parties could no longer build support across sectional lines, the system was doomed. The sectional political stakes that arose after the Compromise of 1850 created such dissension within these two parties that neither could maintain its Northern and Southern coalitions. Essentially what happened is this: The Democrats became a pure Southern party, and the Whigs, unable to support a purely sectional party, disappeared.

## The Free Soilers

The passage of the Kansas-Nebraska Act illustrates how divisive the issue of slavery in new territories had become to the two dominant political parties. Northern

Democrats, especially, paid a heavy political price for their support of the Kansas-Nebraska bill. The Northern Democrats who had supported the measure in the House and Senate (and had given the bill the margin of victory to ensure its passage) were roundly defeated in the next congressional elections as outraged Northern voters turned to other parties more in line with their antislavery views. The Democratic Party became more allied with the view of the South alone. The Whigs lost support as Southern members deserted them to join the Democrats. Northern Whigs lost members to other splinter parties that rose up in protest to the passage of the Kansas-Nebraska Act. One such group, the *Free Soil Party,* which grew to prominence in 1848, supported the Wilmot Proviso (see Chapter 1) that endorsed no extension of slavery into new territories. The new party attracted dissatisfied Democrats, antislavery Whigs, and others generally disaffected with abolitionist radicalism. Free Soilers were closely connected to the free labor ideology (see Chapter 1 also), reflecting an interest in limiting the expansion of slavery into the territories, but not necessarily an interest in offering Blacks any special advantages. In other words, free soil for many in the party was intended for whites only.

## The Know-Nothings

Another party was the *Know-Nothings,* which grew from a secret fraternal organization in New York in 1849. Any member, when asked about his affiliation with this organization, responded with the cryptic phrase "I know nothing." The Know-Nothings drawing support from Whigs in both the North and the South, peaked in 1855, claiming a million members. The main attraction seemed to be this: If you were tired of listening to arguments over slavery, the Know-Nothings offered their version of 100 percent Americanism by opposing the growing voting power of Irish and German immigrants. With a strong anti-Catholic bent (because many German and nearly all Irish immigrants were Catholic), the Know-Nothings demanded a 15-year naturalization period before being allowed to vote, and limits on the production and sale of alcohol. This, too, was directed at the immigrants, whose consumption of strong drink was part of their culture. Because their pure anti-immigration message had little traction, the Know-Nothings disappeared as a political party in 1856. As political power shifted in the North, the Know Nothings drifted into other parties, most notably in the emerging Republican Party. Ironically, the growth of the Know Nothings, largely as a result of the defection of many voters from the Whig Party, helped to bring about the Whig Party's final disappearance in 1855.

## The Republican Party arrives

By 1856, a new coalition of antislavery Whigs, Free Soil Party members, and Know-Nothings had been formed to become the Republican Party. The catalyst for this action, like that for other new parties, was the Kansas-Nebraska Act. To many observers, the South had won a clear political victory; to forestall any further advances, this new party would base its support on one issue — to keep slavery out of Kansas and all other territories.

One of the most powerful spokesmen for this new party was a former Whig congressman from Illinois, Abraham Lincoln (see Figure 2-1). Lincoln was not an abolitionist; like many Northerners, he felt slavery was the source of all troubles within the country. He expressed it in this way: "The real issue in this controversy — the one pressing upon every mind — is the sentiment on the part of one class that looks upon the institution of slavery *as a wrong*, and of another class that *does not* look upon it as a wrong." Lincoln's party had no intention of interfering with slavery in the states where it currently existed. The Constitution guaranteed slavery there — it was unquestioned. The Republicans also had no interest in the most radical abolitionist position that demanded Blacks become the social and political equals of whites. In fact, Lincoln expounded the Free Soil Party view that the new territories should be "an outlet for free white people everywhere."

**FIGURE 2-1:** Abraham Lincoln, Republican Party spokesman and future presidential candidate.

*Hesler, Alexander / The Library of Congress / Public Domain*

In the midst of political turmoil, with parties shifting support bases and other political parties disappearing, Lincoln masterfully and most often gave expression to the thoughts and feelings of many moderate Northerners, regardless of party. He soon became the leading spokesman for the Republican Party, traveling throughout the North addressing huge, enthusiastic crowds. By 1856, the year of the presidential election, the Republican Party already dominated most legislatures in the North.

# The Republicans and the 1856 Presidential Election

Today, we decry political leaders who are all symbol and no substance, thinking this is a product of our own times. If you take a look at the election of 1856, you'll find plenty of trends familiar to you. The Republicans nominated John C. Frémont, a famous western explorer known as "The Pathfinder." He was a former Free Soil Party leader, but it was his youth (43 years old) and his connection to the romance of the West rather than any clear political vision that made him an attractive candidate to many.

## The Democrats: Choosing a safe candidate

The Democrats nominated a pro-Southern Pennsylvanian, 65-year-old James Buchanan, whose only real qualification for office seemed to be that he had been out of the country for several years as ambassador, and thus out of the line of fire in the sectional dispute. Stephen A. Douglas, who engineered the passage of the Kansas-Nebraska Act in part to build political support in the South for his presidential ambitions, was rejected as too controversial.

## Millard Fillmore for president

The remnants of the Whigs and Know-Nothings combined to nominate Millard Fillmore, a man who has come to personify the political nonentity in our history. The Know-Nothings refused even to mention slavery, preferring to say only "the Union is in peril."

## THE LINCOLN-DOUGLAS DEBATES

In 1858, Abraham Lincoln, a Whig, ran against incumbent Democratic Senator Stephen A. Douglas. The two held a series of debates around the state arguing popular sovereignty versus limiting slavery in the territories, the basic idea expressed in the Wilmot Proviso. Lincoln faced an uphill battle against one of the most dynamic and important political leaders in America. Lincoln used the debate to smoke Douglas out on the issue of Supreme Court guarantees for slavery existing in the territories. Douglas clung to popular sovereignty and won the election, but lost the support of the South, which had been relying on the Supreme Court to guarantee slavery's extension. Douglas's denial of that position eventually brought an end to his presidential ambitions. Essentially, Lincoln sacrificed his chance to be a senator to cripple the sectional balance the Democratic Party relied on for survival.

# Politics becomes sectional

The 1856 presidential election is important because it revealed the realignment of national politics by region. Although the Republicans lost the election to Buchanan, the party dominated the North, with the exception of a few key states (Pennsylvania, New Jersey, Illinois, and Indiana). This win was to be the South's last political victory. The growing power of the Republicans in the Northern states and the number of Republicans who would enter the House and Senate were frightening prospects for Southerners. Political power was clearly shifting to the North.

As time went on, the South found fewer and fewer options in the face of the Republicans' open hostility to the expansion of slavery. Southerners believed that if slavery could not expand naturally, the South would then be hostage to the interests of the North. Many Southern leaders had called for leaving the Union, or *secession*, as the only hope for the future. A few Southern hotheads, soon called "fire-eaters," had threatened this in 1850, but their arguments were discounted. As Republican power grew in the North after 1856, however, Southerners began to take the words of the fire-eaters more seriously.

## ABRAHAM LINCOLN: EARLY CAREER, 1809–1860

Abraham Lincoln is most likely the greatest mythical character in all of American history. His image is commonly known to every schoolchild: the tall, lanky, homely man in plain dark clothes and a stovepipe hat. Born in poverty in Kentucky, Lincoln lived on the Indiana and Illinois frontier, where he developed a reputation as a man of ambition and intelligence, despite his lack of formal schooling. After several attempts at different careers, including a short term as a militia leader during the Black Hawk War in 1832, he settled on politics. From 1834 to 1842 he served in the Illinois state legislature. At 25, he read law and joined the bar in 1836. In 1846, he was elected to a term in Congress. After one term, he retired from politics and returned to law. The Kansas-Nebraska Act brought him back to politics. Refuting popular sovereignty, he spoke earnestly of his dislike of slavery and the necessity that it be banned from the new territories. In 1856 he joined the Republican Party, and the same year he was a contender for the vice presidential nomination. In 1858 Lincoln challenged Douglas for the U.S. Senate seat. In the famous Lincoln-Douglas debates, Lincoln lost the election, but gained a large following in the North for his ability to speak plainly and sincerely about the issue of slavery and its expansion into the territories. With a presidential election only two years away, Lincoln was on his way to political greatness.

# Southern reaction to the Republican Party

Many influential leaders in the cotton South came to believe that separation from the Union was inevitable to save their way of life. To many Southern partisans, Northerners were cold, self-righteous and mercenary, all too willing to impose their beliefs on others. Others cited the economic and social benefits of the slave-based cotton economy. Slaveholders controlled most of the wealth in the United States. The value of slaves as property exceeded $3 billion dollars – more than all the nation's accumulated wealth in manufacturing and transportation. Still others spoke of *filibusters*, quasi-legal military expeditions to Central America and Cuba, to secure new American territory for slavery.

More and more moderate Northerners and Southerners began to see their opponents as threats to their way of life, leading to a growing sense that no solution was possible. As a result, every event after 1856 created a heightened sense of danger. Events moved decisions to a crisis point very quickly in the years between 1856 and 1860.

It is not surprising that in the midst of this intense sectional debate over constitutional rights and slavery that the Supreme Court should become involved. Many hoped the Supreme Court's decision on the legality of extending slavery in the territories would put the issue to rest once and for all. Of course, many of these same people had hoped the Kansas–Nebraska Act would settle the issue forever, too.

## SOME COLD, HARD FACTS TO CONSIDER

As both the North and South became increasingly hostile to each other, both regions rhetorically wrapped themselves in the mantle of purity and righteousness. It needs to be made clear that neither section was free of the fear and hostility to Blacks, whether free or slave. In the South, the slave system, however beneficent and humane, depended in the end on the threat of violence to compel obedience and compliance. In this way, it was a tyrannical system and a damning charge against the institution. The North, which was more than 98% white in 1860, was hostile to Blacks. Laws restricted civil liberties, such as voting; schools and many churches, theaters, restaurants, rail cars, and hotels were strictly segregated. Blacks could not testify against whites in court, and some Midwest states banned Blacks from entering their states altogether. Blacks in the cities of the North lived in bleak conditions. Jobs were scarce, as whites preferred to hire Irish immigrants. Violence directed against Blacks was commonplace, and sympathetic support was rare. Thus, the larger problem in America was not slavery, per se, but the fact that Blacks and whites were coexisting in two vastly different and separate worlds.

# The Dred Scott Decision

Dred Scott, a slave belonging to an army doctor, had been taken from Missouri, which allowed slavery, to two non-slaveholding states, Illinois and Wisconsin, in the 1830s. After the doctor's death, Scott claimed he was no longer a slave because he had resided in free states. The case wound its way through the lower courts until it came to the Supreme Court in 1856. Lawyers are sometimes more confusing than historians. Essentially, Scott's lawyers argued that a slave once in free territory was a free man.

In retrospect, the Supreme Court could have avoided a great deal of trouble by simply ruling in favor of the lower court's decision, which pointed out that the Constitution did not recognize slaves as citizens. But because slavery and its extension into new territories had become such a contentious issue, the Court took on Scott's case with the goal of settling the issue once and for all. Unfortunately, the Court was involving itself into a highly volatile political situation. This was not the time for another view to be added to a very angry debate. Nevertheless, Roger B. Taney, the chief justice (and a Southern Democrat), lit the fuse on the powder keg.

The Court ruled seven to two against Scott's claim. Interestingly, each judge decided to write his own opinion. Taney's became the decision of record. On the basic issue of Scott's freedom, the Court agreed with the lower court's determination that Scott was not a citizen of either a state or the United States, and therefore could not bring a suit before a court. Taney could have stopped there, but he went on to find that Scott was still a slave because neither Congress nor any territorial legislature had the authority to restrict slavery *anywhere*.

## SECESSION, NORTHERN STYLE

People tend to associate the concept of secession only with the South. Actually the first region to threaten to secede, or leave the Union, was New England, which was a stronghold of the Federalist Party. Despairing over the United States' apparent defeat in the War of 1812 and never supporting the war in the first place, New England threatened to leave the Union. In fact, the Federalists began organizing a convention to take the New England states out of the Union. The enthusiasm for this bold act quickly disappeared as news of American battlefield victories and a peace settlement arrived. The Federalists slunk away in shame and soon disappeared as a national political party.

# The reaction to the decision

The reaction to Taney's ruling was predictable: The South celebrated, crowing that the constitutional guarantees of property (described in the Fourth Amendment) were secured once and for all. No governmental body had the authority to restrict the movement of slaves, who had been declared inviolable property by the highest court in the land. The North condemned the ruling, describing it as a politically motivated act by a pro-Southern Supreme Court. The Court, they noted, seemed to ignore the fact that the Constitution also spoke of guarantees to freedom in the same sentence that it guaranteed property in the Fourth Amendment. Northerners complained that Taney also forgot to look at Article IV, Section 3, of the Constitution, which clearly gives Congress the power to administer territories.

## The can of worms is opened

In one blow the Supreme Court unwittingly toppled the delicate house of cards built since 1820 to maintain sectional harmony over the issue of slavery's expansion. Neither popular sovereignty (the authority for people in the territories to decide whether to allow slavery to exist) nor the geographical limitations laid out by the Missouri Compromise were valid any longer. The Court's decision opened all of the United States and its territories to slave owners. Congress (with its Northern voting bloc majority in the House of Representatives) could do nothing about it. By declaring that no law could restrict the movement of slaves, the Court placed human beings in the same category as furniture or livestock. Property has no rights to itself, and as such under the Constitution, people cannot be deprived of their property without due process of law.

## The firestorm in the North

Northern radical abolitionists, were, of course, outraged by the Dred Scott decision, but, more importantly, Northern moderates were greatly upset by it too. The decision was too much for Northerners to take, so they declared that they would not obey the Court. This is the first instance of "Massive Resistance" to a Supreme Court decision. Several Northern state legislatures passed resolutions declaring the Court's decision invalid and nonbinding. Some state legislatures refused to provide any assistance to the federal government in prosecuting anyone who violated the Fugitive Slave Law (see Chapter 1).

# UNCLE TOM'S CABIN

In 1852, in reaction to the Fugitive Slave Law, Harriet Beecher Stowe (see the following image), a member of a prominent abolitionist family, wrote *Uncle Tom's Cabin*, a novel portraying the problems of slavery in the South. The novel, typical in many ways of the sentimental writing of this period, nevertheless tells a powerfully effective story using characters that have become stock characters in American culture: Little Eva, the pure little girl destined for heaven; Uncle Tom, the kindly, Christ-like Black servant; and Simon Legree, the brutal and degraded slave owner. It sold 100,000 copies in two months, and 300,000 in its first year. For 1852, these are impossibly large numbers. Like the bestseller *Jaws*, which made the idea of shark attack so real that everyone was afraid to swim in the ocean, *Uncle Tom's Cabin* created frightening images of the South in the minds of its readers. Despite howls of outrage from Southerners, Stowe's image of a benighted South and Southerners as a collection of depraved sadists became reality, convincing thousands of Northerners that slavery's very existence was a moral blight on the soul of America. When Abraham Lincoln met Mrs. Stowe in 1862, he reportedly said, "So you're the little woman who wrote the book that made this great war."

*Harriet Beecher Stowe / The Library of Congress / Public Domain*

## The results of the Dred Scott decision

The Dred Scott decision was a disaster for the South. Rather than protecting slavery, it brought many Northerners to the Republican Party, who now saw the party as the only bulwark against a Southern legal and political conspiracy to open the entire nation to slavery. The Court's decision also unwittingly dealt a deathblow to the Democratic Party's chances to maintain an intersectional political organization. Stephen Douglas's popular sovereignty, whatever its merits, was the one issue that brought Northern and Southern Democrats together. It had allowed the party to win the presidency in 1856. Now that the Dred Scott decision declared popular sovereignty invalid, the party had no hope of winning the 1860 presidential election against a united and powerful Republican Party.

## The Underground Railroad

Some common citizens, angered by the government's policy and spurred by strong moral convictions, turned to clandestine methods. This loose organization, called the *Underground Railroad*, sought to move escaped slaves and free Blacks to Canada, beyond the ability of the U.S. government to touch them. The Underground Railroad's effectiveness as an organization has grown to mythical proportions over the years. While many noble and courageous people were involved in this act of defiance, many others took advantage of such altruism. Unscrupulous groups would entice escaped slaves by pretending to be part of the Underground Railroad. Instead of guiding them to freedom, however, they would turn the slaves over to federal authorities and collect the reward money.

# John Brown's Raid

Tensions between North and South in 1859 were very great; for years, emotions never seemed to reach a peak. Every new incident drove emotions to new heights, but there never seemed to be a limit to how high they could go, or where they would take the antagonists. In this overwrought atmosphere of crisis and tension, John Brown reenters our story.

As mentioned earlier in this chapter, John Brown and his followers had murdered several suspected pro-slavery Kansas settlers. After this attack, Brown and his group spent some time in Canada until the heat was off. By 1859, he had concocted a new and more ambitious scheme than simple nighttime murder and terror. He had become impatient with the lack of action in the country over slavery. What was needed, he kept saying, was action — do something, once and for all, to bring about the destruction of slavery in fire and blood.

His fanatic dedication to ending slavery led him to believe that he could be a one-man instrument of its destruction. His plan to do this called for nothing less than instigating and leading a nationwide slave revolt and race war. Supported with money and arms from wealthy antislavery sponsors who wished to remain anonymous, Brown prepared to carry out his plan.

## Harpers Ferry

Brown selected Harpers Ferry, Virginia — the site of a federal arsenal located at the junction of a key transportation intersection only a few miles from Washington, D.C. — as his target. After he captured the arsenal and its weapons, he planned to use the town as his base of operations to receive the thousands upon thousands of slaves who would escape and join him. He would then arm the slaves as they arrived and create a stronghold. As more slaves arrived, he would expand the area under his control through violent action until he had created a free Black nation. On the night of October 16, Brown and his 18 followers entered Harpers Ferry and had no trouble gaining control of the arsenal and its production facility. Brown was so focused on the first phase of the operation — capturing the arsenal — that he had not thought through exactly how all the slaves in Virginia and the rest of the South would be notified that Brown and his conspirators were waiting at Harpers Ferry to arm them for a race war. Faced with this daunting reality, he did what terrorists usually do: He took hostages, swore he'd never be taken alive, and waited for the inevitable.

## Sending in the Marines

The inevitable made its appearance soon in the form of a detachment of U.S. Marines hastily gathered from the Washington Navy Yard and sent by train to Harpers Ferry. This ad hoc force had an army colonel as its leader. This colonel just happened to be available when the news arrived at the War Department in Washington. His second in command was an army cavalry lieutenant, who just happened to be visiting the colonel and decided to come along. Arriving soon after the Marines at Harpers Ferry, the colonel conducted a reconnaissance, made an assessment of the situation, and gave orders for his force to prepare for a direct assault on the building where Brown and his group were holding their hostages. As you can always expect when Marines are given such orders, the battle was both fierce and over in a few minutes. John Brown was wounded and captured. The calm and decisive colonel was Robert E. Lee, one of the U.S. Army's most capable officers. His lieutenant friend was a cadet at West Point when Lee was superintendent and a frequent guest at his quarters. His name was James E. B. (Jeb) Stuart. Both Lee and Stuart play important roles in the upcoming war.

## The results of John Brown's raid

If this foolish act of a misguided fanatic had transpired ten years earlier, it would have certainly raised little attention outside of Virginia. In 1859, however, after all that had already occurred in the troubled decade, John Brown's raid (as the incident became known) lost all proportion and became a national calamity. The truth is that many Northerners shared the Southern outrage at Brown's insane act. The voices of reason were largely drowned out, however, as everyone heard only what he or she wanted to hear. Today, a common expression states that one man's terrorist is another man's freedom fighter. So it was in 1859 with sectional reaction to the incident at Harpers Ferry. Southerners viewed Brown as a tool of abolitionist Republicans and a murderer; Northerners hailed him as a martyr who was willing to sacrifice himself for the holy cause of freedom. These extreme opinions only hardened hearts further, and raised emotions to a fever pitch. By now, both sides were ready to jump at the least provocation, if only to release those long pent-up emotions in some grand violent act of retribution against the perceived enemy.

## John Brown's end

Just two weeks after his raid, John Brown was tried and executed by the state of Virginia. On the day of his execution, the governor ordered militia and the Corps of Cadets from the Virginia Military Institute to guard the execution site against a possible abolitionist rescue attempt. The units formed a hollow square around the scaffold. Brown was hanged without incident. He faced death impassively, without any sign of fear. Another impassive and fearless man, the commander of the VMI detachment, watched Brown's death. His name was Major Thomas J. Jackson, a Mexican-American War veteran and a quirky instructor at the school. Jackson, who appeared to be a very unlikely hero, would be heard of again very soon.

### "JOHN BROWN'S BODY"

At the beginning of the war, Union volunteers marched off to war singing a song called "John Brown's Body." The first line of the song reflected how Brown had become a prophetic figure to many in the North:

"John Brown's body lies a'moulderin' in the grave! But his soul goes marching on!"

Julia Ward Howe heard soldiers singing the song as they marched below her hotel window in Washington, D.C. Filled with inspiration by the massed voices, she immediately sat down and composed new, more strident, words to the tune she heard. That tune and her lyrics became more famous than the original as "The Battle Hymn of the Republic," a song that still stirs a powerful sense of patriotism. Listen to the Mormon Tabernacle Choir sing it, and you'll never forget it. The original tune for "John Brown's Body" (again with new lyrics) has become the battle song of U.S. paratroopers, titled "Blood on the Risers." Unfortunately, it is doubtful that you'll ever hear the Mormon Tabernacle Choir sing that version.

# The Fighting South, the Angry North

Following John Brown's raid, the atmosphere became extremely tense. When people believe they are trapped and are threatened with destruction, they take the only option left — to fight. In 1859, many of the Southern states certainly viewed the situation in this way. The North's opposition to slavery as an institution left the South with very few options. Southerners were defending constitutional guarantees, as they saw it, and those guarantees were worth fighting for.

The North also felt trapped by the debilitating effects slavery had on the nation. As long as the South maintained its hold on political and economic power, the nation would continue to stumble from one crisis to the next. The implied threat of the South using the Constitution and the Supreme Court to impose its repugnant system on the country angered and frightened many Northerners. Many believed the time was coming to resist such attempts at destroying freedom.

By 1859, without a broad national consensus and the ability to see beyond this growing sense of fear, the United States was spinning out of control. At one time, most Americans believed that sectional trouble could be blamed on radical agitators on both sides; this was no longer the case, however. Many Americans came to see some sort of armed clash between the North and South as inevitable, an "irrepressible conflict" in the words of William Seward, a Northern Republican.

# The Election of Abraham Lincoln in 1860

Almost a year after Brown's death, Americans voted in a presidential election. Abraham Lincoln, whose voice over the past three years had become the voice of the Republican Party, was nominated for president. Lincoln had made speeches in Ohio, Indiana, Illinois, Iowa, Wisconsin, Kansas, and New York, proclaiming as eloquently as anyone of his century that slavery was a moral wrong, "founded on both injustice and bad policy" as he put it. Quoting the Bible, the source of his most inspired speeches, Lincoln told his audiences that the country was "a house divided against itself." "I believe," he said, "this government cannot endure, permanently half *slave* and half *free*." He dissected the Southern defense of slavery, exposing it in a way that the average man could understand.

Although the party had several stronger and more politically powerful candidates, Lincoln emerged as the compromise nominee at the Republican convention because he had the approval of both the very fractious right wing (former Whigs) and left wing (abolitionists) of the party. The Republicans adopted a strong sectional platform, supporting the Wilmot Proviso, internal improvements, a transcontinental railroad, and immigration. The astute reader will note that slavery is missing from this platform. High moral ideals often take a back seat when the political stakes (like the presidency) are so high. Even though clearly a sectional party, the Republicans hedged their bets a bit to try and capture votes outside the North.

## A new party emerges

The Know-Nothings, who had changed their name to the American Party in the last presidential election, now became the Constitutional Union Party. Their strategy, true to form, centered on ignoring the slavery issue completely. Their platform was summarized in a slogan that couldn't possibly insult anyone: "We are for Constitution and Union." This party (such as it was), with its clever matching name and slogan, nominated John Bell of Tennessee, who had strong support from voters in Maryland and Kentucky.

## The Democrats divide

After the Dred Scott decision, the Democrats could no longer maintain a North-South coalition. The party broke into two separate parties, each nominating a candidate advocating a sectional platform. The pro-North wing nominated Stephen Douglas, the author of the Kansas-Nebraska Act and the man who had defeated Lincoln in the 1858 Illinois Senate race. These Democrats vaguely supported both popular sovereignty and the Dred Scott decision. Because there was no clear-cut statement that supported congressional protection for slavery in the territories, several Southern states took action to force the issue. South Carolina, Alabama, Mississippi, Louisiana, and Georgia delegates established a pro-South wing of the party and nominated John C. Breckinridge of Kentucky, Buchanan's vice president.

## Lincoln wins by electoral vote

Thus the election of 1860 had four candidates, each appealing to the voters as the only true defender of the Union. The Democrats spent a great deal of effort attacking each other. The well-financed Republicans spent their money on large and enthusiastic demonstrations on behalf of their candidate. This left Lincoln to say very little at all, in spite of Southern Democrats decrying Lincoln as an enemy of the South. At this time, Lincoln might have been able to calm fears and explain his views, but he decided not to, thinking that the South would not believe anything he said. At any rate, the Republican strategists had written off the South and concentrated on the populous states in the Midwest where the electoral votes were concentrated. Of course, presidents are not elected by popular votes (individual votes cast by citizens), but electoral votes.

**TECHNICAL STUFF**

Electoral votes are a number value assigned to each state based on its population. Whoever wins the greatest number of popular votes in a state wins those electoral votes; whoever wins the most electoral votes wins the election.

The Republican strategy worked. Lincoln won every state in the North except New Jersey. Oregon and California joined to give the Republicans 180 electoral votes and the presidency. Breckinridge won most of the South with 72 electoral votes. Bell captured 39 electoral votes with Tennessee, Kentucky, and Virginia. Douglas took 12 electoral votes in two states, New Jersey and Missouri. Although the aggregate popular vote didn't count, a breakdown of these votes is instructive. The three other candidates received 1 million more popular votes than Lincoln did. In the popular vote, interestingly, Lincoln received no votes *at all* in ten Southern states. In the rest of the South, he had a negligible tally. Another interesting fact emerges about Southern voting. The popular vote in the South was split between the three other candidates, indicating no agreement about the future of the nation, except to prevent Lincoln's election.

One of the interesting quirks of democracy that fascinates and puzzles the non-democratic world is the way that the voters whose candidate does not win accept the judgment of the majority, allowing the business of the nation to go on. In reality this unstated agreement is a very fragile condition, which forms the base of the democratic process. In November 1860, that base was shattered. For the first time in American history, the voters of the losing party refused to accept or abide by the results of an election.

## The South's view of the election

Here's how the South analyzed the results of the election. The Republicans won 180 electoral votes. This meant that even if only one candidate had opposed Lincoln, with the entire South united in support, Lincoln would still have won the election. The South simply lacked the electoral votes to offset the advantage of the Northern states.

Clearly, Southern political power had disappeared, and the Republican Party now could dominate the House and the presidency at will. There would be no congressional guarantees of slavery or protection of Southern rights coming from a House of Representatives dominated by the North. Without any words of conciliation coming from the Republicans, many Southerners in the cotton South feared the worst and began to contemplate the last option they believed they had left — leaving the Union.

## Chapter **3**

# Secession and War: 1860–1861

After the election of 1860, only a few Southern states took the drastic step of secession. The actions of James Buchanan, the outgoing president, and Abraham Lincoln, the incoming president, would determine whether other Southern states would follow. With very few options and time running out, both men sought to satisfy two conflicting conditions at the same time — to assert the rights of the United States and to avoid war.

On the other side, the seceded states created the Confederate States of America. Although wanting to leave the Union peacefully, the new president of the Confederate States of America, Jefferson Davis, was not afraid of fighting for his new nation's independence. For both the United States and the Confederate States of America, Fort Sumter became the dominant symbol of each nation's prideful determination not to back down.

# The First Secession: South Carolina and the Lower South

On December 20, 1860, 169 delegates of the state of South Carolina met in Charleston to consider leaving the Union. The convention was organized to mimic the first state convention that assembled for voting to join the United States in 1788. The logic of secession went like this: Each state was sovereign after independence from Great Britain. In 1788, the states entered into a federal union under the Constitution voluntarily. The Constitution was thus a compact, an agreement of sovereign, independent, and self-governing states allowing the central government to have specific powers as outlined in the Constitution. According to the Tenth Amendment, all other power resided with the states. Therefore, any state, if it so desired, could voluntarily leave the Union (secede) and could become a sovereign state again. This was not a rebellion, the South Carolina delegates insisted, but a legal act.

Given the climate after the election of 1860, and the growing fear of what the Republican Party would do to the South after taking control of the government in March when the new president was inaugurated, South Carolina took the first drastic step to dissolve its fraternal bonds with the United States. To the surprise of many Southerners, there was no reaction. After all of the emotionalism, the threats, and the sense of high purpose enmeshed in their world–shaking event, *nothing happened.* The people of South Carolina must have felt a bit sheepish and uneasy in the roaring silence coming from the federal government. Congress, with its members divided along sectional lines, could take little action, even if it wanted to and President Buchanan had no interest in making waves at the moment. The new citizens of South Carolina also felt a bit lost, lacking any means whatsoever to function independently. The newly declared nation awaited help from her sister states in the lower South, or some indication from Washington. That help came quickly and raised morale higher. Mississippi voted on January 9, 1861, to secede. Two more days passed with two more states, Florida and Alabama, leaving the Union. By the first of February, Georgia, Louisiana, and Texas had also voted themselves out. These states of the lower South had the most to lose from a national government controlled (probably permanently) by Republicans hostile to slavery and condemning the institution to a slow death, which meant eventual economic ruin and social chaos.

The rationale for secession can be summed up in one sentence taken from the Mississippi ordinance of secession: *"Our position is thoroughly identified with the institution of slavery — the greatest material interest of the world."* The key words here are "material interest." Slavery was the basis of the cotton economy, the greatest generator of wealth in the world. These seven states were not willing to risk their wealth, economic security, and social dominance on the Republican-dominated government. This material interest is highlighted by the fact that whites in these states made up only 32% of the South's total population. Slaves in these states made up 47% of the total slave population. In fact, in Mississippi and South

Carolina (the first two states to secede) the enslaved population actually exceeded the white population.

# Building a New Nation: The Confederacy

These newly independent states decided to unite in another compact, one more to their liking. A new Constitution was quickly adopted, very much like the original (except for ironclad guarantees of slavery, a six-year term for the president, and increased power to the sovereign states). On February 18, a new nation, the Confederate States of America, was established in Montgomery, Alabama.

Jefferson Davis, former Mississippi senator, heroic Mexican-American War veteran, one-time secretary of war, and strong supporter of Southern rights, became the first president. One of Davis's first acts as president was to call for 100,000 volunteers to serve the new Confederacy as soldiers for a period of 12 months. Davis didn't anticipate trouble, but he wasn't going to take any chances.

As a matter of course, the new Confederacy began taking control of all federal property within its territory. Military installations, post offices, and customs houses came routinely under control of the Confederate government. All but the two most important pieces of federal property, Fort Pickens at Pensacola and Fort Sumter at Charleston, fell under Confederate control. A few days earlier, the delegates who had formed the new government met in session as the first Confederate Congress and authorized the use of force, if necessary, to remove U.S. troops from Fort Sumter and Fort Pickens. For the new Confederacy, Sumter was a bone in its throat. As long as Sumter remained in the hands of the United States, the new government had little claim to legitimacy as an independent country.

## WORDS HAVE MEANING

The choice of words is very important; after all, a lot of thought should go into what you name your new country. It has to have significant meaning. So why the word "Confederate"? The Southern states in forming a new government harkened back to the original document that first created the United States in 1781 — the Articles of Confederation. To protect the states from a too-powerful central government, the Articles clearly outlined that the powers of the individual states were dominant. In fact, the Articles only pledged the states to enter into "a firm league of friendship." It was this spirit of the Confederation that led to the naming of the Confederate States of America. The creation of the Confederacy can be seen as a conservative revolutionary act, intended to go back to the original form of American government.

# JEFFERSON DAVIS: EARLY CAREER, 1808–1860

Jefferson Davis, born in Kentucky, moved to Mississippi where his father made his fortune in cotton. Davis (see the following image) attended West Point, graduating in 1828. As a lieutenant, he participated in the Black Hawk War and commanded a regiment of volunteers in the Mexican-American War. He served as U.S. secretary of war under Franklin Pierce and served Mississippi as a U.S. senator. Davis was one of the leading advocates of the Southern way of life, defending slavery and the right of secession. His role as a strong Southern spokesman, combined with his reputation for courage and his strong background in military affairs, made him the logical choice to become the president of the Confederate States of America. Davis, it seemed, was the man destiny had selected to lead the new nation.

*War Department / The U.S. National Archives and Records
Administration / Public Domain*

## The growing crisis in Charleston: Fort Sumter

Major Robert Anderson was the U.S. commander at Charleston, South Carolina. In late December he had abandoned his original location in Charleston, Fort Moultrie.

Moultrie was too close to the city, now filling with pro-Southern rowdies (fortified by a few quarts of liquor), who bragged they would take care of the problem by waltzing into the fort and convincing the soldiers they weren't welcome any longer. Fort Sumter, in the middle of Charleston harbor, was the most defensible place. Anderson secretly moved his entire command of 85 soldiers (along with 45 women and children) to the fort to prevent any confrontations. Begun in 1829, Sumter was still incomplete and had only a few operational cannons for defense. Nevertheless, with walls anywhere from 8 to 12 feet thick, it was the most formidable defensive position in the Western Hemisphere. In the coming days, Fort Sumter for the North would become far more than just a piece of military real estate. Very soon it would become a symbol of national resolve to defend the flag and the Union.

## Walking the tightrope: President Buchanan

In the midst of all this activity, President Buchanan was waiting out the last few weeks of his term. His Southern sympathies and his unwillingness to stir the already troubled pot led him to pass assurances to South Carolina that he would take no aggressive action.

As much as Buchanan would have liked to wait, events set into motion by a number of individuals forced the president to take action. Several commissioners from South Carolina had arrived in Washington to meet the president and negotiate a peaceful settlement that would allow the new Confederate nation to go its own way. At the top of their list was the removal of the U.S. garrison from Fort Sumter. Buchanan would have gladly acceded to such a request, but he was faced with threats from his cabinet to resign *en masse* and the possibility of certain impeachment proceedings from Congress if he showed such weakness. He had to walk a political tightrope, so he took another course. Here is what he needed to do:

>> To satisfy the North, he had to show that the U.S. government would maintain its possessions in the seceded states.

>> To avoid antagonizing the South (states both seceded and not seceded), he had to assure them that his intentions were nonthreatening.

This would be a tough call for any political leader, let alone a lame duck president with only a month left in office. Nevertheless, he put a plan together to meet both requirements. Buchanan ordered that Sumter be resupplied and reinforced. But rather than use a warship, which could be seen as a provocation, a merchant ship, the *Star of the West*, was dispatched with supplies and troops from New York. The plan was supposed to be a secret, but then as now, nothing is a secret long in Washington. Pro-Southern spies had the information to Charleston in a flash. While useful and dramatic, this act of espionage was unnecessary. The War Department, as it had done for years, sent all of its orders and information to Major Anderson through the U.S. mail, having forgotten that the U.S. Post Office no longer existed in the sovereign nation of South Carolina. All mail addressed to Fort Sumter had been intercepted and read. It seemed that everyone knew about the resupply effort except Anderson. Sitting in a fort surrounded by water and cut off from all information, Anderson knew nothing about what the government had planned.

On the 9th of January, as expected, the *Star of the West* arrived outside Charleston harbor. Everyone was waiting. Most expectant of all were cadets from the Citadel, the military college of South Carolina, who were standing by heavy cannons on the shore. A cadet fired a cannon aimed at the *Star of the West* — a miss. This could have been the first shot of the war, with all honor and glory going to the Citadel, but the Citadel was denied such an important historical footnote because there was no response from the cannons at Fort Sumter. Other cannons around the harbor joined in, causing no damage to the *Star of the West*. Enough lead was flying, however, to convince the ship's captain to turn away. Anderson watched this display from Sumter and almost returned fire to respond to the Confederate batteries, but, not knowing what the ship was doing in the harbor or why it was being fired upon, he decided to wait. A war would have to come on another day.

## Confederates at Charleston: Waiting for a sign and heavily armed

In the wake of the *Star of the West* incident, the new Confederacy waited for the U.S. government to respond. *Nothing happened.* As the days went by, Charleston harbor became one of the most heavily armed places in the world. Cannons surrounded Fort Sumter on three sides. Both confidence and contempt rose among the population of Charleston. Some thought the North's silence meant that the federal government wouldn't interfere with Southern independence. To others the lack of response meant that the Yankees were cowards and afraid to fight. (*Yankee* was a term of disparagement for Northerners. Originally a term used for generations throughout America to describe business-minded New Englanders, Southerners applied it to all Northerners.)

### WHAT ABOUT FORT PICKENS?

The commander of the garrison at Fort Pickens was a first lieutenant, who defiantly refused to turn the fort over to the state of Florida. Unlike Sumter, Pickens's position at the mouth of Pensacola Bay kept it out of the reach of any Confederate cannon. Thus, it could be resupplied and reinforced easily. Ironically, Fort Pickens was named after Thomas Pickens, a famous Revolutionary War leader and the father of the 1860 governor of South Carolina, who was now leading his own revolution. Fort Pickens remained in federal hands throughout the war.

## Sitting quietly: The outgoing president beats the clock

Although certainly justified to retaliate for the attack on the *Star of the West*, Buchanan discovered two things. First, public support in the North for direct military action was weak, with many differing opinions on what to do next. No politician goes to war without the strong backing of the public. Buchanan, even if he wanted to take action (and he didn't), had no clear support to do so. Second, with the exception of a few warships, the U.S. government had no armed forces to speak of available to do anything. Total military strength of the U.S. Army in 1860 was about 16,000 officers and enlisted men, who were scattered over the continent in small groups. In fact, Anderson's garrison of almost 90 men represented 10 percent of the entire U.S. Army strength east of the Mississippi River. These conditions allowed Buchanan to sit quietly until the new president was sworn in.

# Taking Office: Lincoln's First Inaugural Address

On March 4, 1861, Abraham Lincoln took the oath of office to become the 16th president of the United States. As all presidents have done before and since, he swore an oath to "preserve, protect, and defend the Constitution of the United States." Ironically, the Constitution no longer existed in seven Southern states. Lincoln used his oath as the basis for his message to the nation and to those seven states. He made four points:

>> Secession was illegal and unjustified.

>> The seceded states were still in the Union.

>> No federal troops would be sent against the states, nor would the federal government interfere with slavery where it already existed.

>> The government would "hold, occupy, and possess" all federal property in the seceded states.

In essence, Lincoln told the Confederacy that the U.S. government would take no aggressive action against it. But if the Confederacy attacked federal property (obviously referring to Sumter and Pickens), the government would take action. The ball was now in the Confederacy's court.

# The Sumter crisis renewed

The situation wasn't as simple as Lincoln made it appear in his inaugural address. Almost as soon as he arrived at the White House for his first day of work, Lincoln received an urgent message from Major Anderson at Fort Sumter. Anderson reported his food supplies would last about 40 more days. After that, he would have to give up the fort. The strength of Confederate batteries now covering the fort and the approaches to the harbor would make any attempt to reinforce or resupply impossible. This was an awkward moment; the new president had just committed the government to "hold, occupy, and possess" Sumter. And now it looked as though the fort would have to be given up anyway. Politically, such a scenario was unthinkable. Now, instead of waiting the Confederacy out, something would have to be done. The danger was that a misstep would lead to war, with the North standing before the world as the aggressor.

To make matters worse, the new Secretary of State William Seward, the man who thought he should have been elected president, began leaking information to the press and to pro-Southern acquaintances that Lincoln would not hold on to Sumter after supplies ran out. History shows that some things in Washington *never* change. The information, of course, reached its intended audience, but Confederate President Davis decided to wait and see. If anything, time was on his side at this point. Nevertheless, he knew that his military situation was even more precarious than Lincoln's was. Davis needed as much time as possible to establish some sort of credible military force in the coming days.

# The decisions that led to war

Over the next month, Lincoln and his advisors wrangled over what to do. General Winfield Scott, the senior military officer, saw no chance to gather enough men, ships, and ammunition to relieve the fort before Anderson's food ran out. He therefore recommended that the fort be given up.

Close to despair, Lincoln granted a request from his postmaster general for a special meeting. Montgomery Blair proposed a plan to Lincoln: Resupply the fort secretly, with Blair's brother-in-law as the leader of the expedition. The plan called for several support ships to arrive secretly outside Charleston harbor. Tugs working under cover of darkness would ferry the men and supplies to the fort. Lincoln liked the idea and gave instructions to the War Department to carry out the plan.

Almost immediately, nothing went right, and Lincoln began to have second thoughts about the secret resupply mission. Lincoln then notified the governor of South Carolina that he intended to resupply the fort. He had two conditions: If the relief ships were not fired on, they would only offload food. If fired upon, the ships would offload food, ammunition, and troops. At the same time, Lincoln sent a message to Anderson informing him of the resupply plan and instructing him to hold out as long as possible. In the same message, the president gave Anderson the authority to surrender the fort if the situation made it necessary. Anderson must have found those instructions confusing. On one hand, he was to hold out as long as possible; on the other hand, he could surrender the fort. Essentially, Lincoln had placed the decision for peace or war in the hands of an army major.

Now it was Davis's turn to sweat. Davis could not allow the federal government to resupply Sumter without a fight. The Confederacy had to demonstrate to the world that its independence was legitimate. He ordered the commander of the Confederate forces in Charleston, General P.G.T. Beauregard, to resist any efforts to resupply Sumter. A few days later, responding to popular pressure to do something about Sumter, Davis instructed Beauregard to demand the fort's immediate surrender and to fire on the fort if the demand was refused. On April 11, three Confederate officers, one a former senator with the new rank of colonel, made a visit to Fort Sumter. With proper military courtesy, the group presented Major Anderson with the formal surrender demand. Anderson refused to surrender but made it clear that by April 15 there would be no more food, and he would give up the fort. Yet they both knew that some of the ships of the relief expedition had arrived that night but without the tugs necessary to transfer supplies. The Confederate officers returned to Sumter at 12:45 a.m. for Anderson's final answer. Again he refused to surrender until his food ran out. Given this reply, the Confederate officers responded that the fort would be fired on in one hour.

# Firing the First Shot

At 4:30 a.m. the signal gun fired, its shell exploding 100 feet squarely above the fort (see Figure 3-1). A furious artillery barrage began and lasted for 34 hours. Although exploding shells caused widespread fires within the fort, neither side did any serious damage, nor was anyone killed or injured. On the 14th of April, with no food and little gunpowder left to fire his cannons, Anderson surrendered Fort Sumter. His garrison fired a salute to the flag (in the process killing one soldier and wounding five accidentally) and was picked up by the ineffectual relief expedition.

## Calling for the 75,000 and another secession: The upper South

The day following the bombardment of Sumter, April 15, Lincoln declared the seven states of the Confederacy in rebellion and issued an order for 75,000 volunteers to serve 90 days. This call went to every state still in the Union. Upon receipt of this order, Virginia, North Carolina, Tennessee, and Arkansas seceded and began efforts to join the Confederacy. During the post-election crisis, most of these states had opened conventions like the other Southern states but had refused to make any decision on secession. The delegates to these conventions held long and rancorous debates over whether secession was justified. Many placed all hope on several attempts at a last-minute compromise or any indication that the Republicans would ease their position on slavery.

**FIGURE 3-1:**
The firing on
Fort Sumter.

*Library of Congress Prints and Photographs Division [LC-DIG-ppmsca-35361]*

## DOUBLEDAY UP TO BAT

Captain Abner Doubleday, second in command at Fort Sumter, aimed and gave the command to fire the first Union cannon shot of the Civil War. Although he became a major general, commanding a division, Doubleday's name is more associated with baseball rather than the Civil War. Doubleday was believed to be the inventor of baseball in Cooperstown, New York, in 1839, a claim now discounted.

But Lincoln's call for the 75,000 troops changed minds quickly and dramatically. It was one thing to debate whether the Constitution was a compact of voluntary association or an insoluble bond, but it was quite another thing for the federal government to use force against the states to enforce its will. None of these states would allow troops to be sent against fellow Southerners. Thus, when Lincoln declared the states in rebellion and intended to use coercive military force, the states of the upper South issued their own ordinances of secession. But these were different. There was no mention of slavery; instead, they asserted their rights as sovereign states to leave the Union voluntarily.

To top it off, Maryland, Missouri, and Kentucky, all slaveholding states, threatened to leave the Union as well. A large and powerful group of angry people now confronted the U.S. government. Lincoln suddenly found himself with double the problem that he had before the fall of Fort Sumter.

The bloodless battle that opened the war unleashed the torrent of long-held pent-up emotions. In both the North and the South, people laughed, cried, danced, sang, and prayed for joy at finally reaching a resolution to the tensions. Young men from all over America ran eagerly to join volunteer units forming up to fight. The excitement of adventure and glory was almost overwhelming. The North responded to Lincoln's call for 75,000 men with over 100,000 volunteers.

## The hardest choice: Robert E. Lee takes his stand

While the rookies jumped at the chance to play soldier, the professional soldiers were far less enthusiastic. For many of them, the army was all they had known. They had served where the country had sent them, often to desolate places with poor pay and little to do. But the secession of their states forced many to make a choice they never had thought would be necessary. The following facts help to tell the story of painful decisions made in the crush of events no one ever dreamed would happen:

>> Of the 1,098 officers in the U.S. Army in 1860, 286 resigned to join the Confederacy.

>> Of the 824 West Point graduates serving, 184 joined the Confederacy.

>> Of the 900 West Point graduates who were civilians in 1860, 99 joined the Confederacy.

>> Over 200 officers and midshipmen serving on U.S. naval ships resigned when their states seceded.

**KEY PLAYERS**

One of these officers who faced this terrible decision was Colonel Robert E. Lee. He had served his country all his life. Lee was a graduate of West Point and served as its superintendent. He was an officer on General Winfield Scott's staff in the Mexican–American War, whose intrepid gallantry led to major U.S. victories. He had commanded a cavalry regiment and in 1860 was in charge of the military department of Texas just before the state seceded. He was in Washington when Fort Sumter surrendered.

Lee opposed secession and mistrusted the motives of the cotton states. But when Virginia left the Union, he saw (like many others) that his duty lay with his native state. He did not make his decision lightly; he knew it would cost him greatly. General Scott, who knew Lee well and admired his skills, offered him the opportunity that any professional soldier with talent covets — wartime command of the nation's armies. Scott knew Lee's sympathies but hoped the offer of command would change his mind. Lee's answer was firm and eloquent: "I cannot raise my hand against my birthplace, my home, my children." He offered his resignation from the army and sadly abandoned his wife's family estate, Arlington, overlooking Washington. He never saw it again. The property was later confiscated and today is the site of Arlington National Cemetery. His decision made, Lee traveled to Richmond and, facing an uncertain future, offered his services to Virginia.

# So, Who Started the War?

This is a good question to ask about now. Who gets the blame for bringing the nation to such a terrible fate? The answer can very much depend on your partisan point of view. You can blame Lincoln for maneuvering Jefferson Davis into a confrontation, knowing that Davis had no choice but to resist the resupply effort. Lincoln even told him about the relief expedition just to make sure that Davis's forces would be ready when it arrived. You can blame Jefferson Davis for being overly aggressive, seeking confrontation with the U.S. government over Sumter out of a misplaced sense of Southern national pride. You can also blame both of them equally for setting conditions neither could fulfill.

The problem was that compromise was impossible for either president. It was inevitable that shots would be fired. Lincoln had pledged to save the Union in March; 40 days later, he was at war. If Lincoln did not force a decision, the Confederacy would have gone on unmolested, mocking Lincoln's oath. Davis pledged to defend the new Confederacy in February; 50 days later, he was at war. If Davis didn't force a decision, the Confederacy would have no legitimacy, and the act of secession would be meaningless.

By authorizing the attack on Sumter, Davis made a conscious decision, knowing that the Confederate states could not leave the Union peacefully as he had hoped. He was perfectly willing to risk war, however, to secure the independence of the Confederacy. Lincoln, too, made a conscious decision by calling for 75,000 volunteers to crush what he now called a rebellion. The Confederate attack had put the Union in danger and the Confederate states had initiated armed aggression against the nation. He knew full well that his action risked losing *all* of the slave states to the Confederacy and thus initiating a war of terrifying magnitude. Yet he was willing to risk such a war for the principle of the Union.

Well, there you have it — plenty of blame to go around. Like it or not, history shows us that sometimes there just aren't simple answers. Issues of war and peace can be mighty tough to sort out, and leaders can find themselves in a crisis with no other option except war. You pick your position and come out fighting.

# 2 Making War

Get a fast and furious overview of military systems, military terminology, the difference between strategy and tactics, and the relationship of battles to campaigns.

Understand the relationship between the science and art of war.

Get an understanding of the basic principles and processes of prosecuting war.

IN THIS CHAPTER

» Defining war

» Understanding the principles of strategy that shape the conduct of war

» Discovering the three levels of war and how they interrelate

» Examining the art of war and how commanders apply the art

» Breaking down the military organization of Civil War armies

Chapter **4**

# Civil War Armies: Structure and Organization

War is both an art and a science. The way in which knowledge is applied and principles are employed is an art. But, because it deals with specific principles and knowledge, it is also a science. To understand what happened during the Civil War, you must become familiar with some basic military concepts and learn a bit of vocabulary. This way, when you read accounts of battles in this book, or more detailed accounts of the campaigns and battles of the Civil War in other books, you will have some idea of what the author means.

This chapter walks you through some terms and concepts that give you just what you need to understand and appreciate what happened during the war and why.

# Understanding the Basics of War

When the existing unfavorable conditions between states (or nations) can no longer be tolerated, there is a resort to armed force called war. War, in essence, is a contest of wills in which the opponents employ armed violence against each other to compel a change favorable to the state. The victor in war is the state that breaks the other's will to resist. The outcome of the contest is defined in political terms. Thus, wars are fought for political objectives, but are motivated by fear, or interests related to security or survival, or prestige. Note that the first part of this book focuses on the political struggle between the North and South to establish the reasons for the war. All three of these motivations played a part in bringing the war about.

## The offensive and the defensive

War employs all types of force: physical, psychological, economic, diplomatic, and moral. The physical force of armed conflict is also called *combat power* — the collective efforts of humans, animals, and mechanical-industrial power harnessed to fight or strike an opponent at a vital spot. This combat power is organized into armies. Armies employ combat power in two ways, through the *offensive* and the *defensive*. In the offensive, one army chooses to advance, find, and defeat enemy forces by employing decisive combat power at the right place and time. In the defense, an army attempts to protect itself by minimizing its vulnerabilities and forcing the attacking army to expend combat power until it is too weak to attack any further.

## Strategy and tactics

Military operations are divided into strategy and tactics. *Strategy* directs armies into designated geographical regions to accomplish broad objectives defined by the political leadership. Armies in turn design *campaigns* — a series of battles and engagements intended to accomplish the assigned strategic objectives. *Tactics* deal with the way battles are fought, usually by organizations below army level (a corps, division, or brigade, for example). In summary:

>> **Strategy:** The art and science of designing military campaigns to achieve the objective of the war

>> **Tactics:** The art of employing armed units on the battlefield

The last few paragraphs give you the basics — a definition of war and the three concepts that determine the conduct of war: Strategy determines how a state's military capabilities will be used to achieve the objectives of the war. Campaigns are designed to employ military forces to fulfill the strategic objective. Tactics are the method military units employ to fight battles.

# Creating a Strategy: Three Basic Questions

A state or nation must have a strategy to fight a war. Otherwise the war has no direction or purpose. To determine a strategy, leaders must answer three basic questions that form the base of a wartime strategy:

>> **What are you trying to do?** In war, an ironclad connection exists between political objectives and the conduct of war. Both President Lincoln and President Davis had to determine their political objectives for the war. For Lincoln and the North, the initial political objective was to end the rebellion of the Southern states and restore the Union. For Davis and the Confederacy, the political objective was to gain and maintain its independence as a sovereign nation. These broad political goals become the means to determining a military strategy. War aims can change, depending on the outcome of campaigns and battles. The Union could not justify the war and its costs on its original objectives; another objective had to be added after 1862, which will be revealed soon,

>> **What do you have (or need)?** Answering this question involves an assessment and comparison of both your own and the enemy's resources. Remember, this means resources in the broadest sense — a nation's manpower, material stockpiles, finances, industrial capacity, and farm production. You need all of these things to fight and sustain a war. Another critically important national wartime resource is morale. *Morale* is the national will — how willing are the people (men, women, children) to suffer and endure to achieve victory? It is an intangible, but critical, strategic resource. A nation's leadership can sustain and nurture morale or squander it. Likewise, a nation can have very little in terms of resources, but with high morale it can overcome limitations and hardships to still win the war. Another important factor is will. How willing is the population to suffer the strains and terrible costs of war to achieve the political goals the leaders have outlined that define victory? You can have all the resources in the world and still lose a war because the people and the leadership do not have the will to employ them because the costs are too high to sustain. In the same way, will can make up for many deficiencies if the people and leadership are willing to commit everything to achieve victory. For both the Union and the Confederacy, national morale and the will to sustain the terrible fight played a significant role in both the conduct and outcome of the war.

>> **How do you use what you have?** All of the elements of national power must be employed in the proper proportions and at the right time to assure victory in war. This sounds simple, but it is not! There are many important questions national leaders must ask. Here are a few examples: How are the nation's strategic objectives (or war aims, as they are sometimes called) accomplished by the use of these elements of power? How do you bring in and orchestrate

economic power, moral power, diplomatic power, and military power? Where is one more effective than another? When should a nation employ its power? In what kind of mix? How will these elements of power weaken or negate an enemy's strength? These were questions that both President Lincoln and President Davis struggled to answer (as have most political leaders throughout history). Although neither leader ever answered these questions sufficiently, Lincoln, of course, in the end addressed them well enough to bring about the final defeat of the Confederacy.

# Uncovering the Principles of War

This section looks at the principles that guide the formation of strategy and tactics in war — the science of war. The principles of war have existed in one form or another since military forces first existed in human history. Civil War generals certainly were familiar with them, although in a different context. The principles have been codified now, and the following list is what military professionals study today:

>> **Objective:** Every military operation at all levels of war must have a clear, decisive, and attainable objective. You cannot win a war without an objective. Strategically speaking, the objective is the national political goal. Tactically, the objective is usually an enemy force or position.

>> **Offensive:** Wars are most often won through offensive action. The offensive provides the attacker the opportunity to impose its will on the enemy. In doing so, the attacker gains the initiative both strategically and tactically. The enemy then is unable to take any independent action and is forced to conform to the will of the attacker.

>> **Mass:** Gather overwhelming combat power at the decisive point and time. At both the tactical and strategic levels of war, mass is critical to success.

>> **Economy of force:** Forces must be employed judiciously and always with a purpose. An economy of force operation strategically and tactically can free forces from one point to mass with other forces for a decisive attack at another point.

>> **Maneuver:** Moving forces to gain an advantage over the enemy. Maneuver is applicable to both offense and defense. Maneuver allows an army to employ economy of force or mass. An enemy can be defeated through maneuver alone, without ever having to fight a battle. The greatest generals in history have always been masters of strategic and tactical maneuver.

- » **Unity of command:** Forces must be kept under one commander responsible for planning and directing their employment. Subordinate commanders act in accordance with the commander's plans to achieve the strategic objective by assigning their own forces objectives at the tactical level.

- » **Security:** Protect forces from being surprised by the enemy. The best security is a thorough knowledge of the enemy's plans and intentions.

- » **Surprise:** Strike the enemy at a time and place least expected. Surprise multiplies combat power immensely and can achieve decisive results. Speed, maneuver, deception, and mass can be employed strategically and tactically to achieve surprise.

- » **Simplicity:** The KISS (Keep It Simple, Stupid) principle. War is a complex business. Plans and orders at every level of war must be simple and concise so that everyone understands the plans and intentions of the commander.

# Developing Campaigns: The Art of War

Military commanders employ the art of war by following the principles of war to develop campaigns (see the "Strategy and tactics" section earlier in this chapter to refresh your mind) that support the nation's strategic objectives by seeking the best and quickest way to defeat the enemy. In developing a campaign, an army commander must first decide whether to conduct an offensive or defensive campaign. The goal of the offensive campaign is to break the will of the enemy through battlefield dominance, thereby destroying the military and/or political structure that allows the enemy to fight the war. The strategic offensive seeks out the enemy army, holds it in position so it cannot escape, and brings the enemy army to battle under conditions favorable to the attacker. The attacker has the advantage of making the first move with speed and decisiveness to overwhelm the enemy with superior combat power.

The ultimate goal of the defensive campaign is to protect a vital area or wear down the enemy to a point where further attacks are ineffective. An army on the defensive delays or wards off an attacking army by keeping it off balance, with the goal of not allowing the attacking army to use its superior strength. The defending army may seek to avoid battle altogether if the defender's combat power is significantly less than that of the opposing army. Although a defensive campaign seeks to limit direct contact with the enemy's strength, the defender still seeks to fight the attacker at a place and under conditions that offers the defender the best advantage. A commander will also use the defensive as a temporary measure to build combat power in order to shift to the offensive or lure the attacker into a disadvantageous position to be in turn attacked. This is called a *counterattack*.

# Interior and exterior lines

Strategically and tactically, the defender uses *interior lines* to avoid combat or collect combat power at vulnerable points exposed to an attacker (see Figure 4-1). Interior lines represent the area the defender occupies, usually an arc. Because the interior distance to all points in the arc is shorter than the exterior distance, the defender has the advantage. A commander can shift forces more quickly to meet an enemy attack than the enemy commander can shift forces to attack a vulnerable spot in the defender's lines. Interior lines, therefore, can negate the combat power of an attacking army and allow the defender to set the pace of battle. If a defender uses interior lines, an attacker almost always operates on *exterior lines.* Exterior lines have some advantages, allowing the attacker to maneuver to surround the enemy, threaten a number of weak points all at once, or attack simultaneously all along the enemy's defensive line to prevent any opportunity to mass forces against the threat.

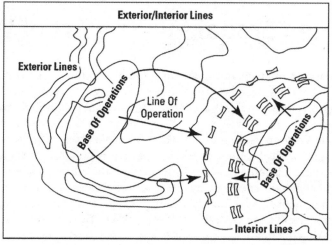

**FIGURE 4-1:** Interior and exterior lines.

John Wiley & Sons

# Lines of communication and supply

An important part of interior and exterior lines is how a commander establishes a *line of communication* and *line of supply.* These lines may be one and the same. Every army on the march has to have a means of continual resupply. Supplies are usually stockpiled and kept as close to the front as possible. Because of the massive amount of supplies a Civil War army consumed every day, boats and trains were the best means to move the amounts necessary to sustain the army for a week or so. Large wagon trains, 5 to 20 miles long at times, carried the immediate necessities (food for both men and animals and ammunition) with the army as it moved.

Like the major arteries in the body, the line of supply is the lifeline of a modern army. If an artery is blocked, cut, or damaged, the body dies. If a line of supply is blocked, cut, or damaged, the army can no longer function. Soldiers and animals starve; their weapons are useless for lack of ammunition, and even the clothes and shoes they wear fall apart.

## Supply is critical in war

Commanders in the Civil War were fully aware that supply lines required protection. The longer the supply line (usually a railroad or river line) the more exposed it became to attack and destruction. Many commanders chose to minimize their vulnerability of dependence on long lines of supply by living off the land for short periods of time. This meant soldiers were sent out in small parties to purchase (or seize) food and livestock from civilians in the countryside where the army was camping or marching. No army can do this forever. Eventually, the line of supply must be restored, or the army will simply cease to function. An army cannot exist without the means to sustain it.

## Information: Orders and critical intelligence

The line of communication is also important to an army. Orders, information, and intelligence information travel along these lines to allow the commander to make timely and effective decisions. In the Civil War, lines of communication were either telegraph lines or individual riders on horseback, known as couriers, carrying dispatches. Information also traveled with supply trains or boats. A commander without the information he needs is blind and can only guess about where the enemy is and can be led to make disastrous mistakes. So just like the line of supply, the line of communication keeps the army effective. A threat to the line of communication represents a serious danger and must be eliminated.

## The Indirect Approach

Clearly, one can fight an enemy force on a battlefield to win a decisive victory. But there are other ways to defeat an enemy army by attacking or threatening the enemy's line of supply, destroy or control its supply depots, or destroy or capture supply transports. Another nifty trick is to cut the enemy's line of communication. Whatever a commander can do to weaken the enemy, either by blinding or starving the army, will contribute to the enemy's defeat. After this is accomplished, an enemy is often vulnerable to direct attack and defeat. Therefore, a commander must always be vigilant to these threats and take the necessary actions.

## Taking the initiative: Who is on top?

When a commander has prevented the enemy from employing its tactical or strategic plans, whether on the offensive or defensive, this commander is considered to have the initiative. Whoever has the initiative dictates what will happen next on the battlefield. Tactically, the initiative can be lost, regained, and lost again depending on a variety of factors. The strategic initiative is usually up for grabs until one side begins to dominate. Victory in war is predicated on one side clearly gaining the strategic initiative.

# Putting It All Together: Strategy to Campaigns to Battles

Now that all the terms and concepts are straight, I will walk through the whole process that characterizes war. After the political leaders have decided on the broad objectives of the war, those objectives become the guide for all military activities. In a *campaign*, the army commander can decide to initiate an offensive or defensive campaign, depending on the ability of the army to conduct operations (the status of supply, morale, training, and leadership all play a role in this decision), whether to operate on interior or exterior lines, or in response to enemy movements or activities. The purpose of a campaign is to achieve the strategic objective through *movement* (the act of physically moving a military unit by road, rail, or water to a specific place for a specific purpose) and *battles* (fighting), using maneuver to employ superior combat power against an enemy army's weakest spot. Depending on the outcome of one movement, or even a series of movements in a campaign, the result is usually one or more battles.

## Fighting battles

Given a strategy with an objective, an army commander develops a *campaign;* within the campaign the commander seeks to meet the enemy force at the most advantageous place and time. When these forces encounter each other, it is called a *battle.* Battles in a campaign are supposed to be planned events, meant to move the campaign toward its ultimate objective. Commanders now employ tactics (methods of employing troops in combat) to defeat or destroy enemy forces. As you may expect, what was originally planned to work according to the proper application of the principles of war often ends on the battlefield as a set of improvised tactical actions in the midst of a maelstrom of death and destruction. Regardless of how well the plans are followed, battles are

>> Won

>> Lost

>> Have no effect

A battle is called *decisive* when success on the battlefield translates into attaining or significantly furthering strategic objectives.

# Win the battles — lose the war

This may sound strange but winning all the battles in a campaign and yet still failing to meet your strategic objective and thereby losing the war is possible. Such an event happened to the British army in the Revolutionary War and to the United States in the Vietnam War. The opposite holds true as well; you can lose all your battles, but still win your strategic objectives if the enemy no longer has the will to continue fighting.

# The commander's choices

In a battle, a commander uses tactics to attack or defend, depending on that commander's assessment of the situation. In the attack, the commander can use *maneuver*, which is the positioning of forces to gain an advantageous position against the enemy. There are three basic choices in the attack:

>> Advance forces head-on to break through the enemy defenses

>> Envelop the defender from one or both flanks (the left and right limits of an army's defensive line) by maneuvering forces around the enemy's defensive line and then attacking

>> Attack from the rear (usually the result of maneuvering behind an unsuspecting or unprepared defender)

The rear area is where the supply depots are located and where the lines of supply and communication are located. The frontal attack is the least desirable (that's usually where the enemy has concentrated combat power and is expecting to repel an attack), a flank attack is better (the enemy has less or sometimes no combat power on the flanks), and the attack from the rear is the best of all (no combat power and vulnerable, easy to destroy targets such as wagon trains and rail and telegraph lines).

These different types of attack can be combined into *main attacks* and *supporting attacks*. A main attack is where a commander employs the bulk of a unit's offensive combat power. The intent of the main attack is to defeat the enemy quickly and decisively. Often, a commander will use a supporting attack — a smaller portion of a unit's offensive combat power either to occupy enemy forces so they cannot *reinforce* (adding additional combat power to support other friendly forces), or deceive the enemy as to where the main attack will take place. Think of it in terms of a boxer who first comes at his opponent with a fake right cross to make his opponent react, then lands a roundhouse left. Like boxers, military commanders use tactics to try to employ more than one type of punch, usually in combinations, to put their opponents off balance and gain the initiative. In military terms, commanders employ a *feint*, in which the commander maneuvers forces to appear as if he is committing most or all of his combat power at a certain point. The feint is intended to deceive the enemy into thinking that this is the main attack. As the enemy responds, a vulnerability opens that can be exploited when the actual main attack is launched and can expose the enemy army to defeat and destruction. This type of employment of forces in space and time requires a masterful commander who appreciates the art of war.

## Terrain and the defensive

The defender tactically seeks to present the strongest position to the attacker, with sufficient combat power to overwhelm the attacker at his point of attack. If the defender has chosen well, the *terrain* (the lay of the land) will strengthen the defense and weaken the enemy's ability to maneuver and employ combat power. On a battlefield, some terrain is considered critical. As the name implies, critical terrain means that whoever controls this specific piece of ground will have a significant advantage over the enemy. Troops and artillery occupying critical terrain can mass firepower to destroy an attacker. If the defender loses this terrain, the army usually would be exposed to further attacks on its flanks or rear and be unable to defend itself effectively. The loss of critical terrain spells defeat and disaster. In the Civil War, critical terrain was usually single hills or ridges.

## Ending a battle

At any time in a battle, either commander can order a *withdrawal,* better known as a *retreat.* The intention of a withdrawal or retreat is to end the fighting to avoid further losses or escape from a disadvantageous position. In the Civil War, the retreat or withdrawal signified that the army commander had had enough of battle and needed to regroup and decide what to do next.

# Looking at the Civil War Army Organization

Because both Union and Confederate armies came from the American military tradition, they had the same organization. Within each army were three branches, corresponding to a particular combat skill: the cavalry, the artillery, and the infantry.

## Eyes and ears: The cavalry

The cavalry — mounted soldiers lightly armed and able to move fast and far — served as the eyes and ears of the army. (See Figure 4-2 for an illustration of the 1st Virginia Calvary.) It provided information about the enemy's location and intentions (attack, defend, withdraw). Cavalry served an important role in *screening*, a tactic that employed friendly cavalry to prevent enemy cavalry from finding out anything about the friendly army commander's intentions. Cavalry also conducted *raids.* Raids are a special type of offensive operation, usually conducted by a small force that enters deep into enemy territory to disrupt communications, destroy or threaten vulnerable lines of supply, capture supply wagons or trains, or frighten and demoralize the civilian population. In some instances, cavalry could fight as infantry, but only in an extreme defensive situation to delay or slow down the enemy force until friendly infantry could arrive.

**FIGURE 4-2:** 1st Virginia Cavalry.

*Waud, Alfred R / The Library of Congress / Public Domain*

Because of its mobility and ability to operate in small numbers that are hard to detect, cavalry also provided an invaluable service to an army commander — *reconnaissance.* Reconnaissance is the process of finding out about the enemy's size, activity, location, disposition (how an army has arranged its forces), morale, equipment, and intentions (attack, defend, and retreat). If a commander can gain information about the enemy while keeping the enemy's reconnaissance from finding out anything of value about his own forces (through screening — see the preceding paragraph), he will — if he's any good — be able to use this information to outfight and defeat his enemy.

## Providing firepower: The artillery

The artillery provided the long-reaching firepower on the battlefield. The army's cannons (see Figure 4-3) were organized into *batteries* of four to six guns each. Posted behind the infantry on high spots on the battlefield, or on the flanks of the line, the artillery supported infantry attacks with fire, or fired on attacking infantry in the defense with cannons. Artillery was often massed when possible to concentrate the devastating effects of the weapons on unprotected infantry formations of the enemy. When placed behind earthworks or breastworks, and sufficiently supported by infantry, artillery made such positions impervious to attack.

**FIGURE 4-3:**
The 12pd Napoleon — the standard artillery piece of both armies.

*Forbes / The Library of Congress / Public Domain*

# Fleet of foot: The infantry

Infantry units use foot marches and massed rifle fire in the attack or defense to accomplish the commander's battle plan (see Figure 4-4). The infantry contains the bulk of an army's combat power, because it is the decisive arm of war. Everything that has happened in war for thousands of years can be reduced to this one exquisite bit of simplicity — nothing is accomplished until soldiers on foot close in on and kill the enemy in close combat and occupy terrain. Infantry units marched to the battlefield in column, usually four soldiers abreast. Once on the battlefield and in proximity to the enemy, the column would make a flanking movement to form two lines facing the enemy. From this formation, units (usually regiments) would advance to a point where they could engage the enemy infantry effectively with massed rifle fire. While this seems simple, moving thousands of men like this took a high level of skill. The best units of the Civil War were those that had a high level of discipline based on time invested in drill, and skilled commanders who had mastered the intricacies of moving large bodies of troops over varied terrain in the face of artillery fire, gun smoke, and noise of battle.

**FIGURE 4-4:** Infantrymen of the 6th Massachusetts Volunteer Militia.

*The Library of Congress / Public Domain*

# Other important branches

When people think of war, they often think only about the fighters (infantry, cavalry, and artillery). This is natural, because they are the ones who make the story exciting. In actuality, the numbers of fighters in an army are usually the minority. Most of an army is made up not of fighters, but of units whose job is to support the fighters. Modern armies — and Civil War armies are a part of modern warfare — consume enormous amounts of *everything*. Whether in camp or in the field, armies consume tons of food and water every day. And not just people do all this consuming, either; the tens of thousands of animals that provided mobility for the cavalry and artillery needed to be fed as well. Anyone who has ever had to feed even one horse or cow knows how much forage it takes every day to keep them happy. In battle, an army consumes ammunition at incredible rates. Also, inevitably, men are killed or wounded.

In the general mess that is war, somebody has to haul every bite of food and every bullet and cannonball fired. Somebody has to provide clothes, shoes (for horses and men), equipment, and repair or replace whatever is lost or broken. Somebody has to keep records to make sure supply stocks are maintained, so that no shortages occur. Somebody has to deal with the sick, dead, and wounded. Somebody has to house the troops when they go into camp. Somebody has to build the bridges and rail lines to supply the army. You get the idea.

## Hauling food and ammo: The quartermaster

The *quartermaster* (or in modern terms, the *logistician*) has the unromantic but all-important job of providing everything the army needs to fight. The quartermaster supervised the rail depots and the supply trains (the long line of wagons) that followed the army on the march. In the Union army, the standard was 25 wagons for every 1,000 men. The *medical corps* treated casualties (the sick, dead, and wounded), taking them from the battlefield, burying the dead, and evacuating the wounded or sick to the rear for treatment and (the all-too-rare) recovery.

Orders for the movement of armies and combat information were passed through the *signal troops*, who maintained the critical lines of communications for the army. In the Civil War these troops used signal flags, mirrors, torches, balloons, couriers (messengers), and the telegraph to pass orders and instructions. Throughout the war, both sides established a highly organized communications system that went from the national leaders to the armies in the field and down to the company level — and back up again. For the first time in the history of war, the telegraph became an indispensable means of almost instantaneous communications. It allowed presidents Davis and Lincoln an unprecedented opportunity to maintain contact with generals in the field. The telegraph also allowed them at times to meddle in their generals' affairs. The armchair strategists in Richmond and Washington also enjoyed using the telegraph to provide field generals with commentary and criticism. Civil War leaders were the first to discover what people today know all too well: Communications technology can be both a blessing and a curse.

### Mastering the terrain: The engineers

*Engineers* planned and built fortifications (both temporary and permanent), built roads and bridges (both temporary and permanent), and made terrain maps (probably temporary and permanent, too). As the war went on, the skills of engineers became of increasing importance when both armies began to use entrenchments and breastworks, using sandbags and logs covered with earth to protect their forces while having a clear shot at the attacking enemy. Both Richmond and Washington were protected by extensive fortifications.

# Building a Basic Civil War Army Structure: The Regiment

The basic building block of the Civil War army was the *regiment*. The *regiment* had 10 *companies* of 100 men each for an official strength of 1,000. A *colonel* commanded the regiment. A *lieutenant colonel* (second in command), a *major* (third in command), and a small staff (which took care of the administrative needs of the regiment) assisted the colonel. Four regiments formed a *brigade*, commanded by a *brigadier* (obviously) *general*. This makes an official total of 4,000 men. Three brigades made up a *division*, commanded by either a *brigadier* or *major* (not so obviously) *general*. This makes an official total of 12,000 men. Three divisions made up a *corps* (pronounced "core"), commanded by a *major general* (if a Union division) or a *lieutenant general* (if a Confederate division). This works out to an official total of 36,000 men. See Table 4-1 for a comprehensive reference of army structure. See Table 4-2 for army hierarchy.

**TABLE 4-1**

## Army Structure

| Unit | Unit Multiples | Number of Soldiers |
| --- | --- | --- |
| Company | | 100 |
| Regiment | 10 Companies | 1,000 |
| Brigade | 4 Regiments | 4,000 |
| Division | 3 Brigades | 12,000 |
| Corps | 3 Divisions | 36,000 |

**TABLE 4-2**

## Army Hierarchy and Command

| Unit | Commanding Officer |
|------|--------------------|
| Regiment | Colonel Lieutenant or Colonel Major |
| Brigade | Brigadier General |
| Division | Brigadier General or Major General |
| Corps | Major General or Lieutenant General |

In 1861, two divisions made up a Union or Confederate army. In 1862, Union and Confederate armies were made up of corps, usually made up of three divisions, but an army could have any number of corps (which is why Civil War armies had such wide variances in numbers). Union armies were primarily named after major rivers (the Potomac, the Cumberland, the Ohio, the James). Confederate armies were named after locations or rivers (the Army of Northern Virginia in the east, the Army of Tennessee in the west). A major general commanded Union armies. A general commanded Confederate armies.

## Strength and size of units

The official numbers are good to get an idea of structure and organization, but in reality, Civil War armies had wide variances in unit strength. Sickness, desertions, battle deaths, wounds, and furloughs (time off from military duty, usually to go home) took their inevitable toll. Regiments often were 500 men or below. By 1863, some veteran regiments in both armies were down to 200 men or fewer. The reason for this lies in the method by which regiments were initially recruited and organized. Volunteers filled the initial ranks of new regiments. After several months of combat, the original (and now understrength) volunteer regiments were rarely brought back up to original strength with other volunteers; instead, entirely new regiments of recruits or conscripts (individuals enrolled in the army by compulsion through law) would be added to the army. This was especially true for Union units. Needless to say, this caused tremendous organizational and administrative headaches for a division or corps commander. This situation also caused problems on the battlefield. Veteran units had to be assigned to divisions composed of mostly untested recruits. This practice kept the overall fighting quality of the Union army uneven. After the institution of *conscription* (compulsory military service), replacements for both Union and Confederate armies were brought into existing units to bring them up to nominal strength. As the war went on, brigades filled out their strength by adding a number of understrength but very combat-capable regiments. Near the end of the war a brigade contained anywhere from five to six regiments.

## UNION AND CONFEDERATE CAVALRY: A COMPARISON

An interesting difference between the Union and Confederate cavalry was that the government provided a Union cavalryman a horse in the same way it provided a uniform and equipment. In the Confederate armies, a cavalryman had to provide his own horse. Needless to say, this led to a large number of well-off men joining the cavalry, although anyone who could procure a horse by any other means could become a cavalryman. Many Confederate cavalry raids in the war were launched specifically to capture horses. For a large part of the war, Confederate cavalry outperformed Union cavalry, because most of the troopers already had well-developed horsemanship skills. In the early part of the war, most of the Union troopers were still learning how to ride a horse, let alone fight on one.

## Roles of different units in an army

In a campaign, armies and corps conduct large-scale maneuvers to gain an advantage and set the conditions for battle. Divisions are assigned objectives to attack — usually a piece of terrain (a hill, ridge, trench line, woods) occupied by an enemy force. Capturing this piece of terrain would give the attacker a significant advantage and cause the defender to be exposed to other attacks. In the defense, a division is given a stretch of ground to cover with its brigades, usually a critical piece of terrain that must be protected if the army is to survive. The division commander passes orders to his brigade commanders, who in turn pass the orders down to the colonels in the regiments. And anywhere from 400 to 1,000 men grimly take their places shoulder to shoulder on line. After all the strategy, campaigning, and maneuver, after all the generals have made their decisions, the battle is fought, and won or lost, at the regimental level.

## Cavalry regiments

Union and Confederate cavalry regiments were organized much in the same way as infantry units, except cavalry companies were (and still are) called *troops*. A cavalry regiment had 12 troops. Cavalry units were considered independent and usually not deployed with infantry. Artillery batteries were attached to infantry brigades and divisions. An artillery reserve would be under control of either the corps or army commander.

# Comparing the Science versus the Art of War

Anyone can master the principles of war. There is no secret to conducting military operations according to the principles of war. This is the knowledge base all military leaders use when employing military forces in war. But not every military leader is successful in war. The science of war alone cannot win battles — the art is what makes the difference. The mystique of warfare and its attraction, some may say, is in observing how well a military leader translates principles of war into action in real situations of life and death when the fate of the nation is at stake. A number of generals throughout history have gained immortality through their ability to take the science of warfare and translate it into something uniquely theirs, something that people call art. The American Civil War displays the talents of some of these masters of the art of war.

Chapter **5**

# Union and Confederate Strategy

Wars are fought with armies. But what guides the actions and purpose of armies in war? That's where strategy comes in. Strategy is developed at the national level. In the case of the Civil War, the president and his military advisors dictated the strategy.

Strategy takes into account a number of important considerations. One of these is an assessment of the resources of the nation — essentially a measurement of its ability to conduct a war and sustain armies in the field. Another is the analysis of the geography. Geographical features can serve as an advantage or disadvantage, depending on your strategic approach.

## Comparing Northern and Southern Resources

For the Union and the Confederacy, any strategy had to be based on an assessment of resources. What were the nation's elements of power? How could they be used to accomplish the war aims of each nation? These elements of power become the resources (both tangible and intangible) that the Union and the Confederacy would rely on to fight this war. Whoever would win would apply these resources in the best manner over time. Sometimes, as in the case with the Union, some resources were not instantly apparent before the war. During the course of the war, the Union's moral power proved to be a very important factor in negating the Confederacy's resources. But no one understood it or appreciated it until two years after the war began.

Let's take a look at the resources the Union and the Confederacy possessed at the beginning of the war and compare them by category. The military men of both sides had a very tough assignment in assessing strategic resources and deciding how to marshal them to support the conduct of the war. No one had any experience in taking on such a monumental task to support military operations across a vast territory that stretched from the Mississippi River to the Chesapeake Bay. Physical and material resources would be required in as yet unimaginable quantities. The will of each country to sustain such a monumental effort would play an important role in determining victory or defeat.

## Industrial power

Industrial power includes raw materials (coal, iron, salt, niter, oil, copper, tin) and the factories to produce weapons, clothing, equipment, train engines, rails, and munitions. Southern factories were insignificant in comparison to the production capacities of factories of the North. Northern factories were already producing shoes, clothing, rails, and locomotives and were able to respond quickly to making these items available to the Union armies. Other factories were able to convert to producing weapons or weapons components very quickly. The Northern industrial base was capable of manufacturing every item (no matter how insignificant) needed to sustain an army in the field. From the onset, Southern factories were undermanned and overwhelmed early by wartime production demands. Although building an impressive capacity with limited resources, the Confederacy continually struggled.

## Agricultural advantages: Food and crops

Agricultural resources include food for the population and their animals, as well as nonfood crops (dyes, tobacco, cotton, hemp, timber); they also include the numbers of animals available both for food and for transportation. The South, a predominantly agricultural society, produced some food crops, but, ironically, not the amount that Northern farms did. The reason for this was the heavy reliance on staple, or cash, crops — tobacco and cotton. "Cotton is King!" was the motto of the prewar South. Indeed, it was. The South's money and wealth came from cotton and tobacco, not food crops. The Southern economy depended on being able to sell both cotton and tobacco on the international market. No other region of the nation, or the world for that matter, could grow these crops in abundance. It is not surprising, then, to see that economically, food production in peacetime was less important to the South than cotton and tobacco production. In wartime, however, it made a great difference.

### Cotton: The double-edged sword

In peacetime, all the world, but especially Great Britain and France, needed Southern cotton to feed their factories. For the South in wartime, though, cotton became a double-edged sword. Cotton hurt the South by taking up acreage that could be used to produce food for the Southern armies and civilian population. On the other hand, cotton represented a powerful strategic weapon for the South. Without cotton, European industries would have to shut down, causing great economic distress. European manufacturers could put pressure on their governments to do something about the lack of cotton. Cotton for the Confederacy could become a political bargaining tool to gain diplomatic recognition from the European nations.

### Cotton as collateral

Financially speaking, cotton was white gold. Cotton shipped to European markets would fetch high prices, especially when the Europeans began to feel the pinch of cotton shortages as a result of the war. In turn, money from cotton sales could be used to purchase the weapons and supplies for Southern armies that the Confederacy could not produce itself. In addition, cotton could be used as collateral for foreign loans to support the Confederate government. Cotton became both a diplomatic and a financial advantage that President Davis hoped would be the decisive factor that would win the war for the Confederacy.

## Soldiers and laborers: Population

Large-scale war requires enormous human resources, both in terms of soldiers to fill the ranks of the armies and workers to produce the means to sustain those armies as well as support the civilian population. The several million immigrants who flooded into the North between 1830 and 1860 provided recruits, agricultural laborers, and industrial workers. Few immigrants came to the South, leaving the Confederacy to rely on its white male population for soldiers. Slaves were a critical strategic resource, providing in some cases the skilled labor in factories and logistical support for the armies, as well as working on the farms to produce food. Women also were employed in a variety of roles in supporting the wartime production effort. During the Civil War, about 45 percent of the eligible males in the North served in the army. In the South, about 90 percent of eligible men served in the army.

## Financial wealth

The financial advantages include the structure and soundness of the banking system, availability of credit, debt structure of the government, and the financial system, as well as the government's tax system. The availability of ready cash reserves (gold and silver) and numerous banks in the North allowed the government to borrow and pay for the costs of raising armies. The South, lacking these financial resources because most of its wealth was tied up in land and slaves, was crippled from the very beginning to finance the huge expenditures necessary to fight a war. The short time between the creation of the Confederate government and the onset of a war for independence caused enormous challenges simply to organize a system of taxation and obtain credit.

## Analyzing the statistics for both sides

Statistics and numbers can be a useful tool, but the insightful interpretation of them actually makes the picture of events crystal clear. See Table 5-1 for the major resources of the Union and the Confederacy (excluding the Border States) in 1861. Without making too much of these statistics, some points need to be made. At first glance, the manpower resources of the North appear dominant. In actuality, the South had a slight strategic advantage. As an industrial society, a significant proportion of the North's manpower was tied up in the factories. Also, many farmers needed to remain home to produce food, further cutting into the manpower pool. The three and a half million slaves in the South, a predominantly agricultural society, allowed white Southerners to serve in the army in far greater numbers, proportionately, than Northerners.

**TABLE 5-1:** ### Distribution of Major War Resources

| | North | South |
|---|---|---|
| **Population** | | |
| | 18.5 | 5.5 million |
| | | 3.5 million (slaves) |
| **Agricultural** | | |
| Corn | 396 | 280 millions of bushels |
| Wheat | 114 | 31 millions of bushels |
| Oats | 138 | 20 millions of bushels |
| Cotton | 0 | 5 million bales |
| Tobacco | 58 | 199 million pounds |
| Rice | 0 | 187 million pounds |

| | North | South |
|---|---|---|
| **Animal Resources** | | |
| Mules | 330 | 800 thousand |
| Cows | 5 | 2.7 million |
| Beef Cattle | 5.4 | 7 million |
| Sheep | 14 | 5 million |
| Hogs | 11.3 | 15.5 million |
| **Industrial Capacity** | | |
| Railroad Mileage | 20 | 9 thousand track miles |
| Number of Factories | 100.5 | 20.6 thousand |
| Skilled Workers | 1.1 million | 111 thousand |
| **Financial** | | |
| Bank Deposits | $189 million | $47 million |
| Gold/Silver on Hand | $45 million | $27 million |

Clearly the Union had all the advantages in the areas of railroad mileage, manufacturing, and finance. Railroads became a strategic asset quickly in this war to gain the advantage over the enemy. For the first time in history, men and equipment in wartime were moved across long distances by rail. Railroads also moved supplies to the armies and raw materials to factories. They became the lifeline of modern war. Do not get the idea that just because the North had more advantages than the South that the war was a predetermined victory. If that were the case, the war would have been over very quickly. Remember, these advantages do not by themselves determine victory. It is how well they are used to support the war's ultimate goal that makes these resources decisive. The South used its fewer resources more efficiently than the North at first, giving the Confederacy an initial advantage. It took the Union far longer to harness its resources and apply them to the war effort.

# Wartime Strategy: Union and Confederate

As the political leaders of each nation had made their determination to move toward war, they now had to huddle with their military advisors and determine how the military strategy would be shaped to support the overall political goals each president had defined for his nation.

## The Union's strategy

Based on the political objectives and the assessment of its resources, the Union had a simple military strategy: divide and conquer. Union armies would have to invade the Confederacy, split it in half, and capture and control its territory. General Winfield Scott, the commanding general of the U.S. Army, developed what was termed "the Anaconda Plan." His strategy for defeating the Confederacy contained three objectives. The first goal of the strategy was to capture the Confederate capital at Richmond, Virginia, only 100 miles from Washington, D.C. The second goal was to strangle the Confederacy through the use of a blockade. This blockade would employ the U.S. Navy in a cordon around the 3,500-mile coastline of the Confederacy to prevent any seaborne commerce from entering or leaving Southern ports. The third part of the strategy was to advance down the Mississippi River, cut the Confederacy in half, and defeat its armies. It all looked good on paper, but the prospects of achieving these three goals were daunting.

## The Confederacy's strategy

Confederate military strategy can be stated in far simpler terms — *survive*. To win, the Union had to invade and attack Confederate resources and its military strength. By remaining on the strategic defensive, inflicting heavy losses on invading enemy armies, and protecting its critical weak points, the Confederacy could conserve its limited resources and simply hold out until the Union leaders gave up. If the Union did not give up easily, the Confederacy included as part of its strategy a plan to end the war through the intervention of a major European power on the Confederacy's behalf. This scenario may sound familiar. It is the same strategy that won the 13 colonies their independence from Great Britain in the American Revolution, when France entered into an alliance with the Americans. Another option was to gain a decisive victory on the battlefield that would convince the Union to seek peace, or convince the Europeans that the Confederacy had the capability to survive as an independent country.

# Geography and Strategy: Theaters of War

In formulating these two strategies for the Union and the Confederacy, geography played an important role. The Confederacy's land area of 750,000 square miles roughly equaled that of Europe, minus the Scandinavian countries. This is a huge area of land — extremely difficult to conquer and equally difficult to defend with limited resources. Geography in strategic military terms signifies the general layout of the land and how it assists or hinders the movement of armies or naval forces. Strategists look for barriers to movement (mountains, rivers, coastlines, swamps, forests); areas that allow rapid movement (rivers, mountain passes, all weather roads, major rail lines, valleys, plains); and key areas (industries, cities, ports, road/rail junctions).

From the point of view of Union and Confederate strategists, the geography of the southeastern United States divided itself into three main areas, or *theaters*. A theater is a subdivision of a larger geographical area where military operations take place.

## The Eastern Theater

The first of the three main theaters was the Eastern Theater, a relatively small triangle of territory in Virginia bounded by Washington, D.C., in the north, Norfolk to the east, and the Cumberland Gap in the west. Within the three points that made up this triangle was Richmond, the capital of the Confederacy. The capital cities of both nations became strategic priorities. Both had to be protected at all costs — the effect on each nation's morale would be devastating if either city was attacked and captured.

In strategic terms, Richmond was also a critical road and rail network, and the location of one of the Tredegar ironworks — one of the most important factories in the South. At Norfolk was the Chesapeake Bay, a water invasion route that led both to Washington, by way of the Potomac, and to Richmond, by way of the James River. Norfolk and the Chesapeake Bay had to be controlled by friendly naval forces. As a major outlet to the Atlantic, the Confederacy needed Norfolk and the access to the mouth of the Chesapeake Bay to sustain commerce and protect Richmond. Just as importantly, the Union forces had to cut off Confederate commercial and military access to the Chesapeake Bay. The western leg of the triangle included the Shenandoah Valley, a critical food-producing region for the Confederacy, as well as a major invasion route into and out of Virginia. Over the next four years within the Eastern Theater, hundreds of thousands of soldiers would be killed or wounded.

## The Western Theater

The Western Theater was a vast area that stretched from the Appalachian Mountains in the north, south to the Gulf coast, and west to the Mississippi River. The Mississippi was a significant east-west barrier to movement but an excellent north-south corridor for invasion. The Confederacy had to keep the river under its control to avoid being split in two, which was part of the Union's strategy; for the Union, control of the river was a key to success. To control the river, you had to control *both* New Orleans and Vicksburg, the two main cities on the river. Other important rivers, such as the Tennessee and the Cumberland, served as invasion routes deep into the interior of the South that also had to be defended against invaders. The ability to build a strong naval presence on these critical rivers would support land forces. Keeping river access open to friendly forces while denying the same access to enemy forces was a critical factor to achieving victory.

The Western Theater also had most of the South's agricultural land and its east-west railroad lines. The railroads were vital to the Confederacy's survival. There were a number of these lifelines: One was the Corinth–Chattanooga–Knoxville–Richmond line; another was Vicksburg–Montgomery–Atlanta–Charleston line; a third was the Columbia–Wilmington–Raleigh–Petersburg–Richmond line. Each of these moved supplies and troops between theaters. Thus, if Union forces could cut off these lines, the Confederacy would be unable to defend or sustain itself for very long. Protecting these lines and the cities that had major rail junctions became a centerpiece of Confederate strategy.

The coastline of the Confederacy offered invaders opportunities to strike from the sea inland at harbors, ports, inlets, sounds, and rivers. The Confederacy's major port cities of Galveston, New Orleans, Mobile, Savannah, Port Royal, Charleston, Wilmington, and Norfolk had to remain open. Both sides knew that the Confederacy's survival depended on international commerce for critical supplies and funding. Union strategy would focus on maintaining a tight, effective blockade to shut down the ports; the Confederate strategy would focus on breaking the blockade or minimizing its effect to allow the ports to operate freely.

## The Trans-Mississippi Theater

The third theater was the Trans-Mississippi Theater, which covered the territory west of the Mississippi all the way to New Mexico. Although not an area where there would be much fighting, Texas, Arkansas, and Missouri were nonetheless critical for the Confederate war effort. Food grown in these areas, as well as war supplies from Mexico, moved by rail from these states to the east. The Trans-Mississippi Theater shared a border with Mexico, a prime trading partner for the Confederacy. Mexico also offered blockade-free access to European suppliers. Military supplies brought in through Mexico had to travel through this theater. Some of the most famous fighting units in the Civil War came from the states of the Trans-Mississippi Theater. Confederate control of the Mississippi River would ensure that this theater would continue to sustain the Confederacy with supplies and manpower. If control of the Mississippi fell to Union forces, however, this important lifeline would be severely limited.

# Civil War Strategy in Retrospect

Despite all of the different angles, advantages, disadvantages, and elaborate strategies, winning the war would depend on who could hold out the longest, although this fact was not obvious to most strategists in 1861. Many strategists believed that a couple of big, largely bloodless battles would settle the matter and bring peace. In their view, the war, such as it was, would only last a few months, six at the most. Only a very few understood what this war actually meant and what it would cost to win. Very soon, both sides would learn hard lessons about modern war and adjust their strategies to adapt to the new circumstances they found themselves in.

# Chapter 6

# Organizing and Training the Armies

The Civil War was a war fought by amateurs. Only a very small number of men in America had military experience. Volunteers and militia units called up for active service for a specific period of time had always fought in earlier American wars. These units were of notoriously poor quality, unless thoroughly trained and properly led.

As the new soldiers found out rather quickly, joining the army didn't necessarily mean wearing a fancy uniform and impressing the women (although that certainly was a motivator for signing up). It often meant tedious hours of marching, standing in formation, inspections, waiting, and learning how to use all the equipment the army issued to you. It meant learning to follow orders, working and thinking as a unit, and developing the skills necessary to survive in battle. The American men who rushed to join the colors in 1861 weren't always too thrilled to conform to the ways of the military. For them, experience would be a stern teacher.

## Making Civilians into Soldiers

Between Fort Sumter in April 1861 and the battle of First Manassas in July 1861, the Union and Confederate governments worked to take tens of thousands of eager civilian volunteers with a smattering of professional officers and enlisted men and train, equip, and deploy them in organized military units that were capable of more than just looking good and consuming supplies. This is not a rapid process in the best of situations. Both armies had far too few experts in military training available to do the teaching. It took months, even over a year for everyone to learn this new trade. Even then, the quality of training in units varied widely. Often, it was the test of combat that determined whether a unit was capable of functioning properly. Those lessons learned in combat were then applied in earnest. Training improved over time, but the period between the onset of the war in 1861 and the spring of 1862 was chaotic.

## Fighting in the frontier: The regulars

The Union had a core of over 16,000 regular (semiprofessional) soldiers who were capable of overseeing conditions on the frontier but were far from capable of providing the leadership and training necessary to turn masses of unruly volunteers into soldiers. The U.S. government as a result kept regular units separate from volunteers. Thus, the regular army remained small throughout the war, much of its strength still parceled out on the western frontier guarding against American Indian raids. The Confederacy, of course, had no regular army, but did make the best use of those regulars who had joined the Confederate army. These officers were integrated into the volunteer units to provide valuable leadership and training. For both armies, the process of turning civilians into soldiers fell to a combination of professional officers and former West Point graduates who returned to active service.

## Responding to the call: The militia

Nearly every state had militia units, the forerunner of our National Guard units today. Militia units were locally recruited volunteers that the state intended to use in an emergency or to be called up to join the regular army during a war. Over the years, largely due to neglect from the state government, they had become more social drinking organizations than military units. The few called up for the Mexican-American War were so poor that they were never used in combat. In reality, other than having a rudimentary knowledge of military formations and use of weapons, the vast majority of militia units were of no immediate use.

## Joining to fight: Volunteers — then Conscripts

Volunteer units were the most common military organizations at this early stage of the war. Young men from towns and cities formed ad hoc military organizations, usually companies, volunteering for military service for 90 days (others volunteered for three years). These units would report to their state capital, where they would be combined with other volunteer units to form regiments. Volunteer companies elected their own officers, usually the most popular or best politician among the group.

## ELECTING OFFICERS IS A BAD IDEA

While a good idea for the Kiwanis club, having the rank and file elect leaders in military units is not wise. Military leaders have the unenviable task of ordering their soldiers to do things that will result in possible wounds or death. Friendship in this case must be set aside, and those who are ordered to face such danger have to have confidence in the man giving the order. The one who won the popularity contest might not necessarily be up to such a task or the responsibility. Although the election of officers continued for some years (especially in the Confederate armies), the practice mostly died out, and a system of merit promotions based on demonstrated ability took its place.

**TECHNICAL STUFF**

While volunteers are usually plentiful at the onset of any war, wars do not grow in popularity after the onset of combat. The pool of volunteers quickly dries up, leaving the government only one choice: conscription, or as the U.S. government in 1862 conveniently put it, "universal military liability." This meant all able-bodied male citizens by law could be enrolled in the army by compulsion (force). Both the Union and Confederate governments resorted to conscription early in the war to maintain manpower requirements.

After volunteer regiments were formed (initially made up of about 1,000 men), they were shipped to an assembly point, most often the capital city (either Richmond or Washington), were equipped as best as possible, organized into brigades and divisions, and then into a corps. Once the command structure had been established, the new soldiers were introduced to the discipline and drill necessary to maneuver and fight in battle. In most cases, the regimental, brigade, division, and corps commanders of these new units had only a bit more experience than their soldiers did.

# Qualifications of Union and Confederate Officers

In the Union army, state governors gave rank to officers of the newly formed regiments. Some of these officers inevitably were political friends, given a plum assignment because they had influence at election time. President Lincoln appointed generals. While many generals he appointed had experience as regular army officers, a fair number of appointments went to Democrats or influential Republicans in key states who helped Lincoln maintain his precarious wartime coalition. Others — representatives of key immigrant groups with powerful voting blocs (the Irish and the Germans) — received general's stars. West Point graduates, who had some exposure to military discipline and structure, were highly valued and contributed a great deal to molding capable units.

In the Confederate armies, officers with political influence at the state level were usually former U.S. senators or rich planters hoping to make a name for themselves. President Davis initially relied on his available pool of experienced army officers for generals. Later, he did not usually promote an officer to general's rank until that officer had displayed battlefield leadership.

When comparing the overall quality of officer talent between the Union and the Confederacy, the advantages initially clearly lay with the Confederacy. Some of the most capable officers in the U.S. Army had joined the Confederacy. The South was also blessed with a superior cadre of mid-level officers who had graduated from the many military colleges found in nearly every Southern state. These men easily integrated into the army and immediately made their presence felt, providing leadership and discipline for the often unruly volunteers. The depth of military talent and experience within the Confederate officer ranks helped them to create a viable military force within a relatively short period of time, especially in the Eastern Theater. Regardless of their officer leadership, both the Union and Confederate armies would discover that the battlefield would teach the hardest lessons.

## Military bloopers: The political generals

The political generals, as the generals who were appointed for solely political reasons were known, continued to plague both armies throughout the war. Lacking any military talent and blundering from one disaster to another, they nonetheless remained as a symbol of the critical link between politics and war. Most of these generals sought more useful (and safer) opportunities for national service outside of the army after their first taste of combat. To be fair, some officers who received their commissions through political connections displayed skill and talent, but these were the exceptions.

## Rookies learning a new trade: the blind leading the blind

In the early months of the war, it was not unusual to see newly commissioned captains, majors, colonels, and generals in the camps of both armies pouring over instruction manuals, trying to stay one step ahead of their trainees. Because so many officers were required for the large new armies, there was not enough expertise to go around. Officers with military experience were usually promoted to high rank early in the war. That left all the ranks of junior officers to be filled with volunteers who often had no idea what their role was in a military organization. Not only did the privates have to learn what soldiers did, but also the new officers had to learn soldier skills in addition to learning their own jobs. Even President Lincoln took time to study military science to acquaint himself with the terms and concepts of military operations — in just about the same way you are doing now!

Chapter **7**

# Significant Weapons of the Civil War

Technology was on the fast track in the 1860s. New and more efficient (deadlier, more accurate) weapons came into use. New weapons meant training and practice. While Americans were quite familiar with firearms, they were not familiar with the tactical employment of individual weapons in battle. Nor were they familiar with purely military weapons, like artillery. New recruits had to be trained to maintain and properly employ these weapons in battle. Cavalrymen had to learn how to fight both mounted and dismounted with three different weapons (pistol, saber, and carbine). Firepower, unless effectively employed on the battlefield, is useless.

## The Weapons You Need to Fight

The Union and the Confederacy had to equip tens of thousands of men pouring into camps, eager for battle. To the chagrin of the volunteers of both sides, these new soldiers had to learn far more than just picking up a gun and shooting at somebody. Part of the basic skill training of the Civil War soldier involved the employment of massed firepower in the form of a regiment standing shoulder to shoulder delivering aimed fire in a single volley at the enemy. Everyone loaded his weapon at the same time, everyone shouldered and aimed his rifle at the same time, and everyone fired his weapon at the same time. Loading and firing took practice until the process became automatic, which was important in the stress and confusion of battle. Likewise, new artillerymen had to learn how to put the cannons into firing position, learn what kind of shell to use at what distance against what target, and learn the intricacies of loading and firing without killing themselves in the process (something that happened with unfortunate regularity), while also under fire. Cavalrymen had to be able to use their limited firepower effectively enough to delay an enemy force from gaining an advantage over friendly forces.

## Struggling with the smoothbore

Part of the problem with arming the soldiers was the lack of modern weapons. At the beginning of the war, the Confederacy had only about 25,000 modern rifled weapons available. The vast majority of weapons on hand were antiquated flintlock *smoothbore muskets*, castoffs from federal stocks delivered to militia units before the war. These types of weapons had been in existence since the early eighteenth century. A smoothbore musket fired a round lead ball from a barrel (the long metal tube). The barrel was smooth all the way down to the bottom, thus the name smoothbore. The ball was tamped into the barrel with a powder charge and wadding (to keep the ball from falling out of the barrel). When the trigger was pulled, a hammer containing flint would strike a steel plate, igniting the powder-ball charge at the bottom of the barrel. The resulting explosion of the powder would expel the ball. The effective range of this weapon was 40 yards, meaning that to kill someone, you had to be pretty close. At 100 yards, the weapon was useless. It was heavy (weighing about 11 pounds), and at best you could get off one shot a minute.

Many Southerners owned weapons like this and brought them to their units. Others brought shotguns, fowling pieces, and other oddities. The shortage of modern weapons limited the effectiveness of many Confederate units in battle in the first encounters in 1861 and early 1862. However, the Confederacy made up for its lack of rifled muskets through domestic manufactures. Facilities in Richmond, Virginia, and Fayetteville, North Carolina, turned out over 64,000 high-quality rifles using the arms-making machinery from Harpers Ferry. The Confederacy also purchased quality foreign weapons, including the British Enfield and the Austrian Lorenz. The Confederate armies also took advantage of scrounging the battlefields for discarded Union weapons.

## Rifled muskets for the infantry

The Union army had little difficulty procuring modern rifled weapons. Unlike the Confederacy, which controlled only the arsenal and weapons production facility at

Harpers Ferry, the North could rely on some of the most sophisticated commercial arms manufacturers in the world. The primary weapon on the Civil War battlefield was the *rifled musket*, which marked a significant improvement over the smooth-bore weapon. In addition to an improved firing system (using a percussion cap made of copper that contained a small bit of explosive material to set off the charge), the barrel of the new weapon had small spiral grooves from top to bottom. These grooves caused a bullet leaving the barrel at high speeds to spin. The spin allowed the bullet to travel farther and straighter. Think of a quarterback throwing a football; the spin put on the ball in the act of throwing creates a tight spiral, allowing the ball to travel long distances accurately. Rifling does the same thing for a bullet.

## Spinning faster: The Minié ball

Speaking of bullets, a French army officer named Minié (pronounced "Minnie") developed a new design to replace the round ball used in the smoothbore musket. The new bullet was a conical soft lead projectile with a hollow base. When fired, the gases created by the burning powder pushed against the hollow base, sealing it against the rifling, and forcing it to spin along the grooves of the barrel. The Minié ball, as it was known, was the standard bullet used in the war. The rifled musket and its Minié ball allowed a soldier to kill an enemy at ranges of 200 to 300 yards. The new rifle weighed about 9 pounds, and a well-trained soldier could get off three shots a minute.

# The Rifled Musket and Tactics

Although it was more accurate, lighter, and more reliable than the smoothbore, the rifled musket had the same loading process as the older design. The bullet and powder were wrapped in paper called a *cartridge*. The soldier stood with the rifle in front of him. He then had to tear the cartridge open with his teeth, pour the powder into the barrel, drop the bullet down the barrel, and then ram both the bullet and the powder down to the base of the barrel with a ramrod. Next, he pulled the hammer back, attached a percussion cap, and, finally, raised and fired the rifle. Ostensibly, an order given by an officer in the ranks preceded each step of the process (nine in all). These orders were believed to be a necessity, because in the fear and confusion of battle, soldiers often lost track of the loading process. With every soldier following the steps by order, this ensured (in theory) that the unit would deliver the massed fire that infantry units had relied upon for decisive effect since the 1700s. In actuality, soldiers would fire an initial volley under orders, then just load and fire as fast as they could.

While the rifled musket was more accurate at longer distances, it did not significantly change the basic tactics of the Napoleonic wars. Units had to be held together in tight ranks to hear and respond to commands, units would advance against an enemy position, and, instead of a deadly bayonet charge, one of two things would happen: the enemy fire would be heavy and accurate enough to stall the advance, forcing an orderly retreat (or a headlong run to safety), or the advance would be strong enough with enough momentum to force the defender to retreat (or run away as fast as possible). Especially early in the war, units neither advanced nor retreated but instead stood facing each other, pouring fire into each other's ranks.

Because battles were decided by close combat, not massed musket fire, the bayonet was an essential infantry weapon. It was a long, thin, pointed instrument placed over the end of the musket barrel that turned the musket into a fighting spear at the ends of their weapons weapon. (See Chapter 4, Figure 4-4, which shows infantrymen armed with one version of the bayonet.)

# The Really Big Guns: Civil War Artillery

Artillery, like the musket, was classified as either rifled or smoothbore, and identified by the weight of the projectile it fired. And like the rifled musket, it was loaded from the muzzle (the front opening of the gun barrel) and had a prescribed order of actions to load and fire. Artillery units were organized into batteries of four to six cannon commanded by a captain. *Field artillery*, as it was called, was light and mobile enough to be used to support infantry on the battlefield. The standard Civil War artillery piece was the 12-pound smoothbore model 1857 Napoleon (see Chapter 4, Figure 4-3). This gun could fire a variety of ammunition depending on the target. It fired a 12-pound shot a maximum distance of 1,600 yards. Rifled artillery, which just like the musket, was more accurate and came in many different types, from 10-pound to 24-pound guns. The most common rifled guns found on the battlefield fired a 9.5-pound shell between 1,800 and 1,900 yards. In smoothbore cannons, the powder and shot were loaded as one package; in rifled artillery, the powder and shot were loaded separately.

Every artillery piece had a horse-drawn caisson and limber, which carried the ammunition, tools, and equipment for the gun. The gun was attached to the limber, and the crew of nine cannoneers rode to battle on top of the ammunition chests — a slightly dangerous method of transportation, to say the least. It took about 91 horses to move an artillery battery. As the war went on, the need for horses to replace battle losses became a prime concern of both Union and Confederate artillerymen.

# Artillery ammunition

Solid shot (cannonball) was used against large troop concentrations and fortifications. A shell contained a bursting charge that would cause it to explode while still in the air, showering troops with metal. Canister was used against close-range targets (up to 350 yards). Canister resembled a tin can. Inside the cylinder were 27 pieces of cast-iron round shot. Canister turned the smoothbore into a giant shotgun. Needless to say, it had a devastating effect on approaching infantry and was the most dangerous of all the ammunition available. The cannon had no aiming system, other than the sharp eye of the cannoneer, who had to see his target and guess at the distance.

# Using artillery

Few generals on either side were familiar with the proper tactical employment of artillery. But when used properly, and served by capable gunners, artillery could be the decisive weapon in battle. Not surprisingly, from the beginning of the war, the Confederacy was hampered by a lack of dependable cannon and ammunition. The Confederacy had only a few facilities capable of casting cannon barrels. Not surprisingly, most of the heavy casting mills were located in the North. Union artillery captured on the battlefield were easily incorporated into Confederate batteries.

# Cavalry Weapons

For centuries, the horseman and his *saber* (a curved sword for cutting and slashing) was a feared combination. However, by 1860, the horseman was vulnerable to rifle fire, which would knock down scores of horsemen before they ever got close enough to use their sabers. So, the saber was outmoded, a relic of a romantic past. They were noisy and awkward to wear and carry, but they were a symbol of the dash and bravado of the cavalry, so almost every horseman carried a saber at one time or another.

## The carbine

In both the North and South, the prized weapon of the cavalryman was the *breech-loading carbine*. A carbine is essentially a short rifle (see Figure 7-1). A breech-loading carbine is a weapon that was loaded with a brass cartridge from the rear, near the trigger. (The breech is where the end of the barrel meets the firing mechanism.) A lever moved to open or close the breech, sealing the cartridge in the barrel and making it ready to fire. Several advantages are apparent:

FIGURE 7-1:
Cavalry troops
with carbines.

Waud, Alfred R / The Library of Congress / Public Domain

>> First, a breech-loading carbine is easier to load and quicker to fire —
   something a soldier appreciates when being shot at. The breech-loading
   carbine could get three shots off to every one fired by a muzzleloader.

>> Second, a breech-loading carbine is small and lightweight (about 8 pounds),
   which comes in handy when you are seated on a horse.

The U.S. government purchased large numbers of breech-loading carbines, but
the Confederacy had very few and could only produce a few inferior copies.
Confederate cavalrymen scrounged them from battlefields whenever they could.
The Confederate cavalry also had muzzle-loading carbines, but these were less
than useless after the first shot; nobody could reload one of those things while
mounted. Many Confederate horsemen preferred the sawed-off shotgun — an
American original that came to be greatly feared in close combat.

## The revolver

Of course, every cavalryman carried one or more pistols to use at close quarters in
a cavalry fight. The preferred pistol was the *revolver* — a pistol that had a rotating
cylinder containing powder and ball that moved to align with the rifled barrel to
fire when the trigger was pulled. Cavalrymen used various types of pistols, but the
most prized were the legendary pistols of Samuel Colt. The U.S. government supplied Colt revolvers to its mounted troops. The Confederates manufactured a few
pistols using Colt's model, but most revolvers used by Confederate horsemen were
obtained from captured supplies or battlefield scrounging.

# 3

# Opening Moves, 1861–1862

**IN THIS PART . . .**

Explore the who, what, when, where, and why of each battle.

Understand how battles fit into a campaign plan.

Watch as the armies begin to advance, and see why the initial encounters between largely untrained troops and inexperienced leaders are bloody and indecisive.

Watch as heroes are born, martyrs are created, and once-promising leaders disappear quickly in failure.

# Chapter **8**

# Starting the War: Bull Run (First Manassas), July 1861

The battle of Bull Run as the Union called it, or Manassas as the Confederates called it, was the first major engagement of the war. Many honestly believed that one large battle would decide the outcome of the war, almost like a Super Bowl — whoever lost would allow the other side to pursue its strategic goals unmolested. Also like the Super Bowl, civilians from Washington came with picnic lunches to watch the battle and cheer for the Union army. Everyone who volunteered wanted to get in the fight, afraid that the war would be over before they had a chance at glory.

As they quickly learned, war is not sport. Battles are contests of will, involving unimaginable confusion, excitement, and horrific violence. The shock of combat is unforgettable, and it convinced many an eager volunteer that he had seen enough of war to last a lifetime. Battles also create (and sometimes destroy) heroes. Bull Run created one of the greatest and most well-known heroes in American military history: "Stonewall" Jackson.

# The First Rumblings: "On to Richmond!"

The war began with neither side fully prepared to do anything. Neither side had a campaign plan to accompany the national strategy. Each side was more interested in putting together an armed force capable of defending its capital city. Nothing resembling an army would emerge for several months after Fort Sumter. Davis and the Confederacy, of course, had time on their side. With a defensive strategy, the Confederate armies (a generous term at this time) simply had to train and wait for the Yankees to invade. It was the Union side, and especially President Lincoln, who felt the mounting pressure to do something. Months had gone by, and so far all the Union army had done was to build forts around Washington and capture the two undefended Virginia cities of Arlington and Alexandria across the Potomac River.

## Taking command of Union forces: McDowell

General Irvin McDowell (see Figure 8-1), a West Point graduate and Mexican-American War veteran who had been promoted from major in the regulars to general only two months earlier, commanded an army of about 35,000 men. McDowell had no one available with any real expertise in training large numbers of men and organizing them into brigades and divisions. Most of the men in his army were 90-day volunteers, who by this time had had enough of both the tedium of camp life and the oppressive heat of a Washington summer. They were ready to go home, battle or no battle. Lincoln, knowing the political implications of his army melting away in a few short weeks, and despite his best judgment that the army was not capable of performing effectively in battle, bowed to public pressure. People were anxious for the government to do something. In the Northern press and in the halls of Congress came the cry "On to Richmond!" These amateur strategists thought it was all so simple: The army just had to march the short 100 miles down to the Confederate capital and turn the rebel government out. Before that, there had to be a battle, a great spectacle that would decide the entire contest. There just happened to be a rebel force only 30 miles away at Manassas, Virginia, just waiting to provide the drama and excitement of war. The road to Richmond, then, would have to lead through Manassas.

## Waiting: Beauregard and the Confederates

The Confederate force, with about 22,000 men, was located at the small town of Manassas, a strategic road and rail junction that connected Washington and the northeast to the Shenandoah Valley, Richmond, and Lynchburg. A number of major roads also intersected there. Thus, it was an ideal place for an army to defend a key transportation hub that allowed access to much of Virginia. It was also far enough away from Washington to be safe from a surprise attack, but close enough to pose a potential threat to the Union capital. This fact certainly did not go unnoticed among politicians in Washington, no doubt causing some sleepless nights. Perhaps fear for their personal safety led certain individuals to bellow "On to Richmond!" more enthusiastically than others. General P.G.T. Beauregard (see Figure 8-2), the hero of Sumter, commanded the Confederate army. His troops were just as poorly organized as McDowell's, and his 90-day heroes were also getting restless as their time of service was close to expiring.

**FIGURE 8-1:** Major General Irvin McDowell.

*Brady's National Photographic Portrait Galleries / The Library of Congress / Public Domain*

Not only did McDowell and Beauregard both have trouble training and organizing their armed mobs, but they also had some operational planning problems. McDowell examined the possibility of maneuvering his army to cut off Beauregard's line of supply and communications with Richmond. This would force him out of Manassas and lead to a battle on terms favorable to McDowell. McDowell figured he could accomplish this with about 30,000 men. It was a good plan, but it depended on the cooperation of another commander. Although not exactly sure of Beauregard's strength, McDowell believed he outnumbered his enemy.

**FIGURE 8-2:**
General P.G.T
Beauregard.

*The Library of Congress / Public Domain*

McDowell cast a wary eye to the northwest part of Virginia near Winchester, the gateway to the Shenandoah Valley. There, a force of 12,000 Confederates under General Joseph E. Johnston stood guard. Johnston was one of the most outstanding soldiers of the prewar army, and one of the highest-ranking officers to resign from the U.S. Army to join the Confederacy. A West Point graduate, American Indian fighter, and one of the heroes of the Mexican-American War, he was a model of courage and competence. Confronting this force and this commander was an army of 18,000 Union troops under Major General Robert Patterson, also a Mexican-American War veteran, but a veteran of the War of 1812 as well. His military experience had been with the Pennsylvania militia. McDowell's plan depended on the Confederates at Manassas not receiving any reinforcements from the Confederate army at Winchester. General Patterson's job was to keep an eye on Johnston and to keep him from sending reinforcements.

Beauregard knew the size and plans of the Union army, thanks to numerous spies and leakers in Washington. He realized that without Johnston's Confederate army to come to his aid, McDowell would have the advantage, forcing him to abandon this key position. Thus his orders to Johnston were to move by rail to Manassas after McDowell's army began its advance, while also somehow convincing Patterson that the Confederate army hadn't left Winchester.

# Marching into Battle (Sort Of)

The largest army ever seen in North America up to that time began its advance on July 16, 1861. Irvin McDowell had over 35,000 men organized into five divisions; each division had from two to four brigades, thirteen in all. Because of fears among the politicians that Washington would be completely exposed to attack if McDowell took all his army, he left behind about 5,000 men to guard roads and secure the lines of communication to Washington. A well-trained army could have made the march quickly and efficiently in less than 48 hours and still have been ready for battle. McDowell's troops moved at a snail's pace. Not only did McDowell carefully check the routes of advance for any potential enemy forces, but his troops seemed to think they were on an extended camping trip. Tens of thousands of men marching on dry dirt roads raised enormous clouds of dust so thick that breathing became difficult; the day was hot, and the men were not used to walking such a distance. So, whenever the men got hot, tired, or thirsty, they simply jumped out of ranks to pick blackberries, crowd around wells for a drink, or lie in the grass until they felt like walking again. The first day the army made 5 miles. On July 18, McDowell again halted the army to wait for the supply wagons to catch up and to gather his army together. They were about 6 miles away from Bull Run.

# Organizing the Armies: Disposition of Forces on the Battlefield

Beauregard, using the terrain available, decided to defend along a steep-banked stream called Bull Run. The main road McDowell was following crossed the stream at a large and sturdy stone bridge. Beauregard stretched his forces to cover the *fords* (shallow places where troops or horsemen could cross in large numbers). His *flanks* (the left and right limits of a deployed force) were open and unguarded, however. As long as McDowell didn't discover this, Beauregard would accept the risk. He was also feeling confident. Johnston and his Confederate army were on the way, traveling by rail. Union General Patterson was fooled by the vigorous activities of Confederate cavalry into believing Johnston's army was about to attack *him*. The conductor of this well-performed ruse was Jeb Stuart, who had accompanied Robert E. Lee to suppress John Brown's Harpers Ferry raid in 1859. After service with the U.S. cavalry out west, Stuart joined the Confederacy and was now displaying exceptional talents with his horsemen.

## RAILROADS: A FIRST AT FIRST MANASSAS

Johnston's arrival by rail to Manassas marks the first time in military history that the railroad had been used to bring troops quickly into battle. Without the railroad, Johnston's army would have had to spend many days on the march, arriving tired and worn out. The use of the railroad cut the movement time significantly, allowing Beauregard to mass Confederate forces at a single place to achieve a decisive effect on the enemy. After Manassas, generals would use railroads to concentrate widely dispersed forces and fight a battle. Troop movement by rail is still a hallmark of modern war.

Interestingly enough, McDowell and Beauregard had battle plans that were exact mirror images of each other. McDowell wanted to make a limited frontal attack with a small portion of his army at the stone bridge to keep Beauregard looking to his front, while the remainder of the army swept around the Confederate left flank and crossed Bull Run at an unguarded ford to get behind Beauregard's army. Beauregard, for his part, wanted to place his main defense at the stone bridge to protect the main road, but he intended to use most of his army to swing around McDowell's left flank and get behind *his* army. Both were good plans. It would become a question of who would be able to get his ill-disciplined and sluggish troops to move first.

# Opening Moves: Key Decisions and Events

McDowell got going first on the morning of July 21 with an artillery bombardment in front of the stone bridge. According to plan, the rest of the Union army crossed Bull Run and began to move slowly and deliberately against the Confederate left. The Confederates were equally slow to respond, and Union forces soon were in the rear of the Confederate army. Beauregard tried to shift his units to face the enemy, gathering forces to occupy the critical terrain on the battlefield, a hill owned by a widow named Henry called, not surprisingly, Henry House Hill.

As the battle lines shifted back and forth around the hill, Beauregard shored up his defenses with Johnston's troops arriving on the battlefield from the Manassas depot. (See Figure 8-3 for a map of the battle.) Johnston's lead brigade, which had arrived on the 20th after a rail and road movement of 57 miles in 25 hours, anchored the Henry House Hill defensive line. The same impassive commander who had overseen the execution of John Brown — Thomas J. Jackson — commanded the brigade. Jackson, a Mexican-American War veteran and erstwhile college professor, had no illusions about war. Known for his unstinting devotion to duty, Jackson was not popular with either his soldiers or his fellow Confederate officers. This mattered nothing to him; he drilled and disciplined his brigade with a single-minded intent to have them ready for the shock of combat. Protecting his brigade behind a fold in the ground behind the brow of the hill, Jackson waited for the enemy.

**FIGURE 8-3:** Map of the battle of First Manassas (Bull Run).

**FIRST BATTLE OF BULL RUN.**

*Getty Images*

**KEY PLAYERS**

As the Confederate lines were breaking under the advancing Union masses, Confederate General Barnard E. Bee, attempting to keep his men together, shouted to them, "Look! There stands Jackson like a stone wall! Rally behind the Virginians!" These were Bee's last words — he was killed immediately afterwards. But what last words they were! Bee had bestowed immortality on a man and his soldiers. From that moment on, and for as long as people talk about the Civil War, they will talk about Stonewall Jackson and his Stonewall brigade. Jackson became the anchor that allowed the scattered Confederates to rally and find their courage again. Jackson's skillful defense, combined with a steady number of fresh troops arriving on the battlefield, gave the Confederates superiority at the critical point.

# Advancing to Victory: The Outcome

By four o'clock, the Union troops had had enough. They had been moving since before dawn, and most were tired, thirsty, and suffering from sensory overload. Without any orders, many simply quit the battlefield, drifting to the rear, convinced that they had done their fair share for the day. As a result, McDowell found his army steadily shrinking while Beauregard's grew steadily larger. The Confederates now began to advance. This was too much for the Yankees. A half-hearted attempt was made to withdraw in an orderly manner, but an increasing sense of panic seized the soldiers, and they began a stampede to cross the stone bridge and escape with their lives. They ran the entire 30 miles back to Washington. A gaggle of civilians, watching the battle while picnicking on the hills on the other side of Bull Run, got caught up in the traffic jam and contributed to the overall sense of panic.

## BATTLE CAPTAIN'S REPORT: FIRST BATTLE OF BULL RUN (MANASSAS), JULY 21, 1861 — CONFEDERATE VICTORY

- **Commanders:** Union: Brigadier General Irvin McDowell, 35,000 men. Confederate: General P.G.T. Beauregard; General Joseph E. Johnston, combined force 32,000 men.

- **Phase I:** McDowell initiates the battle with a movement to turn the Confederate left flank, while using artillery in front of the stone bridge to mask his movement and deceive the Confederates into thinking that the main attack is coming from the front. Beauregard, with the bulk of his forces spread down the wrong end of Bull Run, is initially fooled. He finds himself outflanked and outnumbered. He gathers his forces to defend Henry House Hill, the critical terrain on the battlefield. Thomas J. Jackson's brigade, an advance unit from Johnston's army, moves to a defensive position on the hill.

- **Phase II:** Union forces are stopped on the Hill. Jackson's brigade serves as the anchor point for the defense of the Hill. Both he and his men earn the nickname "Stonewall." Reinforcements from Johnston's army arriving by rail and road begin to threaten the Union right flank. The fresh troops make the difference, and a general Confederate advance causes the Union army to fall back in confusion that soon becomes a *rout* (panicked retreat). The Confederate army is too disorganized to take advantage.

- **Casualties** (those killed, wounded, and missing): Union 2,900, Confederate 2,000. Some of the missing were captured, some were dead on the field but never identified, and some just ran away in panic and came back days later or not at all. Different sources give different figures for casualties in every battle.

Equally overwhelmed by their battlefield experiences, the Confederates blundered after them, stopping about 4 miles from the battlefield, too exhausted and disorganized to follow any further. The Confederacy had won the first major battle of the war. Confederate President Davis, too anxious to wait in Richmond, arrived on the battlefield just as the panic among the Union troops had begun. The Confederate quartermaster gratefully collected the large numbers of arms, ammunition, equipment, and supplies abandoned by the Union army in its haste to return to Washington. The loss was a terrific shock to Northern morale and a great boost for Southerners, who bragged that they had proven their invincibility.

# Analyzing the Battle

Tactically, the battle displayed the weakness of both armies. From top to bottom, this was a battle of amateurs that devolved quickly into a brawl between two armed mobs. Beauregard placed his troops in a poor position, almost inviting a flanking movement by the enemy, and was surprised when McDowell took advantage of this weakness. He was unable to respond as he intended with his own flank attack and found himself in a dangerous position. Neither commander used his forces effectively. Both were slow in organizing and moving forces, and after the shooting began, they had little control over what happened. For the most part their orders were ignored, lost, or forgotten in the confusion. McDowell never used half of his army. Beauregard left about a third of his force idle. To be fair, neither of these commanders had ever led an army before. In fact, neither commander had ever served in the combat arms: McDowell had been the adjutant general (a personnel specialist), and Beauregard had been an engineer.

## A NEEDLESS ERROR

After the Battle of Manassas, President Jefferson Davis promoted several officers to the rank of full general; among them were Albert Sidney Johnston (see Chapter 9) and Robert E. Lee (see Chapter 12). Joe Johnston was not among them. Highly incensed, he wrote a scathing letter to the president, making it clear that he held the highest rank in the U.S. Army before joining the Confederate army. Rather than mollifying his disgruntled commander, Davis answered the letter with the same level of bitterness. The rift between the two was never completely healed, to the larger detriment to the Confederacy, as we shall see.

Cavalry and artillery had little effect on the battlefield because they were all misused or improperly employed. On the other hand, Beauregard's use of the telegraph and railroad to mass forces and Johnston's skillful deception made the Confederate victory possible. The battle had lasted about seven hours. In that time about 3,500 men had been killed and wounded. These were shocking numbers. Americans had never known such losses before in wartime. After the Civil War, Americans would not confront such a high number of battle deaths until World War II. But even then, casualties never reached the one-day totals of Civil War battles. For example, the Marine assault on Tarawa in 1944, considered one of the toughest battles in the Pacific war, resulted in 3,100 casualties over *four* days.

## Immediate and long-term results

The sting of defeat stiffened the resolve of the Union to continue the war. The wishful thinking and Pollyanna attitude toward war ended. Public outcries for action stopped, which allowed the soldiers to do their primary jobs of drilling and training to become an effective, disciplined fighting force. Both sides realized that war was serious business, and both governments began to mobilize resources for the long haul. Lincoln asked for 500,000 three-year volunteers and then authorized an additional 500,000. The Confederacy, after recovering from the general euphoria, also saw the writing on the wall. Davis called for 400,000 volunteers. The possibility of European recognition of the Confederacy rose after the battle, giving Southerners hope for additional support, while giving Union leaders nightmares. Strategically, the gateway to the Eastern Theater remained under Confederate control, along with the important road and rail junctions. Washington remained under continual threat of Confederate attack.

## Naming schemes of the Union and Confederacy

Each side named the battle differently. To the Union, it was Bull Run, named after the stream that ran through the battlefield. To the Confederacy, it was Manassas, named after the important railroad junction that played such a large part in the Confederate victory. This became a standard pattern for the rest of the war. The Union would usually name a battle for a stream, river, or creek on the field. The Confederacy would name the battle after the town located on or near the battlefield.

# Heroes and Goats

Battles, like ballgames, have their heroes and goats. The actions of the heroes and goats usually determine the outcome of the contest. The heroes are the ones who stand out, who have done well, whether in victory or defeat. The goats are outstanding for their failures and contributions to the eventual defeat. The great difference is that in war, the stakes are very high, and men die because of error.

## Heroes

These are the soldiers who stood out in the aftermath of this battle:

>> **Stonewall Jackson:** His cool courage under fire and his well-placed brigade of disciplined troops saved the Confederate defense of Henry House Hill. He became a superstar overnight (much to his confusion and embarrassment).

>> **P.G.T. Beauregard and Joseph E. Johnston:** They came out winners as Southern enthusiasm over victory allowed some blunders to be forgotten. They were considered brilliant military strategists and the primary hope of the Confederacy.

>> **Jeb Stuart:** Stuart's brilliant cavalry action allowed Johnston's army to move to Manassas unmolested. His great talent and flamboyant style made him a rising star.

## Goats

Here are some soldiers who also stood out, but for all the wrong reasons:

>> **Robert Patterson:** Patterson was long past his usefulness in the field, and completely outclassed by General Johnston, who was a far better soldier. Bamboozled even after warned to expect Johnston to try something sneaky, he was responsible for making the Confederates look better than they really were.

>> **Irvin McDowell:** He proved to be a less-than-gifted commander of troops and never had another chance at army command. Despite his professional recommendation that the unprepared army not be sent into battle, McDowell became the scapegoat for the shortsightedness of others.

# CONFUSION AT MANASSAS

The volunteer units that joined the Union and Confederate armies in 1861 came dressed and equipped according to their personal tastes and expense accounts. Neither side had established a standard uniform. One New York unit was made up largely of Scots kilts, although they changed into trousers for battle. Some Union troops wore gray uniforms; some Confederate units wore blue. In the confusion, dust, and smoke that engulfed the battlefield, nobody could tell friend from foe. Many soldiers shot their comrades, thinking they were the enemy. When fighting in the open, as Civil War units did, regimental battle flags were extremely important markers for soldiers. At Manassas, even the flags were of no use to either side. The original Confederate battle flag was red, white, and blue (the Stars and Bars, as it was known). There was no wind on the battlefield that day, so the U.S. and Confederate flags looked exactly alike. Troops from both sides ran to gather under what they thought was their unit flag, only to find themselves in the midst of the enemy. After the battle, the Confederacy adopted a new battle flag based on the cross of St. Andrew (designed by General Beauregard) so that it would not be mistaken for the U.S. national flag. This new battle flag became the most famous symbol associated with the Confederacy.

Chapter **9**

# Trouble West of the Mississippi and the Road to Shiloh, August 1861–April 1862

Between the summer of 1861 and the spring of 1862 Union and Confederate forces clashed in all three theaters of war. As I discuss in Chapter 5, each theater of war had unique conditions that dictated how campaigns and battles would be fought. As I mention, the area between Washington and Richmond would be the centerpiece of the Eastern Theater. Now, this chapter turns to events elsewhere, including how control of territory became a main goal for both Union and Confederate armies in the Trans-Mississippi and Western Theaters. Whichever army could control the critical geographical (and political) areas in these theaters early in the war would gain an early important strategic advantage. Check out how these first battles help shape the conduct of the war, first in the Trans-Mississippi Theater, then in the Western Theater.

# Focusing on the Early Battlegrounds of Missouri and Arkansas

In between the battle of Manassas in the Eastern Theater and the battle of Shiloh in the Western Theater, Missouri and Arkansas in the Trans-Mississippi Theater became the focus of action. A major battle there could determine control of a significant portion of valuable territory along the Mississippi River, as well as a potential source of supplies and reinforcements.

In 1861, the commander of the Confederate at army Fort Smith, Arkansas, was Brigadier General Benjamin McCulloch of Texas. McCulloch fought in the Texas war for independence and the Mexican-American War before joining the Confederate army. McCulloch was ordered to move his new army of 8,700 Arkansas, Texas, and Louisiana troops into Missouri to counter the advance of Union General Nathaniel Lyon, who, with about 5,400 men, was pressing the Missouri State Guard under Sterling Price. Price had no formal military training but had gained a reputation as a war hero in the Mexican-American War, which he successfully used to launch a political career, elected as a congressman and governor of Missouri. Price's State Guard was both a military and a political instrument. Although it had no formal organization, lacked any semblance of military organization or discipline, and its numbers rose or fell depending on the whims of the members, it was still a formidable group, numbering anywhere between 6,000 and 8,000. In Missouri in 1861, such a group of armed individuals could shape the destiny of the state. Its presence was enough to allow a pro-Confederate shadow government to be established and recognized by the government in Richmond as a legitimate member of the Confederate States of America.

McCulloch combined his force with Price and took command of the collective of 11,000 effectives now called the Army of the West. Lyon made a surprise attack on McCulloch's assembly area at Wilson's Creek on August 10, 1861. The battle, such as it was, seesawed back and forth until sheer numbers won the day. Lyon was killed (the first high-ranking Union officer to die in this long war) and by nightfall his army had retreated. Price, who had no skills as a commander, reflected the attitude of his militia, refusing to abide by orders or make any effort to respect rank. He had developed an extreme dislike of McCulloch and defiantly remained in Missouri while McCulloch returned to Arkansas.

# The Union offensive into Arkansas

On December 25, 1861, Union Major General Henry Halleck, commander of the Department of the Missouri, ordered Brigadier General Samuel R. Curtis to take command of the newly formed Army of the Southwest, numbering about 12,000 men, about half of whom were German. His orders were to advance against the Confederate Missouri State Guard and eliminate it as a threat to the Union control of Missouri. Winter campaigns were rare in the Civil War. The fact that this campaign occurred very early in the war indicates how unfamiliar Halleck, especially, was with real soldiering. Curtis began his move on January 13, 1862, in freezing weather, but succeeded in catching Sterling Price by surprise. Price quickly retreated into Arkansas. Curtis followed him with the intent to bring Price to battle. But he was in a dangerous position as he spread his forces, mostly to seek food and forage.

# A new commander arrives

While Curtis was making his advance south, President Jefferson Davis sought to organize a coherent defense. In January, he created the District of the Trans-Mississippi, essentially a sub-theater, which covered Missouri, Arkansas, north Louisiana, and the Indian Territory (Oklahoma). He only wanted a West Point graduate, believing them to be the best capable of higher-level command. The daunting and thankless prospect of defending this gigantic area with a miniscule army (and no prospect of reinforcement) was a difficult sell for the president. A number of prominent officers turned him down before he offered the command to a friend from Mississippi, Major General Earl Van Dorn. The West Pointer had resigned his commission to join the Confederacy, taking a colonel's commission. He had a reputation as a fighter, earning it in both the Mexican-American War and in campaigns against the Indians in Florida and in the West. Van Dorn was in Virginia at the time of his appointment, and he had every intention of making the Trans-Mississippi a decisive theater of war. Van Dorn was a man in a hurry, not always a good trait for a senior commander. His first thought was to go on the offensive and wrest control of the state of Missouri from Unionist control, dictating terms from St. Louis.

Van Dorn, as commander of the District of the Trans-Mississippi, promptly pulled rank on McCulloch and Price, designating their forces as divisions, which now made up what Van Dorn grandiosely designated the Army of the West. At the same time, he declared himself the commander of the new army (such as it was). McCulloch had 8,000 troops, while Price had about 7,000 men, a combination of both Missouri militia and Confederate troops. Van Dorn now decided to take his new army and seek a decisive battle with Curtis. Van Dorn ordered Brigadier General Albert Pike to organize Indian units to bolster his strength. Van Dorn began a move north on March 4 with 16,000 men and 65 artillery pieces. A formidable force on paper, but Van Dorn was in such a hurry that he made no effort to get to know his division commanders, ignored logistics completely, never even thinking about how the army would be resupplied with the essentials of war: food and ammunition, and assumed that his barely trained troops could make a high-speed march over mountains on nearly nonexistent roads in the middle of winter. The results were predictable. New soldiers had trouble marching any distance in good weather, let alone in the brutal cold and snow that engulfed them. Union troops fared little better. Curtis recognized the danger he was in and began to pull his scattered units into a consolidated defensive position.

Because his advance was so slow and his troops and animals were suffering from a lack of food, Van Dorn missed the opportunity to attack Curtis's scattered units. Van Dorn developed an elaborate plan, dividing his army and sending each unit on a flanking maneuver behind a high rock feature known as Pea Ridge and uniting behind Curtis, cutting off his line of retreat. It was a plan that experienced, disciplined, and well-drilled and well-led soldiers could have performed. Although McCulloch's troops had been in a fight before, they were still raw recruits. Price's force was hardly a military organization, and a Cherokee unit (such as it was) was completely independent, looking for an opportunity to get into a fight.

## The Battle of Pea Ridge

The two-day battle of Pea Ridge, March 7–8, was marked by great heroism, and a breakdown of command and control on the Confederate side. McCulloch, forgetting his role as a senior commander, was killed as he advanced ahead of his troops. His second in command, James McIntosh, was also killed. Colonel Louis Hébert, now the new commander of the division (although he did not know it), led an unwise attack, got lost in the woods, and was captured. A spectacular cavalry charge that included many Cherokee fighters failed to dislodge the Union defenders as the cohesion of the division fell apart, incapable of further action. The other wing under Price met Union forces at Elkhorn Tavern. It was a bitter, indecisive brawl. Van Dorn could not unite his divided army, leaving the initiative to Curtis, who took every advantage. During the night, Curtis consolidated his army and, most importantly, massed his artillery in preparation for a counterattack. On the morning of March 8, Union artillery completely disrupted the Confederates. Van Dorn had forgotten to resupply his men with ammunition and had neglected to resupply or position his own artillery. When the artillery bombardment ended, Curtis launched a coordinated infantry attack on the Confederate flank and center, forcing a rapid retreat down the only available road leading away from the battlefield. The battle losses, like those at Manassas, were shocking: The Confederates suffered about 2,000 casualties and Union casualties totaled 1,384.

The commander of the Trans-Mississippi did not stay in the area long. Van Dorn essentially abandoned Arkansas and Missouri to the enemy, led his army across the Mississippi River, and ended up in northern Mississippi, in an attempt to join Albert Sidney Johnston's forces moving toward Shiloh. He was too late, and his army was incorporated into the Army of the Mississippi at Corinth. Major General Thomas C. Hindman replaced Van Dorn as the new (and unfortunate) commander of the Trans-Mississippi. The Confederacy had surrendered the initiative to the Union in the Trans-Mississippi Theater. It was to have fateful consequences.

# Dictating a Strategy in the Western Theater

The Confederacy found itself in trouble almost immediately in the Western Theater. The Confederate defensive strategy, as dictated by President Davis, was correct in its concept, but fatally flawed in its execution. Ideally, you want to defend all your territory and be strong everywhere, but you cannot execute such a strategic approach if you do not have the forces available. The size and experience of the Confederate armies at this point in the war should have dictated a more conservative strategy. However, President Davis decided that Confederate forces should defend the entire area from the Appalachian Mountains to the Mississippi River, a distance of about 500 miles. The problem in doing this was that to cover everything, you have to divide your forces into small groups — and therefore you defend nothing.

This was what the Confederate commanding general in the theater, Albert Sidney Johnston (pay attention — this is a different Johnston than the one at Manassas [see Chapter 8]), ended up doing. Johnston (see Figure 9-1) was from Kentucky and a graduate of West Point. Johnston and Jefferson Davis were good friends. When the shots were fired at Sumter, Johnston resigned from the U.S. Army and offered his sword to the Confederacy. Davis, remembering his friend, made him a full general (one of only five in the entire Confederate army) and gave him command of 75,000 men in the Western Theater. Using rail transportation, Johnston had the advantage of *interior lines*. (Remember what you learned in Chapter 4. The use of interior lines gives a commander the ability to move shorter distances and concentrate forces more rapidly than the enemy can.) The railroad also provided his army with a line of supply south into Georgia, Mississippi, and Alabama, and a line of communication east to Richmond. This all looked good on a map, but unfortunately, the distribution of his troops across the theater (they were scattered everywhere to defend all the major invasion routes) somewhat negated these advantages.

In trying to defend the most vulnerable areas first, Johnston built Fort Henry on the Cumberland River and Fort Donelson on the Tennessee River to control Union access to the Mississippi River and to prevent Union forces from using these rivers as invasion routes into the center of his defenses.

The Library of Congress / Public Domain

**FIGURE 9-1:**
Albert Sidney
Johnston.

# Struggling with Rank: Union Command

Facing the Confederates were two large Union armies; the one under Brigadier General Don Carlos Buell had 45,000 men, and the other, under Henry W. Halleck, had 91,000 men. Halleck was the department commander who oversaw the Western Theater. His headquarters were in St. Louis. Halleck had no authority over Buell. Unlike the Confederate army, which had one general in charge of a theater, the Union army's highest rank was major general. Thus, every major general in a theater had the same rank, leaving no one in overall control. You can imagine what happened when the generals all got together. The clash of egos must have been truly Homeric. In fact, this violation of the unity of command principle was nearly the Confederacy's salvation.

Johnston was certainly hoping that his opponents, struggling as they were with determining who was first among equals, would somehow make a strategic error and give him an opening to attack and defeat any stray Union forces that happened to move south. Just as in the Eastern Theater, these collections of armed men were called armies. In reality, however, they were raw, untrained, ill-disciplined conglomerations of armed civilians.

# The Importance of Kentucky

Strategically speaking, Kentucky was of great importance to both sides. A slave state, Kentucky announced its neutrality in April 1861, although both sides recruited units there. Loyalties were so divided in Kentucky that control of the state became a major strategic objective. It was clear that Confederate control of Kentucky would put the Confederacy in position to control the Ohio and Mississippi rivers, threatening the Union's critical lines of supply and serving as a major invasion route into the Midwest. Kentucky's rich farmland would support Confederate armies in the field with meat, grain, horses, and mules. But neither side wanted to be the first to violate Kentucky's neutrality. Whoever did so would probably drive the state into the enemy's camp.

When Union forces, led by Ulysses Grant (see Figure 9-2), moved to Cairo, Illinois, as a not-so-subtle threat to Kentucky's pro-Southern governor in September 1861, a Confederate force under Leonidas Polk invaded Kentucky and seized Columbus, a critical position that controlled travel down the Mississippi River. Although this was a sound military move, the invasion was a bonehead political move. The pro-Union state legislature then invited Union troops to drive out the invaders. Grant promptly moved his 20,000 troops into Paducah, threatening the newly built Confederate forts Henry and Donelson. Union Brigadier General Buell occupied Louisville with about 26,000 men. Johnston countered with a movement of 25,000 men to Bowling Green (see Figure 9-3).

**FIGURE 9-2:**
U.S. Grant.

*Brooks, Alden Finney / The Library of Congress / Public Domain*

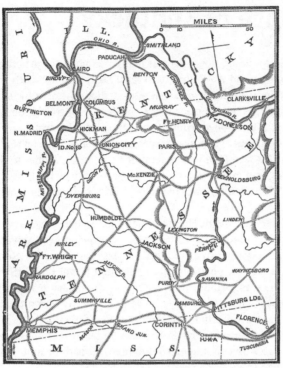

**FIGURE 9-3:**
Map showing the
area around the
Cumberland and
Tennessee rivers.

MAP OF CUMBERLAND AND TENNESSEE RIVERS.

*Getty Images*

# U.S. GRANT: THE MAN NOBODY KNEW

Ulysses S. Grant was a less than standout West Point graduate and a veteran of the Mexican-American War, but the postwar assignments led him to drink to excess out of boredom, leading him to leave the army and pursue a number of mostly dead-end jobs. By May 1860, he was working as a clerk in his father's store in Galena, Illinois. He seemed destined to be a nonentity until the war came. With the demand for experienced officers, Grant was appointed a brigadier general and found himself in command of 3,000 men headed down the Mississippi to prevent Confederate forces from occupying the area opposite Columbus, Kentucky. The battle of Belmont, in Missouri, was fought on November 7, 1861, and it left Grant in possession of the field. It was a small battle, but it opened Grant's eyes to his own potential as a commander.

# Attacking the Forts: Grant Teams with the Navy

On January 19, 1862, Union forces under Brigadier General George H. Thomas, a Virginian who did not join the Confederacy, fought a battle at Mill Spring, in eastern Kentucky, defeating poorly positioned and poorly led Confederate troops, who retreated to Murfreesboro. A small victory, but enough of a badly needed boost for President Lincoln to order a broad attack of the Union armies in the Kentucky region. In February 1862, Major General Henry Halleck, overseeing all Union military operations in the theater, ordered Grant to attack and capture Fort Henry. Halleck attached Commodore Andrew H. Foote's flotilla of gunboats and transports to support the attack. Grant and Foote moved rapidly. Foote's gunboats smashed the poorly constructed fort and Grant's troops captured it with ease. The loss of Fort Henry caused Johnston to abandon his forward base at Bowling Green, Kentucky, and order a retreat to Nashville, Tennessee, to reinforce Fort Donelson. Hesitant to commit everything, he only sent about half of his available force to Donelson.

Grant's army now made an overland march of 11 miles to Fort Donelson, while Foote backed out of the Tennessee River and moved around to bombard Donelson on the Cumberland River. Foote dispatched three gunboats on a 150-mile raid down to the Tennessee–Alabama border, causing havoc and demonstrating the reach of naval power to disrupt lines of communication and supply.

Unlike Henry, Donelson was well built and had powerful cannons that swept Foote's little flotilla off the river. With 25,000 men, Grant decided to starve the Confederates out. In making this decision, Grant had placed himself in a tricky position — Donelson had 17,000 troops with plenty of food and ammunition to withstand a long siege. Besides, if Johnston decided to take action, he could use his army from Nashville to trap Grant's entire force between the fort and the river.

## Military misfits at Fort Donelson

Luckily for Grant, his opponents in charge at Fort Donelson were the equivalent of two of the three stooges: John B. Floyd and Gideon J. Pillow. Floyd, both an incompetent and a coward, commanded the fort. He had been secretary of war in James Buchanan's administration but was a politician and had absolutely no business wearing a uniform, let alone controlling the most critical piece of terrain in the entire Western Theater. Pillow, another civilian masquerading as a general and more of an incompetent than a coward, was second in command. Simon Bolivar Buckner, a competent professional soldier, was third in command, but had no say in the decisions being made.

Floyd and Pillow snatched defeat from the jaws of victory by scaring themselves into believing that they were trapped. In a panic, they concocted a plan to break out of the fort and join Johnston in Nashville. Their attack actually succeeded, throwing Grant's army into turmoil, inflicting 2,800 casualties and opening the road to Nashville. But at the critical moment, Floyd lost his nerve and ordered everyone to retreat back into the fort, where he held a meeting with his officers and decided to surrender. One officer, filled with contempt for Floyd and the other weaklings, refused to surrender his men. He was Nathan Bedford Forrest, a volunteer cavalryman with no military experience. He led his men through icy streams that night to escape to safety and have the chance to fight again.

## Grant's terms: "Unconditional surrender"

Declaring themselves too valuable to be captured, Floyd and Pillow abruptly turned over command to Buckner and abandoned the army, crossing the river to safety in small boats. Buckner was left holding the bag. He contacted Grant and asked for surrender terms. Buckner was shocked by Grant's reply: "No terms except unconditional and immediate surrender can be accepted. I propose to move immediately upon your works."

No one had ever heard of unconditional surrender before — there were always terms or conditions attached. Since the rise of professional armies in the 17th century, surrender had been an elaborate ritual, with the victor granting the vanquished some measure of dignity. Buckner must have been nonplussed for another reason: Buckner and Grant were friends; when Grant was down on his luck after resigning from the army, Buckner had loaned him money to get him back on his feet. Now Buckner found himself facing a man who cared not for the formalities of war even when it involved a pal to whom he was beholden. Grant had opened a new chapter in the way of war of the United States. With no other choice, Buckner surrendered about 15,000 men, 65 cannons, 20,000 rifles, and about 4,000 horses. All of these were vital resources, most of them irreplaceable. The surrender was a disastrous blow to the Confederacy.

Grant had given the Union its first substantial victory. When word got out about his unique surrender demand, some clever newspaperman attached "Unconditional Surrender" to the initials of Grant's name. Instead of Ulysses S. Grant, he was now known as "Unconditional Surrender" Grant, and he became the first Union hero of the war (much to Hallek's disgust — he did everything he could to take the credit for the victory). Soon afterward he was promoted to major general (angering Hallek even further).

# The Shiloh Campaign

The fall of forts Henry and Donelson caused an immediate strategic realignment for the Confederacy. Johnston's army in Nashville was now exposed to attack from two directions. He rapidly moved south, initially to Murfreesboro, Tennessee, and then to Corinth, Mississippi, to protect his lines of communication and supply. Buell's Union army quickly occupied Nashville. A Confederate army would not return to the city until late in 1864. Confederate forces left Columbus, Kentucky, just over a week later. Thus, by the beginning of March 1862, Johnston, in one fell swoop, had lost western Kentucky and the enormous resources of central Tennessee (including Nashville, a critical manufacturing center), along with the control of the Tennessee and Cumberland rivers that led, as Foote demonstrated, directly into the heart of the Confederacy. The Union armies had unmolested access to the upper Mississippi and an open route into the Deep South. Johnston was heavily criticized in the Southern press, and some people loudly demanded his resignation. This was not Johnston's best day, nor could the Confederacy ever make up for the lost supplies and resources that it drew from this part of Tennessee.

Fortunately for Johnston and the Confederacy, Henry Halleck was given command of all Union forces in the Western Theater. The 47-year-old Halleck was known as "Old Brains," because he had written a (largely plagiarized) book on strategy and translated several other similar works. As a commander, Halleck violated every principle he had outlined in the book. A slow, cautious bureaucrat more worried about Washington in his rear than the enemy to his front, he hesitated over and over again to take decisive action and launch an offensive to destroy Johnston's weak and scattered forces.

Halleck finally decided to concentrate his forces and capture Memphis. He sent Grant's reinforced army of 42,000 men down the Tennessee River to an area near the Tennessee–Mississippi state line (see Figure 9-4). There he was to wait for Buell's army of 51,000 men to move 135 miles overland. After they combined, they would move due west to Memphis. Halleck had forgotten what he had written in his strategy book — the objective of a campaign is not a city, but the enemy's army.

Halleck sent Grant and Buell on an expedition to the backwoods of Tennessee, ignoring entirely the fact that Johnston had a steadily growing army assembling in Corinth, Mississippi, defending a critical rail junction only about 20 miles distant from the place Grant had encamped. Pittsburg Landing, Tennessee, was a convenient spot on the river to tie a boat, just two miles from a little crossroads church called Shiloh.

Grant's army was heavily laden with new recruits, so a great deal of time in camp waiting for Buell was spent on drill and inspections. Security was lax, and no one thought of employing the cavalry to screen and collect information. Worst of all, no defensive works had been constructed — no trenches dug, not even trees or fence rails piled up to provide cover in case of attack. To the discerning eye, Pittsburg Landing was not favorable defensive terrain if the army was attacked. Grant had placed five divisions in the area; the other division of his army was located 6 miles away. Creeks bounded the camp on the left and right, and a large, deep river bounded its rear. An attacker could trap the army and slaughter it on the riverbanks. Grant had put himself in a tricky situation, just as he did at Donelson. He was lucky the first time — Johnston did not move against him. This time, Grant's luck ran out. Johnston was on the way to destroy Grant's army before Buell could arrive.

**FIGURE 9-4:** Union transports on the Tennessee River.

*Library of Congress Prints and Photographs Division [ LC-DIG-ppmsca-32988]*

## Taking the initiative: Johnston's plan

Polk's army of 10,000 that had evacuated Columbus reinforced Johnston's 15,000-man army. General Beauregard, who had arrived from the Eastern Theater, helped to assemble another 15,000 men moved by rail from as far away as Florida. The railroad again served the Confederacy well. By the end of March, Johnston had 40,000 men in Corinth. On April 3, Johnston began his march. Like McDowell's march to Bull Run, discipline broke down immediately for the Confederates, assisted greatly by a heavy rain that turned the narrow, rutted trails into thick muck. Units got lost in the woods, traffic jams caused long delays, and, to top it off, nervous recruits started shooting at noises in the woods, thinking the Yankees were attacking. It took Johnston three days to move 23 miles.

After arriving at the point of attack, about 2 miles from Shiloh church, Johnston took a day to organize his forces and calm the fears of his subordinates who urged retreat, arguing that the Yankees had to know they were there. To a group of professional soldiers, their fears appeared justified. The unwitting Confederate volunteers had roaring campfires, were making bugle calls and drum rolls, and generally conducting business as if there was not the slightest danger in the world. Yet, even more surprising, the mostly untried Union troops, lulled into a stupor by weeks of camp boredom, and equally ignorant of any possible danger, paid absolutely no attention to what was going on to their front. William T. Sherman, the Union commander on the scene, bears a great share of blame for this unprepared state. Scouts had warned him that the Rebel forces were coming, and Sherman not only didn't believe them, but scoffed that they were just being frightened by noises in the woods. He still issued no orders for defenses to be built. Johnston won the debate with his subordinates and the order went out to attack at dawn the next day.

On April 6, Johnston's army began a highly complicated attack. He divided his army into three corps and lined them up one behind the other, creating one giant column. Each corps had its divisions spread out side by side to cover the battle-front. On an open field with trained, disciplined troops where the commanders could see every unit properly arrayed, this plan would have worked great. Unfortunately for the Confederacy, the Shiloh battlefield was a mess of ravines, small farmer's fields, and thick stands of timber where you often couldn't see more than 75 yards. On top of the difficult terrain, the Confederate soldiers were soldiers in name only.

## The plan's weaknesses and advantages

Two problems arose almost immediately in putting this plan into action. First, no one can command a 2- to 3-mile-wide battle line. The division and corps commanders essentially lost control after the first shot was fired. Second, the terrain broke up the neat linear formations quickly. The result is that units get lost or separated easily, and leaders cannot issue orders because they can't find their troops. All this contributes to one thing: The momentum of the attack is stopped. Other units pushing from behind get caught in the mess and add to the confusion. Now consider what happens in such a situation when the troops have had only the slightest amount of training. The battle of Shiloh, like Manassas, quickly became two armed mobs in the woods and fields fighting desperately for survival.

The Confederates had one advantage that initially, at least, offset this poor plan of battle. They had surprise. An attacker who surprises an enemy force multiplies his combat power tremendously. Union troops awoke that Sunday with nothing to do but look forward to breakfast. Grant was sleeping late, across the river waiting for Buell to arrive. There had been some firing early that morning, but few took much notice. Quite unexpectedly, they found tens of thousands of men with guns crashing through the woods seeking to kill them.

# The Fighting Begins: The Battle of Shiloh

By 6 a.m., the Confederates had charged into the front Union camps. Soon the entire Confederate line was engaged and, by 7:30 a.m., all Confederate forces had been committed, piling by the thousands into the woods and fields. Popular legend has it that they were shooting Yankees as they emerged from their tents in their camps. In actuality, even without orders from above, lower officers could literally hear the Rebels coming and had tried to get men organized to resist. Discipline and control broke down quickly on both sides; some Confederates could not resist plundering the Union campsites. Most of the Union troops vanished from their units, fleeing as quickly as they could to the rear and the perceived safety of Pittsburg Landing. Those who stayed and fought were overrun. Both right and left flanks of the shocked Union army collapsed under the onslaught and fell back toward Pittsburg Landing (See Figure 9-5).

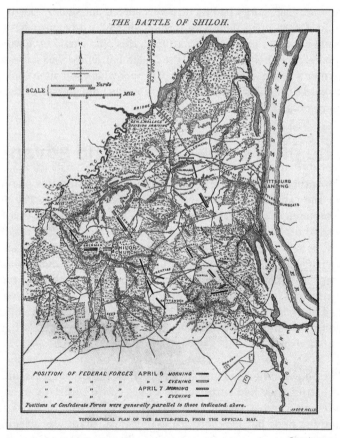

**FIGURE 9-5:** Map of the battlefield of Shiloh.

*Getty Images*

## Key decisions and events

On both sides, individual leadership played a significant role. Groups of lost and frightened soldiers suddenly found a leader in their midst, giving orders and restoring their courage. Lacking any ability to coordinate their attacks or support units that had achieved success, Confederate generals had to lead from the front. Some, such as Patrick Cleburne, became legends; others, such as Braxton Bragg, who petulantly ordered a thousand men to their deaths in ineffective piecemeal attacks, should never have been near troops. In the confusion and terror that seized much of the Union army initially, a small number of generals such as William T. Sherman set a personal example of courage and determination that caused men to stop running and turn and fight. In doing so, the Union army had a chance to save itself.

Grant, arriving on the battlefield and assessing the situation, demonstrated extraordinary personal courage, observing the fight and assessing the situation where the bullets were flying thickest. At the same time, he laboriously formed a new defensive line of badly frightened troops supported by artillery. He also made several critical decisions. He called for reinforcements from his last division located six miles away and ordered the advance units of Buell's army to come with all haste to Pittsburg Landing. The situation was desperate. It was a race against time. Who would arrive at the Landing first — Johnston or Buell?

## Johnston's last battle

Johnston himself realized that he had Grant in a trap. He had only to close it shut. But his forces were scattered, he had no contact with his corps commanders, and the Union defense was stiffening. If he could drive a wedge between the Yankees and the river, he would have a clear shot to Pittsburg Landing. Johnston took personal command of some scattered Confederate units and led an attack on the Union left flank. The attack broke down, and Johnston was wounded, a bullet severing an artery behind his knee. Johnston ignored the wound and continued to rally his troops for another attack. He soon lost consciousness and slumped forward on his saddle. The officers with him were helpless and sadly stood by while he died. Doubtless today anyone with a basic knowledge of first aid could probably have saved Johnston, but given the status of medical knowledge in the 19th century, nothing could be done. So, one of the highest-ranking officers in the Confederacy and the commander of western forces died on the battlefield at a critical time.

# Critical action at the Hornet's Nest

General P.G.T. Beauregard took command and pushed forces away from the flank that was now wide open and moved them toward an area where the fighting was heaviest, a heavily wooded spot by a sunken road where Union forces stubbornly refused to retreat. Called forever after "the Hornet's Nest," the locale was a natural defensive position, and a place where retreating Union troops tended to gather. All in all, about 11,000 men and 38 artillery pieces congregated there, forming a horseshoe. It earned its name from the heavy fire that these Union soldiers were enduring from attacking Confederate troops. To the Confederates, the noise of thousands of bullets sounded like swarms of angry hornets. For nearly six hours Union forces endured seven separate infantry assaults and the combined fire of 62 guns, the largest concentration of artillery in North America up to that time. Attacked on three sides and no longer able to retreat, the Yankees surrendered at about 5 p.m. The victory was an empty and costly one. The courage of the Union troops and their commander, General Benjamin Prentiss, defending this critical piece of terrain bought time for Grant to organize his defense. The Hornet's Nest had fallen, but time — the most crucial and precious element of battle for the Confederates — had been lost.

The Confederates finally focused their efforts on cutting off the Union left flank, nearly four hours after Johnston had last made the attempt. As the assault began in the waning hours of daylight, the long-awaited General Don Carlos Buell's troops began offloading from steamboats just several hundred yards from the weak Union defensive line.

Sensing ultimate victory, the Confederates made a brave assault, but were thrown back. Just as another, stronger assault was being organized, orders came from Beauregard to halt the attack and withdraw for the night. Beauregard, miles behind the front and completely ignorant of the current situation, decided that the army had had enough. Believing he had effectively destroyed Grant's army, he wanted to reorganize his forces for the final push the next morning. It was the last, and perhaps worst, leadership decision made in a day characterized by bad decisions.

Throughout the night Grant collected his last division, lost in the backwoods for several hours, and did what he could to reconstitute his army. Meanwhile, Buell brought about 15,000 fresh troops to Pittsburg Landing. It rained heavily that night, adding to the misery of the survivors. On top of that, two Union gunboats fired their cannons throughout the night in the general direction of the Confederate army. They did little damage but succeeded in keeping everyone awake.

# The second day of Shiloh

The morning of April 7 would find the Confederate army the victim of surprise. Nathan Bedford Forrest's cavalry had discovered that Buell was now on the battlefield. The reports never reached Beauregard, who told no one where he could be found. During the night and early morning, the Confederate army was essentially leaderless. A slow, deliberate Union attack beginning early in the morning appeared to be nothing more than small patrols. But the attack built up momentum, and by the early afternoon the Confederates discovered they were in a fight as desperate as the day before. Under heavy pressure, they were driven back across the fields and woods that they had taken from the Union troops the day before. By now, the Confederates had had enough. Out of ammunition and exhausted, men began leaving the field on their own. Eventually Beauregard realized what was happening and ordered a retreat. The two armies literally stumbled apart from each other — one too tired to run, the other too tired to chase.

## BATTLE CAPTAIN'S REPORT: THE BATTLE OF SHILOH (PITTSBURG LANDING), APRIL 6–7, 1862 — UNION VICTORY

- **Commanders:** Union: Major General U.S. Grant, Army of the Tennessee, 40,000 men; Don Carlos Buell, Army of the Ohio, 23,000 men. Confederate: General Albert Sidney Johnston/P.G.T. Beauregard, 40,000 men.

- **Phase I:** Johnston gains surprise and attacks unprepared Union troops in camp around Shiloh church and Pittsburg Landing. Massing his forces, he attempts to push the Union army back to the Tennessee River and destroy it. The Union army is shattered, leaving 7,000–10,000 panicked and demoralized soldiers huddled in the rear. As the Union army's flanks collapse, the center holds at the Hornet's Nest against repeated attacks. Valuable time is lost reducing this strongpoint. Command and control on both sides fall apart. Johnston, attempting to lead a major attack on the Union left, is wounded and dies on the field about 2:30 p.m.

- **Phase II:** Grant organizes a defensive perimeter around the Landing. At the end of the day, he fights off a final attack by the Confederates with the timely arrival of Buell's troops. Beauregard, taking command for Johnston, orders a withdrawal, believing Grant is finished. Overnight, Grant's last division of 7,000 men, commanded by Lew Wallace, arrives; Buell continues to deploy his army on the battlefield. The following day, Grant and Buell attack with fresh forces and retake most of the battlefield after a long day of difficult fighting. Beauregard eventually recognizes that he is not facing a beaten army and orders a retreat about 3:30 p.m.

- **Casualties:** Union 13,000, Confederate 10,700.

# Aftermath of the Battle

Both sides declared Shiloh a victory. But no one was celebrating. The battle of Shiloh affected Americans as no event ever had before. A total of 24,000 men — one-quarter of the forces involved — had been killed or wounded in less than 48 hours. The losses at the battle of Bull Run, which had shocked most people, now seemed inconsequential in comparison. Shiloh was the bloodiest battle fought in America up to that time. The dead lay so thick on the ground in some places that walking without stepping on bodies was impossible. Besides the Hornet's Nest, Shiloh also coined names of nondescript places that still reverberate with the shock of battle: Bloody Pond — a place where so many men were killed and wounded that the water turned red; the Peach Orchard — not very descriptive, but a place where the firing was so heavy that the peach blossoms in the orchard were all shot off the trees, as though a fierce wind had passed through. Indeed, it had.

## Immediate effects

Concerning the immediate effects, the Union army underwent a quick change of command. Halleck took charge of the united armies, a total of about 120,000 men, and put Grant in his place as second in command. Grant took a heavy bashing for his decisions that led to the battle, because many claimed that he should have entrenched his army. The goal of the army, as Halleck had originally planned, remained Memphis, with the capture of Corinth, the important rail center an intermediate objective. After Shiloh, the entire southwest portion of the Western Theater was open to his army; Beauregard, though reinforced, could not oppose Halleck's massive force. Halleck's moment of glory had come. Yet ever the wise bureaucrat, Halleck put his reputation ahead of strategic priorities He moved the army toward Corinth at a glacial pace, entrenching the army at the end of every day's short march. No one would accuse him of being unprepared as they did Grant. By the time he crept into Corinth, Beauregard was gone. An undefended Memphis would fall shortly thereafter.

**TURNING POINT**

The Confederate defeat at Shiloh indirectly allowed Union army and navy forces under Brigadier General John Pope to isolate and capture the last Confederate fort on the upper Mississippi, at a place called Island Number 10. His victory effectively placed all of western Tennessee in Union hands. Shiloh left the Confederates significantly weaker and facing a combined Union army. The vital Kentucky–Tennessee frontier had been lost, and the three strategic waterways into the heart of the Confederacy — the Mississippi, the Tennessee, and the Cumberland — were under Union control.

## HARDBALL ARMY POLITICS

Just after Grant's victory, Halleck waged his own energetic campaign — against his subordinate. He ordered Grant removed from command with a vague charge of disobeying orders. In justifying his actions, Halleck also hinted broadly to Washington that Grant had resumed his old drinking habits again. Halleck's ultimate reasons are unclear, but it may have been that Halleck believed a ne'er-do-well like Grant didn't deserve such attention after his victories at forts Henry and Donelson. About a week went by before President Lincoln got wind of this injustice. He ordered Halleck to provide details of the charges against Grant. Halleck suddenly found that the whole situation was just a misunderstanding, and that there really were no charges. Halleck promptly restored Grant to his command and began to cover his own rear with a flurry of paper. Halleck had learned the prime directive of politics: You can only stab in the back those who do not have a powerful patron. Halleck did not realize that Lincoln had taken notice of the tough, resolute fighter.

## Long-term effects: The war becomes real

The long-term effects are harder to measure. Perhaps the most important effect was the realization among the people engaged in the war that nobody was giving up easily. Largely untrained and untested in battle, two armies fought continuously (and mostly on their own) for nearly two days. Shiloh revealed the almost superhuman courage and determination of the Union and Confederate fighting men that would manifest itself on numerous other battlefields of this war. Nevertheless, Shiloh marked the last opportunity of the Confederacy to hold Tennessee or control western Kentucky. More importantly, the Mississippi Valley was all but lost to Confederate control.

# Heroes and Goats

The early part of the war was a testing period for many leaders. Most had little practical experience; others had seen combat as junior officers in the Mexican-American War. Some would rise to the challenges of war, others would not. We see here some rapid winnowing out of those who have the determination and skill to continue in the profession of arms.

## Heroes

Heroes can be real or imaginary. Sometimes soldiers become heroes by accident or by misfortune, their symbolic role as hero more important than their actual deeds. Others are true heroes, marked by deeds that stand out for all time. The following shows an interesting mix of these two types of heroes.

>> **Albert Sidney Johnston:** His undeniable courage on the battlefield and tragic death made him the Confederacy's first martyr. The question remains: Was he really as great a commander as everyone in the South initially believed?

>> **Patrick Cleburne:** This Irish immigrant who had served as a corporal in the British army demonstrated extraordinary command presence and inspired great loyalty among his men. His courage at Shiloh propelled him toward higher command.

>> **William T. Sherman:** During the first year of the war, Sherman suffered a nervous breakdown when assigned to administrative work and had been relieved of command. Recovering from this setback, Sherman displayed both a gift for strategy and a determination to win that impressed Grant. From this point on, Grant and Sherman became the dynamos of Union victory.

>> **John Pope:** Bold and brash, he made the most out of a small opportunity from his capture of a Confederate river fort. Looking like a fighter and making noises like a hero, he attracted the attention of politicians who promoted his name around Washington. He would soon get the chance he was seeking — command of an army.

## Goats

With expectations of victory so unrealistically high in the early stages of the war, those who failed on the battlefield often came under sharp criticism. For the two officers in this list, criticism is blunted by presidential intervention. For the Union, saving Grant later proved essential to victory. In the case of Bragg, the Confederacy was ill-served with his ascension to high command.

>> **Braxton Bragg:** Bragg bungled his first attempt at high command, ordering a series of futile frontal attacks against the Union strongpoint at the Hornet's Nest. In spite of his acerbic personality and tactical ineptitude, Bragg came away from Shiloh as an officer worthy of higher command in the eyes of Jefferson Davis, especially with the death of Johnston. He would soon play a pivotal role in the disasters that would befall the Confederate army in the Western Theater.

>> **Ulysses S. Grant:** Ravaged in the press, criticized as a drunkard and incompetent, he almost quit the army, but endured humiliation in silence as Halleck enjoyed a bit of revenge by taking his command. Nevertheless, he still had a man in his corner who made all the difference. Lincoln refused to relieve Grant, saying, "I can't spare this man, he fights!"

Chapter **10**

# Union Navy Victories and Union Army Defeats, March–July 1862

The army at Bull Run and Shiloh (see Chapters 8 and 9) had accomplished very little for the Union. The Union army had been defeated at Bull Run and although winning a victory at Shiloh, the staggering losses seemed to negate the important strategic advantage of controlling western Tennessee. At the same time, however, the U.S. Navy served as an important strategic weapon that provided the Union with several important victories. The effects of these victories would gain importance over time, as they contributed to the overall weakening of the Confederate war effort. Meanwhile, in the Eastern Theater, a new Union commander, George B. McClellan ("the young Napoleon") with a new army he named the Army of the Potomac was on its way to Richmond to end the war in a climactic campaign. For the Union, as well as the Confederacy, the war would teeter back and forth with successes and failures, leaving strategic conditions unsettled and confusing.

# Bringing in a New Commander: George B. McClellan

As soon as the defeated and shamed Union soldiers streamed back into the capital after Bull Run, Lincoln began a search for another commander. The brightest star on the horizon seemed to be the man the press called "Young Napoleon," George B. McClellan (see Figure 10-1).

MAJOR GEN'L. GEO. B. McCLELLAN.

Entered according to Act of Congress in the year 1861, by M.B.Brady, in the Clerk's office of the District Court of the District of Columbia.

**FIGURE 10-1:**
Union General George B. McClellan.

*Library of Congress Prints and Photographs Division[LC-DIG-ppmsca-08368]*

President Lincoln summoned McClellan to Washington on July 22 and gave him command of the dispirited forces in and around the capital. McClellan set to the task with energy and enthusiasm, displaying a remarkable talent for training and organization. McClellan was the perfect man for the job of taking a dispirited and disorganized conglomeration of armed men and turning them into soldiers and organizing an army. He reorganized supply and administration practices and drilled the troops into a disciplined fighting force numbering 130,000. He also gave the army a name: the Army of the Potomac.

## A STAR IS BORN

George B. McClellan was an 1846 graduate of West Point. An engineer by trade, he served in the Mexican-American War building roads and bridges. McClellan's military career was primarily related to various engineering tasks. As a captain, he was an instructor at West Point and a military observer during the Crimean War. In 1857, McClellan left the army to work for the Illinois Central Railroad, where he was very successful in organization and administration. Like many other West Point graduates, McClellan was offered general's stars when he offered his services to the governor of Ohio. He found himself with 5,000 partially trained troops moving into Virginia (now West Virginia) to counter a buildup of Confederate forces, numbering a modest 1,300. A series of encounters, first at Philippi on June 3 and then at Rich Mountain on July 11, forced the Confederates into a rapid retreat, leading to the surrender and capture of a number of unlucky secessionists. The casualties were negligible — 46 Union to 300 Confederate — but from McClellan's point of view it was the most significant victory in American history. McClellan's heroic pronouncements, echoing Napoleon, became good press copy, and in the wake of the defeat at Bull Run, McClellan looked like a winner.

McClellan loved his men, and they returned that affection. Whenever the dapper, diminutive 34-year-old general appeared on his dark horse, they cheered him with great gusto. They affectionately called him "Little Mac." He seemed to enjoy his army so much that he had no plans to use it other than for splendid parades and reviews. In November 1861 George B. McClellan replaced General Winfield Scott as the general-in-chief of the Union armies. "I can do it all," he bragged.

# Taking a Gamble: The Blockade

Five days after Fort Sumter fell in April 1861, Lincoln proclaimed a blockade of the Southern coastline. At the time, the U.S. Navy consisted of about 7,600 officers and men and 42 warships, 16 of which were more or less abandoned for lack of funds and crews. The navy grew exceedingly fast; by the end of 1862, it had over 28,000 officers and men but still struggled to build a sufficient force. Not surprisingly, the Confederacy had almost nothing resembling a navy, with the exception of a number of excellent officers who had resigned their commissions. The Confederacy by necessity had to find innovative and unorthodox ways to protect the vulnerable coastline and weaken the effectiveness of the Union blockade. The capture of the U.S. Navy yard in Norfolk in April 1861 gave a giant boost to the development of the Confederate navy.

Lincoln took a gamble in declaring the blockade. Not only did he not have a force capable of establishing a blockade, but he was technically granting the Confederacy legal status as a nation. According to international law, a blockade was a legal war measure one sovereign nation used against another sovereign nation. Lincoln understood that this fact was also irrelevant if the Confederacy was effectively shut off from international commerce. Thus, a dedicated effort began to establish an effective blockade and begin *interdicting* (stopping and seizing) Confederate ships. At the same time, the Confederacy, under President Davis's order, dispatched a number of privateers to capture Union cargo ships and divert Union warships from blockade duties.

# Patrolling the Coast: Union Naval Victories

While the government began to spend enormous amounts of money to build a navy overnight, something had to be done to establish a Union presence off the 3,500-mile coast with 189 harbors and ports that had to be patrolled and covered. Navy ships began their patrols out of Hampton Roads, Virginia, where the Union still controlled the waters due to its control of Fort Monroe. In August of 1861, using troops from the fort, a naval expedition moved to the North Carolina coast to capture two forts near Hatteras Inlet, a major point of arrival and departure of Confederate trading ships heading to Europe and a base of operations for numerous privateers.

Although it would seem that the presence of a few hundred Union troops occupying a spit of sand would not have much of an effect, it was enough to give Union ships a base to patrol from and shut off the Confederate shipping lane. Several months later, Union forces effectively shut off every river access to the sea in North Carolina except Wilmington, which was protected by geography and a formidable coastal fort, Fort Fisher. Blockade runners could slip in and out of the mouth of the Cape Fear River undetected by Union ships, which were kept at a distance by the big guns of Fort Fisher.

In November 1861, a Union fleet with soldiers and marines captured Port Royal, South Carolina. Union forces had a toehold on the Confederate mainland and established a major naval base there to deal with Confederate blockade runners coming out of Charleston, South Carolina, and Savannah, Georgia. From Port Royal, a combined Union army-navy expedition captured St. Augustine, Florida.

In February 1862, a joint army-navy expedition captured Roanoke Island off the North Carolina coast, which covered access to Pamlico Sound and Albemarle Sound, further cutting off intercoastal traffic moving supplies for the Confederacy. The army commander, Brigadier General Ambrose E. Burnside, gained national fame overnight as his troops, closely supported with effective naval gunfire, proceeded between March and April of 1862 to capture the North Carolina port cities of New Bern, Beaufort, and Morehead City.

On the heels of the North Carolina expedition, the Union navy achieved its most important naval victory of the year with the capture of New Orleans in April 1862. Admiral David G. Farragut (see Figure 10-2) was a man who joined the navy when he was 9 years old, working as a cabin boy and powder monkey. Now 60, he did handsprings to impress his sailors. Aggressive and looking for a chance to take the fight to the enemy, Farragut led an expedition of 24 warships, 19 *mortar boats* (flat-bottomed platforms that carried a mortar, a gun that fired a 216-pound artillery shell at very high angles), and 15,000 troops under command of General Benjamin Butler (a highly placed politician now turned warrior) to capture the Confederacy's largest city and most important commercial center. Using the mortar boats to bombard the two forts guarding the mouth of the Mississippi River, in a daring move Farragut then sent his flotilla upriver in total darkness to sneak past the forts. A spectacular fight ensued, with hundreds of cannons firing and fire rafts sent downstream by the Confederates to destroy the wooden Union warships. A number of Confederate gunboats attempted to halt the fleet but were overwhelmed.

**FIGURE 10-2:** Admiral David G. Farragut.

*Charles D. Fredricks & Co. / The Library of Congress / Public Domain*

## SETBACKS FOR THE BLOCKADE

Although a number of ports were under Union control in early 1862, significant ports like Wilmington, Charleston, and Mobile were still open. The coastline from North Carolina to Texas offered innumerable places for ships to exit and enter Confederate waters. Because the demand for all manner of goods, both military and commercial, rose rapidly in 1862 (and would continue to do so throughout the war), blockade running was a relatively low-risk, high-payoff business. Fortunes could be made with the right cargo arriving safely from Europe past Union navy patrols. The navy did not have sufficient ships to be everywhere, leaving a number of exploitable gaps that blockade runners took advantage of throughout the war.

Through it all, Farragut was undisturbed, even when his ship temporarily ran aground and was set upon by a fire raft. With minimal damage to his flotilla and the loss of only one ship, Farragut passed the forts and could move unmolested to New Orleans. The Confederate troops within the forts were now cut off from the city and faced inevitable capture from the Union infantry and marines now occupying the city as mobs resisted their arrival. The Confederacy now owned a small stretch of the Mississippi River from Baton Rouge to Vicksburg. New Orleans, with its commercial access to Europe and Mexico, became an occupied city for the rest of the war. It was a clear unmitigated disaster for the Confederacy and a much-needed triumph for the Union. Britain and France, watching carefully, were more cautious in their assessments of the Confederacy's survival.

# Discovering the Political Price of Failure and Inaction

In October 1861, McClellan sent a few regiments up the Potomac to investigate reports of Confederate units moving near Leesburg, Virginia. At a place called Ball's Bluff, the detachment met disaster: Nearly 900 men were killed, wounded, or missing. Among the dead was Colonel Edward Baker, a former senator from Oregon and a personal friend of the president. As the bodies of dead Union soldiers drifted on the Potomac River past Washington, Congress established a special joint committee to supervise the conduct of the war. The politicians would have their say in how McClellan would run his war.

Pressed by public opinion to do something, Lincoln wanted to see McClellan actually "do it all." All the president's requests for plans were rebuffed. In desperation, Commander-in-Chief Lincoln even published his own "War Order No. 1" in January 1862, ordering McClellan to move his army, which hadn't moved since Bull Run, against the Confederate force still sitting outside Washington. Beguiled and flattered by all the attention of the Washington political establishment, McClellan was in no hurry to leave his comfortable quarters just blocks from the White House for the rigors of the field. He had nothing but contempt for the president, going out of his way to insult the commander-in-chief. He was so cautious against information leaks that he refused to share his plans with even Lincoln. He hated Republican politicians with their harping on emancipation and believed his only role was to preserve the Union and the authority of the national government at the lowest possible cost. Even though Lincoln was ordering McClellan to advance on General Joseph Johnston, who had been sitting outside Manassas for months behind apparently well-established defenses, McClellan ignored Lincoln's order. Dismissing the president as a rank amateur with no business to direct military operations, he believed that it would be the height of foolishness to play into the Confederate's hands and conduct a direct attack against an army he believed vastly outnumbered his. Nevertheless, McClellan realized that he must move the Army of the Potomac in spring. At last, he condescendingly gave in to Lincoln's request and briefed the president on his plan to end the war.

# The Peninsula: A New Campaign

McClellan's plan was to bypass Johnston's defenses near Manassas and do an end run to capture Richmond before Johnston could react. He proposed to use a similar approach that had worked so well in the West — combine naval power with land maneuver. Looking southeast of Washington, McClellan proposed to move his army by ships to Fort Monroe at Hampton Roads. The Union-controlled fort sat at the tip of a peninsula that led directly to Richmond (see Figure 10-3). Bordered by the York River on the north and the James River on the south, this was historic territory. On this peninsula was the site of Jamestown, the first permanent English settlement in the New World; nearby was Yorktown, the site of George Washington's victory against the British that ensured American independence; and Williamsburg, once the colonial capital, now a sleepy, forgotten village. Armies had marched and fought here before. The peninsula had played an important part in the American experience. It would do so again. McClellan was supremely confident that by operating on exterior lines he could move the 90 miles up the peninsula to Richmond, his flanks protected by gunboats, faster than Johnston could respond.

Lincoln was not so sure about this plan. He began poking holes in it immediately. What if Johnston moved on Washington instead of retreating to Richmond? With McClellan's army gone, wouldn't the capital be defenseless? McClellan must certainly have done some tap dancing, trying to convince the president that he really hadn't intended to ignore the seat of government and leave it defenseless. Lincoln allowed McClellan to sweat a bit. He was tired of McClellan's overblown ego and delays, but he had a great deal of political capital tied up in the "Young Napoleon." Lincoln approved McClellan's campaign plan with two important modifications: Sufficient forces must be left in Washington to defend the capital, and a force must be sent to Manassas to keep Johnston from heading toward the capital once McClellan left. Lincoln then helped to remind his general who was really in charge, relieving McClellan of his duties as general-in-chief and appointing Halleck.

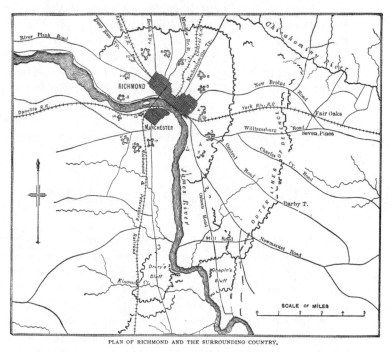

**FIGURE 10-3:**
Map of the Peninsula Campaign.

PLAN OF RICHMOND AND THE SURROUNDING COUNTRY.

*Getty Images*

The Army of the Potomac reached Fort Monroe near the end of March and was ready to advance up the peninsula. Almost immediately, McClellan's plan began to fall apart. About the same time McClellan had landed his army, Lincoln discovered that McClellan had ignored his conditions. There was not, in Lincoln's mind, sufficient force to protect the capital. The numbers of troops in the capital were sizeable, but Lincoln was not confident they were sufficient. He ordered the secretary of war to retain an entire corps of McClellan's army (commanded by McDowell) to remain in Washington and not join McClellan as had been planned. What had concerned Lincoln was the appearance of a Confederate army led by Stonewall Jackson near Winchester, Virginia, just a few days' march from Washington (see Chapter 13). In Washington, no one knew how big Jackson's army was or what it intended to do. It appeared that Lincoln's fears were becoming reality. Therefore, McDowell stayed.

## ALAN PINKERTON: INTELLIGENCE FAILURE

Alan Pinkerton was a former policeman and an ardent abolitionist who founded the Pinkerton National Detective Agency. Pinkerton gained notoriety early as President-elect Lincoln's bodyguard. Warning Lincoln of an assassination being planned in Baltimore, he convinced Lincoln to let him bundle him up and hustle him to Washington incognito. Lincoln arrived in the capital a bit confused and embarrassed. No one knew he was coming. McClellan put Pinkerton in charge of military intelligence for his army. Pinkerton had no skills as an intelligence collector or analyst and he had no military background. Pinkerton and his other agents traveled behind enemy lines, collecting information and interrogating Confederate prisoners. He gathered every possible scrap of information he could get. He apparently consolidated all the reports of his agents and passed them up to McClellan without any comment or clarification. Thus, the reports provided McClellan with outrageously inflated numbers of Confederate troops.

Another event upset his plan. The navy was to provide protection for McClellan as his army marched up the peninsula. But the Confederates, getting wind of the plan, had built batteries along both rivers to prevent the gunboats' passage; in addition, the Confederates had played hell with the Union navy at Hampton Roads with a new ironclad vessel that was impervious to cannon fire and had wrecked several warships. The army, at least initially, was on its own, and in McClellan's mind, without sufficient manpower to succeed. McClellan, with 100,000 men, believed he faced a Confederate army of at least 100,000 near Yorktown. In reality, the Confederate force was 10,000 at best, but trickery and aggressive actions had given McClellan the impression that the enemy he was facing was much stronger. He also was receiving information from Alan Pinkerton (his secret spy name was "E.J. Allen") and his operatives serving as Union intelligence collectors. Pinkerton passed on fantastic stories of tens of thousands of Confederate troops in the area. McClellan, naturally cautious, now became even more careful.

# Writing a New Chapter in Naval Warfare: The Ironclad

In April 1861, after Fort Sumter, Union navy personnel hurriedly attempted to destroy its most important facility in Norfolk, Virginia, to prevent it from falling in the hands of the newly seceded state of Virginia. The group botched the job badly, and Confederate troops recovered vast amounts of ammunition, cannon, stores, repair facilities, and machinery. Also recovered was the scuttled (sunk) steam-powered warship the *Merrimack*. The Confederate naval department knew very well that breaking the blockade was their prime mission. Necessity being the mother of invention in this case, an engineer proposed that the Confederacy build a fleet of armored ships. These ships, protected from cannon fire, would patrol the Southern coastline and chase off Union ships, making the blockade ineffective.

The idea of building a few armored ships, called *ironclads*, was radical to say the least, but because the Confederacy had no navy and wasn't about to build anything to match the Union fleet, the idea was quickly accepted. The design was for a ship that had a pointed bow for ramming, a shallow draft (it floated in shallow water), and a wood casemate (resembling a blockhouse) with sharply slanting sides covered with iron on top of a deck that just barely cleared the waterline. Several heavy cannons would be mounted in the casemate.

Before long, the engineers decided that the *Merrimack*, now recovered from the muck of the harbor, would serve as an ideal base for an ironclad. When construction began in May, it became obvious that the ship's engine was less than satisfactory. In fact, the engine had been scheduled to be completely replaced before the ship had been scuttled. The time spent in the water didn't help much. A new engine was impossible; the Confederacy had no means to build one. So, they made do with what they had. Even finding enough iron to use as armor was difficult. Work on the ship went on around the clock. By mid-February 1862, she was given a new crew and recommissioned the CSS *Virginia*. She had ten cannons, housed in a 24-inch oak casemate with 4 inches of armor plate.

## Washington panics!

In the North, the news of the Confederate monster ship was out. Fears arose quickly along the East Coast. Mayors of major cities imagined horrible scenes of destruction as the Confederate monster churned into harbors, laying waste to Union shipping. Washington, too, felt naked and undefended. It was just a short trip up the Potomac from Norfolk. The monster ship could park near Georgetown and shell the Capitol and the White House! Given such fears, it is not surprising to discover that the normal peacetime bureaucratic hurdles involved in approving money for military procurement magically disappeared. A board was appointed to review design plans for an ironclad ship and approve immediate construction.

John Ericsson, a Swedish-born engineer, had an ironclad ship design already in hand. Its radical new design, incorporating several innovations, was given the go ahead. Actually, Ericsson was none too popular with the U.S. Navy. Years earlier, he had been awarded a contract to design a new naval cannon. During its initial test in 1844, the gun exploded, killing the Secretary of State and several others who had come out to watch the test. Only a crisis such as the one the Union faced in 1861 could have brought Ericsson back into the government's good graces. The stakes were indeed very high, and his design was quite radical. The ship was essentially an armored raft, with most of its hull underwater, and pointed at both ends. Its deck floating less than a foot above the waterline, the ship had a small armored box at one end just big enough for the pilot's head and shoulders so he could see to steer the ship. At the other end was a low smokestack. In the center was a flat rotating cylinder containing two large naval cannons. The ship was completed in record time in New York and commissioned the USS *Monitor*.

## The Virginia goes hunting

On March 8, 1862, the CSS *Virginia*, commanded by Franklin Buchanan (see Figure 10-4), set out on her first cruise. There was no time for a shakedown — the *Virginia* was going into battle against the Union fleet at Hampton Roads. The crew, in fact, had no time to become acquainted with the ship. Up until the very last hour, workers were still onboard. Once underway, the ship's critical weakness soon became apparent. The engine could only produce about 5 knots, and she steered very awkwardly; it took 30 to 40 minutes just to turn.

**FIGURE 10-4:**
Franklin Buchanan, Commander of the CSS *Virginia*.

Brady's National Photographic Portrait Galleries / The Library of Congress / Public Domain

When the Union fleet realized the *Virginia* was coming to them, there was a great panic. One sailor described her as a "half-submerged crocodile." Ships scattered, three running aground trying to escape. The USS *Cumberland* was not so lucky. It was a powerful ship for its time — but its time had passed. In less than an hour, the *Virginia* had rammed and sunk the *Cumberland* after blasting huge holes in its hull with its heavy guns. The cannons of the *Cumberland* had no effect at all on the *Virginia*. The USS *Congress* was next. The ship's crew fought valiantly but was no match for the ironclad. The *Virginia*'s gunfire was so effective that the *Congress* struck its colors and surrendered. It was soon a blazing hulk. With darkness falling, the *Virginia* began what appeared to be a leisurely trip back to Norfolk. She had proven herself. The next day would bring the destruction of the Union navy at Hampton Roads.

Just as the *Virginia* retired, the *Monitor* arrived after a treacherous, problem-plagued voyage. It was her initial trial as well. She anchored near the USS *Minnesota*, the most likely target for the Confederate ironclad the next day. There was nothing more for her crew to do but make what repairs they could and await dawn.

## The Monitor versus the Virginia

The next morning, the *Virginia* appeared again, heading straight for the *Minnesota*. The *Virginia*'s captain ignored what at first appeared to be a floating piece of iron junk. But as the *Monitor* (see Figure 10-5) slipped close by, rotated its turret, and fired a near point-blank shot, it became obvious that the *Virginia* had a fight on its hands. The *Monitor* was far more maneuverable than the *Virginia*, and the two circled each other, blasting away, neither causing any noticeable damage to the other. Because the guns didn't seem to have an effect, each commander attempted unsuccessfully to ram and disable the other ship. As the battle went on, both ships experienced a host of mechanical problems, but the *Virginia* had the most trouble, leaking badly and displaying a noticeable crack in her armor. The *Virginia* did get a shot off at the pilothouse, severely wounding the pilot and causing the *Monitor* to drift away uncontrolled. Thinking she had won a decisive victory, the *Virginia* made her way slowly toward home. By the time the *Monitor*'s officers regained control, the *Virginia* had steamed away. After more than four hours of fighting, both ships were glad to be done for the day, each believing it had won. Neverthe-less, the presence of the *Virginia* was enough to keep the Union wooden ships from moving upriver to support McClellan's turtle-like pace up the peninsula.

March 9, 1862, was a historic day in the history of naval warfare. Wooden ships such as the *Congress*, the *Minnesota*, and the *Cumberland* were obsolete. The indus-trial age had created a new ship that would serve as a model for warships through-out the 20th century. From this point on, warships all over the world would be designed incorporating armor and a rotating turret. The steel navy was born.

**FIGURE 10-5:**
USS Monitor
(July 1862).

*Gibson, James F. / The Library of Congress / Public Domain*

# Getting Fooled at Yorktown

Beginning in April 1862, McClellan inched his way toward Yorktown with the intention of laying siege to the defenses there. As an engineer by training and experience, and seeing the effects of siege operation in the Crimea, it was an obvious choice. For a full month, he waited while his troops dug elaborate trenches and gun emplacements, and heavy artillery and mortars capable of blasting the Confederate entrenchments to bits were laboriously hauled up narrow roads. By the 4th of May, McClellan was prepared to initiate his grand siege. There was only one problem: The Confederates had quietly left their defenses the night before.

## The other Johnston

Joseph E. Johnston (no relation to Albert Sidney Johnston, killed at Shiloh) was 55 years old, a capable and courageous soldier but also a man of pride (see Figure 10-6). As we have seen in Chapter 8, he held a bitter grudge against the commander-in-chief. Davis appreciated Johnston's considerable talents, but the president grew exasperated with Johnston's constant criticism of his decisions and attacks on the government's conduct of the war. Nevertheless, Davis charged Johnston with the responsibility for dealing with the Union offensive.

The Library of Congress / Public Domain

**FIGURE 10-6:**
Joseph
E. Johnston.

# Johnston advances

By the time McClellan's army had begun its creeping pace up the peninsula, Johnston's army had also arrived on the peninsula. He had more than enough time to establish a relatively strong defensive position near Yorktown. But nothing happened, because McClellan took so much time in making siege preparations at Yorktown that Johnston was able to meet with Confederate President Davis and his advisors to plot out a more practical defensive strategy. Although Johnston had argued for a defense in front of the Confederate capital of Richmond, he was overruled in favor of a defense farther down the peninsula.

After Johnston abandoned the Yorktown defenses, McClellan declared Yorktown a victory and began a slow, rain-hampered slog up the peninsula to catch Johnston. Johnston held off the pursuit at Williamsburg, where a sharp fight resulted in about 3,800 casualties for both sides but accomplished nothing more than allowing Johnston to continue his retreat. Union forces did gain an important victory at Norfolk, where Confederate forces abandoned the city after Johnston's army withdrew from Williamsburg. The Confederates also destroyed the Norfolk navy yard, which had been under their control since Virginia had seceded. In the process, the Confederate ironclad, the CSS *Virginia,* was also destroyed. Not only did the U.S. Navy own all of Hampton Roads, but also the James River was now open nearly up to Richmond. The navy could now provide support for McClellan's army.

## LINCOLN TAKES NORFOLK

On May 6, 1862, just after the fighting at Williamsburg had ended, President Lincoln arrived at Fort Monroe to get an assessment of the situation and to find out why McClellan was taking so long to do anything. Lincoln had requested that McClellan meet him at the fort, but McClellan refused, claiming he was at the front and too busy to meet his commander-in-chief. Lincoln, with time on his hands, asked why the Union army and navy had not seized Norfolk. No one had thought of that yet, so Lincoln ordered that the city be taken. He energized the navy to initiate a bombardment of Confederate forts, and he personally supervised the reconnaissance of possible landing sites for the army. The city was abandoned on May 9.

Both armies dragged their way up the peninsula to Richmond, slogging their way through constant rain that saturated the ground, made a muddy paste of the dirt roads, and swelled the rivers to overflowing. Johnston, with 60,000 men, returned to the capital without having fought a major battle, in direct contradiction to Davis's instructions. Right behind him were McClellan's 100,000 soldiers. A Union flotilla attempting to reach Richmond on May 15 was halted at Drewry's Bluff, less than 10 miles outside the city. The crew of the lost ironclad *Virginia* served the guns that stopped the Yankee ships.

# Battle of Wills: The Presidents versus the Generals

Davis and Johnston waged a quiet battle of wills over what to do next. Davis pressed for action to drive McClellan away from Richmond, but while Johnston agreed that action was necessary, he wanted to launch an attack only if it would be decisive. They could afford to hold these chats — McClellan had halted his army and, convinced that Johnston's army had now grown to 200,000 men, bombarded Washington with requests for reinforcements.

McClellan blamed Lincoln for taking McDowell's corps away from him at the start of the campaign. He pushed, begged, and squawked until Lincoln gave in and ordered McDowell to move to Fredericksburg, about halfway between Richmond and Washington, to reinforce McClellan. Lincoln thought he could release McDowell for two reasons:

>> Stonewall Jackson's army (for the moment) had disappeared and was no longer considered a threat to the capital.

>> McClellan was so close to winning the war that the arrival of McDowell's corps would be the event to push him into action.

However, the president was wrong on both counts.

# McClellan Makes a Mistake before Richmond

By the end of May, the Army of the Potomac was entrenching itself six miles from Richmond, occupying a broad front from the James River to the south, up to the Pamunkey River in the north. Union ships controlled both rivers, and McClellan had his main supply base on the Pamunkey River. Bisecting this front was another river, the Chickahominy. Usually fairly shallow and very sluggish, the Chickahominy bordered White Oak Swamp. The rains throughout May had turned the normally placid river into a fast-moving, muddy monster, washing out bridges and spilling over her banks. McClellan had placed his army on either side of the Chickahominy. Tactically, this caused problems — if one part of the army was attacked, the Chickahominy would serve as a barrier preventing the other part of the army to come to its aid. The Young Napoleon had just halved the strength of his army and gave Joe Johnston the opportunity to launch the decisive attack he had been looking for.

» **Exploring the setting for the campaign**

» **Understanding why people still study this campaign today**

# Chapter **11**

# Stonewall Jackson's Valley Campaign, March–June 1862

Jackson's series of battles from March to June 1862 are considered a master-piece of military campaigning. Thomas J. Jackson, known as Stonewall Jackson throughout the Confederacy, emerged as a hero. There was no great battle fought in the Valley Campaign on the scale of Bull Run or Shiloh; actually, the number of soldiers involved was rather small. But the overall effects for Confederate morale were immeasurable.

Collectively, these battles formed the components of a campaign supporting a strategic design developed by Robert E. Lee. Jackson's Valley Campaign served to keep the mesmerized Army of the Potomac commander General George B. McClellan from receiving any reinforcements. Convinced he was outnum-bered, McClellan would not move against Richmond without additional troops. Jackson's efforts enabled Lee to take the initiative outside of Richmond and open his first offensive against the Union army.

# Creating a Hero: Stonewall Jackson

**KEY PLAYERS**

Jackson (see Figure 11-1), born in 1824 in what is today West Virginia, became an orphan as a boy and was raised by his uncle. Although his education was scanty, he obtained an appointment to West Point, but because of his rudimentary schooling he found that he had to apply himself mightily to pass his courses. Here he gained a reputation as a quiet, almost withdrawn, young man who had within him a deep resolve to make something of himself.

**FIGURE 11-1:**
Thomas J. (Stonewall) Jackson.

*Library of Congress Prints and Photographs Division [LC-DIG-ds-03251]*

Jackson was commissioned as an officer in the artillery and soon found himself in a war. The United States was involved in a war with Mexico, where many prominent Civil War officers learned about fighting firsthand. Jackson certainly did. In several important engagements in and around Mexico City, the young officer distinguished himself while expertly and courageously employing his cannons against the enemy. General Winfield Scott, the commanding general himself, made note of Jackson's accomplishments.

Jackson stayed in Mexico for a while and served in various Army posts, including Florida, where his exacting sense of duty and strict adherence to regulations and orders brought down the wrath of his lackadaisical post commander. This experience soured Jackson on the peacetime army, and he accepted an appointment as a college professor of natural philosophy (physics) and artillery tactics at the Virginia Military Institute in Lexington. Lexington was a small, tidy town at the end of the Shenandoah Valley.

As an instructor, Jackson earned the cadets' respect over time, but his methods and personality were hard to get used to. Each night after supper, Jackson would laboriously memorize his lesson for the next day. In class, he would repeat the lesson verbatim. If interrupted by a cadet's question, he would simply repeat word for word the last section he had just spoken. Needless to say, he became a legend. Cadets called him "Tom Fool" Jackson.

He was also a hypochondriac, always imagining some imbalance in his body. As a result, he ate only milk and corn or whole-wheat bread to assist his digestion, and sat bolt upright in his chair, like a sculpture of an Egyptian pharaoh, to ensure that his internal organs were properly aligned. He was also deeply religious, following the rules of the Bible as if they were a set of military regulations. He established a Sunday school for slave children in town.

He married twice. His first wife died in childbirth — not an uncommon occurrence in 19th-century America — and he remarried and bought a house in Lexington and was very happy with his situation. Jackson and the VMI corps provided a military presence for the execution of John Brown (see Chapter 2). John Brown was not the end but only the beginning of sectional strife that would lead to war. When the war came, Jackson, like so many others living quiet, contented lives, joined the colors when his home was threatened. Taking a detachment of cadets to Richmond to assist with drilling new recruits, Jackson was dispatched to Harpers Ferry to train new soldiers there.

REMEMBER

Jackson had a full beard and piercing blue eyes. He was awkward in his manner and careless in his dress, wearing the military coat he wore in Mexico, and a battered cap pulled low over his eyes. Jackson had no time for the relaxed atmosphere of sunshine soldiers and no interest in the pomp and circumstance of the parade ground or the privileges of rank that some officers sought. Quiet, serious, seemingly preoccupied, Jackson always put his duty as a soldier first above everything else and was uncomprehending when others did not do the same. He drilled the men hard and established firm discipline. Although thoroughly disliked by his new trainees, Jackson cared not a whit. War was serious business and called for stern measures. He would follow his orders and do his duty. Jackson did his job well. The same unit he trained at Harpers Ferry he led on the Manassas battlefield in the first major action of the war. The brigade stood out as calm and ordered amid the confusion and terror of battle — a direct result of Jackson's stern and demanding discipline. As a reward for his exceptional performance at the Battle of Manassas, Jackson was given command of a small army of 4,200 men with the mission of defending the Shenandoah Valley.

# Stonewall's Valley: The Shenandoah

For centuries, the Shenandoah Valley had been a heavily traveled natural thoroughfare. It is a broad open valley about 30 miles wide between the Blue Ridge Mountains and the Allegheny Mountains, stretching 160 miles from Harpers Ferry to Lexington. The American Indians used the valley as a trading route for goods throughout the southeast. Later settlers followed the American Indian paths in wagons to settle in the valley or move on to lands farther south and west. By the 19th century, the valley had a packed, hard-surface, all-weather road that made travel easy and relatively quick. The Shenandoah Valley became one of the most important producers of grain, fruit, and cattle in the state. These products could easily be moved northward, via the railroad at Harpers Ferry, or through the mountain gaps down to Richmond.

## The Valley's strategic importance

Militarily speaking, the Shenandoah Valley was of vital importance to Virginia and the Confederacy. It was a natural invasion route for Union armies moving into Virginia or for Confederate armies moving northward into Maryland or eastward to Washington. Its all-weather road enabled troops to move rapidly from one location to another. Its mountain passes gave armies access to the center of Virginia, or they could be controlled by a small number of defenders to prevent an army from entering or leaving the valley. Near Harpers Ferry was the Baltimore and Ohio railroad, a strategic line of communications and supply for the Union. Finally, its agricultural wealth sustained Confederate armies in the field. Such an important source of supply had to be protected; from the Union perspective, control of the Valley crippled the Confederacy's armies by cutting off a major food supply source. Jackson knew very well the importance of this strategic territory. If the Shenandoah Valley was lost, he said, then Virginia was lost.

## Looking for Jackson: Banks enters the Valley

In February 1862, Union Major General Nathaniel Banks entered the valley with an army of 38,000 men, cautiously looking for Jackson's troops in Winchester, a major town at the northern end of the valley. Banks was a career politician, a former governor of Massachusetts, a prominent Republican vote getter, and a former Speaker of the U.S. House of Representatives. When the war came, Banks collected some political favors along with the two stars of a major general. He also was given an army and a department in which to operate. That department included the Shenandoah Valley.

Banks certainly looked like a general, but that was as far as his military ability went. His orders were to push Confederate forces out of the Shenandoah Valley and then prepare to join McClellan as reinforcements near Richmond. Banks dutifully chased off Stonewall Jackson's Confederate troops, pursuing them until he was satisfied that they must have left the Valley. Banks detached a division under Brigadier General Shields with about 11,000 men to occupy Winchester while the rest of Banks's force left to join McClellan's army, which at this time was making a laborious approach up the Peninsula to Richmond.

## Jackson disappears and reappears

By no means had Jackson left the valley. Although he couldn't fight all of Banks's army, he certainly could fight a portion of it. When he learned that Shields was on his way back to Winchester, Jackson moved his little army rapidly in pursuit, moving 50 miles in two days. On March 22, he pounced on Shield's division just outside Winchester at the village of Kernstown. Even though outnumbered, Jackson pressed the attack. By the end of the day his army had been outfought and had left the battlefield in disorder, having lost nearly 700 men — killed, wounded, or missing. The Union force moved to Winchester, having lost about 500 men.

## Using the defeat: Lee's strategic vision

TIP

Kernstown was a clear Confederate defeat, yet this little battle had very big consequences in the overall operations of the Union and Confederate armies in the Eastern Theater. An interesting element of warfare is that battlefield victories or defeats are not as important as how the battles themselves affect the operational and strategic picture. Even though a Confederate defeat, Kernstown surprised everyone. Jackson's force was supposed to have been inconsequential and chased out of the Shenandoah Valley, yet there it was, fighting toe-to-toe with an army nearly three times its size. No one in his right mind would have attacked with such fury unless it had been reinforced. This mistaken assumption changed the course of activities in the Eastern Theater for the Union forces. On the Confederate side, Jackson's defeat actually created more options for maneuvering against the multiple Union threats.

Banks's army was going nowhere — it would stay in the valley. McClellan would have to wait for any further reinforcements. President Lincoln also stepped in and ordered that McDowell's corps, initially bound for McClellan's army near Richmond, hold in place to protect Washington. Lincoln also ordered Banks's army reinforced. Thus, the little battle of Kernstown suddenly reshaped McClellan's entire campaign plan. Banks was ordered to pursue Jackson, but Banks now saw Confederates behind every tree. His advance slowed to a crawl.

In the face of Banks's minuscule advance, Jackson had time to reorganize his army, procuring supplies and equipment. Jackson wisely sent out a group of engineers to map the Valley in preparation for further action. He also received a series of communications from Confederate President Jefferson Davis's military advisor, Robert E. Lee. Lee began to sense that McClellan was not in any hurry to get a battle going in front of Richmond, which would give Confederate forces time to prepare for offensive action. But something had to be done to prevent McClellan from getting any stronger. Lee proposed a bold strategy and would use Jackson's army as a diversion. Even though Johnston's army was badly outnumbered and needed help holding a defensive line at Yorktown, Lee proposed reinforcing Jackson in the Shenandoah Valley. According to Lee, after Jackson was reinforced, he could attack Banks and attract other Union forces to the Valley. By forcing Lincoln to look nervously out of the corner of his eye toward the Valley, no additional Union forces would be sent to McClellan's aid if the politicians believed Washington was exposed to even the slightest danger. This meant that Jackson with a small force could occupy much larger forces in a chase around the Valley, leaving McClellan sitting before Richmond without any additional forces to count on.

Lee's plan was all well and good on paper, of course, but it assumed Jackson could fight outnumbered over three to one and still survive. It was a tall order and a bold gamble. But something told Lee that Jackson was a fighter, and that given additional troops, he just might make a miracle happen. Thus, into the valley came 9,000 additional infantry and cavalry commanded by Richard S. Ewell (pronounced "Yule"). Ewell and Jackson made an interesting pair. Ewell was a hard-bitten American Indian fighter, swore a blue streak, and had mannerisms and an appearance that reminded many of a bird. Ewell's arrival eased only slightly what was becoming a dangerous situation for Jackson.

Not only was Banks creeping toward him (under renewed pressure from Washington), but also another army in western Virginia was approaching on Jackson's flank to link up with Banks. Former 1856 Republican presidential candidate and prewar explorer-hero John C. Frémont, known everywhere in the United States as "The Pathfinder," commanded this army. Frémont had no real soldier skills but received a general's commission anyway because of his connections to the party in power. A small Confederate army of 2,800 men observed Frémont's activities. As part of Lee's plan, this army also came under Jackson's command. Jackson now had a force of 16,000 men. He was still outnumbered. This bothered him not a bit. Placing his faith in God and the marching prowess of his men, Jackson lined up on Frémont.

## Jackson disappears and reappears — again

Ewell's troops came through the Swift Run Gap to reinforce Jackson. To everyone's surprise, Jackson left Ewell and a small body of troops to watch Banks. Jackson never told anyone his plans, not even his subordinate commanders. He loaded the rest of his army on trains heading out of the Valley. Receiving this information, Banks telegraphed Washington that Jackson had left the Valley and was heading toward Richmond to reinforce Johnston. Jackson had the trains make a loop back into the Valley and detrained in Staunton. From there he conducted a rapid march to meet the advance units of Frémont's army on the mountain road near McDowell. The fight was not an easy one, but Jackson's men drove the Yankees off. Jackson had lost nearly 500 men; the Union forces had lost half of that. After blocking the road, Jackson moved to reunite his army, confident that Frémont would not pursue.

Banks, unaware of Frémont's defeat and blithely confident that he no longer needed such a large army in the Shenandoah Valley, detached most of his army under Shields to aid McClellan as originally planned. Banks had only about 8,000 men with him, and he headed back toward Winchester, stopping at a crossroads on the Valley turnpike called Strasburg. By this time Jackson had reunited with Ewell, who hadn't known where Jackson had gone or when he'd come back. Jackson then gave orders to follow Banks. Jackson soon crossed over the backside of a small mountain range that split the valley. Again, Jackson had disappeared, and nobody knew where he was headed.

### "COMMISSARY" BANKS

From Strasburg to Winchester, Banks had strewn the road with every conceivable item of military equipment (which the gleeful Confederates were happy to have), including nearly 10,000 new rifled muskets. Winchester served as Banks's supply depot. It was crammed with supplies of all types, but most important to the Confederate army were the medical supplies, already growing scarce in the South. Because he had left such abundance behind for the resupply of Jackson's army, General Banks became known among Confederate soldiers as "Commissary" Banks, after the military term for a source of supply.

## Jackson strikes again

Jackson used the mountain range as a screen, hiding his army's movement from Banks. It just so happened that Strasburg and Banks's army sat at the end of this mountain range. Jackson was using the terrain to his advantage to get around and behind Banks's army. At Front Royal, Jackson overwhelmed a Union detachment guarding the railroad line that led to Manassas (now under Union control) that served as a major line of communication and supply to Banks. Capturing more than 600 men and a wagon train of supplies and inflicting 900 casualties with a loss of only 50 men, Jackson turned his hard marching army left and headed for Banks at Strasburg. Banks was better at retreat than any other military maneuver. Completely surprised by Jackson's maneuver, Banks drove his army as fast as it could go, headed for Winchester. Jackson caught up with him there and made short work of his thoroughly demoralized troops, who ran for their lives across the Potomac. In three days, Banks had lost 3,300 men; Jackson had lost 400.

## Lincoln sets a trap for Jackson

REMEMBER

Jackson had cleared the Shenandoah Valley of Union troops in a most spectacular fashion. After all the bad news of the terrible spring of 1862, Stonewall's victories were welcomed in the Confederacy with near desperate joy. He became the hero of the nation overnight. In Washington, Jackson was anything but a hero; the capital was in turmoil with rumors that Jackson was on his way to capture the defenseless city. President Lincoln had other plans for the new hero. Lincoln ordered a triple attack on Jackson's forces now enjoying Winchester's bounty. Frémont was ordered to march toward Strasburg in Jackson's rear. Lincoln stopped McDowell's movement toward McClellan and detached 20,000 men under Shields and ordered him to march back into the Shenandoah Valley, move through Front Royal westward, and meet Frémont at Strasburg. Together, they would block Jackson's escape route. Banks was ordered to push Jackson out of Winchester toward Strasburg, where the three armies would destroy Stonewall once and for all. It was a bold plan that revealed the president as a fast learner in the art of war.

Lincoln's plan almost worked. If Lincoln had any other generals to execute the plan, Jackson's army would have been in serious trouble. As it was, Lincoln had three incompetents who moved slowly, if at all. Banks never got started; he'd seen enough of Jackson. Shields and Frémont took their time, got lost, and made a complete mess of the plan. Jackson's men got away, though just barely, due to fast marching (25 miles a day or more for the Confederates) and the iron will of their commander. The trap shut on empty air — Jackson had escaped and was moving to a defensible position at a strategic crossroads in the Valley.

At Cross Keys, Jackson and Ewell watched as a bold Union officer on a white horse led an attack on the Confederate lines. Ewell, in a burst of admiration, ordered that no one kill such a brave man. Jackson immediately countermanded Ewell's order. "The brave and gallant Federal officers are the very kind that must be killed," Jackson explained. Then he added tersely, "Shoot the brave officers, and the cowards will run away and take the men with them."

Jackson's knowledge of the Shenandoah Valley's terrain enabled him to stay one step ahead of his enemies. Nevertheless, he faced a serious problem; two Union armies, each equal to his, were moving against him. Heavy rains made movement slow, and Jackson's cavalry had destroyed the bridges to slow down the pursuit. High water also impeded the march. Jackson chose the only road intersection Shields and Frémont could use to unite their armies. Jackson proposed to fight and defeat each one separately. He did just that.

## The campaign ends

On June 8, Ewell defeated a half-hearted Frémont attack at Cross Keys. Leaving a small force to watch Frémont, Jackson and Ewell joined together the following day with about 6,000 men to fight a portion of Shields's army (4,000 men) at Port Republic. It was the biggest fight of the campaign. Union troops fought resolutely and inflicted heavy casualties on Jackson's forces. By the end of the day, Jackson had outflanked and outfought them. His losses were 800, while the Union losses totaled about 1,000. The following day, both Shields and Frémont had retreated. Banks was still approaching Winchester, having contributed nothing at all.

# The Valley Campaign: An Appreciation

The Valley campaign stands as part of one of the most brilliantly executed campaigns in U.S. military history. Here you can see the importance of linking strategic goals with a plan of operations that then fulfills the strategic goals through a series of interconnected battles that composed a campaign. The Valley campaign served as a strategic diversion, preventing McClellan from receiving the reinforcements he thought he needed to win before Richmond. McDowell had been ordered three times to move his troops to reinforce McClellan, and three times McDowell received orders to stay put because of what was happening in the Valley. The Confederates used interior lines, shuttling Ewell by railroad to the

Shenandoah Valley to provide Jackson with sufficient combat power for him to employ the principles of war — maneuver, surprise, security, and the offensive — to defeat several enemy armies.

With never more than 16,000 men, Jackson held off 64,000 Union troops, fighting four large battles and six small engagements that resulted in 7,000 Union troops killed, wounded, or captured. Jackson's casualties numbered about 2,500. In about 48 days, Jackson had marched his army an astounding 676 miles. Jackson marched his soldiers until they could hardly stand, and then threw them into battle with little regard for their condition and even less regard for the losses they suffered as long as a Union soldier stood on the field. Yet they won battles over and over again under his command. In his communications back to Richmond after a battle, he would credit God with the victory.

The string of victories made the soldiers believe they were something special, and the Confederate army began to gain a sense of pride and esprit that never left them. Jackson's men began calling themselves "foot cavalry" because they seemed to move as fast on foot as men did on horseback. Jackson's brilliance in this campaign has fascinated military professionals for generations. This campaign continues to be studied as an appreciation of Jackson's masterful translation of the principles of war into the art of war.

Chapter **12**

# The Seven Days of Robert E. Lee, June–July 1862

Stonewall Jackson's last battle in the Valley campaign coincided with important events taking place on the outskirts of Richmond, Virginia. On May 31, while Jackson was enjoying the fruits of his victory at Winchester, fellow Confederate General Joseph E. Johnston had fought a battle just six miles outside the capital at a place called Seven Pines (or Fair Oaks). His army was repulsed with many losses, including Johnston himself, who was severely wounded while directing the battle.

## The Confederacy in Crisis: Seven Pines

McClellan had moved his army toward Richmond and set it astride the Chickahominy River, usually a small stream easily crossed. But recent heavy rains in May had turned it into an impassable obstacle, essentially cutting McClellan's army in two. Johnston, who had been waiting for just such an opportunity, made the decision to attack the weaker right flank of the Union army. A Union corps stood at the intersection of three main roads at a place called Seven Pines.

**REMEMBER**

Johnston called his subordinates together and outlined his plan. It was simple enough: The army would divide itself into three columns, each of which would march on a separate road and converge at the Seven Pines intersection to crush the Union forces. What Johnston discovered, however, was that the simplest things in war are often the hardest things to accomplish. The plan implied a rather intricate timetable of movement, precisely coordinated so that everyone was moving at the same speed on the correct route to arrive at the same time. This is exactly what *didn't* happen. The roads became jammed with units marching fast, slow, and in between; the ones on time and in the right place were now merging with those units that had gotten a late start and were in the wrong place. Any commuter will recognize this scene. On top of all this, it had rained the night before, turning the roads into mud bogs. Needless to say, Johnston's units arrived very late and in ineffective bits and pieces. Although forced back, Union troops held off the repeated attacks.

## RISING STAR: ROBERT E. LEE

The Lee family name is indelibly linked to the American Revolution and the new nation it created. Robert E. Lee, born in 1807 at Stratford Hall, the Lee mansion in Virginia, was the son of "Light Horse Harry" Lee, a famous cavalry commander of the Revolutionary War and was a distant relative of Founding Father Richard Henry Lee (who proposed the resolution of colonial independence from Britain). In 1829 Robert graduated from West Point (along with Joseph E. Johnston), standing second in his class. He married the daughter of the adopted son of George Washington, who owned a beautiful mansion at Arlington. He had seven children; three of his sons would serve in the Confederate army. He fought in the Mexican-American War as a member of General Winfield Scott's staff, conducting reconnaissance missions that led to several brilliant victories for the U.S. Army. In 1852, he became the superintendent of West Point and later served with a cavalry regiment on the frontier.

While on leave in 1859, he took charge of the Marines who ended John Brown's raid. He was appointed commander of the Department of Texas, serving until December 1860. When Winfield Scott offered him command of the armies of the United States in 1861, he sadly refused. Virginia had already seceded. Although he loved his country, he could not remain in a "Union maintained by swords and bayonets, and in which strife and civil war are to take the place of brotherly love and kindness." His duty lay with his state. Lee became one of the highest-ranking generals in the Confederacy, serving as President Jefferson Davis's military advisor.

Johnston, moving up front to get a better view of the action, was hit in the shoulder with a bullet and, seconds later, hit in the chest with a shell fragment. He was taken off the field with what many believed to be a mortal wound. The battle was indecisive in the short term. The Confederates lost 6,000 men, and the Union lost about a thousand less. In this time of crisis, with no other choice, Jefferson Davis, turned to his military advisor to take command of the army. This officer had held command in late 1861 but had done poorly in the mountains of western Virginia. The commander's name was Robert E. Lee. Lee's mission was simple. Somehow, in whatever fashion, he had to take control of an army whose leaders were strangers to him, defeat an enemy that outnumbered him at least two to one, and, in the process, save the Confederate capital. As impossible as the tasks may sound, he did all of that and more.

# Results of the Battle: McClellan Falters

Although the Confederates had taken more losses and the Union defenses held firm, McClellan began to show some troubling signs. Having brought his army to the battlefield, he could not bear the sight of his magnificent soldiers being killed and wounded. The battle convinced him more than ever that the Confederates outnumbered him; otherwise, why would they attack? By the end of May, McClellan had convinced himself that as things stood, he had no chance of taking Richmond. Learning that Johnston had been wounded, McClellan had a low opinion of the new Confederate commander. He believed Lee was timid, cautious, and lacking in moral firmness. Ironically, he was describing himself rather than his opponent.

**REMEMBER**

Even after it was obvious that the Confederates sought to take advantage of the Chickahominy River barrier and strike the army's right flank, McClellan made no effort to improve his position there, other than to build bridges over the river to allow the rapid passage of reinforcements. He believed that he faced 200,000 Confederate troops but never considered the possibility that he would be attacked. Instead, he kept hoping for the arrival of McDowell from Fredericksburg to tie into his right flank. But as long as Stonewall Jackson was in the Shenandoah Valley, McDowell's force was going nowhere. What McClellan failed to notice was that his right flank also guarded the Union army's supply depot on the Pamunkey River. A crushing blow to the right flank would also cut off the army from its supplies, leaving McClellan in serious trouble. He would be forced to retreat toward the James River, or fall back down the Peninsula. Either way, McClellan's position presented Lee with numerous options to attack portions of the Union army or trap it in the swamps near the city and destroy it. Lee quickly took notice of this opportunity as he studied his maps and prepared a campaign plan to drive the Yankees from Richmond.

# Taking Command: The "King of Spades"

**KEY PLAYERS**

Lee (see Figure 12-1) took about a month to organize himself. He had the troops begin digging elaborate trenches to protect the Confederate capital of Richmond, an action for which he was roundly criticized. The soldiers, tired of waging war with shovels and pickaxes rather than rifles and cannon, called him "the King of Spades," and others repeated a name he had picked up from his earlier command in western Virginia, "Granny Lee." Despite the grumbling, Lee used the time afforded him well. He began to draw troops by rail from all over the lower South to Richmond. After Jackson's victory at Port Republic, Lee secretly brought Jackson down to the outskirts of Richmond to prepare for an attack.

**FIGURE 12-1:**
Robert E. Lee.

*Library of Congress Prints and Photographs Division*
*[LC-DIG-ppmsca-35446]*

## Jeb Stuart's ride around McClellan

**KEY PLAYERS**

In the meantime, Lee sent cavalry leader Jeb Stuart on a reconnaissance mission to determine the location of the Union army. Stuart did this with 1,200 men and great aplomb, not just collecting valuable intelligence on the enemy forces but also riding around McClellan's entire army as though it was the simplest thing in the world to do. He destroyed supplies, humiliated his pursuers, and returned to a hero's welcome. Another Confederate legend had been born (see Figure 12-2).

**FIGURE 12-2:**
Jeb Stuart.

*Library of Congress Prints & Photographs Division (LC-DIG-ppmsca-38003)*

The most important piece of information Stuart provided to Lee was that McClellan had indeed left his right flank unprotected. Jackson's army was arriving at the proper location to fall on the Union flank and rear, while Lee attacked from the front. Lee had 88,000 men against McClellan's 115,000. But only 30,000 men were covering the Union right flank. Lee had the advantages of surprise, mass, and maneuver. He took a fantastic gamble, leaving only 25,000 men in the entrenchments protecting Richmond. If McClellan got wind of Lee's plan, the remainder of the Union army could sweep into the capital of the Confederacy almost unopposed. Everything depended on McClellan's passive battlefield leadership. McClellan heard that Jackson had arrived but took no action. He didn't seem to understand that things were serious now.

# The Seven Days begin: Lee at Mechanicsville (Beaver Dam Creek)

Lee's orders for the attack on the Union right flank on June 26 were very similar to Johnston's at Seven Pines. Again, the orders envisioned a coordinated assault by four different commanders. But, like before, inexperience, impatience, and an overly complex battle plan led to the Confederate army conducting piecemeal frontal assaults against heavily entrenched Union troops. This battle, called Mechanicsville or Beaver Dam Creek, achieved very little. Only one Confederate division, A.P. Hill's, actually got into the fight. The Confederates lost nearly 1,500 men; Union losses numbered 360. See Figure 12-3 for a depiction of the battle.

**FIGURE 12-3:** Scene from the Seven Days Battles.

Waud, Alfred R / The Library of Congress / Public Domain

That night, McClellan ordered his corps commander, Fitz-John Porter, to retreat to a less exposed defensive position at Gaines's Mills. Lee followed, and the next day again attempted the same type of coordinated attack against the flank and rear of Porter's corps. Again, A. P. Hill carried the brunt of the fighting while Jackson's army wandered lost in the woods, hearing the noise of battle, but unable to find the battlefield. Finally, about 7 p.m., Jackson arrived and ordered his men to sweep the enemy from the battlefield with the bayonet. As Jackson appeared on the flank, Texas soldiers commanded by John Bell Hood broke the Union center after one of the most courageous charges of the war. The Union defenses dissolved, leaving 6,800 casualties. The Confederates, again forced to make frontal attacks against dug-in infantry and artillery, lost 8,700 men. McClellan's army was now across the Chickahominy — but the Union supply depot belonged to Lee.

## McClellan calls it quits

Even though Porter had been pushed back and suffered significant casualties, the Union line had actually become stronger than it was before. Also, Lee had engaged only one Union corps. The rest of the Union army had been untouched. True, McClellan had lost his supply base, but he still had the navy at his rear on the James River, and he had already initiated orders for a new base of supply on the James River at Harrison's Landing. McClellan held all the cards. But the Young Napoleon had had enough. Shaken by Lee's audacity and the tenacity of the enemy's assaults, he ordered what he termed a "change of base" and headed for the James River. Everyone, from President Lincoln on down to the lowest private, called it something else: a retreat.

Lee, sensing what McClellan had in mind, ordered every unit he could find, including the troops from the trenches protecting Richmond, to make contact with the enemy and drive him to destruction. The result was again a lost opportunity to coordinate separate and dispersed units for a single, overwhelming attack. The attacking Confederates found the center of the Union line, and in brutal fighting over two days, first at White Oak Swamp (Savage's Station), and then at Glendale (Frayser's Farm), succeeded in only speeding the pace of the Union army's retreat to a stronger defensive position. As McClellan's army moved closer to the James River, the more concentrated it became, and the more firepower it could bring to bear on an attacking enemy.

## WHERE WAS JACKSON?

Jackson's history-making combat performance in the Shenandoah Valley was followed by a dismal performance in the Seven Days battles. In his plans, Lee repeatedly placed Jackson's force at the critical point of the attack, confident that Jackson would move rapidly and strike hard. But Jackson was always late, or lost, or not moving at all, even at times when within earshot of battle (Jackson, an artilleryman, was hard of hearing anyway). Jackson's reputation suffered a bit in the aftermath, and Jackson himself never had an explanation for his performance. Historians and biographers tend to agree that by this time Jackson was suffering from combat fatigue and exhaustion, compounded by a lack of familiarity with the terrain. Benumbed by the accumulated fatigue and stress of the Valley campaign, he simply could not respond to the new situation he found himself in. Unsure of what Lee wanted of him at times, he fell back on his very strong sense of duty by strict adherence to orders as given. This put him and his forces out of the fight at critical times, leading to incomplete and unsatisfying victories.

# The end of the Seven Days: Lee's final push at Malvern Hill

The last defensible piece of terrain before the river was a place called Malvern Hill, which was fronted by a wide, open plain. Here, the Union cannoneers placed 100 guns to the front and 150 guns on the flanks. Porter's infantry, eager for revenge, waited nearby. Lee, certain that one more attack would crush the enemy and trap them against the river, ordered a massed infantry assault to take Malvern Hill. The attack, led by Brigadier General Lewis Armistead (who would die the following year in a more famous, but equally doomed charge — Pickett's at Gettysburg) was a disaster. Successive and equally ineffective assaults failed to dislodge the defenders, who repeatedly blasted the approaching infantry with high volumes of cannon fire. The Confederates lost 5,000 men on the field; the Union suffered fewer than 3,000 casualties. McClellan and his army reached the sanctuary of Harrison's Landing, now protected by warships of the U.S. Navy. One of McClellan's first actions upon arriving there was to telegraph Washington requesting 100,000 more men. The Seven Days battles were over.

## BATTLE CAPTAIN'S REPORT: THE SEVEN DAYS BATTLES, JUNE 26–JULY 1, 1862 — CONFEDERATE VICTORY

- **Commanders:** Union: Major General George B. McClellan, Army of the Potomac, 115,000 men. Confederate: General Robert E. Lee, Army of Northern Virginia, 85,000 men.

- **Phase I:** After a slow, two-month movement up the peninsula, McClellan's army is just outside Richmond's city limits. General Joseph E. Johnston, who has been giving ground up to this time, attacks a portion of the Union army at Seven Pines on May 31. He is wounded, and President Davis appoints Robert E. Lee as the new commander. At the end of June, Lee has assembled sufficient force to go on the offensive against the inactive Union army. Jeb Stuart rides around McClellan's army to gather intelligence. Stonewall Jackson arrives with his army from the Shenandoah Valley. Lee seeks to destroy the right flank of the Union army isolated across the Chickahominy River and cut off the rest of McClellan's army from its supply base. At Mechanicsville (Beaver Dam Creek), Porter's Union Corps holds off a determined but poorly coordinated Confederate attack.

- **Phase II:** McClellan orders Porter to fall back to better defensible terrain. Porter does so in time to meet another determined but poorly coordinated attack at Gaines's Mill on June 27. Jackson arrives late but in time to assist in driving off the

Union forces at the final phase of the battle. Lee has pushed the Union army over the Chickahominy and gained control of McClellan's supply base. McClellan now has decided to retreat to the safety of the James River. He orders the army to begin a consolidation at Harrison's Landing.

- **Phase III:** Lee attempts to destroy McClellan's army while it is retreating. Again his battle plans go awry in hard-fought but indecisive battles at White Oak Swamp (Savage's Station) on June 29 and Glendale (Frayser's Farm) on June 30. Essentially, the Union army is fighting to save its life, protecting its vulnerable rear from attack. McClellan breaks contact with the pursuing Confederates and assembles a very powerful defensive force at Malvern Hill to protect his army as it moves to the James River. Lee, believing McClellan's army is about to collapse, orders an all-out attack on July 1. The attack fails as wave after wave of Confederate infantry is shattered by concentrated artillery fire from the hill. McClellan retreats safely back to Harrison's Landing, forming a strong position able to resist any attack. McClellan makes plans to return his army to Washington. Satisfied that the Union army will no longer threaten Richmond, Lee forgoes any further attacks.

- **Casualties:** Union 16,000, Confederate 20,000.

# The Significance of the Campaign

McClellan's campaign to capture Richmond was soundly planned but poorly executed, due largely to McClellan's inability to make the transition from trainer and organizer to field commander. In the office, as the leader and administrator of a training army, he was unexcelled. But in the field, McClellan was cautious to the point of paralysis and slow to the point of lethargy. Unwilling to risk the magnificent military machine he built to losses in combat, he hoped somehow its mere presence before Richmond would cause the Confederacy to collapse.

Superior in numbers and equipment at the outset of the campaign, McClellan's army had the opportunity to overwhelm the Confederates at any time. Yet by moving so slowly, he surrendered the initiative to his opponent. McClellan essentially chose to support an offensive strategy with a tactical defensive. In doing so, he gave himself up to Lee's bold offensive plans.

## Lee takes the offensive to win

Robert E. Lee, in every way McClellan's opposite as a field general, began to make the decisions and take actions to which McClellan had to respond. Lee made quick work of the passive and ineffective McClellan with a sound offensive strategy. Badly outnumbered, he nonetheless assembled a strong army by using rail movement to mass the Confederacy's combat power at a strategic point. Leaving Richmond largely defenseless, Lee took the offensive in a bold gamble to drive the Union army from Richmond and force the enemy to give up the fight.

Yet Lee, too, had his difficulties. The army he had was an ad hoc organization, thrown together at the last minute. Lee compounded this difficulty with very complex battle plans that required a great deal of close coordination and tight control; to do this, he relied on commanders that he didn't know and had only the slightest idea of their capabilities. Lee himself had little control over events after they were initiated. The result was a series of poorly conducted attacks with high losses that failed to meet Lee's overall objective — the destruction of the Union army. This was a change in style for many in the army. Lee was not interested in a draw, or a delay, or a stalemate. His goal was total victory by decisively defeating the enemy on the battlefield. In doing so, he discovered subordinate leaders who would be capable of such an approach to war. Stonewall Jackson certainly appeared to be such a leader, even if he had performed poorly. Lee and Jackson soon became an unbeatable team.

## The Seven Days: The bottom line

The bottom line is that the Seven Days battles were won, not by generals and their battle plans, but by the incredible bravery of the Confederate soldier, who day after day charged into terrible fire and won by sheer willpower. Likewise, the Peninsula campaign was a failure because of the timidity of its commander, not because of the tremendous fighting skills of the Union soldier, who resolutely refused to admit defeat. A year's training and experience had created two very dangerous armies. Just as McClellan had given his army a name and an identity that would make history, so did General Lee. He called it the Army of Northern Virginia.

# Heroes and Goats

In almost every battle, some officers make mistakes, others rise to the challenge, and some just put their time in. In retrospect, depending on the given circumstances of the situation, some names are lost to the sands of time, and others live on, undimmed by time.

# Heroes

These are the officers who employed skill and bravery to make things happen:

>> **Robert E. Lee:** His audacity and unrelenting attacks unhinge McClellan and the Union army. Although his plans are often too complicated and ambitious for the command structure, his ability to determine what must be done makes him successful. He becomes the miracle the Confederacy had been praying for. Joseph E. Johnston, for now, is forgotten.

>> **Jeb Stuart:** With his ride around McClellan's army, he becomes the romantic ideal of the dashing Southern cavalry commander. Publicity plus skill make him a national figure.

# Goats

Here are the officers who could've performed better during these battles:

>> **George B. McClellan:** He has victory in his grasp and perhaps could have ended the Civil War with just a simple order for his army to advance. But because he waited, Lee would gain the upper hand and defeat his plans. Lincoln is increasingly exasperated with McClellan's complaining and timidity in the face of the enemy.

>> **Stonewall Jackson:** An example of how quickly in war a commander can go from brilliant to nothing in 24 hours. His performance is simply terrible. Lee's opportunity to deliver perhaps the killing blow to the Union army is lost because of Jackson's failure to act at the right time. He will recover his reputation quickly.

# Chapter **13**

# Second Bull Run (Manassas), August 1862

As President Lincoln attempted to create some order out of the mess that was the Eastern Theater, he brought in a new general from the Western Theater to help. John Pope, big-talking and swaggering, arrived to take care of Lee and his army. But Lee was not about to let Pope teach him any lessons about waging war. He therefore dispatched Jackson to provide Pope with a tutorial.

Jackson's victory after a sharp fight at Cedar Mountain and the now predictable slowness of McClellan provided Lee with an opportunity to change the entire strategic picture in the Eastern Theater and perhaps win the war. Using maneuver and deception, Lee placed Jackson's entire command across Pope's line of supply and communication at Manassas. With an enemy force between him and Washington, Pope made haste to clear away the threat. This set up Pope's army for what was to become the famous one-two punch of Lee's Army of Northern Virginia.

## Reshuffling the Union Command Structure

Lincoln recognized that having the general-in-chief also serve as a field commander had its drawbacks. McClellan was not only supposed to command the Army of the Potomac, but he was also supposed to deal with the day-to-day activities of *all* the Union armies. In effect, with McClellan gone from Washington, Lincoln and his secretary of war, Edwin M. Stanton, had to run the war effort. Just a few days after Malvern Hill, Lincoln brought Henry "Old Brains" Halleck to Washington to become the general-in-chief of all the Union armies. "Old Brains" had just achieved an empty victory by capturing Corinth, Mississippi (the Confederates had abandoned it long before Halleck's 100,000-man force arrived).

**REMEMBER**

Lincoln also made a decision concerning the scattered armies of Nathaniel ("Commissary") Banks, Irwin McDowell, and John C. Frémont. These forces were combined into a single army, named the Army of Virginia. He gave command of this army to a friend, General John Pope (see Figure 13-1), who had made a name for himself as an independent commander in the west after capturing a Confederate stronghold called Island No. 10 on the Mississippi River. Frémont resigned in protest, angry that he had not been selected for the position. Pope made no secret of his political opinions, declaring that the war must be waged vigorously, and that slavery must be eliminated.

**FIGURE 13-1:**
John Pope.

*Brady's National Photographic Portrait Galleries /*
*The Library of Congress / Public Domain*

While popular in some political circles, Pope had a habit of stirring up bad blood, swaggering around, and bragging about his victories, implying that eastern soldiers were less courageous than western soldiers. Some of his subordinates called him "a bag of wind," while others simply called him "an ass." Nevertheless, he was willing to fight, a quality Lincoln valued, especially after his experience with McClellan. Perhaps as a way to show his aggressive nature, Pope began to address his daily reports with the unorthodox headline "headquarters in the saddle." Once the Confederates got wind of this practice, many remarked that Pope seemed to have his headquarters where his hindquarters ought to be.

Pope certainly amused his enemies with his posturing, but they were less than amused with the Union general's declaration that his army would forage for food and supplies in Confederate territory and threatened to kill any Southern civilians who disobeyed his orders. This was a frightening prospect of war against non-combatants, something that at this time was incomprehensible. Pope seemed willing to make his threat real. He moved the bulk of his forces to Warrenton, covering both the access to the Shenandoah Valley and the main road to Washington, while threatening Richmond and two key railroad junctions that connected western and southeastern Virginia.

# Giving Lee an Opportunity: "Old Brains" Miscalculates

While Pope organized his new army, Halleck ordered McClellan to return to Washington. By giving this order, "Old Brains" handed Lee a golden opportunity. With McClellan's army in transit and no longer a threat to Richmond, Lee was now free to attack Pope or threaten Washington directly. Somehow this possibility had eluded "Old Brains," the master of strategy. Once Lee understood what was happening, he ordered Jackson, with 24,000 men, to head for Gordonsville and develop the situation. In Jackson's mind, this order meant one thing — attack. At Cedar Mountain, he found an isolated portion of Pope's army, commanded by General Nathaniel Banks, one of Jackson's opponents in the Shenandoah Valley in 1862. The outcome was the same as it had been in the Valley. As Banks retreated, Jackson pursued until he ran into McDowell's forces. Jackson hoped to bring on a fight, but none came. Instead, Lee, with the rest of the Confederate army of 30,000 commanded by Major General James Longstreet (see Figure 13-2), came via rail to join Jackson.

## Jackson appears, disappears, and reappears

Lee had waited until McClellan's army safely boarded ships and headed for Washington. Lee now outnumbered Pope and intended to destroy Pope's army before McClellan could get back into the picture. Pope had captured orders from

Lee and understood his plans. Pope pulled his forces back behind the Rappahannock River to wait for Lee's attack and for reinforcements from McClellan to arrive. But Lee had no interest in attacking across a river or allowing Pope to be reinforced. With no time to lose, he again detached Jackson, but this time Lee sent him on a long secret march to get behind Pope's army and cut off his line of communication and supply at Manassas. With Jeb Stuart's cavalry providing a screen, Jackson's troops accomplished a nearly impossible feat — they marched 60 miles in two days, arriving at Pope's supply depot at Manassas. There, the hungry, ragged, tired soldiers enjoyed one of the greatest bonanzas of the war. There were train cars filled with military supplies, food, ammunition, uniforms, and equipment, but there were also mountains of delicacies — candy, liquor, canned seafood, and cigars. The men carried off everything they could in wagons, knapsacks, or pockets, and burned the rest.

**FIGURE 13-2:** James Longstreet.

GEN. LONGSTREET, C. S. A.

*The Library of Congress / Public Domain*

Pope, learning of the disaster at Manassas, ordered a retreat. Ignoring the rest of Lee's army, Pope became focused on destroying Jackson's force in his rear. Jackson knew that he had to take action in order to survive until Lee and the rest of the army arrived, following the same route that Jackson had taken. He selected a wooded ridge near the main road to Washington, north and east of the original Manassas battlefield. The area provided concealment for his troops and allowed

Jackson to observe the road that Pope's army would have to travel. It also put him closer to the route that Lee and Longstreet would have to take to join him as planned.

## Looking for Jackson: Pope advances

The Union army was scattered over the countryside looking for Jackson. Pope himself believed Jackson was retreating. When Jackson attacked and mauled a Union division on the main road to Washington, Pope ordered his forces to concentrate on the old Manassas battlefield. In the meantime, units from McClellan's army began arriving, not sure what to do. Halleck was supposed to coordinate the process of joining McClellan's troops with Pope's army, but he did nothing, and McClellan was more than happy to do nothing to assist Pope. Rather than consolidating his position, Pope sent these reinforcements off looking for Jackson as well. Jackson had chosen to attack to draw Pope's army to a place where the combined Confederate army could finish it off. Lee and Longstreet were not far away.

The following day, General Pope, believing in his own mind that Jackson was retreating, sent his forces up the open slope into the woods to attack Jackson. The Confederates had chosen their ground well. An unfinished railroad bed, which served as a natural trench line for the defenders, was at the top of the ridge. As the Yankees came through the woods, they were met by heavy gunfire. Throughout the day, brigade after brigade hurled itself against Jackson's defensive line. But the defenders held, though just barely in some places. Lee and Longstreet arrived on the battlefield and began assembling forces for an attack. But Longstreet convinced Lee that a thorough reconnaissance was necessary before attacking. Lee allowed Longstreet to wait.

Pope's army had fought poorly that day, suffering about 8,000 casualties. He had received reports that Longstreet's troops were on the battlefield. Yet Pope was still convinced that the Confederates were retreating. In a telegram to Washington the next day, he even claimed that he held the ground that the enemy had abandoned. He believed he could still, as he put it, "bag the whole crowd." Pope spent the morning and early afternoon organizing what he thought was a pursuit. But when he sent in a division to attack Jackson's right flank, the commander was surprised to find the woods full of Longstreet's Confederates massing for an attack. General David Porter's corps from McClellan's army, which had arrived on the field the previous day and had caused Longstreet to delay his attack, was sent in against Jackson's right flank. The battle was intense; with their ammunition exhausted, some Confederate units had to resort to throwing rocks at their attackers.

Confederate artillery fired into the flanks of the attackers and broke up reserve units as they were sent in to support the attack. With superb mistiming and completely ignorant of Longstreet's arrival, McDowell ordered units guarding the Union left flank to move in support of Porter, just as the first Confederate units advanced.

Longstreet began his long-expected attack on the exposed Union left flank, headed for Henry House Hill and the stone bridge crossing Bull Run. If the Confederate troops could get around and behind the Union army, they could block the Union line of retreat to Washington at the stone bridge. Henry House Hill was a key piece of terrain that dominated the battlefield. With Confederate artillery on the hill, the Union army would be exposed to accurate and deadly fire from their rear. The Union troops, although initially disordered, rallied and stood firm late in the day. Longstreet's attack ended in a terrible struggle for control of Henry House Hill as darkness fell. The following day, Pope left the field and headed for Washington. He did not get away easily, however. Lee again sent Jackson on a flank march in the hopes of trapping the Union army and destroying it. The result was a short but desperate battle fought in a raging thunderstorm. With Jackson's maneuver halted, the rest of the Union army slipped into the safety of Washington's defenses. See Figure 13-3 for a depiction of the battle.

**FIGURE 13-3:** Battle of Second Manassas.

*Waud, Alfred R / The Library of Congress / Public Domain*

# BATTLE CAPTAIN'S REPORT: THE BATTLE OF SECOND MANASSAS (SECOND BULL RUN), AUGUST 29–30, 1862 — CONFEDERATE VICTORY

- **Commanders:** Union — Major General John Pope, Army of Virginia; 70,000 men (including reinforcements from McClellan's Army of the Potomac). Confederate — General Robert E. Lee, Army of Northern Virginia; 55,000 men.

- **Phase I:** Pope faces Lee's army at the Rappahannock River in a good defensive position, awaiting McClellan's army, which has departed Richmond by ship, to join him upon its arrival in Washington. Lee knows he outnumbers Pope and must defeat this army before McClellan arrives. Lee divides his army, sending Stonewall Jackson on a wide flank march to place his force in between Pope's army and Washington, cutting Pope's line of supply and communications. Jackson swiftly marches and captures Pope's undefended supply depot at the rail junction at Manassas. Pope immediately moves to Manassas to catch and destroy Jackson's small force and then turn and defeat the remainder of Lee's army.

- **Phase II:** Jackson occupies excellent defensive ground not too far from the old Manassas battlefield of 1861. He awaits Pope's army. In the meantime, Lee and the rest of the Confederate army under Longstreet move along Jackson's route to the battlefield. There, Lee hopes to catch Pope in a viselike attack that leads to his destruction. Jackson makes his presence known on August 28, fighting the first elements of Pope's army. The following day, Pope launches attack after attack against Jackson's line, but his attacks are poorly coordinated and badly led by his inept corps commanders. Amazingly, at the end of the day, Pope believes it was Jackson, not his own army, that had failed. He believes Jackson is retreating. Meanwhile, Lee and Longstreet have arrived on Jackson's right flank, but no attack is made that day. Longstreet has convinced Lee that further reconnaissance is necessary.

- **Phase III:** Pope dithers all morning on the 30th organizing a pursuit. With reinforcements from McClellan, Pope begins another movement toward Jackson's lines. A desperate fight again takes place along the unfinished railroad, a natural defensive strongpoint. Jackson's worn-out troops snatch rifle cartridges from the dead and wounded, and some throw rocks in a last-ditch effort to hold the line. At last, Longstreet begins his attack on Pope's exposed left flank. Perfectly timed, it throws the Union army into disarray. Only determined and heroic fighting at the base of Henry House Hill as the sun goes down prevents the Union army from being overrun. Pope is able to retreat from the battlefield the next day.

- **Casualties:** Union 14,000. Confederate 9,000.

# The Aftermath of the Battle

Lincoln's plan to put separate armies under one commander (Pope) and to appoint a separate general-in-chief (Halleck) demonstrated his growing understanding of a critical fact of warfare: One commander must be in charge of the total effort. But Halleck and Pope both failed him in this situation. By withdrawing McClellan to Washington, Halleck allowed Lee to take the initiative again. Pope began his campaign well but faltered when he was faced with Lee and Jackson's capabilities to maneuver forces. Pope never clearly understood what the enemy was doing. Lee took advantage of this and succeeded in damaging Pope's army but not destroying it as he had planned. McClellan could have changed the entire battle but, as always, moved his units offloading on the Potomac with extreme slowness toward Manassas.

**REMEMBER**

Pope talked big but failed to deliver and was clearly outfought by a commander of superior skill. Upon his arrival from the west, Pope was seen as a rising star. Some thought he would be the man to replace McClellan, who had fallen into disfavor among the Republicans in the administration. But Pope's spectacular failure ensured that McClellan would remain the top dog in the Union army, at least for a while longer. As the beaten units of Pope's army slunk into Washington, Lincoln and Stanton had no one else to turn to. No other general was capable of restoring the army to fighting trim. Swallowing their pride, the president and the secretary of war went to McClellan to ask that he again take over the reins and rebuild the Union army. The news of McClellan's return was like a tonic to the dispirited soldiers — they sent wave upon wave of cheers to the Young Napoleon whenever they glimpsed him riding by.

# Heroes and Goats

The brilliant Confederate victory at Second Manassas enhanced the reputations of Lee and Jackson, while causing the eclipse of the career of Union General John Pope.

## Heroes

The heroes, along with a survivor:

>> **Robert E. Lee:** His aggressiveness and confidence created a new hero in the Confederacy. Lee showed a brilliant understanding of using maneuver to offset lack of numbers, and he seemed to know what the enemy was thinking even before the enemy did. From the doorstep of disaster in June, Lee outfought two Union armies and saved Richmond.

>> **Stonewall Jackson:** Still the quirky and mysterious commander, Jackson's brilliant maneuver to threaten Pope's rear is one of the great marches of the war. Jackson regained his form after a poor performance in front of Richmond. At this point, he and Lee learned to cooperate and formed a partnership that kept the Confederacy alive for another year.

>> **James Longstreet:** Tough, relentless, and indomitable in the attack, this battle helped make Longstreet one of the major leaders in the Army of Northern Virginia and an officer Lee increasingly relied on.

>> **George B. McClellan:** During the Peninsula campaign, he was inept and inert. He could not fight because he believed that he was outnumbered nearly two to one, when in actuality he had overwhelming combat power. In hot water with Lincoln after that campaign, he nevertheless came out of the Seven Days debacle back in control. The army's great personal loyalty to him, and the political necessity Lincoln faced to keep the wartime coalition of Democrats and Republicans together, gave McClellan (a Democrat and the darling of the party) a second chance at glory.

## Goats

Here are some goats:

>> **John Pope:** His swaggering style and boastful predictions returned to haunt him. Completely confused and lacking any sense of command, he was outgeneraled and outfought. Pope was quietly transferred to Minnesota to deal with the Sioux uprising.

>> **Irvin McDowell:** A two-time loser. As inept as Pope and unable to have any appreciation of battlefield conditions, McDowell makes a significant contribution to the army's defeat.

>> **Pope's Army of Virginia:** The subordinate commanders were beaten individually by Jackson in the Valley, and then beaten again by Lee and Jackson at Second Manassas. The soldiers of this poorly led army deserved better than they got. Like Pope, this army quickly disappeared.

# Chapter **14**

# The Bloodiest Day: Antietam (Sharpsburg), September 1862

The summer of 1862 found the Confederacy on the offensive. In the Eastern Theater, Lee's Army of Northern Virginia had driven the Union armies away from the Confederate capital, Richmond, and was preparing to invade Maryland. In the Western Theater, the Confederate armies were also on the move, pushing into Kentucky. At the same time, indications from Europe pointed to the success of King Cotton diplomacy. France and Britain were beginning to feel the pinch as the supply of Southern cotton trickled away. Perhaps Confederate battle-field victories in Maryland and Kentucky would convince Europe that the Union could not win, leading to an open alliance with the Confederacy (and a steady supply of cotton). President Jefferson Davis became willing to take a bold step that could lead to victory.

President Lincoln was also thinking of taking a bold step to ensure victory. He began to see clearly that the war needed to take a different direction. His strategic goal to restore the Union was not sufficient to sustain the will of the Northern states for continuing the war. He had decided to give the Union a new reason to fight and the Europeans a good reason to stay out of the matter, but he needed a victory to use as a backdrop for this change in strategy. The problem was how to announce this new direction before the Confederate armies broke the back of Northern morale with victories on the battlefield.

# Winning the War Now: The Confederate Strategic Situation

Early on, President Davis had adopted the strategic defensive. Essentially, this meant keeping the Confederate armies on guard against Union attacks, by shifting forces and resources to meet the threat with the hope of wearing out the opponent by making it too expensive in terms of blood and treasure to conquer the Confederacy. But Davis recognized that an opportunity existed to win the war by taking the offensive.

While Lee and Jackson were battling the hapless Pope at Manassas, Confederate General Kirby Smith and 12,000 men had defeated a patchwork Union force at Richmond, Kentucky. By the end of August, Smith's army arrived at the state capitol at Frankfort, Kentucky, and having chased away the pro-Union legislature, raised the Confederate national flag. Could the same thing be done in the east? Nearly two months of constant marching and fighting had battered Lee's army. Nevertheless, Lee was strongly in favor of abandoning the purely defensive strategy and taking the war to the enemy.

**REMEMBER**

Some military factors favored an invasion of the North. Virginia had borne the brunt of fighting since 1861, and therefore could not easily supply the Confederate army. If Lee's army operated outside of the state, both the army and Virginia could benefit. The upcoming fall harvest in Virginia could be collected without interference. Additionally, the rich farmland of Maryland could easily sustain Lee's army. Clothing and shoes were available in Maryland as well. This may sound like a minor issue, but the Confederate soldiers were literally wearing rags, and most were without shoes. Everything had worn out long ago; remember that while the cotton was grown in the South, the mills to turn it into cloth, as well as factories that made shoes were in the North. Finally, Lee hoped that Maryland men would volunteer for the army and that the state as a whole would eagerly throw off the yoke of Union control once a Confederate army entered the state.

Beyond the practical matter of sustaining an army in the field and neutralizing Union influence in a pro-Southern state, Davis was also watching the situation in Europe carefully. Great Britain was heavily dependent on Southern cotton (very similar to the West's dependence on foreign oil today). Eighty percent of Britain's cotton for its mills came from the Confederate states. With the blockade, exports of cotton to England shrank from 816 million pounds to 6 million pounds in the first two years of the war. British cotton mills were closing down, putting tens of thousands out of work. British Foreign Minister John Russell seemed ready to recommend recognition of the Confederacy to the prime minister, who held out for another convincing Confederate military victory to take such a major diplomatic step.

The French, while not as drastically affected by the loss of Southern cotton, nevertheless sought a joint effort with Britain to mediate a settlement and end the war. An independent Confederate States of America would restore the flow of cotton and improve French ambitions to reestablish a toehold in North America via Mexico. With the South taking the strategic offensive in Maryland and Kentucky, the British took a wait-and-see attitude. Not willing to act unilaterally, the French took the British lead and waited as well.

# Waiting for a Victory: The Union Strategic Situation

President Lincoln faced a tough situation in 1862. Politically, his coalition with Northern Democrats was fraying badly. The Republicans in Congress and in the administration increasingly insisted that the war should be the instrument to destroy slavery and crush the rebellion of the Southern traitors. This kind of talk alarmed Northern Democrats, who desired that the Union be restored to its prewar form, with slavery untouched. The shocking number of casualties had lowered Northern morale. The great enthusiasm that had brought eager volunteers to fill the ranks in 1861 had petered out after Shiloh and the Seven Days. The government's new levy for 300,000 volunteers for three years and another requirement for 300,000 more militia for nine months was filled only with great difficulty. Backroom deals with state governors, monetary incentives, and the implied threat of conscription were necessary to fill the quota. Some states were forced to require compulsory service to meet the militia quotas, leading to a number of violent protests. These problems placed the Democrats — strongly supported by Irish and German Catholics, who opposed conscription — in a good position to win the upcoming congressional elections and make Lincoln a helpless wartime president.

Even as McClellan's Army of the Potomac huddled against the banks of the James River, Lincoln had realized that the broken vessel of the Union could not be put back together as it had previously existed. The status of slaves had been an awkward problem. The government, fighting to restore the Union, treated slaves not as refugees or human beings, but property. Slaves who had fled to Union lines or had been abandoned by their masters were called "contraband," occupying the same category as a horse or other confiscated property. At times, slaves were returned to Confederate lines, a case of old habits dying hard. The Republican Congress passed a Confiscation Act intended to seize slaves and other property used to support the Confederate war effort. The hidden political intent was to make the eventual move to freeing the slaves — *emancipation* in the high-sounding talk of politics.

By late summer of 1862, Lincoln had moved closer to the views of the Radical Republicans on the slavery issue. He came to a brutally simple conclusion: To destroy the South's ability to make war, slavery must also be destroyed. Slavery sustained the Southern wartime economy, freeing thousands of men to serve in the Confederate army. Besides, emancipation could potentially have an added benefit by working on the sympathies of the European powers. Resisting political pressure for now, Lincoln, the master politician, needed good timing for his own announcement on emancipation to be effective. Publishing such a noble proclamation in the midst of panicked Union troops running again for the safety of Washington's defenses would be suicidal. Thus, Lincoln's draft lay quietly in his desk drawer as he waited for McClellan, or any of his generals, to bring him a victory and the public morale boost necessary to issue the proclamation safely.

# The Antietam Campaign

Lee's army crossed the Potomac River into Maryland on September 4. His objective was Harrisburg, the capital of Pennsylvania. On the way, he sought to spread his army around western Maryland, displaying his troops, gathering supplies (purchased with Confederate money, which, of course, was not legal tender outside of the Confederacy) and volunteers, and threatening Washington, Baltimore, and even Philadelphia in the process. Eventually McClellan would come out of Washington to fight him, but Lee knew he would have plenty of time to choose the ground on which to fight the decisive battle that would destroy the Union army and ensure the independence of the Confederacy.

Lee chose to use the Shenandoah Valley as his line of supply. There was one problem: The Union controlled Harpers Ferry at the northern opening of the Valley. Like a foot on a garden hose, this force could cut off Lee's wagon trains of ammunition, the one item that could not be obtained from the local populace in

Maryland or Pennsylvania. Therefore, controlling Harpers Ferry became a key point in Lee's campaign. As the Confederate army marched into Frederick, Maryland, Lee began to issue orders. Lee's army would march west from Frederick, going through the mountain passes at South Mountain to shield his movements from enemy eyes. The army then would split into several parts. Jackson would lead three columns south to capture Harpers Ferry; Longstreet would move north to Hagerstown. Once Harpers Ferry was secured, Jackson would join the rest of the army for its move north into Pennsylvania (see Figure 14-1).

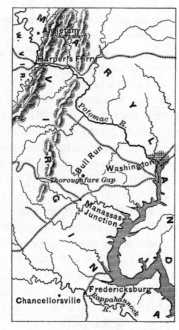

**FIGURE 14-1:**
Map of the Battle of Antietam.

Great battle at Antietam, in Maryland, 1862.

*Getty Images*

These plans were detailed in Lee's Special Order 191 and copied and sent to all commanders. Jackson sent an additional copy of the order to General D.H. Hill, one of his division commanders who had been detached from his command and assigned to Longstreet. The orders, wrapped around three cigars, were accidentally dropped at a campsite near Frederick.

**TURNING POINT**

McClellan had begun his army's typically cautious advance toward Frederick. Just as before, McClellan was convinced that his army of 90,000 was outnumbered. Lee, he believed, had at least 120,000 men. But then came the stroke of luck that, even to this day, is astonishing. One of his soldiers had found the lost Order 191. An even greater miracle was that the order actually got into the hands of the commanding general within hours. The fog of war had lifted for McClellan. He now knew exactly where Lee's forces were, where they were going, and, best of all, that Lee's army was scattered and weak. "Now I know what to do!" he was quoted as saying when he read the order. If he moved now, he could end the war in 24 hours.

McClellan allowed 16 of those precious 24 hours to drift by. Time is the dominant factor in warfare — always has been and always will be. How a general uses his available time to make decisions, to move forces, and to sequence actions on the battlefield will tell you all you need to know about his qualities. How Lee and McClellan used time in this campaign illustrates better than anything the qualitative difference between these two commanders. Within hours of McClellan reading Lee's orders, Jeb Stuart had passed the critical information about the lost orders to Lee. While McClellan telegraphed the good news to the president and Halleck, the general-in-chief, and issued orders for his army to move promptly *the following day,* Lee began immediately to shift the meager forces he had immediately available to defend the two mountain passes his army had recently used. McClellan's army would have to fight to get through South Mountain. Lee recalled Longstreet from Hagerstown, ordered him to support the defense of the passes, and ordered the rest of the army to concentrate at a little crossroads near the Potomac River — Sharpsburg, on Antietam Creek.

The following day, McClellan found the passes at South Mountain guarded. Although heavily outnumbered, the Confederates fought skillfully and tied up several Union army corps. At the end of the day McClellan had the passes, but not much else for his trouble. It was clear that Lee knew that McClellan was aware of his situation. Because Lee knew he was in danger now, the captured plans were increasingly less useful. But even as it was clear that Lee was improvising, McClellan still believed Lee's situation had not changed. Even then, all was not lost; Lee was still vulnerable. But if McClellan and the Union army were to destroy Lee and his invading army, time was of extreme importance. Nevertheless, McClellan again delayed, while claiming victory, declaring Lee's army all but finished. President Lincoln, who understood the difference between words and actions, responded to McClellan's overblown assessment succinctly and directly: "God bless you and all with you. Destroy the rebel army if possible."

# Jackson's Coup at Harpers Ferry

**REMEMBER**

While McClellan claimed victory, Jackson was claiming his own victory, notifying Lee of his capture of Harpers Ferry. By a brilliant use of maneuver and deception, Jackson rapidly convinced the demoralized Union defenders that they had no chance. Jackson's reputation alone seemed enough to clinch the victory. Over 11,000 men surrendered, and the Confederates took possession of 3,000 rifles,

73 cannons, and 200 wagons. While Jackson's nearly bloodless victory was a sterling accomplishment and a brilliant employment of his forces, the capture of Harpers Ferry is largely forgotten because of the events that would overshadow it in the next few days. Lee's reply to Jackson's victory message stressed that he must bring his men to Sharpsburg as quickly as possible. Jackson promptly responded to Lee's orders, as he always did. He left General A. P. Hill's division in charge of handling the prisoners while he took the remainder of his men to join Lee. Hill's men, as ragged and dirty as any in the Confederate army, took advantage of the more than adequate Union supplies at Harpers Ferry, equipping themselves with new rifled muskets, canteens, and shoes. Many put on brand new blue uniform pants and jackets.

When he received news of Harpers Ferry's surrender on September 15, Lee had about 19,000 men from Longstreet's division on the banks of Antietam Creek. The day before, he had decided to retreat across the Potomac. Jackson's message changed his plans, because now, Lee could count on having about 41,000 men on the field. He was outnumbered, but the defensive position he had staked out was good. One advantage that Lee's position did present was that his troops occupied a 4-mile line on a low ridge with woods and small hills overlooking Antietam Creek. This meant that attacking Union troops would have to cross a water obstacle and attack through large wooded areas uphill, for the most part. But Lee's position left his flanks open, and, worst of all, his back was to the Potomac River, a major obstacle. If worst came to worst, Lee's retreating army could be trapped against its banks and easily destroyed. But Lee seemed totally unperturbed by the odds he faced. Lee took the risk for two reasons: First, he knew his opponent. McClellan had never risked a major attack against any enemy force. Second, he understood the stakes involved in the campaign. A victory would most likely lead the Confederacy to foreign recognition and independence.

# Starting the Battle: McClellan Creeps In

While Lee scanned the horizon for Jackson's troops, he watched as the Union army slowly made its approach to the battlefield. A vast sea of blue appeared on the hills opposite Antietam Creek on September 16th. Yet there were no indications of an attack or any aggressive action. In fact, nothing at all happened that day. McClellan had given Lee another precious 24 hours to assemble his army. Jackson's men (minus A. P. Hill's troops still at Harpers Ferry) arrived and took up positions on the vulnerable left flank of the army. What happened?

At this time, there was nothing keeping McClellan and his 71,000 men from advancing and crushing Lee's inadequate force. The only thing stopping the Young Napoleon was his own fears. McClellan believed that Lee had 120,000 men facing him. To McClellan, an attack that day would be foolhardy — best to bring up the entire army, its artillery, and all its supplies, and spend a day in preparation and planning. McClellan had never planned a battle before and had no idea exactly what to convey to his corps commanders, other than vague directions about beginning the battle with an attack on the Confederate army's left flank, followed by an attack on the right flank. He would control the battle with orders issued from his headquarters.

On the morning of the 17th, McClellan ordered the bulk of his army — three corps — to attack Lee's left flank. He ordered another corps to attack the Confederate right flank by crossing Antietam Creek. The problem was that aside from these vague general instructions, once the battle really started, the Union corps commanders could only wait for orders from McClellan's headquarters or, if inclined, to take action as they felt necessary. This is not a good way to conduct a major battle.

Joseph Hooker's corps, numbering 8,700 men, went in first on Lee's right flank. All McClellan had told him was to start the battle. As the men crossed a cornfield, they ran directly into Jackson's troops. For over an hour, thousands of men fought in the terrible cornfield, charging and countercharging. John B. Hood's division of Texans battled the enemy to a standstill. Hooker's corps was shattered — one-third of his men dead, wounded, or missing. But Jackson was only barely holding on — his losses had also been severe. Another Union corps, composed mostly of new recruits, followed behind Hooker. Lee had shifted troops from the right and center to reinforce Jackson. Another hour and a half of brutal fighting passed with another Union corps broken and no ground gained.

## The sunken road

Shortly after this attack ended, yet another Union corps started its attack. The divisions became spread out, and one division headed for the enemy's right flank, where the men became bogged down in a concentration of Confederate artillery and rifle fire that wrecked the division. The other two divisions headed toward the strongest point of the Confederate defensive line — a sunken road that provided the defenders with a natural trench to fight from. These Union divisions also were shattered in vicious fighting, but not before gaining the sunken road, thereafter called Bloody Lane. Lee's center was wide open — only a few remnants of the Confederate defenders stood to resist. Things were so desperate in the center that General Longstreet's staff manned an artillery battery, with Longstreet directing its fire. McClellan had thousands of fresh troops to mount a concerted attack that would have carried the Union army to Sharpsburg and the Potomac. But nothing happened.

McClellan was struck with uncertainty. The battle had been going on for seven hours; he had thrown three corps against Lee's lines without success. All the news he had received from his commanders had been bad. McClellan was convinced that Lee's 120,000-man army was poised for a counterattack. He ordered his commanders to hold their ground where they were and defend. At the point of decisive victory, McClellan was thinking of how to save his army from defeat.

# Burnside's bridge

By late afternoon, General Ambrose E. Burnside's corps became the main (and only) attack. Burnside had been on the field since morning, but he had only made the most tentative attempts to cross the large stone bridge at Antietam Creek. McClellan uncharacteristically ordered Burnside to attack repeatedly and "at all hazards," yet Burnside still had made no progress. Why he never just sent his 12,500 men wading across the 50-foot-wide shallow stream is still a mystery. To the 550 Confederates sitting on the hills above the bridge, it was a sharpshooter's paradise. As soon as the massed attackers tried to run along the bank to reach the bridge, the defenders shot them down in heaps. By afternoon, Burnside had finally succeeded in crossing the bridge and began a slow advance up the difficult terrain toward Sharpsburg. The Confederate defenders were too weak to stop the advance; they could only delay it. Lee was in Sharpsburg rallying troops for a final stand, as his right flank and escape route to the Potomac were in great danger. See Figure 14-2 for a depiction of the battle.

**FIGURE 14-2:** The Battle of Antietam — Burnside's Bridge.

The Library of Congress

# BATTLE CAPTAIN'S REPORT: THE BATTLE OF ANTIETAM (SHARPSBURG), SEPTEMBER 17, 1862 — DRAW

- **Commanders:** Union: Major General George B. McClellan, Army of the Potomac, 75,000 men. Confederate: General Robert E. Lee, Army of Northern Virginia, 38,000 men. (Some authorities believe this number may have been as high as 50,000.)

- **Phase I:** With his plans for the invasion of Maryland in McClellan's hands, Lee orders his army to assemble at the town of Sharpsburg, near the Potomac River. Here, he and Longstreet select defensible terrain and await McClellan's attack. Jackson, minus A. P. Hill's division, arrives from Harpers Ferry, after capturing the Union garrison there. McClellan approaches slowly and with great caution, giving Lee an extra day to assemble his forces and prepare his defense.

- **Phase II:** The battle opens at 6 a.m., with Hooker's corps attacking Jackson's position on the Confederate left flank. A terrible struggle at the cornfield and near the Dunkard Church begins. Hooker is repulsed, but another Union corps under General Mansfield follows Hooker's effort at 9 a.m. This corps is also stopped after close and desperate fighting. Sumner's corps launches a third Union attack at 10:30 a.m. The three divisions of this corps are sent in piecemeal, one headed toward the Confederate left flank, the other two headed for the center of the line. Confederate reinforcements arriving on the battlefield crush the Union attack on the left. Thousands of Union troops fall in a matter of minutes. Fighting in this part of the battlefield ends.

- **Phase III:** The two remaining Union divisions of General Sumner's corps advance mistakenly toward the center of the Confederate line, where the defenders have occupied a sunken road — a natural trench. The attackers cannot see the defenders until they are almost upon them. The Confederates fire at point-blank range. As each division attacks, it suffers terrible casualties, but not before gaining a part of the road and overwhelming the defenders, who are killed in heaps along the stretch of road known thereafter as Bloody Lane. The Confederate center is broken, but the attack is stalled. McClellan orders no more reinforcements to go forward — he is thinking about saving his army when he is on the edge of total victory.

- **Phase IV:** General Burnside's corps has spent all day attempting to cross a bridge over Antietam Creek. Every time Burnside attempts to push forward, his men suffer heavy casualties. By 3:30 p.m., Burnside succeeds, partially because he changes tactics (a direct rush over the bridge rather than moving parallel to the bank to access the bridge) and partially because Lee has stripped men from the right flank all day to save his left and center. Once Burnside crosses, his divisions advance slowly against tough but limited resistance. He nears the outskirts of Sharpsburg and the main road that leads to the shallow part of the Potomac River, Lee's only escape route. The Confederates have no reserves to stop his attack. Burnside has the second opportunity of the day to gain complete victory. At this time, troops appear on Burnside's left flank. They are dressed in blue, but the flags they fly identify them as Confederate troops. It is A. P. Hill's division from Harpers Ferry, arriving at precisely the right time and place. They attack Burnside's tired and surprised men, driving them back to the bridge that still bears their general's name — Burnside's Bridge. The sun sets after 14 hours of battle — the bloodiest day in American history.

- **Casualties:** Union 12,400, Confederate 10,300.

Just then, a large body of troops appeared on Burnside's flank. No one could tell who they were. Through the dust, their uniforms appeared blue — Union reinforcements! But to the shock and dismay of the Union troops, they were A. P. Hill's Confederates; many were wearing captured Union uniforms, arriving on the battlefield from Harpers Ferry at precisely the right time and place. Burnside's attack collapsed, and the disordered divisions retreated to hold the bridge that they had fought so hard to win. After 14 hours of combat, the sun mercifully set on two shocked and devastated armies.

**TURNING POINT**

Although a draw, the Battle of Antietam is considered one of the decisive battles of the Civil War. Politically, Lee's failed invasion gave Lincoln the opportunity to issue the Emancipation Proclamation and change the direction of the war. Diplomatically, Lee's withdrawal from Maryland influenced the European powers to remain neutral and continue to wait for future developments.

# Aftermath of the Battle

As Lee, Longstreet, and Jackson met to survey the battlefield, they quickly realized that the army had been grievously hurt and completely disorganized. "Half of Lee's army was hunting the other half," one staff officer recalled. A full third of his army had disappeared — killed, wounded, or missing. Lee had thrown every man available into the battle. There were no reserves, no fresh troops. On the Union side, four army corps suffered almost all of the 12,000 casualties sustained that day. Amazingly enough, one-third of McClellan's army had not even fired a shot. On both sides, regiments ceased to exist. The fighting had been so fierce and so close that hundreds of men fell dead or wounded in just a matter of minutes. At the end of the day, only a handful of survivors of these brutal encounters were left to answer the roll.

Despite the heavy losses, Lee gave instructions to his subordinates to prepare for another battle. He refused to surrender the field to McClellan. For his part, McClellan expected another battle, but in his mind it was Lee's 100,000 men who would attack. He ordered his army to defend the ground they occupied, even after receiving 13,000 reinforcements. A strange calm followed throughout the day, as soldiers from both sides collected casualties and cooked rations. That night, Lee withdrew silently across the Potomac, the hopes of victory that would lead to independence postponed. A Union attempt at pursuit was savagely beaten back at the Potomac by A. P. Hill's men. The Antietam campaign was over.

## Assessing the Battle and Its Significance

The battle itself was a draw. Lee always considered it one of his finest battles, in which he displayed his mastery of the battlefield against enormous odds. McClellan, too, believed he had demonstrated his superior skills, claiming that it was "a masterpiece of art." Although neither side gained any advantage on the battlefield, the Battle of Antietam had profound significance for America.

**TURNING POINT**

The day after Lee's army crossed the Potomac, McClellan sent the president a triumphant telegram announcing his victory. "Maryland is entirely freed of the enemy," he reported. True, Maryland was freed, but Lee's army was not destroyed as Lincoln wished. Nevertheless, McClellan's report was the first Union success in many long months. It gave the president the cover he needed to alter the nature of the war.

## The Emancipation Proclamation

On September 22, Lincoln issued his Emancipation Proclamation. The Proclamation, a wartime expedient that Lincoln issued as commander-in-chief, declared that unless the Southern states returned to the Union by January 1, 1863, all the slaves in those states "shall be then, thenceforward, and forever, free." By issuing the Proclamation, Lincoln hoped to cripple the South, both psychologically and economically. The Proclamation was intended to break Southern morale and lead to an end to the war; it was also aimed at crippling the South's ability to continue the war. By offering freedom to the slaves who sustained the South's farms and factories, Lincoln was aiming at the Confederacy's vulnerable heart. This wording reflected Congress's Second Confiscation Act of June 1862, which declared fugitive slaves free and allowed the president to use Africans in any manner he thought necessary to support the suppression of the rebellion.

The Emancipation Proclamation also signaled a new direction in the war and a final effort to win the battle for the hearts and minds of the European powers. It was also meant to bolster his political support among Republicans, especially abolitionists. Expanding the original war aim — restoration of the Union — to also include a war for human freedom helped nullify Lincoln's political opposition in the North. The Union armies were now armies of liberation.

## Lincoln's proclamation: The fine print

Lincoln's noble words in 1862 were just that — words. A careful look at the document reveals some interesting legalistic language carefully crafted for political purposes. Let's take a look at the main points:

>> The Proclamation made no mention of slaves held in neutral states or those loyal to the Union. Even after January 1, 1863, the people held in bondage in these states were still slaves. This exclusion helped ensure that these slave states would not join the Confederacy.

>> Slave owners in states not in rebellion could be financially compensated for their slave property. Lincoln also proposed resettling people of African descent (presumably outside of the country).

>> Slaves in territory under Union control, as of the proclamation date, were still in bondage.

>> Lincoln declared freedom for slaves in an area where the federal government no longer had any power. Thus, for the Proclamation to have any effect, the Confederacy would have to be occupied by Union troops.

## Southern reaction

Southern reaction to the Proclamation varied from outright hysteria over fears that the Union was trying to foment a slave rebellion to a cocky response that said, in effect, "Come and get us!" But thoughtful Southerners understood the power of Lincoln's words. Already, the French and British were growing cool to the idea of Southern independence. The Union had gained the moral high ground in world opinion, or at least the part that counted. Also, the slaves themselves could not help but be aware of the promise offered to them. There was no way for slave owners to control their thoughts or emotions, or ensure their loyalty. The Proclamation would also change the course of the war. The Union would no longer be fighting for limited objectives. Southerners understood that the nature of the war had changed. The stakes were now raised to a war for human freedom. Any compromise on the issue of slavery was now out of the question. With this new Union war aim came the unstated understanding that the Confederacy would have to surrender unconditionally. Unconditional surrender meant only one thing — the

South's absolute destruction. It was a fearsome prospect that no one had contemplated in the heady days of 1860 and 1861. The war would have to go on.

# Heroes and Goats

This campaign produced many heroes and one prominent goat, who had the exceedingly rare opportunity given only to a few, to change the course of history. It is interesting to observe how such little things can sometimes turn out to be so important.

## Heroes

Heroes come in all forms. Sometimes even a lowly private can turn the tide of battle. Check out the following:

>> **Robert E. Lee:** His bold plan to invade the North and threaten Pennsylvania and beyond just might have worked. Caught off guard, Lee improvised and fought a battle for the survival of his cause, never once doubting the capabilities of his soldiers or his able commanders to win a victory. But the cost was high — Antietam claimed too many of the best men he ever had.

>> **Stonewall Jackson:** His brilliant victory at Harpers Ferry was soured by events at Antietam. Still, Jackson arrived on the field in time to fight valiantly, even desperately, on Lee's left flank against the better part of three Union corps. His cool leadership during the battle was worth a thousand men. Loved by his soldiers, feared by his enemies, Jackson's value to Lee continued to grow.

>> **A.P. Hill:** He provided as close to a storybook ending as you will find in the history of warfare. Wearing a bright red shirt, Hill rode at the head of his hard-marching division from Harpers Ferry to smash into Burnside's attack that, at the last minute, threatened to cut the Confederates off from the Potomac. He saved the day and became one of the most famous generals in Lee's army. He was clearly destined for bigger things.

>> **Corporal Barton W. Mitchell, 27th Indiana:** He was the soldier who discovered Lee's Special Order Number 191 near Frederick and had the brains and initiative to pass this goldmine of information up the chain of command to General McClellan.

>> **Abraham Lincoln:** He was still far from the status of faultless icon that we know today, but he was on his way. The Emancipation Proclamation, although in many ways an exercise in political double-talk, ennobled both the cause and its author, over time. He became the Great Emancipator of legend and myth.

# Goats

Goats, like heroes, can stand out or remain anonymous. McClellan is an example of amazing opportunities lost. The other goat is an example of why paying attention to little things in war is important. The goats are as follows:

>> **George B. McClellan:** He claimed, for the second time, to have saved the nation from outright destruction. (The first time was at the conclusion of the Peninsula campaign.) Everyone was frustrated with his timidity and aversion to bloodshed. Given a chance of a lifetime, and to change the course of American history forever, he gave Lee every possible chance to survive, and then, when all the cards were in his favor, he was overcome by fears of massed rebels that existed only in his imagination. Time was running out for the Young Napoleon.

>> **Whoever Lost Special Order 191:** For some strange reason, this careless Confederate officer, forever anonymous, decided that a commanding general's critical movement orders for the entire army should be carried about, wrapped around three cigars. What was *he* thinking? On such errors, history is made (or unmade).

Chapter **15**

# Lost Opportunities for the Confederacy in the West: September–October 1862

Both Union and Confederate generals learned difficult lessons about conducting campaigns in the Western Theater. The first and most important lesson dealt with logistics (the means of supplying an army in the field with all its necessities) and lines of supply. No matter how good your army is, it cannot fight effectively without adequate supplies. Movement of forces is the second lesson a general must learn, because it allows you to place your army where and when you want it. The third lesson is maneuvering forces effectively against the enemy to gain an advantage. The final lesson is that once in a favorable position against an enemy force, a general must employ his forces aggressively and in a unified and coordinated fashion. Confederate General Braxton Bragg's advance into Kentucky and Union General Don Carlos Buell's pursuit illustrated that these generals had much to learn about campaigning. Likewise, Confederate Generals Earl Van Doren and Sterling Price showed that they also were lacking in the skills necessary to conduct successful operations. As a result, the Confederacy's hold on the Mississippi River was dangerously exposed.

# The Western Theater: A Lesson in Geography

The southern border of Tennessee is about 400 miles, stretching east across northern Mississippi, Alabama, and Georgia. The Kentucky border is about 100 miles away to the north (see Figure 15-1 to get an appreciation for the land between Kentucky and Tennessee where the armies will move and fight). From the Kentucky border to the key cities of Frankfort (the state capital), Louisville, and Lexington is another 100 miles or so. Within this geographical area are a number of militarily significant cities. Going from west to east across the Tennessee border are Memphis (a source of supply for the Union and a key base from which to launch an attack south down the Mississippi River to Vicksburg), Corinth (another Union supply base and important rail junction controlling access to southern Mississippi, northern Alabama, and western Tennessee), Chattanooga (a Confederate base controlling rail access to eastern Tennessee), and Knoxville (another Confederate base offering access to the Kentucky border). Nashville, roughly in the center of the state, is the state capital under Union control, with a pro-Union governor administering the areas of the state occupied by Union forces. It has both rail and road access north to Bowling Green, Kentucky, and south to northern Alabama. Rail movement of troops and supplies will be essential; overland movement of troops will require marching distances reaching 100 miles. Much of the region is marked by large rivers and hilly terrain. In 1862, much of this land along the southern Tennessee border was sparsely populated and poor; Kentucky offered lush pastures, rich farmlands, large population centers, and opportunities for collecting provisions, but it was far away. The point of all this is to indicate that any commander contemplating a major military campaign in this region, especially covering a distance of 200 miles or more, will demand extraordinary skills.

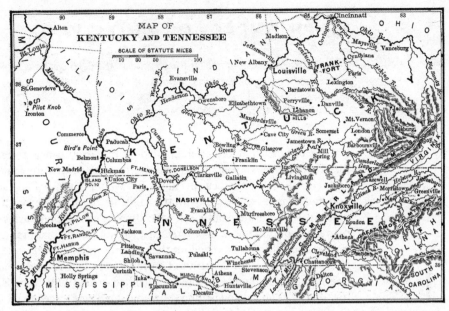

**FIGURE 15-1:**
Map of Kentucky
and Tennessee.

Getty Images

# Confederate Cavalry Dominates Tennessee

Prior to his departure to Washington, D.C., to become the general-in-chief replacing McClellan, Halleck divided the massive army that he had assembled during his snail-like capture of Corinth. Halleck looked at the map and noted that vast areas required troops for garrison and occupation duty stretching west from Nashville to Memphis and from Columbus, Kentucky, in the north to Corinth in the south. These bases were connected by rail, which served as the Union army's primary lines of supply and communication. But these critical lines were still deep within enemy territory, and Union forces were constantly harassed by Confederate cavalry. Nathan Bedford Forrest and John Hunt Morgan were superb raiders. Attacking isolated outposts and destroying or seizing supplies, they wrecked bridges, tunnels, and rail lines with impunity. The Confederate cavalry was such a problem that tens of thousands of troops from Grant's 67,000-man army were dispersed to guard their supply lines and protect the line of communication between Nashville and Memphis.

# KEEPING TRACK OF WHO IS WHO

At the beginning of the campaign, Buell's Army of the Ohio is redesignated as the Army of the Cumberland; Bragg takes command of the Army of the Mississippi, soon renamed the Army of Tennessee.

Halleck decided that rather than keeping his army concentrated and using the Mississippi River to sustain his massive force to move into southern Mississippi and cut the Confederacy in half, he would spread his forces across the 400-mile Tennessee border with the vague intent of dealing with the Confederate units scattered to the south and east. Union General Don Carlos Buell's 40,000-man Army of the Ohio was ordered east to capture the main rail center at Chattanooga. Even though he relied on the rail line from Corinth to Chattanooga (it is about 200 miles from Corinth to Chattanooga), he averaged about 4 miles a day. Nearly every day, Buell (see Figure 15-2) had to deal with Confederate raiders who tore up tracks ahead and behind the army. Buell was forced to move only as fast as his repair crews could work. Another aspect of this campaign became painfully obvious to both Union and Confederate soldiers who would have to endure it: A severe drought in the region made water a precious commodity.

**FIGURE 15-2:**
Don Carlos Buell.

*The Library of Congress / Public Domain*

# Bragg Takes Command

At the end of May 1862, President Davis appointed General Braxton Bragg (see Figure 15-3) as the commander of the Confederate Army of Mississippi, replacing General Beauregard, who was later also relieved of command of the Western Military Department. In June, Bragg became the commander of the Department. As a young officer in the Mexican War, Bragg had won a reputation as a fighter, and he was a close associate of President Jefferson Davis. But Bragg was a difficult man to deal with. His relationship with subordinates was almost uniformly terrible, creating resentment and distrust. He was a no-nonsense type who could get things done, but he was quarrelsome and stubborn. He also had a very high opinion of his own abilities. These traits would do little to further the interests of the Confederacy in the Western Theater.

**FIGURE 15-3:**
Braxton Bragg.

*The Library of Congress / Public Domain*

Bragg was now both a department commander and an army commander. Unable to delegate authority, he could not be on an active campaign while also dealing with the many dangers from Union forces threatening the department. Ignoring the complications and with no enemy pressure against his forces, Bragg used the time to drill and discipline the army of nearly 70,000 men into an effective fighting force. With Buell struggling to move his army to Chattanooga in the face of

Confederate cavalry delaying tactics, Bragg took advantage of his interior lines to move about half of his army (30,000 men) from northern Mississippi to Chattanooga ahead of Buell by rail. At this point in the war, the Confederates had no fear of Union cavalry threatening rail lines. Confederate forces could move rapidly by rail through the interior of the South, which gave Bragg an enormous advantage (this is, after all, what interior lines accomplish for a commander). Bragg left the other half of his army, 16,000 troops under Major General Earl Van Dorn and another 16,000 troops under Major General Sterling Price in northern Mississippi, to protect Vicksburg and keep an eye on Grant. This was a decision that would have serious ramifications. As we have seen, neither Van Dorn nor Price were officers who should have been left to their own devices.

## Bragg's invasion plan

By August, Bragg was ready to take the initiative. General Kirby Smith, in Knoxville with 20,000 Confederate troops of the Army of Kentucky, was not under Bragg's command, but the two commanders had made an agreement to cooperate. Given the distances involved, moving from Chattanooga to threaten Nashville, a political and military target that would unsettle Union control of the state and lead to a major battle on terrain favorable to the Confederate army, seemed within Bragg's capabilities. But Bragg was thinking of an even bigger opportunity — threatening the entire Midwest by moving his army into Kentucky up to the Ohio River. Kentucky supposedly offered great strategic advantages. Like Maryland in the Eastern Theater, Kentucky was believed to be ripe for joining the Confederate cause. Rumors abounded that Kentuckians were eager to be rid of Union control. President Davis was especially in favor of a move into Kentucky. After all, it was his native state, and politically it offered enormous benefits, especially after he suffered so much criticism over losing Tennessee. His only guidance to Bragg was not to lose his army in the process. Encouraged by the enthusiastic endorsement of his ambitious goals, Bragg initiated a bold move north. Smith drove into Kentucky, smashing a patchwork of largely untrained defenders at Richmond in early August, just about the same time Lee had beaten Pope at Manassas. Smith then moved to Frankfort. Bragg planned to support Smith's advance by driving his army north toward Kentucky, while threatening Nashville as well. This would draw Buell northward to protect Nashville with its newly installed pro-Union Governor Andrew Johnson. If Grant moved to assist Buell in the east, Bragg's forces in northern Mississippi could strike and move into western Tennessee, or even into Kentucky, wiping out all the Union gains in the spring of 1862. The plan, such as it was, required great insight into the enemy's actions and intentions, a flexible and imaginative commander, and close coordination between four separate armies, two of which were operating several hundred miles away. It was a lot to ask of Braxton Bragg.

# Bragg in Kentucky

Once his army arrived in Kentucky, Bragg's forces captured a Union garrison at Munfordville and blocked Buell's easiest line of advance northward. Buell had advanced ever so slowly to Nashville, then made his way to Bowling Green. Buell's army was only about 35 miles away from Bragg and headed toward Louisville. Bragg had an opportunity to attack Buell's army, but he seemed to lose his focus. Although he had not fought a battle yet, he wasn't sure what to do next — link up with Smith and invade Ohio? Capture the main logistics base at Louisville and move into Indiana? Fight a climactic battle in Kentucky? Smith, for all intents and purposes, was an independent commander, who, although pledging cooperation with Bragg, could do as he pleased. The two armies were separated, with Smith near Lexington and Bragg near Bardstown, more than 60 miles away. This disjointed command structure (the brainchild of President Davis) frustrated Bragg. In addition, he was greatly disappointed at the response of the people of Kentucky, who showed little or no interest in flocking to the colors. So he busied himself with politics, installing the new pro-Confederate governor, Richard Hawes, in Frankfort. While the new governor was giving his address, his words were cut short by the sound of artillery outside of town. The ceremony ended quickly.

While Bragg wasted valuable time playing politician, Buell accomplished little as well. Prodded into action by Halleck, Lincoln, and an aggravated Northern press, Buell gained reinforcements and made a slow and deliberate McClellan-like movement toward Louisville, arriving there on September 26.

# Lincoln loses patience

Lincoln had actually decided to remove Buell and replace him with George H. Thomas. Thomas declined the command, arguing that the army was ready to move and that it would be improper to change commanders at such a critical time. Buell also had very powerful allies in Congress who made their displeasure known to the president. Lincoln backtracked, putting Thomas as second in command. Buell now began to feel the heat and put together a sound battle plan. With 60,000 men (most of them raw recruits), Buell sent a division to Frankfort to fool the Confederates into thinking that this was his main attack. It was this division that spoiled the Hawes inauguration. At the same time, Buell also launched an uncharacteristically aggressive three-pronged attack with 55,000 men against the divided forces of Smith and Bragg.

# Starting the Fight: The Battle of Perryville

Bragg took the bait; believing Buell's main attack was headed for Frankfort, he shifted forces north in support of Smith. But Bragg never really knew where the enemy was because his orders to his subordinate commanders were confusing and had no connection to the actual situation. Bragg was planning to concentrate his army with Smith's at a point 30 miles northeast of where Buell was actually concentrating his army — Perryville. Buell's estimations of the enemy's movements were not much better — he had no idea where Bragg's main body of troops was located. A northward-moving portion of Bragg's army, 15,000 men under Bishop Polk, ran into a part of Buell's army at Perryville. Polk took up a strong defensive position near the town and waited most of the day for an attack that never came. Buell had planned to attack in the morning, but his subordinates were slow in bringing up their troops. Bragg arrived in the afternoon, finally realizing that the enemy was not where he had originally thought. On October 8, the Confederates launched an attack against the Union left flank, catching the Yankees off guard, as a division moved forward to look for water in a nearby creek bed. The Union forces were driven back nearly a mile after prolonged and very bitter fighting. Most of the new units composed of recruits broke and ran, but some units stood and fought stubbornly (some said the toughest close-in fighting of the war occurred at Perryville). In the center, an aggressive Union division commander named Philip Sheridan advanced against the enemy, driving the Confederates into the town. His success, however, was never followed up because of the Confederate pressure on the collapsing Union flank. While one Union corps fought, the other two corps stood idle.

Amazingly, Buell did not know his forces were in a major battle until late in the afternoon. The temperature or the wind that day had created an effect called an *acoustic shadow,* in which sound travels upward rather than along the ground where it can be heard. Just a few miles away from the fighting, Buell heard nothing. Likewise, Bragg was not aware that Polk had been engaged until he arrived on the scene. It was not until nightfall that both commanders finally had a clear idea of their respective situations. Buell ordered an all-out attack against the vastly outnumbered Confederate defenders; Bragg, realizing that he was facing the entire Union army, ordered a retreat that night. The battle of Perryville was over. Over the objections of his subordinates, Bragg stubbornly refused to take stock of his overall still-favorable position and ordered a retreat out of Kentucky.

# Enduring Another Confederate Disaster: Iuka and Corinth

Bragg had indicated to Van Dorn and Price that at some point (although he was never clear what that point would be) he wanted them to combine forces and move toward Nashville to threaten Buell's line of communication. These instructions, of course, ignored the fact that Grant still had a sizeable army capable of responding to such a threat. Even though Bragg was their commander, Van Dorn decided that he should advance north up the Mississippi to attack Paducah, about 160 miles away as the crow flies but much further overland, of course. As usual, he had no concept of what it would take logistically to sustain an army deep into enemy territory. Even more amazing, he bypassed Bragg and went directly to President Davis and got his approval to be the commander of a combined army with Price as his subordinate. Price, refused to accept this new command arrangement, claiming he was still under orders from Bragg. Acting on his own, he attacked the Union outpost at Iuka, Mississippi, to capture supplies. Taking far too much time to enjoy his success, he had no idea that Grant was about to strike.

Grant saw an opportunity to destroy an isolated element of the Confederate army. He launched a two-pronged attack on September 17 to surround and trap the outnumbered Confederates. Major General William S. Rosecrans, who commanded the southern portion of the envelopment, arrived first just as Price was evacuating the town. He escaped from the trap after a short fight. Rosecrans compounded his error by a slow pursuit. Price and Van Dorn combined their armies to form the Army of West Tennessee and moved against Rosecrans and his 20,000 troops occupying Corinth.

REMEMBER

Corinth had been continually fortified, first by General Beauregard in April of 1862, and then by the Union army, which over the course of several months had improved the Confederate works and expanded several strongpoints around the southern part of the city. The defenses were well built and well manned, arranged in an outer and an inner line. Artillery positions were protected by stout earthworks and were situated to provide a deadly crossfire against attacking infantry.

Van Dorn's army, after a long and wearying march in brutal Mississippi heat, assaulted the Union lines on October 4 with multiple attacks that broke the outer defenses. As darkness fell, and with his troops battered and exhausted, Van Dorn prepared to continue the attack the next day. Until reminded, he had again, as he had at Pea Ridge, forgotten to order a resupply of ammunition. The following day saw desperate fighting that brought the Confederates into Corinth itself. But the attack had culminated. Without further reinforcement and now in danger of being cut off and surrounded, the attackers, who had achieved the near impossible, withdrew to friendly lines. Van Dorn now began to pull his army together for a retreat. The casualties that resulted from attacking fortified defensive positions had been heavy: Van Dorn's army suffered over 4,000 casualties; Rosecrans lost 2,500. Grant sought to take advantage of this repulse with a vigorous pursuit and dispatched a force to cut the line of the Confederate retreat, but Rosecrans was less than enthusiastic and did not assist, allowing Van Dorn to slip away.

# Assessing the Aftermath of the Campaign: Results and Recriminations

Bragg later succeeded in combining his army with Smith's army — about a week too late. Bragg had no interest in another battle. Apparently, Buell did not want another fight either, even though he outnumbered the Confederates. Bragg finally began a long retreat to Knoxville, leaving Kentucky and the prospect for a decisive turnaround in the Western Theater. He had accomplished one of his objectives: The army he brought back to Tennessee was vastly better clothed, shod, and equipped than the one that had left and in possession of vast quantities of supplies, particularly the superb horses of Kentucky. Buell also let an opportunity for decisive action slip away. He followed Bragg too cautiously, to the point of abandoning the pursuit altogether; to make matters worse, he balked at the president's directive to move into east Tennessee, arguing that Nashville should be protected. Lincoln lost all patience and sacked him, putting William S. Rosecrans in charge of the army. Grant, who was disgusted with Rosecrans's poor performance at Corinth and his reluctance to pursue a defeated enemy after the battle, had been ready to relieve him – just before the president rescued him.

On the Confederate side, the finger pointing began in earnest as soon as the army was safely in Tennessee. The Southern press was furious and demanded an explanation from the president. What had gone wrong? Bragg traveled to Richmond to meet with President Davis personally and explain what had happened. Bragg was quick to assess blame — it was all Polk's fault. Davis then summoned Polk to Richmond. Polk said it was all Bragg's fault. Davis made an executive decision. He promoted Polk to Lieutenant General and kept him in Bragg's army (soon to be redesignated as the Army of Tennessee). He placed General Joseph E. Johnston in overall charge of Confederate forces in Tennessee and Mississippi. Kirby Smith was assigned to the Trans-Mississippi Theater, and Major General John C. Pemberton took over command from Van Dorn, who had proven his inability to command an army (Van Dorn would move on to become a rather effective commander of cavalry). Pemberton, who had no command experience, was now commander of the newly created Department of the Mississippi.

Now if this all sounds confusing, it is. Like all executive decisions attempting to balance conflicting interests, this pleased no one and created unnecessary layers of command. Bragg and Davis were friends, as were Davis and Polk, but Davis and

Johnston were not on good terms, and Johnston's role was purposely ambiguous, indicating that Davis was not willing to entrust Johnston with significant responsibilities. Davis could not bring himself to believe that Bragg was incapable of effective battlefield command. This reluctance would ultimately doom the Confederate defense of the Western Theater.

# Significance of the Battles

Compared to other important Civil War battles, Perryville was rather small. But for the forces actually engaged, the casualties were very high — 4,200 Union and 3,400 Confederate. The number of casualties alone illustrates the intensity of the fighting. But for both sides, the battle decided little. However, it prevented the Confederate army from convincing Kentucky, or France and Great Britain for that matter, that the Southerners could sustain an offensive outside of their own territory. Kentucky had been up for grabs; a pro-Confederate legislature and governor were in place in Frankfort. Bragg and his army (along with the freelancing Kirby Smith) had the opportunity to change the balance of the war in the Western Theater. But Bragg seemed to lose track of both his objective and Buell's army. Buell, although only a bit more competent than Bragg in this campaign, was able to take advantage of Bragg's listlessness. The result was an accidental battle that lost Kentucky for the Confederacy and returned the strategic initiative back to the Union, although it seemed that Buell was just as befuddled in victory as Bragg was in defeat. Corinth was a battle that did not need to be fought and Van Dorn's attacks against entrenched troops supported by fortified heavy artillery only depleted Confederate manpower and opened Mississippi up to a Union counteroffensive.

# Heroes and Goats

Heroes in this campaign are hard to find. A hero would have taken advantage of the numerous golden opportunities offered him by his enemy and brought about a decisive result. As it was, no true hero emerged at the army level.

## Heroes

Some heroes stand out because of their individual acts. Some heroes stand out because of their collective acts. Here are some examples:

>> **The Union and Confederate soldiers:** The Battle of Perryville proved, beyond a doubt, that American volunteer soldiers possessed impressive fighting

qualities. Marching for days without water, often poorly led, and even more poorly supplied, these men persevered. They displayed enormous courage and spirit in a battle fought, not by generals but by colonels, majors, and captains.

» **Philip Sheridan:** Feisty, bold, and unafraid, Sheridan made his mark at Perryville. He and his men were always in the thick of the fight. Sheridan saw things his superiors on the battlefield did not. He was quick to take advantage wherever he could. He showed that he would be a great asset to the army.

» **Ulysses S. Grant**: Pushed aside by Halleck and denigrated as a drunk and a nobody, Grant showed great mettle and drive in comparison to Buell. He seemed to have something other Union generals did not — a fighting spirit.

# Goats

Without a doubt, this is one of the sorriest examples of generalship in the American Civil War — a comedy (tragedy?) of errors, compounded by ignorance that is hard to believe at times. As always, the soldiers in the ranks pay the terrible costs of these generals' blunders. A great deal was riding on the skills of these two generals during this campaign. Neither displayed any skill. In fact, it is hard to say who performed worse.

» **Don Carlos Buell:** Buell's caution and inaction drove Lincoln to distraction. Lincoln, perhaps realizing how close Buell came to losing Kentucky, wisely began to move him out of command after the battle.

» **Braxton Bragg:** Bragg's inability to get along with his officers led to the collapse of a well-conceived campaign plan and squandered an opportunity for a decisive action that could turn the tide of the war. He was quickly overtaxed, made a number of poor decisions in Kentucky, allowed Price and Van Dorn to stumble off with only vague instructions, and lost his nerve after Perryville. Despite all this, Bragg retains command.

» **Earl Van Dorn**: A man completely unable to reign in fantasy with reality. His ignorance and neglect of logistics, his inability to command forces in the field effectively, and his ignorance of his subordinates' capabilities hurt the Confederate cause and wasted brave men's lives.

» **Jefferson Davis:** As commander-in-chief, he had the uncanny ability to intercede at the worst possible time, giving Van Dorn command and allowing him to blunder into an unnecessary battle at Corinth, then created a nightmare of command relationships trying to please everyone, while keeping Bragg in command.

Chapter **16**

# War So Terrible: Fredericksburg and Murfreesboro, December 1862

In the Eastern Theater, McClellan had just barely defeated Lee's invading Confederate Army of Northern Virginia at Antietam, but at a frightful cost. Lee was still a powerful and dangerous foe. In the Western Theater, the Confederate invasion into Kentucky had been turned back at Perryville, but General Braxton Bragg and his Confederate Army of Tennessee remained a threat. Other Confederate forces, though battered at Corinth, were able to mount a respectable defense. All the fighting and all the losses had amounted to nothing. The elections had gone badly for the Republicans. Morale in the North sagged. How long could either side take such punishment? The last months of 1862 and the first month of 1863 would be bitter times for the Union; new Union army commanders and new offensives would bring more horrific casualties, but neither would bring the war any closer to a conclusion.

The Confederacy had survived 1862. The Army of Northern Virginia finished that terrible year with another brilliant but unsatisfying victory in the Eastern Theater. In the Western Theater, it was more of the same — one step forward and two steps backward for the Army of Tennessee. But the bottom line was that the Confederate armies were still in the field, and the Union was no closer to victory than it had been at the beginning of the year.

# Making a New Start in the East

After Antietam, Union General McClellan and his beloved Army of the Potomac rested, refitted, and trained, giving every indication that the commander was not eager to use the last months of autumn for any campaigning before entering into camp for the winter. Lincoln arrived at the camp, spent time with the troops, whose morale was good, and had several long discussions with his general. Lincoln was trying to cure what he called "the slows," a condition he believed McClellan had that prevented him from energetically engaging the enemy. McClellan had no problem making the president aware of all the reasons why he was not yet ready to move. After Lincoln's departure — as the Young Napoleon undoubtedly breathed a great sigh of relief to be rid of the silly civilian pest and rank amateur — an order arrived from General-in-Chief Halleck in Washington instructing him to move his army across the Potomac and begin combat operations. McClellan took nearly three weeks to get going. Meanwhile General Jeb Stuart and his Confederate horsemen reprised their celebrated ride around the Union army in front of Richmond before the Seven Days battles. This time Stuart rode into Pennsylvania, disrupted Chambersburg, took hundreds of horses and wagons, and then rode behind McClellan's force, returning to Virginia unmolested. Even though McClellan had promised Washington that he would take vigorous action, nothing happened. Once again, the Confederates had mocked McClellan's immobility, and Stuart added an even greater aura to his reputation as a dashing cavalryman.

McClellan set out with the Army of the Potomac, about 120,000 men. He took his time, crossing the Potomac in nine days. Lee's army, brought up to 68,000 with new draftees and men who had rejoined their units, was resting and refitting in Winchester. After crossing the Potomac, the Union army was actually closer to Richmond than Lee's army. A rapid movement south would place Lee in a disadvantageous position, forcing him to attack McClellan to protect the capital. McClellan, believing Lee had 130,000 men, set his usual creeping pace. This enabled Lee to shift the bulk of his army eastward and easily position it squarely in McClellan's path. Buell's fate should have alerted the Young Napoleon that a slow pursuit of the enemy would get him fired by President Lincoln. The end came quickly. A courier delivered the message on November 7, relieving McClellan and putting the reluctant Major General Ambrose E. Burnside (see Figure 16-1) in command of the Army of the Potomac.

**FIGURE 16-1:**
Ambrose
E. Burnside.

*The Library of Congress / Public Domain*

## BURNSIDE/SIDEBURNS

Ambrose Burnside was a Rhode Islander and a West Point graduate. He was also an entrepreneur, inventing a breech-loading (a cartridge is loaded from the rear of the weapon) carbine that was one of the most advanced weapons of his time. He had fought with the Army of the Potomac since First Bull Run, and had a moderate success as an independent commander, capturing Roanoke Island off North Carolina early in the war. At Antietam, he had shown tenacity, if nothing else, and impressed the politicos in Washington with his apparent aggressiveness. Burnside had a distinctive appearance, having a large, bald head, deep-set eyes, and a flourish of enormously bushy whiskers that stretched from his ears and down his jaw line, crossing below his nose in an elaborate sweeping mustache. His facial hair was so unique that his name, somewhat corrupted by wags, became the word for any hair that extends down the side of a man's face — *sideburns*. Burnside has come down to posterity as one more famous for his hairstyle than his generalship.

# Hurry Up and Wait at the Rappahannock

Burnside, clearly understanding the implied message from the president that he was to get into a fight before the end of the year, sent a plan of action to Halleck, shifting the direction of the army away from its general direction towards Warrenton to Fredericksburg, a small city on the banks of the Rappahannock River, and on the primary road and rail lines to Richmond, which he declared to be the strategic decisive point. He also reorganized the army to simplify the command structure. The six corps of the army would be divided up into three Grand Divisions, with two corps each. Major General Edwin Sumner commanded the right Grand Division, William Franklin commanded the left Grand Division, and Joseph Hooker commanded the center Grand Division. On paper, it eased the complexities of command, but Burnside quickly demonstrated that no system of command and control would help him.

## My kingdom for a pontoon

Burnside lost no time in presenting his plan for approval. The president, in granting his approval, made the qualification that if his plan was to work, Burnside must move rapidly. As part of his plan, Burnside ordered pontoon bridges on November 12 to arrive at Falmouth when his troops did, so the army could cross the river without delay (all the bridges across the river had been destroyed). But Burnside was relying on Halleck, of all people, to provide the pontoons. Meanwhile, he moved Sumner's Grand Division rapidly to Falmouth, a town directly across the river from Fredericksburg, arriving on November 17. Burnside had gotten a rare step ahead of Lee and by November 20, the Army of the Potomac was concentrating at Falmouth.

Lee's army was divided. Jackson's corps with 37,000 men was in the Shenandoah Valley, ready at any time to threaten Washington. Astride the approach to Warrenton was Longstreet's corps with 38,000 men. Lee was in a position to attack or defend as necessary, knowing full well that McClellan would take no aggressive action. The new commander, however, by shifting one-third of his army south, caused Lee some concern. Stuart's cavalry soon provided the information Lee needed to make a decision, and he ordered Longstreet to Fredericksburg, while keeping Jackson alerted and ready to move to support. Longstreet would arrive on November 21 but was not fully closed on the city until November 25.

Why did Sumner wait, when there were no Confederate forces in Fredericksburg? Why did the entire Union army stand still even as Longstreet, who was completely outnumbered, was still on the move?

**REMEMBER**

Here is the answer: Burnside's reluctance to make command decisions that varied from his plan. His plan called for pontoons to build bridges; the pontoons had not yet arrived. In fact, they did not arrive until November 27, after Longstreet had occupied the heights above Fredericksburg. Sumner, who could have forded the river downstream when he arrived ten days earlier, was ordered to remain in place, as Burnside was afraid that rains might cause a sudden flood that could cut off Sumner's Grand Division from the rest of the army — better stick to the plan.

Between November 24 and December 10, Burnside made only minor revisions to his original plan. Meanwhile, Jackson's corps had arrived and extended Lee's line about 17 miles farther south along the Rappahannock. Lee found it hard to believe that Burnside would attack directly across the river through the city. Instead, he thought that a competent commander would seek to turn his flank further south, thus the reason for Jackson watching the river below Fredericksburg. Burnside now decided that the engineers would lay down five pontoon bridges across the river. Three would be set up in front of Fredericksburg; two would be set up downstream. Franklin's Grand Division would cross the river downstream and attack the enemy's flank and open the road to Richmond. Once Franklin had made progress, Sumner's Grand Division, in support of Franklin, would move into the city and attack the Confederates defending Marye's Heights, the decisive high ground overlooking the city. Hooker's Grand Division would remain in reserve to support either attack. It was a plan that inspired no confidence in any of his commanders.

On December 11, Burnside's engineers began to place the pontoon bridges. The downstream bridges were set up with no resistance. The bridges in front of Fredericksburg were another story. Unwilling to make the crossing easy, Lee had sent a brigade of troops to shoot the engineers as they worked. Hidden in and around the buildings, the Confederate sharpshooters drove the intrepid engineers back for cover again and again. The entire attack was stalled by a handful of riflemen. Eventually Union artillery went into action and fired over 9,000 shells for two hours into the town to drive out the Confederates. When this failed, four brigades of Union infantry crossed the river and drove the Rebels out. As soon as the opposite shore was secure, the bridges were rapidly built, and thousands of men began to move into the now ruined city. At the same time, Franklin's troops recrossed the bridges downstream, but as night fell, Burnside decided to wait until morning. Just as he had been at Antietam, Burnside was fixated on bridges. There had been nothing to stop him from ordering Franklin to send his nearly 60,000 men across the river and be in place to begin the attack. But that was not in the plan. Burnside still had to prepare his orders.

## Lee awaits

Lee used well the time given to him. Recognizing that Burnside was actually going to attack head on, Lee ordered Jackson to move to protect the vulnerable right flank. Jackson brought his corps up but was still bringing units on the battlefield at about the time Franklin made his first move. By the time the battle began, Lee had his entire army of 78,000 men stretched along a 7-mile front — Longstreet had one soldier for every yard of terrain, while Jackson's men were hidden, spread along wooded hills on the Confederate right flank.

# The Battle of Fredericksburg

Fredericksburg was the wrong battle at the wrong time at the wrong place for the Army of the Potomac. There is no more difficult attack to conduct in military operations — cross a major river and move through a built-up area to assault an enemy defending high ground. Generals avoid such attacks because they are too costly. Burnside would prove just how costly.

Franklin's Grand Division initiated the attack on December 13. He did not receive his orders until sometime after 7 a.m. Instead of an all-out attack, Sumner was now ordered to make a tentative advance with only a division directed against Lee's flank, while at the same time keeping a line of retreat open. With these completely nonsensical directives from the commander, Franklin advanced a division forward in heavy fog. Delayed and harassed by artillery fire, the division, led by Major General George G. Meade, finally made an attack in the early afternoon. Meade's units had some success, actually penetrating part of the Confederate line, but were driven back with heavy losses; a supporting attack by another division failed to make any gains. A Confederate counterattack in the late afternoon was stopped after heavy fighting and Franklin, although he had tens of thousands of troops available to continue the fight, decided not to make any more efforts against the Confederate line. The focus of the battle shifted to Sumner's Grand Division in Fredericksburg.

**REMEMBER**

By midafternoon, Union brigades totaling 40,000 men had stacked up on the main road leading up the broad, 1,000-yard, open slope to the heights that dominated the town. Just in front of the heights was a 4-foot stone wall in front of a sunken road (see Figure 16-2). Longstreet's troops from Georgia, and later North Carolina, manned this natural trench, standing in parallel lines along the wall. As the Union brigades emerged from the city and crossed into the open, they were met with the massed destructive fire of rifled muskets and artillery. Again and again, the brave Union troops advanced, but the men were shot down in rows. Bodies were heaped on bodies before the stone wall where the Confederate defenders were alternating four, then six, firing lines. As soon as one line had fired, it moved back and reloaded, allowing the next line to fire. The resulting rate of fire was almost like a modern machine gun. By the end of the day, 6,300 Union soldiers lay dead or wounded in front of the wall, none getting any closer than 40 yards.

**FIGURE 16-2:**
Confederate soldiers at the stone wall at Fredericksburg.

COBB'S AND KERSHAW'S TROOPS BEHIND THE STONE WALL.

*Redwood, Allen Christian / The Library of Congress / Public Domain*

Although urged to halt, Burnside, who was far away from the action and believing that Franklin was successful on the left flank of the Union line, ordered Hooker to continue the attack. As darkness fell on that short December day, about 13,000 Union soldiers were casualties; the Confederates had lost 5,300, mostly in the engagement on Jackson's line. Burnside had to be convinced not to renew the attack. After a day of indecision, he withdrew the army across the Rappahannock the next day. As Lee watched the battle from a hilltop that gave him a panoramic view of the battle, he was heard to say, "It is well that war is so terrible — we should grow too fond of it!"

# The Aftermath of the Battle

Fredericksburg had been heavily damaged by artillery fire and pillaged ruthlessly by Union troops. Lee had won another victory, but it had been a hollow one. He had not been able to exploit the Union army's situation with a major counterattack that would have destroyed the Yankees against the river; neither the terrain nor the heavy artillery that protected the Union troops in and around Fredericksburg would allow such an attack. Lee had fought his army skillfully, using the natural advantages of the terrain to increase his strength. As the Army of Northern Virginia went into winter quarters, he would have to be satisfied with the results he had obtained.

# BATTLE CAPTAIN'S REPORT: THE BATTLE OF FREDERICKSBURG, DECEMBER 13, 1862 — CONFEDERATE VICTORY

- **Commanders:** Union: Major General Ambrose E. Burnside, Army of the Potomac, 120,000 men. Confederate: General Robert E. Lee, Army of Northern Virginia, 78,000 men.

- **Phase I:** Burnside plans to cross the Rappahannock River at Fredericksburg and threaten the Confederate capital at Richmond, forcing Lee into an open battle. But Burnside cannot get the necessary pontoon bridges in place to cross the river and loses valuable time. Lee begins to move his army into strong defensive positions in and around Fredericksburg. Delayed most of the day of December 12 by Confederate sharpshooters who prevent Union engineers from laying the pontoon bridges, Union troops finally cross in strength.

- **Phase II:** On December 13, Burnside orders an attack with one of his Grand Divisions on the Confederate right flank, thinking Lee's forces are not all in place. The attack meets Stonewall Jackson's troops in the woods. Major John Pelham of Stuart's cavalry with two artillery pieces disrupts the attack as well. Although the Confederate line is broken, there are no Union reinforcements to exploit success. Meanwhile, Jackson's counterattack drives Union forces back to their starting positions. Union activity on this flank ends.

- **Phase III:** The bulk of Burnside's troops begin an assault through Fredericksburg toward Marye's Heights. The area they attack over is a broad plain covered by artillery and defended by masses of Confederate troops standing in a sunken road behind a stone wall. Virtually impervious to enemy fire, the Confederates wreck the dense Union formations with massed artillery and rifle fire. Again and again the Union units charge, but none come close to the wall. Burnside eventually calls off the attack. After a period of indecision, Burnside brings the remainder of his army back across the Rappahannock.

- **Casualties:** Union 12,600. Confederate 5,300.

Fredericksburg was the greatest defeat of the war for the Union. For Burnside, no battle could have been more poorly mismanaged. His proud army had suffered as many casualties as it did at Antietam — all for nothing. Although Burnside made no excuses for his conduct of the battle, the political ramifications for the Union cause and the president were severe. Morale among the soldiers and officers in the army collapsed, as did the morale of Northern civilians as the casualty lists arrived. Lincoln became the prime target of anger and discontent. He was called "a cowardly imbecile" (among other things), and Lincoln himself said, "It appears to me the Almighty is against us and I can hardly see a ray of light."

## Both the Union and Confederacy fail in Mississippi

Although Rosecrans commanded the troops that had defeated the Confederate assault on Corinth, it was Grant who had played a large role in orchestrating the defeat, ending the last hope for a Confederate military presence in northern Mississippi. Grant followed this up with a two-pronged thrust at the strategic Confederate stronghold of Vicksburg, Mississippi. Using the pattern that had worked so well at Forts Henry and Donelson, Grant planned to send General William T. Sherman with about 30,000 men on naval ships down the Mississippi River to attack the city, while Grant himself mounted an overland march with 40,000 men along the Mississippi Central Railroad to seal off the Confederate retreat. Grant had to move first because, like most Union commanders in the Western Theater, he was entirely dependent upon the railroad for supply. He tried to circumvent this weakness by stockpiling supplies at Holly Springs, Mississippi. Soon after he began his march, Confederate cavalry under Generals Nathan Bedford Forrest (see Figure 16-3) and Van Dorn had a splendid time destroying Grant's Holly Springs supply depot, then tearing up the rail lines for 60 miles. Grant found himself completely hamstrung in a hostile land without supplies or communications. Meanwhile, Sherman's 30,000 men had landed north of Vicksburg. On December 29, he launched an attack against strong defensive positions and was driven off with 1,800 casualties. The first Union movement against Vicksburg ended in total failure.

## Rosecrans takes charge in Tennessee

Rosecrans's success at Iuka and Corinth, Mississippi, led to his promotion and appointment as the new commander to replace Buell. Rosecrans (see Figure 16-4) had begun his rise to command with McClellan in West Virginia in 1861. Like Burnside in the Eastern Theater, he had shown the politicos in Washington some pugnacity, and therefore he was elevated to command of the 44,000-man army in Nashville and told to do something about the Confederate army just 30 miles south. A handsome, intelligent man who looked like a general, Rosecrans had many talents. He also had an explosive temper that sometimes affected his judgment, and he lacked an appreciation for how a commander arranges units and controls the pace of battle.

**FIGURE 16-3:**
Nathan Bedford
Forrest.

*The Library of Congress*

**FIGURE 16-4:**
General William
S. Rosecrans.

*Brady's National Photographic Portrait Galleries / The Library of Congress / Public Domain*

# The Battle of Murfreesboro

After Perrysville, Bragg brought the Army of Tennessee to Murfreesboro along the Stones River. Murfreesboro, the important rail junction between Nashville and Chattanooga, seemed to be just the right place to stay for the winter. The day after Christmas, Rosecrans moved his Army of the Cumberland toward Murfreesboro. Many of the troops were still hung over from the previous day's celebrations. A cold, steady rain made traveling difficult and compounded their misery. Confederate cavalry raids not only wrecked Union supply trains, but also provided Bragg with important information about the location of the Union army. Rosecrans approached slowly, arriving with part of his army before Murfreesboro on December 29. The rest of his army would not arrive until the next day.

Bragg deployed his army in a curious fashion, straddling his two corps across Stones River in front of the town. Although the river was small and easily fordable, nevertheless it both served as a barrier to maneuver and complicated an effective defense. Bragg planned to use his left flank to attack the Union troops in a difficult maneuver that would have worked fine on an open field. But the terrain around Stones River was hilly, rocky, and heavily wooded, which made conducting such a maneuver very difficult.

Rosecrans also made a battle plan. Interestingly enough, it was the mirror image of Bragg's scheme, only without the complicated maneuver thrown in. Rosecrans proposed to initiate the battle by attacking with his left flank against the Confederate right flank. If the attacks began simultaneously, the armies would conduct a giant pinwheel movement. This is just about what they did.

On December 31, Bragg beat Rosecrans to the punch with an attack on the Union right, smashing two divisions. Just as it happened at Shiloh, the complicated plan caused units to become entangled, lost, or to show up in the wrong places. Although the attack did not go exactly according to plan, Major General Pat Cleburne, adding to his already impressive reputation as a fighter and leader, was a key figure in making the attack a success. But the Confederates ran into a commander who had no intention of giving up the field. Brigadier General Phil Sheridan, who had fought so well at Perryville, now blunted the Confederate attack. His men ran out of ammunition and had to pull back along with most of the Union troops to a defensive position nearly perpendicular to their original line. The entire Union army had been forced back, pivoting on a piece of key terrain called Round Forest, but after repeated attacks, the Confederate assault lost momentum, the men too exhausted to continue. Bragg could administer a final crushing blow with his right flank, and he ordered Bishop Polk's men into action. Polk sent his forces in a brigade at a time rather than massing them for one overwhelming attack. The result was predictable. Each individual attack was repulsed with heavy losses to the Confederates. By the end of the day, both sides had fought each other to a standstill — but the battle had decided nothing.

# BATTLE CAPTAIN'S REPORT: THE BATTLE OF MURFREESBORO (STONES RIVER), DECEMBER 31, 1862–JANUARY 1, 1863 — CONFEDERATE VICTORY

- **Commanders:** Union: Major General William S. Rosecrans, Army of the Cumberland, 41,000 men. Confederate: General Braxton Bragg, Army of Tennessee, 35,000 men.

- **Phase I:** Rosecrans advances to fight Bragg's army and drive it from Tennessee. Rosecrans's advance is slow, giving Bragg ample time to prepare. The two armies camp across from each other along Stones River on December 29. The following day both commanders plan the same attack: Strike the enemy's right flank, drive it back, and cut off its line of retreat.

- **Phase II:** Bragg initiates his plan first, smashing into the Union right flank just before dawn. The Confederates drive the Union line back 3 miles, bending it against the Union left until the Union position forms an inverted V. The Union army is saved from disaster by the determined stand of general Phil Sheridan's division, which loses one-third of its men, but holds the line. Rosecrans, abandoning his plan of attack, shifts troops from his left to strengthen his line. At the end of the day, the Union army is battered, but is holding a strong (though awkward) defensive position. Bragg believes he has won a great victory and reports this to Richmond.

- **Phase III:** Rosecrans is not finished; he decides to stay and fight another day. He moves a division across Stones River to lengthen his defensive line. Bragg cannot resist the temptation to attack this division and orders General Breckinridge to assault the Union position. Breckinridge argues that such an attack over open ground against such a position is suicidal. Bragg ignores the protests and orders him forward. The result is a brave but futile attack of infantry attempting to take a position defended by 58 artillery pieces. Breckinridge loses 1,500 men in an hour. Bragg again has wasted gallant soldiers for no result. His subordinate commanders no longer trust him. With no further plan, and facing a resolute enemy, Braggs retreats on January 4.

- **Casualties:** Union 13,000. Confederate 10,000.

During the night, Rosecrans decided to stay and fight rather than retreat. Bragg, believing he had won a great victory (Bragg never thought he had ever lost a battle), simply assumed Rosecrans would retreat. The next day dawned, and Bragg was surprised to find the Army of the Cumberland in a strong defensive position awaiting an attack. Bragg decided late in the afternoon to send General John C. Breckinridge's corps against the Union left the next day. Breckinridge, a

Kentuckian, had been vice president of the United States under Buchanan and the Southern Democratic candidate for president in the election of 1860. Breckinridge was a senator when he resigned to join the Confederacy. Now in command of a division, he knew such an attack could not succeed. He protested, but Bragg's stubbornness was never more pronounced, despite the facts presented to him. The attack was a grand spectacle, the men marching forward with precision and élan. The division struck hard, breaking three understrength Union brigades. The fire of 58 Union cannons against the Confederate flank and a strong counterattack soon met them, however, smashing their charge. The attack cost Breckinridge 1,500 men in about an hour of fighting — all for nothing, except that it earned Bragg the undying hatred of many his officers and men. Realizing Rosecrans was not leaving, Bragg retreated the following day.

# The Results of the Battle

The Battle of Murfreesboro, or Stones River as the Confederates called it, was tactically indecisive but strategically important. The Union troops could claim victory; after all, they had intended to capture the town of Murfreesboro, and they did. Bragg had never intended to fight but did attack Rosecrans's army when he had the opportunity and had come very close to winning, but lost heart and retreated. These were two veteran armies and neither side was giving in or falling back. Both armies had suffered tremendous losses as a result. Union casualties amounted to 13,000 out of 45,000 engaged. Confederate losses were 10,000 out of 38,000 engaged. Many Confederate regiments suffered 40 percent losses; most of their regimental commanders were killed also. One-quarter of the Confederate brigade commanders had been killed or wounded as well. If this battle was a victory, as Bragg claimed, he could not afford another such success.

## Securing Tennessee: Union gains

The Battle of Murfreesboro secured the state of Tennessee for the Union. The capture of the important rail junction set the stage for future campaigns against Chattanooga and Atlanta. The victory, such as it was, did help Lincoln's political fortunes a bit after Fredericksburg. Lincoln sent Rosecrans a letter that reflected a profound sense of relief: "You gave us a hard-earned victory, which, had there been a defeat instead, the nation could hardly have lived over."

## Confederate losses

Strategically, the Union victory also weakened the waning support of Great Britain for the Confederacy. Worst of all for the Confederate Army of Tennessee, Braxton

Bragg's growing problems as commander of the army would weaken its effectiveness in the year to come. All but President Davis, it seemed, had lost confidence in Bragg's leadership. Bragg responded to this with recriminations against the poor conduct of his subordinates during the battle. Davis did consider replacing Bragg with Joseph E. Johnston, but Johnston decided to avoid stumbling into such a cauldron of bitterness and resentment. Bragg would remain in command for the time being.

# Heroes and Goats

In both of these battles, bravery, skill, and opportunity play definite roles in the outcome. Those who can use all three of those things to their best advantage can win a battle, while the ones who don't can lose it even more easily.

## Heroes

The following are men who made their marks on both the battles of Fredericksburg and Murfreesboro:

**KEY PLAYERS**

>> **Robert E. Lee:** Almost outmaneuvered, Lee takes advantage of Burnside's troubles and allows the enemy to attack him where he is strongest. His reputation as the most brilliant Confederate commander is solidified.

>> **Major John Pelham:** The young officer of Stuart's command appears to hold off the entire Yankee army with two artillery pieces. His incredible bravery disrupts what may have been an overwhelming attack on the Confederate right flank. He becomes the symbol of the gallant young men of the Confederacy.

>> **The Union regiments storming Marye's Heights:** Bravery itself is not enough to win battles. Faced with an impossible task, the Union troops never waver in the assault, many of them walking forward with their heads and shoulders hunched into their overcoats as if they were facing a heavy rainstorm.

>> **Philip H. Sheridan:** Always the fighter, Sheridan is skeptical that the Confederates will allow Rosecrans to take his time in launching his attack. While other units are still wrapped in their bedrolls, Sheridan has his men up and ready for combat at 4 a.m. Luckily for the Union, he was ready. His determined stand saves the Union line from collapse.

>> **John C. Breckinridge:** Battling the Yankees was not enough; he had to fight his own stubborn commander. His argument against attacking the Union defensive position on January 1 was sound. He followed orders, but knew what the cost and result would be. He never forgave Bragg.

# Goats

Sometimes winning and victory can have their own problems. Here are a few personalities who could've expedited things a little better:

>> **Ambrose E. Burnside:** Not suited for high command, he bungles this campaign and battle badly, ignoring all the signs of impending disaster. Things become so bad that his orders are simply disobeyed.

>> **William S. Rosecrans:** He wins a questionable victory and the thanks of the president, who needed some good news from the front, but in the process he loses nearly one-fourth of his entire army. Bragg has retreated, but not too far away. His personal bravery is never at question, but does he have what it takes to be an effective army commander?

>> **Braxton Bragg:** First day he claims victory, then the next day he orders a retreat. What kind of commander does this? Bragg never has a concept of what to do with the result of a battle. He appears to know only one way of doing things: make frontal attacks, then fall back and wait. His heavy-handed manner and refusal to listen to his subordinates creates a growing mistrust within the army's command. Bragg's effectiveness is dwindling every day.

## BATTLE CAPTAIN'S SUMMARY FOR 1862 CONFEDERATE REPORT

In the Eastern Theater, the campaign initiating with the Seven Days outside of Richmond and culminating with the failure to achieve success at Sharpsburg (Antietam) led to Lee only holding ground at Fredericksburg. Despite the dramatic successes that drove Union forces from Virginia and Jackson's achievements in the Valley, Lee had been unable to strike the decisive blow to defeat the Army of the Potomac. Fredericksburg was a hollow victory in this sense as it accomplished nothing. The Army of Northern Virginia would have to surrender the initiative to the Union, because Lee, defending the Rappahannock River line, could only wait to respond to the initial move of his opponent in the coming year.

In the Western Theater, the Confederate failed counteroffensives at Shiloh, Pea Ridge, and Corinth were overshadowed by Bragg's botched invasion that lost Kentucky permanently to the Confederacy. His lack of foresight as a theater commander led to the loss

*(continued)*

*(continued)*

of northern Mississippi. The initiative was now in Grant's hands. As always, geography played a decisive role: Vicksburg, Atlanta, and Chattanooga, all critical transportation centers, would have to be defended with inadequate forces and weak commanders.

Politically, the prospect of European recognition, so bright in the summer of 1862, had dimmed considerably. The Emancipation Proclamation was also a powerful counter to the Confederacy's attempts to link its cause with Britain or France.

## UNION REPORT

The year was fraught with folly and frustration. In the Eastern Theater, somehow a massive army had been outfought and outgeneraled on the Peninsula before Richmond. An import from the Western Theater, John Pope had been overwhelmed and his army suffered a humiliating defeat at Second Manassas (Bull Run). McClellan had inexplicably been unable to destroy Lee's army at Antietam, even having his enemy's plans. A new commander, Ambrose Burnside, proved a disaster at Fredericksburg.

In the Western Theater, a series of hard-fought battles at Shiloh, Perryville, Corinth, and Murfreesboro had given the Union an advantage, but at a terrible cost. The door was open to deeper thrusts at the Confederate heartland, but it was a forbidding prospect. The people were hostile and had to be suppressed, while vast swaths of territory needed to be occupied; guerrillas and Confederate cavalry roamed freely against Union supply lines, which the armies depended on to sustain any offensive. To accomplish any success in this theater, commanders with unique insights and capabilities were required. Halleck and Buell were not up to the task, but Grant looked like someone who could and would fight, yet who also seemed to possess the operational and strategic foresight necessary to win.

Politically, the president had taken a great risk in redefining the war in terms of human freedom and the destruction of slavery through the great trial of war. There would be no negotiated peace; there would be no return to the prewar status quo. One side would win only when the other side could no longer continue the fight. This was the terrible reality that both Jefferson Davis and Abraham Lincoln had to face.

# 4
# War to the Hilt, 1863–1865

See how the Confederacy makes its second bid for recognition and independence.

Watch the emergence of Ulysses S. Grant and his coordinated campaign plan to support the national strategy.

Understand how politics plays a role in the ultimate triumph of the Union.

See how and why the war develops into a remorseless, grinding, bitter fight to the end.

» **Accomplishing a military miracle**

» **Enduring a tremendous loss**

» **Winning battles where they count**

Chapter **17**

# The Battle of Chancellorsville, May 1863

In the Eastern Theater, the Union's Army of the Potomac stood at the Rappahannock River, not much farther from Washington than where it had begun the war in 1861. Morale was low, troops were deserting left and right, and Burnside was finished as a commander. Lincoln now had to search for a new general to take charge and find the way to defeat Lee and his army. As for Lee, his army stood behind the Rappahannock at Fredericksburg, Virginia, guarding the main approach to Richmond. His army was in good spirits and had competent, battle-tested leaders. The road to Richmond would not be an easy one to travel, whoever the new commander of the Union army was.

# Beginning a New Campaign in the Eastern Theater

The armies stood essentially where they were since Fredericksburg. Besting Lee and Jackson would take clever planning and skillful maneuvering. It seemed that Lincoln had found a general with the right combination of energy and toughness in Joe Hooker. The Confederates on the other side of the Rappahannock River watched and waited as well. Lee was waiting for the enemy to show his intent; at that point, he intended to strike an offensive blow that would cripple the Union army.

## Another new commander for the Union army

Lincoln culled through his possible candidates for command of the Army of the Potomac in January of 1863. Burnside had been sent off to the Department of the Ohio, a large rear area where it was hoped he would do no more harm. Lincoln tried to find a general who could not only fight, but who would also please the Republican politicos. Unfortunately, Lincoln had trouble meeting his first criterion. It seemed that nobody in the army had a consistent record of competent leadership in battle. All except one — the corps commander known as "Fighting Joe" Hooker (see Figure 17-1). Hooker had a reputation as a hard-drinking, hard-living man, with an eye for the ladies. Nevertheless, he had displayed some ability at higher-level command. He was also a braggart who had both good friends and bad enemies. Politically he was harmless, but he was well liked by the radical Republicans, including Secretary of the Treasury Salmon P. Chase. Lincoln therefore decided to give Hooker command of the Army of the Potomac, hoping that his brash and aggressive nature would be turned to good use against Lee.

Hooker took charge and whipped the army back into shape, adding reinforcements and building morale with better food and furloughs. He gave soldiers the unit badges on their caps that they would wear for the rest of the war. He eliminated Burnside's unwieldy Grand Divisions and returned to a corps structure. He also organized the Union cavalry into one corps instead of having small units parceled throughout the army. With drill and discipline, the army returned to fighting trim, now numbering 134,000 men. Justly proud of this instrument of war he had shaped, Hooker now turned to boasting, beginning his sentences with "When I get to Richmond . . ." and "May God have mercy on General Lee, for I will have none." He boasted (not without a large measure of truth) that he had "the finest army on the planet."

**FIGURE 17-1:**
Joseph
Hooker.

*Brady, Mathew B / The Library of Congress / Public Domain*

# Hooker's plans

Hooker followed up his boasting with an imaginative and innovative campaign plan. Hooker planned to make Lee fight in several directions at once. First, he would send his cavalry out on a deep raid toward Richmond to cut Lee's lines of communication and supply. This raid was intended to draw Confederate forces away from the Rappahannock.

Next, he divided his army into three parts. Hooker would take three corps of his army and move about 25 miles away from Fredericksburg, crossing the Rappahannock and Rapidan rivers and making a broad move around Lee's left flank. The second part, two corps commanded by Union Major General John Sedgwick, would press the Confederate defenses in front of Fredericksburg. The rest of the army, two corps, were the reserve, to move to reinforce either flank as needed. Hooker believed that faced with these multiple threats, Lee would have to abandon his defensive line along the Rappahannock River or be trapped along its banks. If Lee's army had to move, there was the chance that it could be trapped by Hooker's superior forces and destroyed. At the very least, the attack would force the vaunted Army of Northern Virginia to retreat, something it had not done in a long time.

Hooker's planned cavalry raid came to naught due to bad weather and poor leadership. The rest of the Army of the Potomac, however, performed superbly that late April 1863. As Union forces moved into Fredericksburg, Hooker's three corps successfully crossed the river and made their way back towards Fredericksburg. On the way, the Yankees passed through an area of thick undergrowth and dense, second-growth trees cut by numerous ravines and small streams called the Wilderness. At a road junction in the Wilderness stood a large brick house owned by the Chancellor family. The spot was called Chancellorsville, even though the house was the only building at the crossroads. Just past Chancellorsville, the terrain opened up, and a sizeable Union force would be sitting directly on Lee's flank and rear, forming one jaw of a vise that would trap the Confederates in and around Fredericksburg, while the other jaw closed in on the enemy from behind the city. Hooker felt so good about his prospects for the next day that he halted his troops, while he made his way to join them with additional reinforcements for what promised to be a triumphal march leading to Lee's destruction or his ignominious retreat.

## Lee's situation

Lee had about 60,000 men in the area. He was without two divisions and General Longstreet, all dispatched to Suffolk to watch for a possible Union attack from the coast. Lee had not taken the bait of the cavalry attack intended to draw his attention from the Rappahannock. He and his army stayed put, deciding to await developments. The appearance of Union troops on his left flank and the deployment of Union troops in Fredericksburg was not altogether unexpected; Lee had anticipated some kind of movement to force him out of his position. Because the Union troops in Fredericksburg showed no inclination to attack, he reasoned that this was another feint to distract him for the real attack. Jeb Stuart's cavalry confirmed that Union troops were now in the Wilderness. Hooker's plan was now clear. The question now was what was Lee going to do.

Lee had two options: retreat to a better defensive position and leave Hooker holding the bag, or attack one of the elements of Hooker's army and develop the situation. Nine commanders out of ten would have chosen to take the most prudent course and retreated. But Lee was different. He did not see himself in danger — instead, he saw Hooker in danger with his army divided and exposed to a smashing counterattack. Lee decided to defend Fredericksburg with a very small force while he took the rest of the army, Jackson in the lead, to strike Hooker in the Wilderness.

# Fighting Joe Hooker won't fight

Hooker's troops took their time getting ready to move the next morning, expecting to find the Confederates heading toward Richmond. Instead, the Confederates were headed for him. Jackson had very clear orders from Lee: "make preparations to repulse the enemy." For someone like Jackson, those orders were crystal clear. He wasted no time in slamming head on into Hooker's leading units. This unanticipated action stunned Hooker into a near stupor. Even though the units engaged were fighting well, Hooker had had enough. To the surprise and consternation of his generals, he recalled the army back to Chancellorsville and ordered everyone to dig in for the night. The army was stretched about five and a half miles along a narrow dirt road, in the middle of a forest so thick that visibility beyond 50 feet was impossible, with a river at its back. The troops threw up some logs and brush and waited for Fighting Joe to decide what to do next.

**TURNING POINT**

While the troops in both armies rested uneasily in the dark thickets, Lee and Jackson searched for an opportunity. Jeb Stuart provided that opportunity with a report to Lee that the Union right flank lay open. It was simply dangling, not anchored on any defensible terrain. Fortified with Stuart's info, Jackson proposed a plan that made even the bold Lee catch his breath. He intended to take all but 17,000 men, whom Lee would command, to deal with Hooker's entire force, while he took the rest, about 26,000, in a wide march to fall on the open Union flank. Jackson's attack would roll up Hooker's army like a rug, cutting off its line of retreat at the river fords, thus trapping it against the river and destroying what was left. Lee was dividing his army for a second time in the face of a far superior force. He would only risk such a maneuver on the skill of Jackson and the inaction of his opponent. Lee agreed, and Jackson set off to organize his troops for the march to begin at first light.

While Jackson moved his nearly 10-mile column in a slow march in front of and around the Union army, Hooker was awaiting Lee's attack. Of course, he expected the Confederates to come from his left flank, as they had the day before, so his defenses there were particularly strong. He traveled the lines inspecting the preparations, and even thought his right flank, hanging invitingly out in the open, to be adequately protected. About midafternoon, after repeated reports that Confederate troops were moving in large numbers across the front of the Union defensive lines, Hooker came to believe that Lee was retreating and that the troops everyone reported were the rear guard of Lee's army. At the urging of one of his corps commanders, General Dan Sickles, Hooker authorized an advance to find out what was happening. Sickles impetuously sent an entire division out that made contact with the rear guard, but by this time, Jackson's men had already passed and were getting set up for the flank attack. Hooker, still in the dark, was convinced that his plan was working perfectly, and that Lee was abandoning the battlefield.

# Jackson disappears and reappears

Jackson and his 26,000 men made the march and reached the far-right flank of the Union line, but it took two precious hours to put so many troops into formation amid the undergrowth of the Wilderness. That many men rustling around in the underbrush were bound to attract some attention. Messages from Union outposts were passed to the corps commander, who discounted all of them. Everyone seemed to be convinced, as Hooker was, that Lee's army was in retreat. By 5:00 p.m., the men were up, but Jackson took extra time to spread the ranks out over a mile in length, poised directly on the unprotected Union flank. Time was running short; there were only about two hours of daylight left, and the tension and anticipation was growing with each passing minute. Finally, Jackson calmly told his division commander leading the attack, "You can go forward, sir."

By early evening, the men of the Union XI Corps had settled down to cook their meals. Their weapons were stacked, card games were underway, and tents were set up for the night. This corps was made up primarily of German immigrants, led mostly by German officers who were staunch Republican supporters. Some of these units had fought in the Valley in 1862 when Jackson had beaten them once before. Suddenly, there was a high-pitched yell from the throats of thousands of wildly excited men — the Rebel Yell the Yankees had heard before — then groups of startled animals ran out from cover into the camps. Next, the masses of Confederate troops burst in among the startled Yankees. All order was lost as units were overrun. As soon as a defensive line was formed, it was swept away by thousands of panicked men fleeing for their lives, headed for safety somewhere near Chancellorsville. But the Wilderness hampered the charging Confederates as much as it did the Union troops desperately trying to put together some defense. The heavy brush and looming darkness slowed the momentum of the attack; units got lost and small groups of men, Union and Confederate, crashed around in the dark. As panicked men surged through the Union lines seeking safety, Union artillery around Chancellorsville began hammering shells into the wood line and down the road to halt the attack. Jackson called up General A.P. Hill's division and ordered him to press on to take the main ford on the Rappahannock River, which would cut off the Union army's primary line of retreat. It was to be Jackson's last combat order.

**TURNING POINT**

In the chaos of combat in unfamiliar woods, Jackson and his staff began scouting a route to reach the ford and determine the Union front lines. As they were returning, a forward unit of Jackson's mistook the riders for Union cavalry and fired into the group, wounding Jackson in the arm. Shortly thereafter, his arm was amputated at a field hospital and Jackson was moved from the battlefield to Guiney's Station, a supply depot for the Confederate army. He died of pneumonia, a complication unrelated to his wound, eight days later in the presence of his wife and infant daughter. A.P. Hill, who would have taken command, was also wounded while attending to the fallen Jackson. Lee ordered Jeb Stuart to take command of the corps and prepare to attack at dawn to link the two separate wings of the Confederate army.

## Hooker fails to act

The Union situation was serious, but not as desperate as it seemed. Union forces had reacted well and had put up a stubborn defense. Hooker still outnumbered Lee, and the Confederate army was split in half, with Hooker's troops in the middle. All Hooker needed to do was take the initiative and launch a counterattack in almost any direction. But he did nothing. Jeb Stuart resumed his attack the next day, pushing hard to reunite the divided wings of the army. They successfully came together just below Chancellorsville, pushing the crumbling Union lines back toward the river. Sometime during the fighting, a Confederate artillery shell hit a pillar on the porch of the Chancellor house. Hooker had been leaning against the pillar when the shell struck it, throwing him violently to the ground and knocking him senseless for a time. Whether in possession of his senses or not, Hooker had no control over events — he had given up the fight.

With the army reunited, Lee now sought to push Hooker's army into the Rappahannock River, but the Union troops were quick to build a solid line of defensive breastworks in the deep woods protecting the nearby ford — their only escape route. It was apparent that no frontal attack would succeed. A new threat, however, emerged for Lee and his army. General Sedgwick had received orders from Hooker the night before to take Fredericksburg and come to his support. This was a strange request by any stretch of the imagination. Sedgwick, whose force was supposed to be the second jaw of Hooker's vise, could not mount a night attack against a fortified position and then march 12 to 14 miles to help Hooker on a road held in strength by the enemy. Besides, Sedgwick had about 24,000 men with him; Hooker had nearly 90,000 — in what way did Hooker think Sedgwick was going to help him? The day Lee reunited his army, Sedgwick rolled past the Confederate defenses above Fredericksburg and headed toward the Wilderness. Sedgwick did not know that Hooker was already ordering a withdrawal across the river, leaving his subordinate open to an attack from Lee. Lee split his army again, leaving Stuart with 25,000 men to watch Hooker, while he took 21,000 to deal with Sedgwick. Lee struck hard, but late in the day and with soldiers who were physically at the end of their capabilities. By nightfall, Sedgwick had retreated to a ford with the intent to withdraw across the river. The following day, Lee turned his men back toward Hooker to finish him off. But Hooker's troops were already crossing over the ford to safety.

# BATTLE CAPTAIN'S REPORT: THE BATTLE OF CHANCELLORSVILLE, MAY 1–3, 1863 — CONFEDERATE VICTORY

- **Commanders:** Union: Major General Joseph Hooker, Army of the Potomac, 134,000 men. Confederate: General Robert E. Lee, 60,000 men.

- **Phase I:** Hooker divides his army into three groups. With one group acting as a reserve, the first group will cross the Rappahannock River to threaten Fredericksburg. The third group (under Hooker with about 53,000 men) will cross the Rappahannock and Rapidan rivers and swing around Lee's left flank to come around behind, forcing him to retreat toward Richmond. Lee is without Longstreet and two of his divisions, and his army is spread from Fredericksburg southeast along the Rappahannock River. Lee gets wind of Hooker's flanking movement and sends Jackson with troops to develop the situation.

- **Phase II:** By May 1, Hooker has moved his army across the rivers and placed it in a dense undergrowth forest called the Wilderness around a crossroads called Chancellorsville. Jackson's forces would then blunt the initial Union advance out of the Wilderness. Hooker is so confused by the attack that he orders a retreat. He orders the army into a defensive position around the crossroads of Chancellorsville, hoping that Lee will advance to attack him. Lee has left a small force to deal with the Union troops at Fredericksburg, taking the rest of the army to fight Hooker. That night, Lee confers with Jackson, looking for a vulnerable opening. Jeb Stuart reports that the Union right flank is open and undefended — all the troops are facing south; no one is looking west. Jackson proposes to take his corps and march to the open flank while Lee occupies Hooker's front. At 5:15 p.m., on May 2, after an all-day march, Jackson launches his assault. It catches the Union XI corps completely off guard and sends them fleeing toward the Chancellor house. Darkness falls before the full weight of Confederate attack can be employed, and the Union resistance stiffens. Jackson is wounded by his own men while searching in the darkness for a route that will cut off the Yankees from their only line of retreat — the ford.

- **Phase III:** On May 3, Lee realizes he is in danger. Unless he can reunite the two wings of his army, Hooker can counterattack and destroy his force. Jackson's corps, now under Jeb Stuart's command, fights desperately to link up with Lee's force. Hooker, dazed by a near miss from an artillery shell, plays no role in the battle. By midmorning, the Confederates have captured Chancellorsville and the Union army begins to withdraw toward the ford. Meanwhile, the Union force under General Sedgwick has captured Fredericksburg and is moving westward toward Chancellorsville. Lee splits his forces, leaving Stuart to guard Hooker while he attacks Sedgwick. Sedgwick initially retreats, and is attacked again in strength the following day, May 4. Sedgwick then retreats across the Rappahannock River.

- **Phase IV:** Lee turns again on Hooker, hoping to launch an attack with his united army. Hooker has had enough and orders a retreat. The Army of the Potomac skillfully crosses the Rappahannock to safety. The army is still full of fight; 40,000 men in the army had not fired a shot during the entire battle. Richmond celebrates what seems to be another miraculous victory. In Washington, Lincoln in deep anguish can only cry, "My God! What will the country say?"

- **Casualties:** Union 17,000, Confederate 13,000 + 1 (Jackson's death is a loss so serious that some say the war cannot be won without him).

# Heroes and Goats

Certainly, Lee and Jackson pass into the halls of immortal generals with this battle. Jackson's wounding and later death take away the Confederacy's greatest hero. Goats seem to become goats by believing their excellent battle plans are all that is necessary to defeat the enemy. But without a sense of where you are or what your purpose is, once you meet the enemy, you are headed for goatship.

## Heroes

The blending here of commander, key leader, and soldiers is what all military men hope and dream to have. Such a combination of skill, audacity, and courage becomes a nearly unbeatable combination, as the Army of the Potomac learned over and over again.

>> **Robert E. Lee:** Never has Lee's genius as a commander shone more brilliantly than at Chancellorsville. Lee's use of surprise, maneuver, and mass to offset the strength of a superior force is considered one the masterpieces of military art. He begins to believe he can do anything with his Army of Northern Virginia.

>> **Stonewall Jackson:** Jackson is the Confederacy's greatest loss and martyr. He is wounded at the moment of his greatest battlefield triumph. Upon recovering from the anesthetic after his amputation, he dutifully informs Lee that he has been incapacitated and has lost his left arm. Lee replies: "I have lost my *right* arm." Jackson is irreplaceable. He is one of the ablest commanders that the United States has ever produced. Never again will Lee be able to act as boldly or as confidently as he did with Jackson under his command.

>> **The Army of Northern Virginia:** This instrument of battle, so masterfully led and so dedicated to its leader, appears unstoppable. Under trying circumstances, hungry, ragged, and ill, and despite all odds, it continues to win battles. As long as it can fight, the Confederacy can stay alive.

# Goats

Hooker had led soldiers in combat at Antietam and Fredericksburg and had been in some of the toughest fighting there, yet he lacked something to be an army commander. The goat here is obvious; bragging and posturing like a general doesn't make you a general. Also, when generals become goats, often the blame is passed (justifiably or unjustifiably) to subordinates. Here is a bad luck unit that experiences an unpleasant sensation of being at the bottom after everything has rolled downhill.

>> **Joseph "Fighting Joe" Hooker:** Hooker's well-conceived plan is also well executed — for the first 36 hours. Hooker expected Lee to retreat; when he stood and fought, Hooker never got over his surprise. After the battle, he tries to keep the bad news from the president for nearly three days. He makes weak excuses to his corps commanders about protecting Washington and saving the army. Hooker alone lost the battle. His collapse of will, not the Army of the Potomac's fighting ability, caused this defeat.

>> **The Union XI Corps:** The mostly German unit caught by surprise and overrun by Jackson's flank attack is later nicknamed "the flying Dutchmen" within the Army of the Potomac. Its shaky reputation as a combat unit is never repaired in the Eastern Theater.

Chapter **18**

# The Battles of Gettysburg and Vicksburg, July 1863

I n the summer of 1863, both the Union and the Confederacy stood at a crossroads. For each side, victory would hinge on how well the two premier commanders, Ulysses S. Grant and Robert E. Lee, performed. If Grant could capture the Confederate fortress of Vicksburg, the Confederacy would lose control of the Mississippi River and be cut in half — a crippling strategic blow to the Confederacy and its hopes for independence. If Lee could win a decisive victory against the Army of the Potomac on Northern soil, Union morale might collapse and open the way for European recognition of an independent Confederate States of America. Whichever commander gained his objective would determine how the war would proceed to its conclusion.

# The Gettysburg Campaign

The victory at Chancellorsville opened a strategic opportunity for the Confederacy. Lee proposed a bold offensive to invade the North and defeat the Union army on its own ground aimed at altering the strategic balance once and for all. Such a plan was risky, to be sure, but it had a strategic defensive purpose. A battlefield victory at this point could end the war, and if anyone could pull off such a risky maneuver, it was Lee and his Army of Northern Virginia.

The Confederate leadership faced a dilemma in the early summer of 1863. Lee in the Eastern Theater had held the invading Union Army of the Potomac at bay. In the Western Theater, Union forces had moved against the strategic strong point of Vicksburg. Could Lee's army give support to Vicksburg's defenders? Lee was cool to such an idea; he had a proposition of his own. In May, Lee met with President Jefferson Davis and his cabinet to propose a bold thrust. Two driving considerations led the leadership to buy Lee's plan:

>> First, Lee argued that moving the army north would allow Virginia farmers to harvest badly needed food crops without the perils of armies maneuvering around them.

>> Second, invading the North might pull troops away from the Western Theater, or from the threatened coastline of the Confederacy.

Another possibility, of which all were aware, was that another victory, this time in Northern territory, might tip the scales for Great Britain or France to intervene on the side of the Confederacy. Besides, the fact that the Confederacy was running short on everything was no secret. The Confederacy would have trouble supplying an army sitting in a defensive position all summer. A move north would allow the army to live off of the bounty of the rich fields of Pennsylvania, so far untouched by war. Confederate forces moving in the vicinity of Washington would throw Lincoln's government into a panic, leading to all types of opportunities, just as had happened before in 1862 when Stonewall Jackson's small force led Lincoln to pull combat forces from McClellan to protect the capital. But Stonewall was no longer with the army. The measure of Jackson's abilities is seen in Lee's decision to divide Jackson's corps in half, giving one new corps to A.P. Hill (see Figure 18-1), and the other half to Richard Ewell (see Figure 18-2), both of whom had served under Jackson. They were good and capable leaders, but neither man on his best day was equal to the invincible Stonewall in his ability to understand Lee's intentions and develop the pace of events on the battlefield.

**FIGURE 18-1:**
A.P. Hill.

*War Department / The U.S. National Archives and Records Administration / Public Domain*

**FIGURE 18-2:**
Richard Ewell.

*The Library of Congress / Public Domain*

## Moving the armies

Lee's army, together with cavalry, had grown to about 79,000 men, the most he would ever command. Morale was high; everyone from the lowliest private to General Lee himself believed the army was capable of accomplishing anything. Lee began a slow sidling movement west, headed toward the Shenandoah Valley, the gateway to the North and a route that provided a mountain screen to limit enemy observation. The vanguard of the army under Ewell swept into Winchester and cleared the last Yankee defenders away. The route for the invasion lay open.

Moving into Pennsylvania, Lee's army took advantage of the agricultural riches of the land, accumulating food, clothing, horses, livestock, greenbacks, and forage. They paid for it in Confederate money or IOUs to be paid by the Confederate government. To procure needed supplies, the Confederate army had spread itself in several columns, covering nearly 100 miles from Chambersburg to York and as far north as Carlisle. Meanwhile, Lee had sent instructions to Jeb Stuart to ascertain the location of the Union army. Stuart decided that not only could he report on the location of the Union army, but he could also make another grand ride around it as he had done in two previous campaigns. This time, he discovered that the Union army was marching on a broad axis headed north. Stuart had to keep moving farther and farther away from Lee as he spent several very precious days trying to find his way back to the Confederate army, and worst of all, out of contact with Lee. In the meantime, Lee's troops were spread out deep in enemy territory with no information on where the enemy was or what the Army of the Potomac was doing. Alerted by a spy's report on June 28 that the Union army was moving rapidly north through Maryland, Lee sought to concentrate his scattered forces west of the town of Gettysburg. Here he could decide on his next move.

## Hooker waits (again) and is finished

The Army of the Potomac had about 100,000 men available, but about 20 percent of this total represented new recruits, replacements for those whose enlistments had expired at the end of May. The veteran regiments in the army were superb combat units, but they were under strength and scattered throughout the army. Instead of filling old regiments with new soldiers, veteran units were left to dwindle away, while replacements were brought into the army as entirely new regiments. When he got wind of Lee's movement, Hooker pulled the army back toward Washington and waited nearly two weeks before moving his army into Maryland to pursue Lee's army, which was now spreading out into Pennsylvania.

## THE BATTLE OF BRANDY STATION, JUNE 9, 1863

Uncertain of what Lee was doing, Hooker sent his cavalry corps along with infantry units to the town of Culpeper to attack what he thought were Confederate cavalry defending supplies. With 11,000 men, General Alfred Pleasanton crossed the Rappahannock River and arrived at Brandy Station near the suspected enemy location. Pleasanton did not know it but he was riding into the place where the Army of Northern Virginia was concentrating in preparation for its move into Pennsylvania. Protecting this concentration (but not very well) was Jeb Stuart's cavalry. The Union advance took Stuart by surprise, and all day the mounted forces charged back and forth, fighting at close range with sabers and pistols, each side trying to gain an advantage. It was the greatest cavalry battle in U.S. history but largely indecisive in terms of the results. The Yankees retreated, taking about double the casualties as the Confederates, but they had proven that they were a force to be reckoned with. From this point on, Union cavalry would be equal in every way to their Southern counterparts.

REMEMBER

Hooker again seemed to lose his nerve after a prudent initial movement to protect the capital. When Hooker began to use McClellan's old excuse that he didn't have enough men to fight, Lincoln had had enough. Hooker was promptly replaced with George G. Meade (see Figure 18-3), who commanded a corps in the army. When messengers from Washington roused him from his tent, Meade's first question was "Am I under arrest?" To his surprise and dismay, he quickly discovered that he was the newest commander of the Army of the Potomac. Meade was a solid officer who had been with the army through all of its major battles. He was an apolitical soldier with a fierce temper who cared not a bit whether he was popular or not. Although he was junior in rank to other corps commanders in the army, he had their confidence in his abilities. Meade started to make things happen quickly. He ordered the army to move northward into Pennsylvania — initially toward Harrisburg, then to find suitable defensive terrain to place his army. He also sent a cavalry unit to Gettysburg, a town that on the map looked like the hub of a wheel — ten roads from every direction intersected at this little town. Military logic dictated that this key road junction had to be secured before moving the main body of troops forward and to determine if Lee's army was there.

## CALLING OUT THE MILITIA

As Lee's army advanced, panic ensued in Pennsylvania, New Jersey, and New York. The governors of those states called out the militia. Trenches were dug to protect Harrisburg. In Pennsylvania, the militia was more of a danger to itself than to the Confederate army. Wrightsville, a town on the Susquehanna River, was almost burned down when the militia set the bridge on fire to prevent the rebels from using it. Confederate troops arrived and put the fires out. The destruction of the bridge did, however, prevent an attack on Harrisburg that could have been devastating to the Union cause.

**FIGURE 18-3:**
George G. Meade.

Brady, Mathew B / The Library of
Congress / Public Domain

# The Battle of Gettysburg: Day One

On June 30, a Confederate brigade in search of shoes, legend has it, moved toward Gettysburg. To the infantrymen's surprise, there was a unit of Union cavalry in the town. The Confederates pulled back and waited for additional troops to arrive. No one believed Union troops were anywhere near Gettysburg. Mistaking the cavalrymen for Pennsylvania militia, the decision was made to move into Gettysburg the next day. Early the following morning, in a light mist on July 1, the advance units of Lee's army of A.P. Hill's Corps moved down the road toward the town, initiating what would become the greatest battle ever fought in the United States.

The Confederates soon found not militia but nearly 3,000 Union cavalrymen barring the way into the town. These soldiers were armed with breech-loading carbines and could fire much faster than the Confederate infantry with their muzzle-loading rifled muskets. The volume of fire forced the infantry to deploy and take time to maneuver. The cavalry's job was to report what they found and buy time for the Union infantry to arrive and take over the battle. In this case, the Union I Corps was fewer than 10 miles away. After word reached them that Confederate infantry was outside Gettysburg, General John F. Reynolds brought his 10,000 men into battle. This corps had some of the finest units in the Union army. If there was to be a fight, these were the men to depend on. The unlucky XI Corps (see Chapter 17) soon reinforced the I Corps. The two corps held their own, defending McPherson's Ridge northwest of the town and extending the line eastward as pressure grew on the right flank. By the afternoon, however, more Confederate units under command of General Ewell began to arrive on the battlefield from several unexpected directions, primarily the northwest and the northeast. This was too much for the XI Corps. Outnumbered and outflanked, many units broke and ran for the safety of the hills behind the town, followed by the I Corps, which had fought the enemy to a standstill and had lost its commander, General Reynolds, to a rifle bullet. Falling back to Seminary Ridge and then retreating into town, the I Corps took nearly 60 percent casualties. It had virtually ceased to exist as a military organization. Confederate troops chased the fleeing Yankees through the streets of Gettysburg.

## Gettysburg favors the defender

Despite the defeat, the terrain of the Gettysburg battlefield gave the defender (the Union) the advantage. The town was in the middle of a shallow valley made up of two roughly parallel wooded ridges stretching southwest to northeast that had potential as strong defensive positions. The ridge west of the town was called Seminary Ridge after the Lutheran seminary that sat on it. The other ridge behind the town curved at bit, making it look like a fishhook. This was Cemetery Ridge, because the town cemetery sat on part of it. There were also a few rocky hills at the bottom and top of the fishhook-shaped ridge that were ideal for the defensive. Culp's Hill anchored the defensive line east of Gettysburg while Devil's Den and Little Round Top protected the left flank of the Union line. The end of the first day looked like a typical defeat for the Army of the Potomac, but the high ground of Cemetery Ridge just outside of town offered security and a place to reorganize. As Union soldiers naturally sought safety and shelter on higher ground at Cemetery Ridge, they found General Hancock (see Figure 18-4) waiting for them.

Campbell Photo Service / The Library of Congress / Public Domain

**FIGURE 18-4:**
Winfield Scott
Hancock.

On the Union side, things were serious. General Reynolds, the highest-ranking Union officer on the battlefield at the time, had been killed, and General Abner Doubleday (who had ordered the first Union shot of the war at Sumter) had taken his place. General O.O. Howard, commander of the XI Corps, was the senior officer on the field but was soon replaced by II Corps commander Major General Winfield Scott Hancock, who had been sent by Meade to assess the situation. What Hancock saw was not promising, but he made the decision to defend the ground he was on at Cemetery Ridge and Culp's Hill. He began organizing the men into units and getting them into position to defend against an attack. Meanwhile, Hancock must have been relieved to see the arrival of two additional Union Corps, giving him 20,000 troops to defend the ridge that evening.

## Ewell says no

Lee had arrived in the afternoon and surveyed the scene of Union troops streaming away from the battlefield. He had not anticipated nor wanted a battle here; but Hill had brought it on, and some action had to be taken to seal the victory. Immediately he recognized the importance of the hills and the low ridge behind the town. He ordered Ewell to "carry the hill occupied by the enemy," but added the unusual qualifier, "if practicable." Ewell, seeing Union troops massing on the ridge and being unable to collect his disorganized units, decided that there would be no attack. The eternal question remains: If Jackson was still in command, what would he have done on that evening?

# The Battle of Gettysburg: Day Two

Throughout the night, the Confederates heard the sounds of axes and shovels and the low, rhythmic tread of large numbers of men on the move. July 2 would be a hard day for the Confederate infantry spread around the Union line, now squatting from Culp's Hill, along the bulge of the fishhook at Cemetery Ridge and down the straight shank, stopping short of Devil's Den and Little Round Top. Meade had arrived after midnight and was satisfied with the disposition of the forces. Although four corps had arrived over night, he had only about 75 percent of his army on the field. Lee's army, with the exception of one division (George Pickett's) had arrived during the night. Lee knew that if the Yankees were driven off the ridge or the hills at either end of the ridge, they would have to retreat.

Early on the morning of July 2, Lee met with his corps commanders and outlined a plan. Longstreet's corps was to attack the Union left, suspected to be near Little Round Top, while Ewell's corps supported Longstreet with an attack on Culp's Hill. He hoped to cave in both flanks and force a retreat. But the problem was this: Lee didn't know for sure where the enemy line ended or what the enemy's strength was. Without reliable information from his cavalry, such as he had at Chancellorsville, Lee had to guess. Essentially, Lee was ordering a reconnaissance with infantry to probe the enemy's lines. He had given his orders but allowed Longstreet to bring in a late-arriving brigade. By then, it was already noon.

## Longstreet opens the battle

Longstreet was a stubborn fighter and a man of determination. Lee called him his "warhorse." But he was no Stonewall Jackson when it came to taking action and moving troops. Jackson was well known for having his men ready to move at first light and setting a killing pace to do Lee's bidding. Longstreet did not have his troops prepared to execute Lee's orders. Traveling over unfamiliar ground, he got turned around once or twice and had to sort out the traffic jams. When his corps reached its attack position, it took time to array the units properly. But when he *did* get organized, and when he *was* ready to attack, Longstreet's prowess was rarely matched.

While Longstreet was on the march, the Union army waited. Time weighs heavily on the hands of commanders sometimes, and as a result they make bad decisions. This is true of the commander of III Corps, Major General Daniel Sickles. Sickles, a former congressman from New York, had received a commission because he was a Democrat who supported the Republican administration's war policies. Free from any military education or experience, Sickles was not above taking independent action or ignoring good advice. At Chancellorsville, he had moved a division from his corps out of the defensive line to investigate reports of Confederate troops moving to his front. In making this maneuver, he was out of position to assist Howard's XI Corps when it was overrun at the onset of Jackson's flank attack. On the following day, he pulled his corps out of a critical position, allowing Lee to unite his army and crush the Union defensive line. Now, at Gettysburg, Sickles thought the ground in front of him was better than the low ground his corps occupied. Without orders and with colors flying and bands playing, he moved his 11,000 men forward to a rise that had a peach orchard on it. Sickles now had an entire corps sticking out from the Union line like the proverbial sore thumb, with no support and his units facing in opposite directions. There was no other Union unit of any size past his corps — the Union flank was open and exposed. He had just given Longstreet a golden opportunity to do just what Lee had ordered. On top of that, Sickles had just finished making his move by 4 p.m., the time Longstreet launched his attack.

## Longstreet attacks

In a short time, Longstreet's assault had demolished Sickles's corps. A portion of Longstreet's corps swept over the lightly defended Devil's Den and headed for Little Round Top. Little Round Top was unoccupied except for a signaling station. Both sides seemed to recognize this fact at the same time; getting to Little Round Top now became a race.

### DAN SICKLES'S LEG

When his corps was attacked in the peach orchard, Sickles took command at the center of the fight. His exposed position was an artilleryman's dream: With the troops packed together as they were, crossfire would inflict maximum casualties. The Confederate gunners did this quite effectively. In the cannonade, an artillery shell smashed Sickles's leg. He was carried from the battlefield on a stretcher, a cigar clamped between his teeth, giving encouragement to his men. His leg was amputated and he kept it, eventually donating the bones to the Army Medical Museum. After the war, it was put on display, and Sickles would come by to visit his leg. Dan Sickles's leg is still on display today, at the U.S. Army Medical Museum.

Meade's chief engineer, Governor K. Warren, arrived on Little Round Top and discovered two things: The Confederate units were headed his way and somebody needed to defend this hill. Fortunately, two additional Union corps had come up in the morning. Warren diverted two brigades to Little Round Top from the Union V Corps on its way to support Sickles. They arrived just in time to stop the Confederate assault in a very bitter fight that lasted most of the afternoon. As additional Confederate units battered the Union line, additional reinforcements from II Corps and V Corps were just enough to hold the Confederates from breaking through after desperate and heroic fighting. Meanwhile, Ewell began his attack at Culp's Hill at 7 p.m., but Union troops behind prepared positions of logs and rock held firm. Another attack on Cemetery Ridge in the early evening threatened to overwhelm the XI Corps defenders, but darkness was falling and the attack ended. See Figure 18-5 for a look at the Battle of Gettysburg.

**FIGURE 18-5:**
A scene from the battle of Gettysburg.

*The Library of Congress*

# The Battle of Gettysburg: Day Three

The results of the second day did not faze Lee. Although Longstreet's and Ewell's divisions had fought to a standstill, Lee believed he had struck a severe blow to the Union army and that one more attack would finally push them off Cemetery

Ridge. He made preparations for a final assault, using Ewell's and Hill's men plus the recently arrived division of General Pickett from Longstreet's corps.

Lee still didn't know how strong his enemy was. Stuart and his cavalry had arrived that day, having been found in Carlisle by couriers that Lee had sent out to find Stuart. When Stuart arrived, Lee's only comment was "Well, General Stuart, you are here at last." Lee and Stuart had known each other since Stuart was a cadet at West Point and Lee was the academy's superintendent. But Lee's comment, though gentlemanly and understated, clearly indicated his disappointment. Lee now ordered the chastened cavalryman to prepare to attack the Union rear in support of the next day's attacks.

## Meade calls a meeting

In the gloomy darkness of a room in a shabby farmhouse on the battlefield, George Meade met with his corps commanders to decide what to do next. The army had been in a terrible fight but still held the decisive terrain. The consensus was to stay and fight but remain on the defensive to see what Lee would do. Included in the group was General Sedgwick, who had just arrived that evening with his VI Corps. The Army of the Potomac was all together. Meade told his commanders what to expect the next day — Lee had tried the flanks; tomorrow he would try the center.

Initially, Lee desired a full-scale attack all along the Union line, but he gave up on that plan when he found out that Longstreet had not made preparations for an attack. He spent the morning changing his scheme of attack, deciding upon a massive assault aimed at a small copse of trees that marked the middle of the Union line on Cemetery Ridge. Pickett's division, with support from A.P. Hill's corps, would attack across the open area stretching nearly a mile to the enemy position. Simultaneously, Ewell would launch another attack on Culp's Hill. Stuart's cavalry would threaten the Union rear and attack the Yankees when their lines finally broke. The main attack would be preceded by a massive artillery bombardment that would disrupt the defenders and their artillery while blasting a hole in the line for the attackers to move through. Longstreet opposed Lee's plan, but Lee believed his men capable of anything. Most of all, however, he believed that victory was in his grasp.

## The Confederate attacks

The battle at Culp's Hill began, ironically, with a Union attack that was launched just as Ewell's men were beginning their own attack at 4:30 a.m. Intense fighting swirled around the hill — attack was followed by counterattack, which was followed by yet another attack. The fighting stopped just after noon, both sides with heavy casualties and very little to show for it. There was a lull on the field. Stuart's attack also had no positive result, ending in a stalemate that represented no threat to the Union rear.

Longstreet had assembled about 160 cannons, all pointed at the Union line on Cemetery Ridge. During the morning, a collection of different brigades from Hill and Longstreet — all total about 15,000 men — assembled in the woods behind the cannons. The artillery barrage began shortly after 1 p.m. and went on for two solid hours. No one in the United States up to that time had ever witnessed such a display of firepower. For all its ferocity, noise, and smoke, however, it accomplished very little. The gunners shot high, and most of their shells rained down on empty ground. The Union artillery was largely untouched, and the troops lying behind a low stone wall on the ridge near the copse of trees were unharmed. Some Union soldiers even reported falling asleep during the bombardment after they realized that they were not in danger. It was the greatest artillery bombardment ever conducted on the North American continent and the loudest noise ever heard up to that time.

As the intensity of the bombardment trailed off, Longstreet reluctantly gave the order to advance. The units, composed of men from Virginia, North Carolina, and Tennessee and from Alabama, Mississippi, and Georgia stepped out from the trees, aligned themselves on a mile-long front, and began their march toward the Union line. Waiting for them were about 8,000 veteran infantrymen of the II Corps and the remainder of the battered I Corps, somehow sent to this part of the line because it was quiet. Union artillery began to engage the Confederates, not only from the wall and Cemetery Ridge, but also from Little Round Top as well. The cannon fire was effective, forcing the attackers to halt and realign their ranks again before advancing at a run, flags flying, screaming the Rebel Yell. Gaining the wall, the attackers seemed to have won — but only for a moment. The Union defenders were far too numerous and far too determined to give up. Reinforcements were already moving forward, piling into the thinned Confederate ranks. Many were taken prisoner; those who could, fell back. Lee met the survivors as they returned, trying to rally them. "All this has been my fault," he repeated over and over. The magnitude of the failed attack became apparent quickly — nearly half of those who crossed the open field did not make it back. Check out Figure 18-6 for a map of the Battle of Gettysburg.

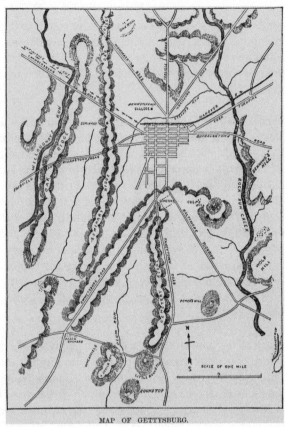

**FIGURE 18-6:**
Map of the Battle
of Gettysburg.

MAP OF GETTYSBURG.

*Getty Images*

## PICKETT'S CHARGE

George Pickett, up to this point, had never commanded troops in battle. He was something of a dandy and was known for his good humor and engaging personality. Because his division was the only unit that had not been assembled ad hoc for the attack, he was given command of the advance. But Pickett did not lead the charge, nor was he visible during the fighting. One of the greatest charges in all military history has Pickett's name attached to it, mostly because he had arrived on the battlefield too late to do anything else. Pickett's Charge is often described as an attack only by Virginians. While it is true that Pickett's division was composed of all Virginia units, a large number from North Carolina participated and performed as formidably as the Virginians. Pickett himself never forgave Lee for his decision on the third day at Gettysburg.

# The Final Moves

The following day, as he had done at Antietam, Lee remained on the battlefield with his bloodied army. Meade did nothing that day, preferring to rest and reequip his army; he certainly felt that a victory in the hand was far better than taking a risk at losing it. Lee knew what he had to do — he gathered up his wounded (those he could get to — he was forced to leave over 6,000 of them on the field), assembling a wagon train 17 miles long to take them on the long, hard road back to Virginia. A heavy rain accompanied the army, and Lee was halted at the flooded Potomac for several days, exposed to the threat of an attack from Meade's army. Meade finally did pursue but slowly and cautiously, despite President Lincoln's entreaties to go after Lee and finish him off. When he found Lee's men protecting their Potomac escape route with heavy entrenchments, Meade waited. While he waited, Lee crossed over the river to safety during the night.

## BATTLE CAPTAIN'S REPORT: THE BATTLE OF GETTYSBURG, JULY 1–3, 1863 — UNION VICTORY

- **Commanders:** Union: Major General George G. Meade, Army of the Potomac, 90,000 men. Confederate: General Robert E. Lee, 75,000 men.

- **Phase I:** Lee's army is spread in an arc from Carlisle to Harrisburg to York, gathering supplies. Lee, without Stuart's cavalry to tell him where the enemy is, decides to concentrate his forces to the east of Gettysburg and plan his next move. The Union army, under a new commander, moves northward from Maryland to the Pennsylvania border, looking for a good defensive position to protect Washington. Meade sends his cavalry out to the crossroads town of Gettysburg to collect information about the enemy. Meanwhile, Confederate troops arrive in Gettysburg looking for shoes and run into the cavalry. A sharp fight ensues, attracting other units to the town.

- **Phase II:** By early afternoon of July 1, two Union Corps have arrived on the field with more units coming. Confederate forces arrive from the north and east, outflanking the defenders and driving them off Seminary Ridge and out of the town of Gettysburg. Union forces under Winfield Scott Hancock organize a defense on Cemetery Ridge and Culp's Hill. As darkness arrives, Lee orders Ewell to take the critical terrain, if possible. Ewell, his regiments scattered after chasing the 11th Corps through town, decides not to, giving the beaten Union army a breather. Lee collects his forces and plans for the next day.

*(continued)*

(continued)

- **Phase III:** On July 2, Lee makes a decision to attack the flanks of the Union army. Ewell's corps is to seize Culp's Hill and Cemetery Ridge, while Longstreet's corps attacks the Union left near the Round Tops. Longstreet takes most of the day to get his men into place — he is not exactly sure where the Union flank is. Meanwhile, Union General Dan Sickles decides to move his corps out to a better defensible spot nearly half a mile out of place, just as Longstreet begins his attack. Sickles's corps is mangled, and the Union left is in danger. The previously undefended Little Round Top is occupied just prior to the arrival of Confederate forces. The Union left and right are both under heavy attack, but terrain favors the defending Union army, which also has the advantage of interior lines, quickly shifting forces to match the Confederate thrusts. The day ends with no advantage to the Confederates. Stuart arrives that evening, contributing nothing more to the campaign for General Lee than some captured wagons and stale information. George Pickett's Division of Longstreet's corps arrives.

- **Phase IV:** Lee decides to attack the center, which he believes has been weakened to supply troops to the threatened flanks. Lee decides to use Pickett's Division as the core unit for a nearly 15,000-man assault on the Union center. Most of the additional troops would come from A.P. Hill's corps, which had not seen action since the first day. Ewell would again attempt to take Culp's Hill. The attack would be preceded with a heavy artillery bombardment of the Union line. Longstreet disagrees with the plan, seeing no utility in it, but Lee is determined to win on this field. The greatest artillery attack in North America begins; almost every shot fired for the next two hours misses its intended mark — the Union defensive lines are largely undamaged. With Confederate guns running out of ammunition, the Confederate attack begins. Pickett's Charge, one of the most famous events in military history, is as magnificent as it is hopeless. After small initial gains, Union reinforcements drive off the survivors. Ewell's attack, begun early in the morning, is hard fought but futile. Stuart also fails to threaten the Union rear. Lee waits a day before retreating and crosses the Potomac on July 13, cautiously followed by Meade, who is glad to see the enemy go.

- **Casualties:** Union 23,000, Confederate 23,000.

# The Battle's Significance

Gettysburg was the largest battle fought on the North American continent. Nearly 160,000 men fought on the field, and 45,000 were killed or wounded. Meade had handled the army well, and his troops had fought with courage and determination on their home territory. Lee had not fought well. Gettysburg was his greatest failure. He made bad decisions, crippled by a lack of information. In the end, he asked too much from the men he commanded. His men responded the best they could and came so close several times to clinching the victory, but even they had limits.

In the immediate aftermath of the battle, its importance was not obvious. Yes, Lee's army had been defeated and driven out of the North for a second time, but what concerned everyone was the terrible cost. The casualty lists brought great shock and grief to families in the North and South. Yet nothing had been decided. The war would go on in all of its terrible fury. Because the war had to go on, Gettysburg gained its true significance in November of 1863 when Abraham Lincoln came to speak at the dedication of the Union soldier's cemetery on the battlefield. His short speech known as the Gettysburg Address is one of the masterpieces of the English language. In it, he captured the essence of the cause the men had died for, validating their sacrifice and laying the foundation for a new nation in the process.

# Heroes and Goats

Gettysburg has entered into American myth — it has come to symbolize the entire Civil War and it is the representative battle that everyone knows something about. There are so many elements of heroism here that they must be selected carefully.

## Heroes

Reynolds and Hancock are at the right time and the right place making critical decisions that saved the battle for the Union. But in the end, this battle gives us the best sense of the heroic quality of the American soldier that transcends time. Valor and sacrifice are the watchwords here.

>> **The Army of the Potomac:** Finally, after years of disappointment, dismal performances, and poor leadership in combat, the army gains a tremendously important victory when it counted the most. With a core of tough, battle-tested veterans, the army is equal to Lee's best. After this battle the Army of the Potomac becomes a dangerous foe.

>> **The Iron Brigade and the 1st Minnesota:** On the first day at Gettysburg, the 1st Brigade of the 1st Division of the I Corps, known as the Iron Brigade, fought a magnificent defense that held the Confederate attack at bay for several crucial hours, expending itself to near destruction in the process. On the second day at Gettysburg, the 1st Minnesota was sent in to stop a Confederate breakthrough. If the Minnesotans couldn't stop them, the Union line would be shattered. Of the 262 men who made the charge against the enemy, only 38 survived. But the Confederate assault was halted and the Union line held.

>> **George G. Meade:** Dragged out of his bed and made commander of the army just days before the army's most critical battle, George Meade came through. He led by consensus, meeting with his corps commanders to gain their approval, but he made all the right decisions and gave the Union the victory that would change the direction of the war in the Eastern Theater.

>> **Winfield Scott Hancock:** Arrives on Cemetery Hill in the midst of a disaster and calmly ascertains the situation. Meade had entrusted him with making the decision to stay and fight or retreat. Making the statement, "I think this the strongest position . . . that I ever saw," he makes one of the most critical decisions of the Civil War. The Army of the Potomac would assemble here and defend.

>> **The Army of Northern Virginia:** The Virginians of Pickett's Division, the North Carolinians of Pettigrew's Division, the Mississippians of Barksdale's Brigade, the Alabamians of Wilcox's Brigade, the Texans of Law's Brigade, all won immortality, even if the battle was lost.

## Goats

Here the Confederates join the ranks of the goats — an unaccustomed situation for the leaders of the Army of Northern Virginia. Debating who was the *real* goat of Gettysburg continues to this day — it has been going on since the battle ended. Saying that one or all of the following are to be blamed as the one who lost this battle for the Confederacy will certainly land you in a fight, verbal or otherwise.

>> **Jeb Stuart, James Longstreet, Richard Ewell:** Pick one, a combination of two, or all three. For years the South sought a scapegoat for the loss of Gettysburg. Lee was held blameless, despite his poor decisions. Stuart was blamed, perhaps with more justification than others, for leaving the army in the lurch when his troops were most needed to collect information about the enemy. Longstreet was blamed because he disagreed with Lee's plan of attack on days two and three and was accused of being slow and sullen in carrying out his orders. "If only Longstreet had been faster," goes the criticism, Lee would have won the battle. Ewell's decision not to take Cemetery Hill on the first day appeared to be a fatal blunder. Because Ewell didn't take them when it was relatively easy, he was unable to take them when the Yankees made it tougher.

>> **Robert E. Lee:** Upon hearing that Hooker had been replaced with General Meade as commander of the Army of the Potomac, Lee said, "General Meade will commit no blunder in my front, and if I make one, he will make haste to take advantage of it." Lee's blunders cost him his army in a place deep in enemy territory, on a field not of his choosing, under circumstances unfavorable to him. Lee wrote Confederate President Jefferson Davis and offered his resignation, holding his subordinates completely blameless. In his account of the battle, he told Davis he never doubted that he could win a victory; otherwise, he would not have given the orders he did. Davis took no action on Lee's resignation, leaving Lee as the commander of the army.

# 1863: The Western Theater

In the Western Theater, Vicksburg loomed as the focal point for all operations. The Confederacy had to hold Vicksburg to ensure continued control with the states in the Trans-Mississippi Theater. The Union had to take Vicksburg to split the Confederacy in half and control the Mississippi River. From Vicksburg, Union forces could strike at will into the largely undefended rear areas of the Confederacy. The all-important rail junction of Chattanooga was also key to the Confederacy's survival. Chattanooga was the gateway into the Deep South, the vital agricultural and industrial base that was essential to the Confederate war effort. Opposing the Union army were Confederate forces under Lieutenant General John C. Pemberton, which occupied a strong defensive position at Vicksburg. Bragg's Army of Tennessee stood guard south of Murfreesboro, protecting Chattanooga. Confederate General Joseph E. Johnston was nominally the overall commander in this theater, but he never seemed willing to take actual control of operations. Into this command vacuum came President Davis, who gave orders to Pemberton without informing Johnston.

# The Vicksburg Campaign

In 1863, Vicksburg, a town sitting on a bluff overlooking the Mississippi River, was the key to victory in the Western Theater (see Figure 18-7). It was the last outpost preventing Union control of the river; without Vicksburg, the Confederacy was cut in half, isolating Texas, Arkansas, and Missouri, and preventing them from providing any support to Richmond. Vicksburg, however, was easier taken in strategy meetings than in actuality. Grant had tried once before (between November and December 1862) and had failed to take the city, suffering heavy casualties. In 1863, he was determined to capture this strategic city.

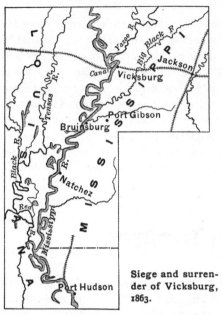

**FIGURE 18-7:**
Map of the Battle
of Vicksburg.

Siege and surrender of Vicksburg, 1863.

*Getty Images*

## The advantages of geography

**REMEMBER**

Anyone who has read Mark Twain knows that the Mississippi River was a treacherous and powerful foe, swallowing up the pilot who paid no heed to her peculiarities. The river was swift and deep in some places, shallow and sluggish in others. The water washed huge trees and other debris into the river, creating underwater barriers and obstacles. The river twisted and turned in hairpin curves. One such hairpin curve whipped right underneath the bluff where Vicksburg stood. On the bluff were powerful cannons that would splinter any navy ship coming into range. Also flowing into the Mississippi north of Vicksburg was the Yazoo River, which formed a large swampy delta that would impede any advance from the north. The only way to get at the city of Vicksburg was to attack from the south or go around the Yazoo to the east and come around the city from behind. To get south, of course, troops in ships would have to pass Vicksburg. To cross the Yazoo, troops would have to move eastward for a significant distance and then cut back through enemy-held territory with a long and vulnerable supply line to protect. It was a tough problem for any commander to handle.

Confederate commander John C. Pemberton had about 20,000 men who had to do nothing except occupy the city. The navy, which up to this point had been General Grant's ace in the hole, would have to play a role no matter what approach to Vicksburg Grant decided to take. Whatever way Grant tried would be very difficult and time-consuming. This was not good because political pressure was mounting to do something quickly. Unlike other Union commanders, Grant fully appreciated the political aspect of military operations related to President Lincoln's strategy for victory. Whatever decision he made, he had to continue to make progress. A retreat, so common during this war, would be yet another admission of defeat and a threat to Grant himself being relieved of command by a frustrated commander-in-chief. Grant arrived from Memphis in late January 1863 to direct the campaign.

The Army of the Tennessee would be supplied by ship from the river; his staging area for the attack on Vicksburg was only 20 miles from the city, but he couldn't get there from here. The swamps, bayous, and water made the task of moving his army impossible. Grant looked at the map and reasoned that he could get south of Vicksburg if the base of the hairpin curve in front of the city was cut by a canal. That way, the Union ships and troops could sail past the city at their leisure. So, a canal was dug (by hand — by lucky soldiers selected for this detail, working in muck up to their waists) for two months before the whole project collapsed, literally and figuratively, when the levee fell in, flooding the entire neck of land. The next project planned was a 200-mile canal to bypass Vicksburg completely and join at the Red River, which would allow Grant's men to attack from the south. The project, however, was far too ambitious and time-consuming to be practical. A river advance down Yazoo Pass in an attempt to reach dry land failed at Greenwood, Mississippi, where the Confederates built a fort of cotton bales and drove the gunboats off. A similar attempt at Steele's Bayou, a more direct approach to Vicksburg via the Yazoo, met with failure as the flotilla was caught by Confederate troops, who felled trees in front and behind the ships, then began to shoot anyone who exposed himself on deck. Sherman's troops were dispatched to provide protection for the navy and get them out of the tangled mess they were in. The troops actually saved the fleet from direct capture.

## Grant's gamble

For three months, Grant had tried to take the engineer's path to victory and had failed; he was now ready to take a chance that would either make him a hero or get him relieved from command. In April, Grant proposed to move the army south on the left bank of the Mississippi River below Vicksburg. Meanwhile, Admiral David Dixon Porter (see Figure 18-8) would sail his fleet right past Vicksburg's defenses and link up with Grant's troops. The ships would ferry his men and supplies sufficient for sustained movement across the river, and he would be able to move on dry land and approach the city from the rear. There were two problems involved in this plan. The first was that Grant would move his army south and operate against the enemy without a supply line. The second problem was that if Porter failed, or if a large number of his ships were damaged or destroyed, the campaign was effectively ended (and with it, Grant's career). As the calls for Grant's dismissal rose with each passing day of no news from Vicksburg, Grant knew he only had one chance to make good. Lincoln could only watch and wait, displaying his full confidence in his general's judgment.

**FIGURE 18-8:**
David Dixon
Porter.

*The Library of Congress / Public Domain*

Grant slowly moved two corps, about 24,000 men, southward along the semi-solid riverbank, while Sherman (with 10,000 men) remained above Vicksburg with his corps to distract and confuse the Confederates. In addition, Grant sent Colonel Benjamin Grierson with 1,700 men to attack Confederate rail lines and supply depots in central Mississippi, which would further distract the enemy's attention. Grierson did this very well, covering 600 miles in just over two weeks and ending up at Baton Rouge; it is considered one of the most successful cavalry operations of the war. Grant's distractions worked — Pemberton was confused and sent troops and cavalry running everywhere to deal with the number of threats he thought were coming his way. As Grant had intended, Pemberton dealt with all but the most dangerous threat.

With the Confederates distracted and Grant in position, it was now Porter's turn. On April 16, Porter sent transports and selected ships downstream at night past the bluffs of Vicksburg. The Confederate batteries were waiting and lit up the night with bonfires and houses set on fire along the riverbank. The Confederate guns fired for nearly three hours and succeeded in sinking only one transport. Nearly a week later, the rest of the fleet with supplies passed successfully. Porter's sailors began to ferry the infantry across the river. Once assembled, Grant was ready to move against the city.

Grant wasted no time after he was on dry ground. He marched rapidly to Jackson, Mississippi, to cut off Pemberton's supply line and block any Confederate reinforcements coming to his aid. Grant was using speed and deception to keep Pemberton guessing. He had abandoned his supply line, something Pemberton never expected. Troops carried three days' rations; after that, they would live off the country. The only extra supplies carried for the army was ammunition. Grant also was outnumbered when he crossed the river. Even after Sherman joined him near Jackson in May, he had only 34,000 men. Pemberton had 40,000 under his command, but he had spread them all over trying to defend everything. Grant easily overcame these isolated groups, and Pemberton never really figured out what Grant was doing until it was too late. Pemberton's confusion was compounded by the conflicting orders he was receiving. From General Joseph E. Johnston, the theater commander, he was told not to allow himself to get caught in a siege but to maintain his mobility. At the same time, Confederate President Jefferson Davis was telling him to stand and hold at Vicksburg. Pemberton was not a man blessed with a great deal of imagination and, given conflicting orders, he was incapable of making a decision at this moment of crisis.

## Grant closes the vise

As the Union forces approached Jackson, Joseph E. Johnston arrived to take charge and prevent Pemberton from being trapped. The Yankees moved too fast; Johnston had only 5,000 men to hold off three times that many men. Grant's forces were also moving west toward Vicksburg to cut off his retreat and block Pemberton from supporting Johnston. The following day, Johnston retreated and gave up the city and ordered Pemberton to move out of Vicksburg to attack Grant's supply lines. It was a good idea but had no grounding in reality. Grant had no supply line. What he did have were two Union corps sitting across Pemberton's supply line and looking for a fight. Pemberton took up a good defensive position at Champion's Hill on May 16 with over 21,000 men, but he was outnumbered as the two Union corps attacked and drove the Confederates back. Pemberton badly misdirected the battle and lost control of his forces, suffering over 7,000 casualties. He found himself pursued into the defenses of Vicksburg with only 20,000 men. Grant now outnumbered him and had linked up with his river supply line north of Vicksburg. From here, supplies and reinforcements would allow Grant to sustain a siege with 71,000 men.

# The Siege and Fall of Vicksburg

Eager for a resolution, Grant tried two all-out attacks against the defenses on May 19 and 22, which were repelled both times with heavy casualties. Grant had to worry about Johnston, who now had assembled an army of about 25,000 men and had reoccupied Jackson in an attempt to break the siege. Grant sent Sherman's corps of 50,000 to watch Johnston, while Grant and the rest of the army resigned themselves to a siege — a steady land and naval bombardment of the city. The Confederate forces returned fire, but each day their food supplies grew smaller. The Confederate defenders also had to deal with a sizable civilian population as well. People lived in dugouts or caves to protect themselves from the incessant shelling. They began to starve, and sickness spread through the 10-square-mile area in the sweltering Mississippi summer heat. No Americans have ever suffered in war as much as the people of Vicksburg did during the siege. Johnston made an attempt to save the city on July 1 but retreated when blocked by Sherman's superior forces. Just two days later, Pemberton asked for terms of surrender. Pemberton had known Grant during the Mexican-American War, and he hoped that friendship would give him some advantage. He was disappointed. On the next day, July 4, the Vicksburg garrison surrendered and was paroled. (This saved the trouble of transporting 30,000 prisoners north on very scarce river transport. By signing a parole, they pledged not to participate in any further military action against the Union army.) Gettysburg had ended with Lee's defeat the day before. "The Father of Waters again goes unvexed to the sea," Lincoln wrote after hearing news of the surrender. Grant's brilliant generalship moved him to the first rank of Union generals.

# Success at Port Hudson

Nathaniel Banks, the commander who had been so thoroughly outmatched by Stonewall Jackson in the Valley (see Chapter 11), took over the Department of the Gulf from General Butler in December 1862. He was responsible for military operations on the lower Mississippi and Louisiana and administering the occupation of New Orleans. One of his tasks was to capture Port Hudson, a Confederate stronghold sitting on high bluffs overlooking a sharp bend on the Mississippi about 30 miles north of Baton Rouge. Unlike Grant's excellent relationship with his navy counterpart, Banks and Rear Admiral Farragut failed to coordinate their efforts. In March, Farragut's squadron was to pass the dangerous batteries while Banks provided a diversion with a ground attack. Farragut's squadron was heavily damaged while Banks failed to order an attack. Later, his clumsy attempts at coordinating his operations with Grant caused Grant finally to ignore Banks and continue with his own plan to take Vicksburg. Johnston waited too long to pull the Confederate defenders from Port Hudson to be used against Grant, leaving badly needed troops to their fate. In May of 1863, Banks had assembled 30,000 troops against about 7,500 defenders holding very formidable earthworks. In over a month, Banks lost over 3,000 men in a number of costly attacks. The Confederate commander, Major General Franklin Gardner, fought effectively, but his soldiers suffered greatly, lacking food and supplies. When Vicksburg surrendered, Gardner surrendered a few days later, after undergoing the longest siege in American history — 48 days. Now the Union controlled the Mississippi and, with it, the strategic initiative. The Confederacy would now be fighting for survival.

# Grant's Accomplishment

Grant had done what few U.S. generals had ever done. Nineteen days had passed from the time he crossed the Mississippi River with his two corps on April 30 to the time he had trapped Pemberton in Vicksburg. Grant had taken enormous risks by dividing his forces in the face of the enemy and cutting his army off from its supply base. He compensated for these risks, however, by deceiving Pemberton and by using speed of maneuver, marching over 200 miles to force Pemberton to protect his own line of supply at Jackson. After he was out in the open, Grant could attack Pemberton and destroy him or send him back into Vicksburg, while threatening any Confederate force moving west either to support Pemberton or relieve the siege. Either way, Grant had the initiative. Pemberton had allowed Grant to take it, and, in a matter of days, Union forces were closed around the city and the relief force had been driven away.

# Heroes

These are pretty obvious.

>> **Ulysses Grant:** Grant displays all of the qualities of a great commander. He gave clear and concise orders and his subordinates carried out maneuvers within a larger concept of operations. Grant showed complete trust in his subordinate corps commanders to accomplish his orders. When one did not, he was quickly relieved (the unfortunate political general John McClernand, who tried a McClellan-style stunt with the press). He took prudent risks, knowing that Pemberton was a weak commander and never lost the initiative, allowing him to impose his will on the enemy.

>> **Admiral David Dixon Porter:** Porter is another hero, who enthusiastically supported Grant even when his army commanders had doubts. In complete harmony with Grant, Porter resolutely risked his entire squadron to bypass the Vicksburg defenses and allow Grant to seize the initiative. Without the navy, there could have been no victory at Vicksburg.

# Goats

The Confederates assembled the same distressing repeat offenders.

>> **Jefferson Davis:** Davis, whose animosity for Johnston leads to the president bypassing him altogether to confuse an already confused commander at Vicksburg.

>> **Joseph E. Johnston:** Johnston, given command authority, does not exercise it. When theater-level decisions had to be made to protect Vicksburg, he refrained from taking any serious action or risks. When he did respond, it was too little and too late.

>> **John C. Pemberton:** Pemberton had no command skills and fewer battle skills. He was outclassed in every way. He was put in command largely because he was a friend of President Davis and he was a Northerner, which in Davis's mind was an advantage to show the North that not everyone in the Confederate army was from the South. On this cracked logic lay the basis for the disaster at Vicksburg.

Chapter **19**

# The Battles of Chickamauga and Chattanooga, August–November 1863

Just a few days before Grant's triumph at Vicksburg, Mississippi, Union General William Rosecrans began to move his army, idle since January, toward Chattanooga, Tennessee. If Vicksburg was the strategic key to the Western Theater, Chattanooga came a close second in strategic importance. The capture of this key rail junction would allow Union armies to strike south to Atlanta and the Carolinas, and even threaten the Confederate capital of Richmond from southwest Virginia. As long as a Confederate army held Chattanooga, eastern Tennessee and

Kentucky were potentially threatened with another invasion. Chattanooga became a place that each side had to have to accomplish its strategic goals in the war.

Unfortunately for both the Union and the Confederacy, commanders whose reputations for applying the military art were less than sterling led the armies facing each other in Tennessee at this time. As Union Major General Rosecrans and Confederate General Braxton Bragg maneuvered, each exposed his army to potential disaster in the woods and thickets along a creek named Chickamauga, from an old Cherokee word meaning *river of death.* In September 1863, Chickamauga would earn its name a thousand times over.

# Rosecrans: Approaching and Taking Chattanooga

In June 1863, Major General Rosecrans and his Army of the Cumberland began a maneuver in which he intended to force Bragg's Confederate Army of Tennessee out of its defenses at Tullahoma with a flanking movement that forced Bragg back toward Chattanooga. Crossing the Tennessee River with 65,000 men, 45 days rations, and plenty of ammunition, Rosecrans, inspired by his maneuver and claiming a great victory, headed into north Alabama and swung across to north Georgia and back into Tennessee, approaching Chattanooga from the rear. Faced with this situation, Bragg's 44,000-man army would be forced to fight at a disadvantage or retreat.

Rosecrans effectively used terrain, deception, and speed to his advantage in outflanking Bragg. He sent a small detachment to occupy Bragg's attention outside of Chattanooga while the rest of his army used the mountainous terrain to screen his movements. He marched lightly (and therefore quickly), without the encumbrances of a long supply train. Rosecrans had help from the commander of the Department of the Ohio, Major General Ambrose Burnside, who decided that he had had enough of locking up *Copperheads* (pro-Southern sympathizers in the North) for the moment and wanted to join the fight. Burnside moved into the Cumberland Gap and east Tennessee, capturing Knoxville, a town within several days' marching distance of Chattanooga. These movements also focused Bragg's attention away from Rosecrans. By the time Bragg discovered that Rosecrans was approaching Chattanooga from the rear, he made a wise decision to abandon the city rather than be trapped in a siege. Rosecrans's troops walked into the town on September 9. Rosecrans's total losses to capture Chattanooga: six men, four of whom were injured accidentally.

Bragg was not a happy man in the summer of 1863. In fact, he was rarely a happy man, no matter what time of year. Bragg had been ordered to dispatch troops to assist Lieutenant General Pemberton, who was commanding Confederate forces defending Vicksburg, which did not make him happy. But he had other problems that added to his unhappiness. Since the battle of Murfreesboro (see Chapter 16) six months previously, Bragg had been quarreling with his subordinates, nagging them so that most were at the end of their patience — especially his two senior commanders, William J. Hardee and Leonidas Polk. Even Polk, an Episcopal bishop, had run out of Christian forbearance. Polk's frustration, mirrored by other subordinates, stemmed from the knowledge that the only reason Bragg remained in command at all was that Confederate President Jefferson Davis approved of him. Davis got involved in the dispute, but instead of taking some generals to the woodshed, he essentially told them all to get along. This, of course, solved nothing and would lead to great problems in the coming days for the Army of Tennessee.

Bragg retreated 20 miles south of Chattanooga to LaFayette, Georgia. By virtue of the fact that his was the only active Confederate army in the Western Theater at this point, he benefited from the strategic shifting of forces to meet the most dangerous threat. A concentration of forces under Bragg could be used to attack Rosecrans and throw the Union's strategic offensive momentum off balance, shifting it in the Confederacy's favor again. Troops that Bragg had previously sent to Vicksburg rejoined his army, along with a corps from Knoxville, as did the advance elements of what would be most of the I Corps of Lee's Army of Northern Virginia — 15,000 men under Lieutenant General Longstreet. The corps was arriving by train, taking the long way around (a 900-mile route by rail) because Burnside's forces occupied Knoxville. This effort had taxed the transportation resources to the limit, but they were arriving. Bragg had an army nearly as large as Lee did at Gettysburg — close to 72,000 men.

# The Chickamauga Campaign

Believing he had Bragg beaten without fighting a battle (Bragg had spread rumors that his army was falling apart and demoralized) and filled with self-confidence, Rosecrans began moving south. His goal was to take Atlanta, and he intended to end the war by Christmas. He moved his three corps — a total of 57,000 men — out of Chattanooga along three separate axes of advance. The distance between each corps was 15 to 20 miles, too far apart to assist each other in case of trouble. But Rosecrans did not expect trouble. In actuality, he had divided his army in the face of a concentrated foe waiting on his flank, which could fall on any one of his corps and annihilate it and then turn to defeat the other corps in detail. This is the kind of opportunity that the great captains of history have used to become the great captains of history.

**REMEMBER**

Despite this opportunity, Bragg was not a great captain. Great captains become great because they build strong bonds of trust with their subordinate commanders. Such bonds are essential to the great captain's success and imprint upon history because these subordinate commanders are the ones who carry out the great captain's battle plans. No one under Bragg's command trusted or believed in his competence. Thus, when Bragg put his plan together to attack the isolated Union corps one by one, his subordinates carried it out poorly and half-heartedly.

In addition, Bragg had a habit of beginning every battle he fought crippled by a startling lack of knowledge about his enemy. He was always surprised by what he found, and it always unnerved him. This situation was no different. Bragg assumed Rosecrans had only two corps, not three, marching toward him. His attack was aimed at the corps he thought was the more isolated of the two. In reality, he was attacking the center corps of three, the worst possible choice when trying to defeat a divided enemy force in detail. Not only that, but he decided to attack before all of Longstreet's corps had arrived.

Bragg's subordinates made no real attacks on the enemy — they accomplished nothing more than alerting Rosecrans that he was not facing a demoralized, retreating Confederate army. More importantly, Rosecrans also recognized that he was in trouble if Bragg could cut off and attack his separate corps individually. He immediately ordered a concentration of the army. Over the space of four days, Bragg waited for Longstreet to arrive while Rosecrans united two of his three corps near Chickamauga Creek at a small town in the woods known as Lee and Gordon's Mill. Rosecrans himself knew very little about the enemy, unaware that Bragg's large army was poised to strike.

Bragg, still believing he faced only one Union corps, planned to strike the defender's left flank and push the enemy southwest into the mountains, thus opening the way to Chattanooga. He first had to cross Chickamauga Creek. General Longstreet had arrived with most of his units, so Bragg decided to attack the enemy on September 18. To his surprise, he found most of the crossings well guarded. Rosecrans, realizing what the Confederates were doing, moved Major General George H. Thomas's corps to secure the army's left flank. That night, most of the Confederate army crossed the creek at various places; at the same time, Union units were marching north to protect the flank. Movement for everyone was slow and difficult. The heavily wooded terrain lacked any distinctive landmarks, and soldiers spent many hours backtracking on small rutted paths in the darkness. By morning, the Union line stretched 6 miles, and the Confederates were there in front of them.

# The Battle of Chickamauga: Day One

The first day's battle on September 19 had no form — it was an intermittent and intense day of combat. Brigades were fed into battle up and down the Union defensive line. Units attacked and were met with counterattacks. Even a dramatic charge by Patrick Cleburne's Confederates failed to make any progress. Thomas's Union troops had been hard pressed but were holding firm. Because of the heavily wooded terrain, neither Rosecrans nor Bragg had a very good idea of what was going on during the day. During the battle, the third corps of Rosecrans's army arrived. Now Bragg unknowingly faced a united Union army.

Bragg had also received reinforcements — the last brigades of Longstreet's corps, along with Longstreet himself. Bragg planned to make his flank attack the next day. He divided the army into two wings, Longstreet in charge of one, Polk in charge of the other. His plan of battle — turn the enemy's left flank and drive him away from Chattanooga — had not changed since the first contact with the enemy, despite what had occurred over the past two days. Polk would attack first, followed by Longstreet.

Because Bragg had created these wings with little knowledge of the actual disposition of his units, division and brigade commanders were not sure to whom they belonged. Orders were lost and confusion reigned the night before the battle. Bragg had intended to begin the attack at dawn, but Polk didn't do so. Bragg became anxious when by 9 a.m. nothing had happened, so he sent an aide to find Polk. Polk at that moment was sitting 3 miles behind the front lines sitting in a rocking chair on the front porch of a house, reading a newspaper and waiting for breakfast.

# The Battle of Chickamauga: Day Two

Polk got a move-on, and the Confederates pressed General Thomas's defenses hard (see Figure 19-1). Thomas had prepared well, building *breastworks* (a temporary fortification built to chest height) of logs to protect his troops from enemy fire and piling up debris to create obstacles for the attackers. But Confederate numbers began to tell, and Thomas's line curled back. Thomas called for reinforcements, and Rosecrans provided units from the Union right flank and center, which weren't engaged. Feeding more units into the battle on the left made his defenses weaker everywhere else. Rosecrans, riding along his lines, noticed what appeared to be a gap in the center of his defensive line. He could not see that one of his divisions was sitting in thick woods covering that part of the line, so he ordered General Wood, a division commander, to fill the gap. Wood, who had been the victim of one of Rosecrans's violent temper tantrums for not following orders earlier, complied with this order quickly and efficiently, without questioning whether such a movement made any sense. Thus, as Wood pulled his division out of the way to fill this nonexistent gap in the line, he unwittingly created a real quarter-mile gap in the line.

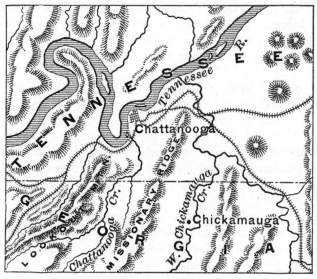

**FIGURE 19-1:** Map of the Battles of Chickamauga and Chattanooga.

BATTLES ABOUT CHATTANOOGA.

*Getty Images*

If you open a gap in your already thin defensive line, the last enemy general you want to see coming toward you is Lee's warhorse, James Longstreet, whose reputation for conducting hammer-blow attacks against the enemy was well known. Where the fighting was toughest, his men were usually there — at Gaines's Mill, Second Manassas, Antietam, Devil's Den, and Little Round Top. Now they were advancing headlong against an unprepared enemy. Rosecrans had given his order to Wood at the precise time Longstreet's wing was initiating its attack. Gettysburg veterans Major Generals Lafayette McLaws and John Bell Hood, along with the Army of Tennessee's finest units, found themselves charging through an undefended opening in the Union line. With the piercing Rebel Yell, the Confederates broke into the open flanks and rear of Rosecrans's army.

The Confederates drove nearly a mile into the Union rear. Rosecrans's right flank collapsed, and soldiers headed for Chattanooga as fast as they could go. Rosecrans and most of his staff had been standing at the gap when the Confederates came through. Frightened and confused men jammed the road, literally sweeping Rosecrans and his staff up in the running mob. Rosecrans discovered he had been carried back to Chattanooga and was unable to return to the battlefield. For all he knew, the entire army had been wrecked.

**TURNING POINT**

But the army had not been completely lost. George H. Thomas (See Figure 19-2) stepped forward and saved the Union army (and perhaps the Union cause) from total disaster. As the right flank gave way, units in the center and left flank formed a horseshoe-shaped defensive line around the only prominent piece of terrain on the battlefield, Snodgrass Hill. Here Thomas took control, gathering men together into ad hoc units and putting them into line, refusing to leave the battlefield, and fighting on against enormous odds. His calm, determined example encouraged the soldiers, and he earned the name the "Rock of Chickamauga."

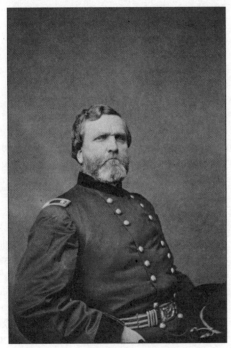

**FIGURE 19-2:** George H. Thomas.

The Library of Congress / Public Domain

## A DIFFERENT VIRGINIAN

George H. Thomas was a Virginian who remained loyal to the Union. He attended West Point and served in the campaign against the Seminoles and in the Mexican-American War. He held various command positions during the first year of the Civil War but did not lead troops in combat until 1862. For a brief time, he commanded the Army of the Tennessee after Shiloh.

Thomas performed well at Perryville and earned a reputation as a tough commander who looked after his men, who referred to him as "Pap." Although Thomas would become one of the finest army commanders to emerge during the war, he could not go home again. Thomas was disowned by his family for choosing the nation above his state. His sisters never mentioned him again and turned his portrait to the wall at the family homestead.

# The Battle Ends

For the rest of the day, Longstreet's troops attempted to break Thomas's defensive position again and again, but Thomas and his men stood firm. Bragg did not order Polk to assist Longstreet's assaults on Snodgrass Hill and allowed the battle to end with the coming of darkness rather than with a decisive attack. Thomas, supported by the reserve, withdrew back to Chattanooga that night. Bragg did not pursue Thomas, nor did he take any action to clinch what appeared to be a significant victory.

Standing on a mountain ridge overlooking Chattanooga and observing the confused mass of Union troops in and around Chattanooga, Bragg's cavalry commander, Nathan Bedford Forrest, sent a message to the commander: "every hour is worth ten thousand men." Forrest, like all the other army leaders, wanted Bragg to pursue the Yankees and drive the army like a wedge between Burnside and Rosecrans. This would force both to retreat, leaving Chattanooga back in Confederate hands and the road open for further offensive action. Unfortunately, Bragg did not believe he had won the battle. The number of casualties that his men had suffered unsettled him, and he had little interest in taking any decisive action. He moved forward and set up his troops around Chattanooga, locking Rosecrans and his 40,000 men in the town. See Figure 19-3 for a depiction of the Battle of Chickamauga.

FIGURE 19-3:
The Battle of
Chickamauga.

Waud, Alfred R / The Library of Congress / Public Domain

## BATTLE CAPTAIN'S REPORT: THE BATTLE OF CHICKAMAUGA, SEPTEMBER 18–20, 1863 — CONFEDERATE VICTORY

- **Commanders:** Union: Major General William S. Rosecrans, Army of the Cumberland, 57,000 men. Confederate: General Braxton Bragg, Army of Tennessee, 67,000 men.

- **Phase I:** Rosecrans outmaneuvers Bragg and his army out of Chattanooga. Bragg retreats into Georgia. Rosecrans pursues, but thinking Bragg's army has fallen apart, separates his three corps in rough mountainous territory; they cannot support one another if attacked. Bragg's army, far from demoralized, is reinforced, including most of Longstreet's corps from Lee's army. Longstreet's men have moved halfway across the Confederacy to join Bragg. Bragg prepares to attack the left flank of Rosecrans's army.

- **Phase II:** Bragg's plans fall apart. Not only do his subordinate commanders fail to do what they are told, but also Bragg thought there were only two Union columns. He mistakenly attacked the center column of the Union army, thereby losing the advantage of surprise. Rosecrans hurries to assemble his forces, while Bragg,

*(continued)*

*(continued)*

awaiting Longstreet's arrival, allows Rosecrans to do so. The battle lines form near Chickamauga Creek.

- **Phase III:** On September 19 Bragg attacks the Union defensive line, hitting the left flank hard but making no headway. This is essentially a battle fought by individual brigades; neither commander has a clear idea of what is going on.

- **Phase IV:** Bragg finally has all of Longstreet's forces on the battlefield. He forms two wings, one commanded by Longstreet, the other by Polk. Polk was to hit the Union left, and Longstreet was to support Polk's attack. During the night the Union troops had pulled back to a better defensive line in the woods and held their positions throughout the day as Confederate attacks forced the Union left flank to curl backward. At this time Longstreet moved his troops forward to the attack, just as a Union division, by Rosecrans's orders, had moved out of the line. This created a gap through which Longstreet's men poured. The right flank of the Union army collapsed, leaving George H. Thomas's corps and the army's reserve to hold off a series of uncoordinated Confederate attacks. By nightfall, Thomas retreats to join the rest of the shattered Union forces in Chattanooga.

- **Casualties:** Union 16,200, Confederate 8,500. This represents a casualty rate of 28 percent for both armies.

# Chickamauga: The Results

No greater opportunities for the destruction of a Union army were ever presented to a Confederate commander in the entire war. Rosecrans several times set his army up for decisive defeat; each time Bragg squandered his opportunity. Bragg had all the advantages: more men, a divided enemy force, a quarter-mile gap in the defensive line — and he still didn't win decisively. His subordinates mangled or ignored his orders; Bragg threw away his numerical advantage in troops by fighting them as brigades in separate and costly attacks; he took no advantage of Longstreet's incredible opportunity at the breakthrough; and he believed himself beaten even in the midst of an important victory, where he had gained the tactical and strategic initiative. Instead of using it to his (and the Confederacy's) benefit, Bragg threw away his advantage by selecting to *lay siege* (surround with military force) to Chattanooga. The Confederacy's last great opportunity was lost.

## The Union: Mixed results

For the Union, Chickamauga was a setback and a humiliating defeat, but not a decisive blow. Union reinforcements arrived in a few weeks and the Western Theater consolidated its forces for another thrust into Georgia. In the aftermath of the Chickamauga campaign, the strategic situation remained as it had been after Rosecrans had captured Chattanooga. Only now, the Union army was stronger and the Confederate army weaker. Rosecrans's reputation was irreparably ruined, even though the men in the army respected him a great deal.

## The Confederacy: Frustration

The news that initially came from Bragg was that Chickamauga was a great victory. It had been for a short while, but as reports from Longstreet and other commanders filtered back, it became clear to everyone that the battle had been a great waste and a golden opportunity lost. Bragg's subordinates, who had urged him again and again to make the most of the victory, burned with anger and resentment. Bragg came under heavy criticism and dissension grew so bad that President Davis himself had to travel to Bragg's headquarters to deal with the problems.

# Heroes and Goats

This campaign highlighted two generals who made excellent plans but were unable to employ their forces once they encountered the enemy. Here we see that plans do not win battle. Generals become goats because they are unable to rise above the images their plans have implanted in their heads and deal with the actual situation on the battlefield. When the army commanders become goats, it is sometimes their subordinates who become the heroes because they are doing the real fighting.

## Heroes

Heroes stand out due to a dramatic action. George H. Thomas simply would not be outfought and would not quit. His careful preparation of the battlefield allowed him to fight effectively throughout the day, even after the rest of the army collapsed and disappeared. The determined attack by Longstreet's men demonstrated what role chance can play on the battlefield. Heroes are born when chance favors the bold. Here are the heroes:

>> **George H. Thomas:** In one of the most dramatic actions of the war, Thomas refused to be scared off and saved the Union army from disaster at Snodgrass Hill. He was rewarded for his efforts with an army command.

>> **Longstreet's Corps:** Fresh from Gettysburg and still believing that they could win the war on their own, these redoubtable men nearly did so. Leading another brilliant attack, Lee's old warhorse took advantage of timing and circumstance to deliver what should have been the killing blow for the Union army.

# Goats

These two goats were undone by their own stubbornness and unwillingness to listen to their subordinates. Thomas demonstrated that stubbornness was sometimes good, but these two generals did not attempt to understand the changes that occurred on the field and how they affected the course of the battle. Without a clear idea of what is happening, a battle degenerates into a confused mob of men fighting without direction or purpose — much of the two-day battle of Chickamauga took this form. Here are the goats that were responsible for the chaos:

>> **Braxton Bragg:** He fought his best battles against his own subordinates, not the Yankees. This lack of trust and support became a fatal flaw to his battle plan. Never having a clear idea of where the enemy was, he spent his army's strength in pointless attacks. When Bragg finally discovered the location of the enemy and saw that the enemy had been beaten, he suddenly became cautious. When the battle was over, he faced an open rebellion among his commanders.

>> **William S. Rosecrans:** Rosecrans began a brilliant campaign of maneuver and then threw it all away by starting a fight with his forces deployed in a manner that invited complete disaster. His poor leadership at Chickamauga led to a near fatal blunder. Within a matter of minutes on September 20, most of his army was swept away — and his future with it. Abraham Lincoln described him as "confused and stunned like a duck hit on the head."

# Turned Tables at Chattanooga

Bragg, as shaken by his victory as Rosecrans was by his defeat, prepared to starve the Yankees out of Chattanooga. Two important terrain features dominated the town — Lookout Mountain and Missionary Ridge. With artillery and troops on these two positions, the Confederates owned Chattanooga. All the roads except one (called the "Cracker Line" by the Union soldiers) were cut off, and supplies coming 60 miles across the mountains were not enough to keep the Union troops and animals fed. Confederate cavalry had a field day destroying wagon trains. As September turned to October, it looked like the Union would face a Vicksburg in reverse.

## Now Rosecrans is out

Rosecrans never regained his confidence after Chickamauga. Abraham Lincoln and General-in-Chief Halleck watched from Washington with dismay, as the

Army of the Cumberland wasted away. Unwilling to face another idle winter, Lincoln consolidated the Union armies into one administrative organization called the Division of the Mississippi, put Grant in charge of this organization, and ordered him to deal with the situation in Chattanooga. Grant's troops had been idle since Vicksburg; they were now headed for Chattanooga, as were two corps from the Army of the Potomac, the unhappy XI Corps and the XII Corps, both under-manned after the fierce fighting at Gettysburg (see Chapter 18). The Army of the Cumberland, trapped in Chattanooga, also got a new commander — George H. Thomas, whose response to orders to hold at all costs was quite simple. "I will hold the town until we starve." Grant himself was on his way to assess the situation in Chattanooga.

## Handling the problem: Davis arrives

Although it appeared that Bragg held all the cards, he was not so secure. The army was angry about the hollow victory, and his generals had sent a letter to President Davis requesting that Bragg be relieved of command. Bragg responded by removing all his senior officers from their commands, beginning with Polk. But if Bragg thought he was having trouble with unruly subordinates up to this time, he faced an entirely different situation with Longstreet.

Longstreet was frustrated with Bragg's caution and lack of initiative. He wrote to Davis, pleading that Bragg be relieved, for the army's sake. He even asked that General Lee take temporary command of the Army of Tennessee. Bragg's problem, in this situation, was that he couldn't relieve Longstreet; he still belonged to Lee in the Army of Northern Virginia.

### FORREST TAKES ON BRAGG

Nathan Bedford Forrest, one of America's great combat leaders, rising from private to lieutenant general, commanded the cavalry at Chickamauga. He watched the enemy retreat and pleaded with Bragg to take action to pursue Rosecrans's defeated army. Forrest refused to serve under Bragg any longer and made his feelings plain, telling his commander face to face: "I have stood your meanness as long as I intend to. You have played the part of a damned scoundrel."

He also warned Bragg that if they ever crossed paths again, Bragg would be a dead man — this from a man who killed 30 enemy soldiers with his own hands. Like other officers who opposed Bragg, Forrest ended up in another region.

The situation within the army was so bad that the President of the Confederacy himself had to travel all the way from Richmond to deal with the problem. As he had before, he did everything but make things right. He ignored the subordinate leaders' blunt assessments of the commanding general and kept Bragg in command, reassigned other commanders, and sent Longstreet off on a mission to push Burnside out of Knoxville. Sending him there had little military merit. Burnside was harmless, and Bragg needed Longstreet's 15,000 men to maintain the siege.

## Grant takes charge

Just as Longstreet departed on his curious mission, Major General Grant arrived in Chattanooga from Vicksburg. He matched Bragg's force when he gathered his reinforcements. He planned to break out of Chattanooga and drive south into Georgia, so he had to sweep Bragg's army off Missionary Ridge. Grant believed a frontal assault against entrenched troops was useless; he placed George Thomas's Army of the Cumberland at the base of the ridge to keep the enemy occupied. Thomas's job was to do nothing more than occupy the front line, as Grant believed the army too demoralized to do any more. The main effort would be directed against the Confederate flanks. Sherman's Army of the Tennessee would attack the Confederate right flank, while General "Fighting Joe" Hooker, rehabilitated somewhat after his defeat at Chancellorsville (see Chapter 17), would attack Lookout Mountain with most of the units transferred from the Army of the Potomac.

Hooker succeeded in taking Lookout Mountain on November 24. Since Longstreet's troops had left, the Confederate defenders on the mountain were now outnumbered by more than six to one. Hooker's men captured the critical terrain quickly and placed an American flag at the top for all to see. On the other flank, Sherman's attack made no progress, bogged down by very rough terrain and a masterful defense by Pat Cleburne's division.

## The soldiers take charge and win

The next day, November 25, Sherman renewed his attack, sending six divisions against Cleburne's entrenched troops. Grant gave orders to Thomas to move his army forward to take the Confederate trenches at the foot of Missionary Ridge and hold there for further orders. He wanted to keep Bragg occupied to the front, so he would not send reinforcements to Cleburne. Thomas sent 32,000 men in a sweeping charge that the entire battlefield could observe. Thomas's divisions took the front trenches but were exposed to enemy fire from above. Eager to prove themselves, they pushed up the ridge without orders. (Refer to Figure 19-1 for a map of the Battle of Chattanooga.)

## ARTHUR MACARTHUR

As an 18-year-old lieutenant of the 24th Wisconsin Regiment, Arthur MacArthur took the colors from a fallen soldier, in the face of intense artillery and rifle fire, and led the men up the steep slope. He planted the colors on the top of Missionary Ridge. He was awarded the Medal of Honor for his act of gallantry. Arthur MacArthur would go on to a distinguished military career as one of the great leaders of the postwar army. His son, however, would achieve far greater fame. Douglas MacArthur, who also received the Medal of Honor, became one of the greatest soldiers in American history.

REMEMBER

Confederate defenders at the top of the ridge were helpless: The infantry could not fire for fear of hitting their own retreating men. The artillery was improperly positioned to shoot at all. It was a spontaneous movement of men in small groups who took the battle out of the generals' hands and made it their own. They dashed up the steep ridge so fast that the Confederate defenders — who had all the advantages and until then put up a stiff resistance — broke and ran for their lives. It was one of the great triumphs of the war for the Union army, a triumph achieved by the soldiers themselves.

# The Battle's Aftermath

Unlike in earlier Civil War battles, Grant followed up this victory with a vigorous pursuit of the defeated enemy. One reason he did this was the relatively small number of casualties — about 5,800 out of the 60,000 men Grant had assembled. Bragg's losses were higher, about 6,700 for the 46,000 in the Army of Tennessee. In fact, many of the losses were prisoners or deserters rather than killed or wounded. Grant also dispatched a force to chase Longstreet away from Knoxville, pushing him into North Carolina. By following up his victory with aggressive action, Grant secured all of Tennessee for the Union.

After weeks of maneuver through southern Tennessee and northern Georgia, days of terrible and costly fighting at Chickamauga, and a month of siege, the strategic rail center of Chattanooga was firmly in Union hands. Bragg had thrown away several chances to change the strategic picture. Given every advantage, presented every opportunity by his opponent, Bragg wasted brave men in pointless frontal attacks. Even then he came close to winning but lost the will to make anything of it. After the humiliating spectacle of his army simply disappearing in the face of the Union army's attack (only Pat Cleburne held his men together to make an orderly retreat), Bragg provided his usual explanation — he blamed it all on his subordinates. By this time, even Jefferson Davis could not ignore the obvious.

Bragg had to go. Davis made the personally distasteful decision to hand over command of the Army of Tennessee to Joseph E. Johnston, a man he disliked intensely, and ordered Bragg to Richmond to serve as the president's military advisor.

# Heroes and Goats

At long last, the Union began to identify its heroes. In the months after Chattanooga, the North came to know these generals as heroes. On the other side, Bragg had ruined an army that had fought so well for so long.

## Heroes

The heroes who emerged from Chattanooga shared the same qualities: determination, a clear-eyed understanding of war, and aggressiveness. The men in the ranks began to sense that they were led by tough commanders who would bring the war to a victorious end. They responded in kind with a dramatic and spontaneous attack. Here are the heroes:

» **George H. Thomas:** Taking over command of the Army of the Cumberland from the dispirited Rosecrans, Grant asked for an assessment of the situation at Chattanooga. Thomas's words were like a tonic: "I will hold the town till we starve." Always levelheaded in planning and decisive when engaged in combat, Thomas's star continued to rise.

» **The Army of the Cumberland:** Shamed at Chickamauga and humbled and nearly starved out at Chattanooga, the men of the army were relegated to a minor role in Grant's breakout plan. Without orders and with nothing more than fierce determination to get the best of their enemies, they took Missionary Ridge in a mass assault.

» **Ulysses S. Grant:** After Chattanooga, he was promoted to lieutenant general, the highest rank in the Union army. Grant proved to be the man who was not afraid to fight. He had the ability to bend the enemy to his will. He accomplished this feat through an understanding of strategic goals, maneuver, deception, combined arms, and mass. Given all the tools of war that the industrialized North provided, he used these tools to their fullest extent. He became the man of destiny.

» **William T. Sherman:** Sherman was another Union commander on the rise. In 1863, he demonstrated the capability to lead armies. He understood Grant's intent perfectly, almost in the way Jackson understood Lee. He was tough, uncompromising, and always anxious to push the enemy hard and fast. Grant trusted him completely.

>> **Philip H. Sheridan:** He was another tough guy who emerged from the Western Theater. As a division commander, Sheridan had a reputation for hard fighting. Grant needed just such a combat leader in later campaigns.

## Goats

Bragg came up a goat in every battle that he fought — something was clearly amiss. His subordinates hated him, and the army disliked him, yet President Davis kept him in command. Finally, enough was enough, and Bragg was replaced. The Army of Tennessee, dispirited by Bragg's failures and demoralized by inactivity, responded in kind and ran from the battlefield.

>> **Braxton Bragg:** No officer ever had better intentions. And no officer, by his own actions, ever did so much to sabotage those good intentions.

>> **The Confederate Army of Tennessee:** How could men who had so often stood the test of battle fall apart like raw recruits? The answer lies in one word: morale. Morale is the fighting spirit of the army that allows it to survive immense hardships and dangers and still function. By late 1863, the distrust between Bragg and his subordinate leaders sapped the army of its remaining morale. The empty victory of Chickamauga and the wasteful siege at Chattanooga broke the bonds of trust between the leaders and the led. When faced with a charge up Missionary Ridge, they had no stomach for it. They fought with great skill and even desperate courage in later battles, but, at this point, they were done.

Chapter **20**

# Lee and Grant: Operations in Virginia, May–October 1864

In March 1864, President Lincoln brought U.S. Grant to the Eastern Theater after Congress passed a bill creating the rank of lieutenant general exclusively for him. George Washington was the only other officer who had held this high rank. Grant, who replaced Halleck, was now in command of all the Union armies — about 550,000 men in all. He began formulating a comprehensive strategy to end the war that would support Lincoln's national political objectives. The focus of Grant's efforts would be directed at two objectives: the Confederate armies in the field and the Confederacy's ability to fight the war. Of course, these objectives should always have been the focus of the military strategy, but no military leader up to this point had been given the authority to orchestrate and coordinate campaigns across several theaters to achieve a single strategic goal. More importantly, there had not been an officer up to this point capable of mastering military operations on a continental scale.

Grant gave both Major General Meade (Army of the Potomac commander) and Major General Sherman (now commander of the Military Division of the Mississippi) a simple mission: take on the Confederate armies until they ceased to exist. This meant not letting them rest, refit, maneuver, transfer forces from one theater to another, or escape to fight another day. Wherever the Rebels turned, a Union army would be there to fight them. Another part of the strategy involved attacking from several directions at once, forcing the Confederates to respond with their minimal forces to a number of simultaneous threats. By operating on strategic exterior lines and pressuring simultaneously in both theaters, the Confederates would be hard pressed to respond.

Grant's opening campaign in the Eastern Theater involved three separate attacks from three separate armies intended to overwhelm Lee and his feared Army of Northern Virginia. Lee's army was not strong enough to defend all of Virginia at once, confronted with threats to the Shenandoah Valley (a critical food production region, also known as "the breadbasket of the Confederacy"), Richmond, and his own force. Faced with such a situation, Lee would have to give something up. Whatever he gave up would weaken the Confederacy's ability to resist.

# Generals Get Their Orders from Grant

The less-than-brilliant but politically well-connected German immigrant Major General Franz Sigel was provided a small force of 6,000 men and ordered to clear the Shenandoah Valley of Confederate forces. Another less-than-brilliant but politically well-connected major general, Benjamin F. Butler, was given the 35,000-man Army of the James and ordered to move up the Peninsula to threaten Richmond. Major General George G. Meade's Army of the Potomac, with a strength of 118,000, would cross the Rapidan River near Fredericksburg and move southward, seeking to defeat Lee's army in battle. Grant decided to put Philip Sheridan in charge of the Union cavalry, now 12,000 strong, and also decided that as general-in-chief, he would accompany the Army of the Potomac to provide Meade with operational direction. Grant applied the lesson he learned during the Vicksburg campaign and at Chattanooga concerning logistics: The army would not be tied to a supply line of over 4,000 wagons. Instead, there would be a much smaller wagon train for resupply; the troops would march with what they initially needed, and ships moving up Virginia's rivers would resupply the army.

Lee's Army of Northern Virginia had a strength of 65,000 to 70,000 men at the beginning of spring 1864. General Beauregard, long relegated to obscure coastal defensive missions, returned to Virginia to command a ragtag force of about

25,000 men defending Richmond. Times were tough; the South had no more men and food was hard to come by. Yet nearly all of the men in Lee's army had voluntarily reenlisted and done so before the Confederate government made their service mandatory. Despite losses and hardships, Lee's tough veterans were just as dangerous as ever. They were ably led and devoted to their commander. They had every expectation of defeating the Union army once again and were not impressed by the reputation Grant had built in the west. Lee had the army spread in a wide crescent along the Rapidan River trying to protect as wide an area as possible and allow the army easier access to food collected from the countryside. The Confederate supply system at this time was so poor that army rations were infrequent and very meager. Increasingly, Confederate armies had to scour the countryside, obtaining food from local farmers. Lee was in a position, as always, to defend or strike out on the offensive if an opportunity presented itself.

## PROBLEMS OF COMMAND

With Grant now accompanying his army, General Meade chafed mightily at what he saw as a demotion. Grant was essentially giving all the orders and Meade and his staff did nothing more than relay them to the corps commanders. The Northern press had a field day with Meade, comparing the proud Pennsylvanian to a desk clerk, which drove him to near apoplexy. His resentment, plus the fact that Grant had inserted another layer of command, created delays in orders being passed that often led to problems on the battlefield. The Army of the Potomac, never a flexible instrument to begin with, was often less than responsive in the 1864 campaign.

## BEN "BEAST" BUTLER

Benjamin Freeman Butler was the archetype for the political general. A lawyer-politician from Massachusetts, he was short, heavy, and slightly cross-eyed — hardly the authoritative military figure. From the very beginning of the war, he developed a bad habit of taking action without authorization, most likely to embarrass or disturb the government. It was Butler who declared early in the war that escaped slaves were "contraband of war" and therefore could be confiscated, like other property. He started as a war Democrat and moved to become a radical Republican, which made him a very important figure for the Lincoln administration.

*(continued)*

*(continued)*

Butler was the commander of the occupation army in Louisiana and was so obnoxious that President Jefferson Davis declared him a criminal, with orders that he be executed immediately if captured. He became known throughout the South as "Beast" Butler. His political connections seemed to act as a magic charm that kept him in the field after many others of his type had given up. In 1864, Ben Butler's name was synonymous with military disaster. Given one more opportunity for glory in 1865, he was dispatched to capture Fort Fisher defending the last open Confederate port of Wilmington, North Carolina. Having all the advantages, Butler squandered them and made an ineffective attack before hastily sailing away at the word that Confederate reinforcements were arriving. Grant had him relieved and sent back to his home state of Massachusetts to await further orders. Since Lincoln had been reelected and Butler's clout in the Republican Party was no longer needed, Butler remained away from the war.

# Day One in the Wilderness: "Bushwhacking on a Grand Scale"

Grant took a page from Joseph Hooker's book and crossed the Rapidan River in an attempt to flank Lee's army, just as Hooker had planned to do at Chancellorsville in 1863. If Lee refused battle, Grant planned to place the army between Lee and Richmond. This certainly would force Lee to fight. His plan had the army crossing through the Wilderness, the same place that had been the scene of Lee's greatest triumph at Chancellorsville (see Chapter 17). The woods and thickets held a terrible meaning to the Army of the Potomac. They would again. Grant did not know how difficult it would be to move his army and the over 4,000 supply wagons through the area; it took longer than he planned. He could not maneuver in the thick undergrowth and lost the advantage of numbers. Lee was acutely aware that Grant was vulnerable and moved forward to take advantage of the situation.

Lee struck quickly with the two corps he had and ordered Longstreet's corps to join them. The initial encounter quickly turned into a large-scale brawl as thousands of men on each side found themselves disoriented, fighting in small groups in the woods filled with smoke from the burning powder from the weapons. Some soldiers refused to call it a battle, instead describing it as "bushwhacking on a grand scale." Officers had no control over the battle; orders were lost, and units joined the battle wherever they could. Artillery was useless in the woods, so the battle was conducted with individual rifle fire alone. A forest fire, compounding the stress and fear of battle, blazed through the day and into the night. Tragically, many wounded soldiers were trapped in the flames and burned to death.

# Day Two in the Wilderness: Grant Doesn't Quit

The following day, both Lee and Grant planned to renew the brutal battle. Grant ordered an attack, with weight directed against the Confederate left. Meanwhile, Lee sought to hold the Union army in place by creating a diversionary attack on the enemy's right flank, while bringing up Longstreet's corps to attack the enemy's left flank. Ewell's Confederate troops launched their attack just before three Union corps began their attack. The battle on the Confederate right halted in stalemate along the entrenchments dug during the night. Meanwhile, General Hancock, one of the army's Gettysburg heroes, drove his corps hard against the Confederate defenders on the right led by A.P. Hill. The Union attack crushed the Confederate line, and it appeared that Lee's army was beaten. Just as Hancock reported his success to General Meade, Longstreet's corps arrived, driving the attackers back and enveloping the Union left. The momentum had shifted suddenly and dramatically.

## Lee attempts a decisive counterstrike

The Confederate flank attack faltered in the undergrowth, and Longstreet suffered a near-fatal wound. Despite the state of medical treatment at the time, he was out of action for fewer than six months and back in command by the end of the year. The battle ended that night with neither side having made any progress and both glad for nightfall. The battle was one of the fiercest ever fought between these two armies (see Figure 20-1). In the end there were 18,000 casualties for the Union and 10,000 casualties for the Confederates. Lee had lost a corps commander and several high-ranking officers. The Confederate troops were in good spirits, believing they had won a victory. The soldiers expected Grant, like every other Union commander, to drag his beaten units back across the river and try again later. That didn't happen.

Unlike previous commanders, Grant had no intention of concluding the campaign. He stuck to his plan, ordering the army to maneuver left to outflank Lee and force him to fight another battle. Spotsylvania Court House was at the next road junction that would allow Grant to do this. Lee sensed that Grant would not follow the standard Army of the Potomac script. Lee then knew he would have to block every thrust Grant made, forcing the Union army to expend men and supplies for each step of the way to Richmond. Anticipating Grant's plan, Lee ordered his own army eastward to get to the key crossroads at Spotsylvania first.

# "GENERAL LEE TO THE REAR"

When Hancock's attack threatened the entire Confederate line, General Lee arrived to find troops running from the fight. As he unsuccessfully tried to rally the broken remnants, he saw the Texas brigades of Longstreet's corps wheeling into lines to engage the enemy. Seizing a battle flag, he ordered a charge that he would lead himself. The troops refused the order to protect Lee and thousands of voices began shouting "General Lee to the rear!" General Longstreet arrived, and convinced Lee to remain back. Longstreet, instead, led the men into battle himself.

**FIGURE 20-1:**
Battle of the Wilderness: Soldiers of the Union Army's II Corps (note the fortifications).

*Forbes, Edwin / The Library of Congress / Public Domain*

Confederate troops built entrenchments as soon as they reached the crossroads. This was the new pattern of the war — no one fought out in the open anymore. The veterans of both armies had learned some hard lessons and recognized the benefits of the defense — especially when protected by strong *breastworks* of logs with entrenchments backed by cannons that gave the defender the advantage against an attacking enemy. Because the Confederates were numerically inferior to the Union army, breastworks negated any manpower advantage the Union had.

The trenches and log breastworks were well built and formed the shape of a rough V, with its bottom tip pointed like an arrowhead at the Yankees. At the point of the V was high ground a mile in length and about half a mile wide, which held 22 cannons. It was the key to the Confederate defensive position. The Confederates called it the "Mule Shoe" because of its shape.

## The battle for the Mule Shoe

From May 10 to May 12, the Army of the Potomac attacked the Confederate trench lines. A late evening attack on the 11th temporarily captured the Mule Shoe, but a breakdown in the plan forced a retreat. The next day, Grant sent 20,000 men from three corps in massed columns to attack the Mule Shoe at dawn. It began to rain in the predawn darkness and continued all day. The Confederates had pulled back to the base of the Mule Shoe to shore up their lines, but with indications of an attack becoming apparent (20,000 men stomping around in the mud make a lot of noise), about 3,000 men and the 22 cannons were returning to the front lines when Union troops burst upon them.

The Union attackers easily captured the entire group with hardly a shot fired. The Confederate line had been broken, and for a second time just over a week, Lee's army was in danger of destruction. Instead of continuing the attack to broaden the breach, the 20,000 Union troops stayed in the narrow confines of the Mule Shoe. Lee pushed forces forward into the Mule Shoe to seal off the penetration. Again, Lee rallied his men, and waving his sword, he attempted to lead a charge into the Mule Shoe. Again, his soldiers prevented him from doing so, grabbing the reins of his horse and yelling "General Lee to the rear!" Before morning was over, the Yankees had been pushed back to the original line, where they stayed all day. Each side battled continuously for 24 hours across a wall of logs and mud.

## FAMOUS LAST WORDS

John Sedgwick, one of the longest-serving corps commanders in the Union army, was killed in front of the Confederate lines at Spotsylvania. Known as "Uncle John" to his men, Sedgwick rode forward to get a better look at the Confederate defenses. A soldier warned him of snipers. Sedgwick replied, "Nonsense, they couldn't hit an elephant from here," and he fell from his horse dead, struck by a Confederate sharpshooter's bullet.

The Union attackers controlled the Mule Shoe's outside, but the Confederates controlled the vital corner where the Mule Shoe connected to the main trench line. Here Union efforts focused on a secondary effort to break the Confederate line. This place became known as "Bloody Angle." There are only a few instances in the history of modern warfare where soldiers have fought with almost superhuman strength — the French and Germans at Verdun in 1915 and American Marines at Bloody Nose Ridge in 1944 at Guadalcanal are examples. The Bloody Angle is another.

REMEMBER

The fighting there was so intense that large trees were cut in half by musket fire alone. You can see one of these tree trunks in the Smithsonian Institution in Washington, D.C. Nothing like this had happened before. In all the brutal battles of the war, where hundreds of men fell in a matter of minutes, there was nothing equaling this. For nearly 20 hours, in pouring rain, thousands of men fought and died, standing a little less than an arm's length from each other. But the Confederate line held. Over the next few days, both sides recovered from the awful carnage before Grant renewed his assault, but the attacks were largely uncoordinated and failed as Confederate artillery fire blasted the Union ranks (see Figure 20-2). Lee also made an attack against the Union right that failed.

**FIGURE 20-2:**
Battle of
Spotsylvania.

Waud, Alfred R / The Library of Congress / Public Domain

By May 20, Grant had suffered 17,000 casualties at Spotsylvania. Lee's losses are unknown but estimated to be about 12,000. Thus, in over three weeks of fighting, the Union army had lost about 35,000 men to the Confederate army's 22,000. Both commanders requested reinforcements that replaced about half of their losses.

## Bad news for Grant

While the battle at Spotsylvania raged beyond his control, Grant received two pieces of bad news that wrecked his strategy for the Eastern Theater:

» After an abortive effort to capture Petersburg, Ben Butler's Army of the James, with 36,000 men, had been beaten in a fight near Drewry's Bluff, on the James River south of Richmond on May 13. Butler would soon be maneuvered into a neck of land sticking out into the James River called Bermuda Hundred. Beauregard entrenched across the base of the neck, sealing Butler's army and preventing it from doing any harm, and sending 7,000 men to support Lee — exactly what Grant did not want to happen.

» Sigel's small army had been defeated on May 15 at New Market, Virginia, by John C. Breckinridge with a patched-together force that included teenage boys from the Virginia Military Institute, where Stonewall Jackson had taught. Breckinridge had held the cadets in reserve, never intending to use them, but was forced to commit the boys in an all-out attack on the Union line. The climactic charge (also in a rainstorm) won the day. Sigel rapidly retreated, allowing Breckinridge to send 2,500 troops to reinforce Lee — exactly what Grant did not want to happen.

From a three-way coordinated strategic offensive, Grant now had nothing but the battered Army of the Potomac and the determination, as Grant put it in a message to Halleck, "to fight it out on this line if it takes all summer."

## Bad news for Lee: Stuart's death

On the heels of Longstreet's battlefield wound came terrible news from a place called Yellow Tavern, just 6 miles from Richmond. Philip Sheridan's 10,000 cavalrymen were given the green light to prove their worth to General Meade, who had little use for cavalry. Sheridan led a raid deep into Confederate territory to threaten the Confederate capital and link up with Butler's forces approaching Richmond from the southeast.

**TURNING POINT**

Jeb Stuart, with about 4,500 men, sought to protect the capital and hit the enemy column at Yellow Tavern. In a pitched battle there on May 11, Stuart was wounded in the stomach by a bullet. Such wounds were beyond the capabilities of Civil War doctors; Stuart died the following day in Richmond. Lee was now without the man who had provided him with the information that had made his greatest victories possible. He also lost a dear friend.

# Lee Loses the Initiative at North Anna

Failing to break Lee's solid defenses, Grant sidestepped and headed southeast. Lee pulled back to the next defensible position, the North Anna River, about 25 miles north of Richmond, to block the Union movement along the main roads that led to the capital. Lee then established a strong defensive position, guarding the main ford across the river. Grant recognized that he could not attack with any confidence of success. Grant decided to slip sideways again, trying to draw the Confederate army out in the open for a decisive battle, but Lee had suffered crippling losses, including many of his best officers; Lee's army was no longer strong enough nor were the leaders in the units experienced enough to take any bold offensive action. Lee could only respond to Grant's initiative, while keeping his army between the Yankees and Richmond.

# Grant's Disaster at Cold Harbor

Frustrated with the failures of his detached commanders, Grant replaced Sigel with Major General David Hunter and ordered him to strike up the Valley with his army to Charlottesville, destroying anything of military use to the Confederates. He also pulled the XVIII Corps under Major General William F. "Baldy" Smith from Butler's inexpert hands to reinforce the Army of the Potomac. On May 26, Grant again moved to outflank Lee. By this time, the Union soldiers had an unmilitary name for such a military operational maneuver: the "jug-handle movement." This time the destination of the army was Cold Harbor, an innocuous crossroads 10 miles northeast of Richmond. Again, Grant was confronted by strongly entrenched Confederate troops backed by artillery. As his troops dug in, Grant looked for an opportunity to attack.

Believing the Confederate army to be exhausted and weak, Grant ordered an assault on the Confederate line on June 3. The Cold Harbor defenses were not only strong, but also well laid out. The trenches were angled in a zigzag fashion so that an attacking force was exposed not only to fire from the front, but also to fire from each side. Lee's engineers had created a 5-mile killing zone. The veteran soldiers behind these imposing defenses were not ready to give up by any means. The Union veterans who understood what the attack meant wrote their names on small slips of paper and pinned them to their backs. This would allow comrades to identify them after they were killed.

REMEMBER

The battle lasted about an hour, but it was all over in 30 minutes. In that time, 7,000 men were killed or wounded. Those not killed outright were caught in a murderous crossfire and couldn't retreat. The men flopped on the ground and began to dig, using bayonets, canteen halves, penknives, and bare hands as they sought some protection from the bullets and shells. Grant regretted his order for the rest of his life. He had become impatient and neither his staff nor Meade's staff had done any reconnaissance or preparation before the attack. Ironically, he had reached the same point Union General McClellan had in 1862 but was no closer to taking Richmond than McClellan had been. And unlike McClellan, he had suffered over 60,000 casualties to get where he was — equal to the number of men Lee had in his whole army when the campaign had begun. Could the North bear much more of this? The already low morale of the North turned lower. For Lincoln and the Republicans, the political costs were enormous. The heavy casualties would only dampen the enthusiasm for Lincoln, who was waiting to be renominated for a second term during the first week in June. The Peace Democrats, gearing up for the 1864 presidential election, began to call Grant a "fumbling butcher" who sacrificed his troops needlessly.

# The Jug-Handle Movement to Petersburg

The Cold Harbor attack nearly ruined the fighting abilities of Grant's army, leaving him few options. He could try another end round movement, but that only would put Lee in the exceptionally strong defenses around Richmond, something Grant did not want. The direct attack had proven ruinous, so that option was out. Never for once thinking of calling off the campaign, Grant decided on a third option: Make Richmond undefendable and pull Lee's army out into the open by taking an indirect approach. The indirect route was the city of Petersburg.

## The strategic importance of Petersburg

Only 23 miles south of Richmond, Petersburg was the hub of five major railroad lines that connected from all over the lower South and southwestern Virginia. From Petersburg came the rail lifeline to the Confederate capital of Richmond. Supplies for the Army of Northern Virginia flowed through Petersburg to Richmond. If the Union army could seize Petersburg, Lee's army would be forced to abandon Richmond and reestablish another supply line.

Thus, Petersburg became the Army of the Potomac's new objective. But to get there, Grant faced some serious geographical barriers. First, the army would have to cross the James River, which was wide and swift, and had no bridge. The other problem was the city's defenses. Since 1862, a heavily fortified trench line with 55 artillery batteries guarded the city. If the enemy was alerted to the Union army's movement, reinforcements could occupy the defenses and make the city impregnable.

# Grant's plan

Grant needed to move the army secretly. He also needed to distract Lee from what was happening to his front. On June 6, Grant dispatched Sheridan and his cavalry to threaten the rail lines to Richmond with a diversionary attack near Charlottesville. To meet this threat, Lee was forced to dispatch his own cavalry force. Without his cavalry, Lee would not be able to scout the Union army's activities. On June 9, Butler dispatched 3,000 infantry and 1,500 cavalry to attack Petersburg, which at this time had about 1,200 defenders, mostly militia, teenagers, old men, and criminals let out of jail. The Union attacks were uncoordinated and half-hearted and had no effect. A sterling opportunity to capture the city and sever Lee's vital supply line with minimal effort had been lost. General P.G.T. Beauregard, who was in command of the defenses, made a number of frantic calls for reinforcements, but all were denied. Lee believed that the lack of activity to his front at Cold Harbor indicated that the enemy was "strengthening his entrenchments." Instead, Grant was already pulling units out of the front lines. He made his move during the night on June 12, heading for the James River and Petersburg, in one of the most skillful movements of forces in American history.

# General Beauregard's greatest moment at Petersburg

The XVIII Corps, under command of "Baldy" Smith from Butler's Army of the James, had been at Cold Harbor and took heavy casualties in the terrible battle there. As part of Grant's plan, Smith was ordered to move 14,000 infantry and 2,500 cavalry across the newly constructed 2,100-foot-long pontoon bridge spanning the James River and move west to attack the Petersburg defenses, which had still not yet been reinforced. Hancock would follow with the II Corps. One division in Smith's corps was composed of U.S. Colored Troops. As the divisions advanced toward Petersburg on June 15, they encountered Confederate cavalry, which delayed the advance and sent the vital information back to Petersburg that a strong enemy force was on the move toward the city. The defense of Petersburg was the responsibility of General Beauregard, who had been invisible since Shiloh. He commanded an under-strength brigade of 2,200 men, which he spread out over a distance of four-and-a-half miles. Most of his command had been sent to reinforce the Army of Northern Virginia at Cold Harbor; the rest were keeping the remainder of Butler's army trapped at Bermuda Hundred. He sent an urgent appeal to Lee, but Lee was hesitant to respond, still believing that the Union Army had not moved.

As his divisions approached the thinly defended Confederate lines, Smith took one look at the formidable earthworks with their heavy cannons and stopped dead in his tracks. This would make Cold Harbor look like a picnic; a thorough reconnaissance was necessary. Meanwhile, Beauregard was given precious time to shift his meager forces. Smith finally made a decision to attack at about 7 p.m. The assault on the defensive positions was made in small groups, rather than a massed assault. This attack succeeded in capturing a large section of the most significant defensive works. The delay, however, had allowed a fresh Confederate division to arrive to bolster the defenses, but even with these additional troops, Beauregard could not have prevented the Union forces from walking into Petersburg, yet the Yankees halted where they were for the night, even after advance units of II Corps arrived on the battlefield.

Lee slowly began to understand what was happening at Petersburg; he hadn't anticipated the enemy making such a great leap across the James. Grant's pontoon bridge, the longest in modern history, was a notable achievement, one of the great engineering feats of the war. It provided the Union army with an operational flexibility that did not exist in the Confederate army and left Lee uncertain of his enemy's exact whereabouts. He reacted quickly when the reports of the action reached him, ordering A.P. Hill's corps to Petersburg. Having dispatched Early, most of his cavalry, and Breckinridge to the Valley a few days earlier (see "The Second Valley Campaign" section later in this chapter), Lee's entire remaining force numbered only 35,000 men. Despite the haste, Hill would not be able to help Beauregard for several days. Beauregard was on his own, facing the ever-growing Army of the Potomac massing to his front.

Beauregard recalled the rest of his troops from Bermuda Hundred to Petersburg. He faced about 60,000 Union troops. During the night, Beauregard pulled his men from the outer line and began constructing a shorter line of defenses. Meade arrived and, like Smith, he was impressed by the apparent strength of the earthworks. Everyone was so impressed that no one thought to ask if such formidable looking defenses actually had any defenders occupying them. He, too, decided to wait and conduct a reconnaissance, while waiting for the IX Corps to arrive. The IX corps and II Corps attacked on the evening of the 16th but were driven back. The men had little heart in going against Confederate entrenchments – they were not going to die needlessly. Cold Harbor had broken their will.

That night, Hill's men began to arrive, along with Lee himself. Confederate strength began to build. Once the Union troops realized this, all the steam went out of the attack ordered for the 18th. No soldier in the Union army wanted to face Lee's veterans holding nearly impregnable earthworks. The attacks, such as they were, made no progress. Grant's bold movement had only succeeded in pinning Lee's army, not defeating it. There was no other choice except siege.

## THE 1ST MAINE HEAVY ARTILLERY

Since December 1863 the 1st Maine had occupied Washington's defenses. Because the threat of attack was nonexistent, it was easy duty. In 1864, Grant pulled this and other units out of the defenses and employed them as infantry. Their first engagement was at Spotsylvania, where they resisted Confederate General Ewell's attack on the Union left flank. On June 18, as part of Grant's order for a coordinated mass assault on the Petersburg defenses, the 1st Maine led the attack. As soon as the Confederate defenders started firing, all but the 1st Maine halted their attack. Of the 850 men who began that charge, 635 were killed or wounded as they crossed the open ground. The 1st Maine Heavy Artillery has the terrible distinction of suffering the greatest losses in one engagement of any Union regiment in the war.

# The Second Valley Campaign

Now that his army was locked at Petersburg, Lee attempted to alter the strategic picture as he had in 1862. Back then, with McClellan threatening Richmond, he reinforced Jackson's army in the Shenandoah Valley and threatened Washington, causing Lincoln to withhold reinforcements to protect the capital. This allowed Lee to take the offensive that became the Seven Days battles. Lee, of course, had no Jackson to depend on, yet the same strategic possibilities beckoned. He could send a Confederate force to threaten Washington and simultaneously take the pressure off the defenders of Petersburg and Richmond by diverting Union troops to protect the Union capital and chase the Confederates out of the Shenandoah Valley.

## Old Jube in the Valley

Jubal Early (see Figure 20-3), a West Point graduate, was a lawyer in Virginia before the war. He was a member of the Virginia convention that voted the state out of the Union. Though he'd cast his vote against secession, he joined the Confederate army to defend his state against invasion. Wounded at Williamsburg in 1862, he returned to the army and became an effective brigade commander. Promoted to major general in 1863, he commanded a division at Chancellorsville and Gettysburg. In May 1864, Lee promoted him to lieutenant general and gave him command of the II Corps to replace Ewell, who was incapacitated by illness (and had not performed to Lee's expectations).

**FIGURE 20-3:**
Jubal Early.

*The Library of Congress / Public Domain*

Early was tough, profane, unkempt, and usually irritable, but he knew how to fight, and his troops respected him. He certainly was not the master of operational maneuver like Jackson, but Lee had little recourse. His pool of talented leadership had diminished. Lee detached the Second Corps from the Army of Northern Virginia and gave it the title Army of the Valley. Early's mission was to disrupt Union forces in the Valley and threaten Washington. He was also to gather whatever supplies he could to send back to the army at Petersburg. Lee hoped that Early's actions would allow Lee to regain the initiative from Grant.

## Early distracts everyone

Early set out for the Valley with 8,000 men after receiving his orders on June 12. He joined forces with John C. Breckinridge in Lynchburg. After the New Market victory, Breckinridge's small army was being pushed hard by a Union force under Hunter, who took great pleasure in chasing the outnumbered rebels and wrecking parts of the Valley as he went. Early's arrival gave Hunter second thoughts. Believing he was outnumbered, Hunter retreated into the mountains, again leaving the Valley open to the Confederates.

## A TRIBUTE TO JACKSON

Along the way to Winchester, Early's army passed through Lexington, the home and burial place of Stonewall Jackson. Early now commanded the same units that Jackson had led. With great emotion, the army paraded past Jackson's grave in salute and viewed the ruins of the Virginia Military Institute, which Hunter had burned in retaliation for the cadets' participation in the battle of New Market. Many soldiers reported that their visit to Lexington inspired them to greater efforts.

Adding Breckinridge to his force along with other scattered groups, Early soon had 14,000 men. Before long he was at Winchester; soon after he was in Maryland, where Lee had opened his first invasion of the North in 1862. There he wrecked the Chesapeake and Ohio canal and held a town ransom for $200,000 (U.S. money, of course). His troops ranged far and wide, looking primarily for shoes. His cavalry threatened Baltimore, putting that city and half of the North into a panic. He fought a small but significant battle at Monocacy as Union troops tried to delay Early's supposed advance to Washington until Grant could dispatch additional troops from the Petersburg front to protect the capital.

As Early pushed toward Washington, he found that units of the VI Corps of the Army of the Potomac, moved by ship to the capital, manned the defenses. There was a small engagement on the outskirts of the capital at Fort Stevens, but neither side wanted to risk a major battle. Early pulled his army back to Winchester, with the VI Corps in pursuit. Along the way, Early's men laid waste to the area — an act of retaliation for Hunter's acts of destruction. The VI Corps followed but soon gave up the chase and returned to Petersburg.

## A VISITOR TO FORT STEVENS

While the Confederates exchanged artillery and rifle fire with the Union defenders, President Abraham Lincoln arrived, wearing his now famous stovepipe hat. To get a better look at the action, he climbed up on the wall. With his civilian clothes and tall hat, Lincoln was a conspicuous target. Just 3 feet from the president, a surgeon was killed by a sharpshooter's bullet. At that moment, staff officer Captain Oliver Wendell Holmes yelled out to his commander-in-chief: "Get down from there! You'll get your head shot off, you damned fool!" Lincoln immediately obeyed Holmes, who later became one of the greatest justices of the U.S. Supreme Court.

Early was a minor annoyance in the large scheme of things. Grant knew this, but the politicians in Washington didn't. Pressure mounted to do something about Early, whose presence in the Valley caused much agitation and swooning in the capital. Grant decided to get rid of the distraction once and for all. He sent Major General Phil Sheridan into the valley with 40,000 men and gave him the order to finish Early. Grant knew Sheridan would not have to be told twice or be closely supervised — that was one reason he brought Sheridan with him from the Western Theater to begin with.

## Early meets Sheridan

Early held Winchester, the gateway to the Shenandoah Valley and the starting point for any offensive action to strike Northern territory. Sheridan gathered his strength, watched Early closely, and then struck hard in September after Early had deployed his troops poorly. Sheridan and Early both lost about 5,000 men in the fight, but Sheridan could withstand such losses far better than the Confederates. It was the first time these Confederate troops had ever been forced to give up a battlefield to their enemy. They retreated with Sheridan in pursuit. He caught up with the Confederates at Fisher's Hill (about 30 miles from Winchester) and drubbed the dispirited defenders again. Early again made the mistake of deploying his troops poorly. He headed out of the Valley. In four days, Sheridan did what no other Union commander had been able to do — defeat Stonewall Jackson's men in the Valley.

## Reversal at Cedar Creek

But neither Lee nor Early was finished with the Valley. It was too valuable to leave to the enemy. A month later, Early returned to the Valley reinforced with 18,000 men, looking for Sheridan's army. He found it 20 miles south of Winchester, camped at Cedar Creek. Sheridan was not with them. He was in Winchester, on his way back to the army after attending a strategy conference in Washington. Grant wanted Sheridan to destroy the railroads and canals that supplied Richmond from the Valley. Sheridan thought that the destruction of the crops in the Valley would achieve the same strategic purpose and allow the army to be used for other purposes. On October 19, during his return trip, Sheridan met hundreds of panicked soldiers fleeing up the Valley turnpike, accompanied by wagons and walking wounded. They told a tale of disaster at Cedar Creek.

Sheridan's 20-mile ride on his horse Rienzi has become the stuff of legend (see Figure 20-4). Waving his hat, he moved among his men, urging them to rally and return with him to Cedar Creek. He reached the field and realized things were not as bad as he had been told (as you can imagine, soldiers running from a battle do tend to exaggerate the situation). Early had caught the Yankees unaware in a dawn attack, but the assault had given out about the time Sheridan arrived. Early did not give any subsequent orders, allowing the Union army to put its strength in numbers to good use by concentrating overwhelming force against the Confederates.

Waud, Alfred R / The Library of Congress / Public Domain

**FIGURE 20-4:**
Philip Sheridan.

By 4 p.m., the counterattack had begun and the Confederate army fell apart. Early gave up what was left of the old Second Corps to Lee at Petersburg and kept a small contingent at Waynesboro as a token Confederate force in the Valley. In reality, the Valley belonged to Sheridan. He mercilessly destroyed all that supported or supplied the Confederate army. The Valley was dotted with burning buildings and fields. In fact, residents of the Valley in October 1864 called this "The Burning," and many still speak of it today (see Figure 20-5).

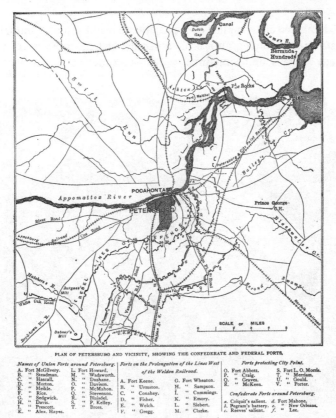

**FIGURE 20-5:**
Map showing Union and Confederate forts established during the siege of Petersburg.

PLAN OF PETERSBURG AND VICINITY, SHOWING THE CONFEDERATE AND FEDERAL FORTS.

| Names of Union Forts around Petersburg. | Forts on the Prolongation of the Lines West of the Weldon Railroad. | Forts protecting City Point. |
|---|---|---|
| A. Fort McGilvery. L. Fort Howard. | | O. Fort Abbott. S. Fort L. O. Morris. |
| B. " Steadman. M. " Wadsworth. | A. Fort Keene. G. Fort Wheaton. | P. " Craig. T. " Merriam. |
| C. " Hascall. N. " Dushane. | B. " Urmston. H. " Sampson. | Q. " Graves. U. " Gould. |
| D. " Morton. O. " Davison. | C. " Conahey. I. " Cummings. | R. " McKeen. V. " Porter. |
| E. " Meikle. P. " McMahon. | D. " Fisher. K. " Emory. | |
| F. " Rice. Q. " Stevenson. | E. " Welch. L. " Siebert. | *Confederate Forts around Petersburg.* |
| G. " Sedgwick. R. " Blaisdel. | F. " Gregg. M. " Clarke. | *a.* Colquit's salient. *d.* Fort Mahone. |
| H. " Davis. S. " P. Kelley. | | *b.* Pegram's battery. *e.* " New Orleans. |
| I. " Prescott. T. " Bross. | | *c.* Reeves' salient. *f.* " Lee. |
| K. " Alex. Hayes. | | |

*Getty Images*

# The Siege at Petersburg: July–October 1864

Sieges, by and large, are boring for the military history writer, mostly because sieges themselves are boring for soldiers as well. In a siege, nothing much happens. One side of a siege has locked the other side into a position, and neither can move without giving up something of strategic value. In this case, the Confederates could not afford to give up the strategic supply lines at Petersburg, especially since they lost the Valley; the Union could not allow Lee's army to escape and fight as it had done since 1862. The troops settled down to watching each other (see Figure 20-6).

Forts ringed the city. Men lived in dugouts (often called bombproofs) and occupied their time with guard duty in the trenches, always watching for an attack. Men were killed or wounded every day, but Grant could replace his losses; the Confederates could not. Grant now had the James River and the City Point railroad, where he established his headquarters and an enormous supply depot that efficiently fed and supplied over 100,000 men and 300,000 animals every day. The Confederates, relying on a broken supply system, often went without food and forage for days, and sometimes weeks, at a time.

O'Sullivan / The Library of Congress / Public Domain

**FIGURE 20-6:** Bombproofs at Petersburg 1864.

## Breaking the stalemate

Bored men can always find ways to occupy their time. And so it was with the 48th Pennsylvania Regiment, the coal miners who created a plan to end the siege. If the army couldn't attack across open ground, and couldn't get around the defenders, why not go underneath them? The coal miners proposed to dig a horizontal mine shaft 586 feet long, from their trench to a Confederate strongpoint. Underneath the strongpoint, the miners would plant explosives that would blow a hole in the enemy's line wide enough for the entire Union army to pour through and capture Petersburg. The 48th Pennsylvania Regiment belonged to the IX Corps commanded by Ambrose Burnside, the erstwhile commander of the Army of the Potomac. He had been rehabilitated, but he was hardly any more competent as a commander than he had been at Antietam or at Fredericksburg or at Knoxville. Burnside liked the idea and Grant approved the plan. The miners began digging on June 25.

# Burnside blunders

The miners performed an exceptional feat of engineering, overcoming many obstacles, not the least of which was lack of cooperation from higher headquarters, which provided almost no logistics support. Nevertheless, they completed the project in about a month and loaded four tons of black powder into the shaft beneath the Confederate position. Burnside, in charge of the operation, made his battle plan. Once the explosion was set off, a division of U.S. Colored Troops would move to hold the right and left flanks of the penetration while three additional divisions followed through the gap into Petersburg.

When presented the concept for the attack, Grant and Meade changed the plan completely, putting the U.S. Colored Troops last and the other divisions driving straight through the gap first, rather than covering the flanks. Two other corps would be lined up behind the Union lines to exploit the breakthrough. Burnside's plan, now completely changed, began to unravel. By drawing straws (of all things!), Burnside selected the division that would make the first all-important assault through the gap. As luck would have it, the division chosen had a commander who had only been in place for six weeks, and as it turned out, was a complete slacker.

# The Battle of the Crater

The explosion occurred at almost 5 a.m. on July 30, and it was incredible. It blew a hole 30 feet deep, 80 feet wide, and 170 feet long. The 278 men and 2 cannons that had occupied that space were obliterated. The Union's lead division marched forward, but instead of continuing through the gap as planned, stopped dead in the crater. Sliding down 30 feet of loose earth is one thing; climbing out of the bottom of a 30-foot hole whose sides are covered by loose earth is another. Brigade after brigade jumped in the hole — nobody could get out. As the men milled about, the Confederates reacted quickly as Lee shifted forces to plug the gap.

While artillery fired into the mass of Union troops, Confederate infantry counterattacked to drive the enemy back. The men trapped in the crater had no chance. Those who could ran back to the protection of the Union lines, leaving behind 4,400 casualties. Lee had lost 1,500 men. The gap was promptly closed, and the siege continued (see Figure 20-7).

In a court of inquiry held in the aftermath, it was discovered that the commander of the first division making the assault and the commander of the U.S. Colored Troops were both in a shelter behind the lines drinking rum when the attack began. Burnside was held responsible for not making any preparations for the attack, such as clearing obstacles from the front of his own trenches or flattening down trench walls. Burnside resigned in the aftermath, finally freeing Union soldiers from paying in blood for the consequences of his decisions.

**FIGURE 20-7:**
Battle of
the Crater.

Waud, Alfred R / The Library of Congress / Public Domain

## The siege continues

After the debacle at the Crater, Grant stopped trying to attack the Confederate defenses directly. Instead, he extended his trench lines southwestward, trying to completely surround the city and cut off the vital rail lines. To protect these rail lines, the Confederates would have to extend their own trench lines to keep the enemy from flanking their defenses. Each one of these movements was accompanied by nearly continuous fighting through the summer and fall until the oncoming winter weather turned the roads into quagmires, preventing any large movement of forces. Throughout these months, Grant deftly handled his forces, continuously shifting corps and divisions in and out of the line to threaten Richmond and force Lee to pull his troops from the Petersburg defenses to meet the threat, while also striking at the rail lines south of the city in small but very violent encounters. Each time an advance was made, strong Confederate counterattacks had to be fought off so that a new fort could be constructed and the siege line extended. Unlike Grant, Lee did not have the manpower to occupy the everlengthening trench lines. At some point, he would be stretched too thin, allowing Grant to attack anywhere along the line and break through. As winter set in, and with only one rail line left under Confederate control, Lee's men, facing starvation, hung on stubbornly.

Chapter **21**

# The Atlanta Campaign and a Guarantee of Union Victory, May–December 1864

While Ulysses S. Grant sent George C. Meade's Army of the Potomac into Virginia to destroy Lee's Army of Northern Virginia in the Eastern Theater, he also sent William T. Sherman, with the combined armies of nearly 100,000 men, into Georgia to destroy the Confederate Army of Tennessee, commanded by Joseph E. Johnston.

Although the objectives of these two campaigns were the same, the campaigns themselves were conducted differently. Grant, overseeing Meade, battered the Confederate army until it was locked into a siege at Petersburg. Sherman used more maneuvering than fighting, but he ended up in the same position as

Grant — locked into a siege. The city under siege was Atlanta, the last important rail center in the west-central part of the Confederacy. By this time, the Army of Tennessee had a new commander, John B. Hood. During Hood's tenure, things took a definite turn for the worse for the fate of the Confederacy.

# Taking Command: Johnston and the Army of Tennessee

**KEY PLAYERS**

With the removal of Bragg, after the disaster at Chattanooga in November 1863, Confederate President Jefferson Davis held his nose and appointed a man whom he intensely disliked as the new army commander. Joseph E. Johnston took command of the dispirited Army of Tennessee and began making changes, instilling discipline, granting furloughs, and offering amnesty to deserters. He obtained clothes and shoes for the men and put the army back in shape to fight a campaign. The army, about 50,000 strong, was entrenched about 20 miles south of Chattanooga. He had two corps, one led by William J. Hardee, a tested officer and the author of a book on tactics that every commander studied and employed during the war. John B. Hood, one of the best division commanders in the Confederate army, led the other corps. Hood had been a mainstay in Longstreet's corps, but he had suffered grievously in the war, having lost the partial use of his left arm at Gettysburg and having had a leg amputated after Chickamauga. Still full of fight, Hood was a favorite of Davis, but Johnston was not sure how Hood would fare as a corps commander. Johnston had a cavalry corps under Joseph Wheeler, who was a raider at heart, not a scout who could provide accurate information about enemy movements. In addition, Johnston was expecting that reinforcements from Bishop Leonidas Polk's Army of the Mississippi (currently in Alabama protecting Mobile) would raise his army's total from about 41,000 to 65,000 men. Unlike Sherman, Johnston had an uneasy relationship with his commanders, who, poisoned by Bragg's abrasive command style, did not hesitate to send backbiting messages to Richmond politicians, including Davis. Davis's intense dislike of Johnston inclined the president to believe the unflattering rumors being passed about the army's commander.

Davis, who had received inflated, self-serving, and totally inaccurate reports from these commanders on how ready the army was to initiate an offensive, urged Johnston to attack Chattanooga and move into Kentucky. Johnston was far too astute to see this proposal as anything more than pure fantasy. He had neither the resources nor the capability to defeat Sherman's forces in an open battle. Chattanooga was a Union supply base, now impregnable, and any movement northward would leave Johnston's army vulnerable to attacks from the flanks and rear. Besides, such a move would leave Atlanta unguarded. On top of that, there was no way the army could sustain itself on such a long march. When a political leader and a military commander do not see eye to eye, there is always trouble ahead.

## AN INTERESTING SIDELINE

Bragg had been removed from command of the Army of Tennessee but was kicked upstairs to serve as President Davis's chief military advisor. It might not have been a surprise, then, that Davis was urging Johnston to conduct an offensive into Kentucky — after all, Bragg had done it in 1862. Of course, he failed for all the intelligent reasons that Johnston cited for not conducting such an offensive in 1864.

# Preparing to Move: Sherman in the Western Theater

Sherman (see Figure 21-1) was given command of the Military Division of the Mississippi, essentially the entire Western Theater. This gave him command of the three armies he consolidated around Chattanooga to begin his campaign. These armies were well balanced with infantry, artillery, and cavalry and included "The Rock of Chickamauga" George H. Thomas's Army of the Cumberland, and the Army of the Tennessee, commanded by James B. McPherson, who had earned the reputation as one of the finest combat commanders in the Union army. In addition, Sherman had an independent corps and a cavalry division designated as the Army of the Ohio, led by John M. Schofield. Sherman had full confidence in his subordinate leaders, and they in him. It was a good team, with each commander both capable of acting independently, as well as operating in support of other army commanders.

**FIGURE 21-1:**
William
T. Sherman.

*The Library of Congress / Public Domain*

## THINK OF RED RIVER

Lincoln made his last foray into influencing military operations by peeling off a sizeable force of 10,000 men under the command of the incomparably incompetent General Nathaniel P. Banks, who had botched every assignment since 1862. Instead of using this force to threaten the Confederate critical port of Mobile, and thus draw off troops from Johnston to defend the city, Lincoln wanted to send a message to Emperor Maximilian, who had arrived as the nominal ruler of Mexico in April 1864 under direction of France's Napoleon III. This political-military expedition led to a comedy of errors as Banks attempted to move his army up the Red River. Between May 8 and 9, Banks was thoroughly outgeneraled by Major General Richard Taylor and defeated in two sharp battles. As Banks retreated, Admiral David Dixon Porter's fleet of gunboats supporting the operation was almost stranded in low water and escaped with difficulty. It is uncertain whether the emperor, still getting oriented to his new situation, took any notice. The units were returned to Sherman in June, who certainly put them to better use.

Sherman knew Johnston was a very capable commander, although not an aggressive one. In some ways, Sherman had to fight with one hand tied behind his back. He could not stray too far from his line of supply, the rail line that stretched several hundred miles from Nashville, through Chattanooga, to northern Georgia. He needed about 14,000 tons of supplies a day to sustain his army. To protect this lifeline from Confederate cavalry and guerrillas, Sherman had to reduce his fighting force by placing guards and outposts all along the tracks. He also had to protect Nashville, Tennessee. If this huge depot was captured or destroyed, Sherman's campaign was finished.

# The Campaign for Atlanta Begins

Sherman began his southward movement on May 4, the same day that Grant began his Virginia campaign. Johnston intended to delay Sherman's progress, to preserve the fighting capabilities of his army, and to inflict high casualties on the Union armies. Time was on his side. It was a presidential election year in the North, and war weariness was growing. A lack of progress by November could lead the voters to throw Lincoln and the Republicans out of office and force the new president to sue for peace. For his part, Sherman did not want to fight head-on battles with entrenched Confederate forces. Instead, he wanted to take advantage of Johnston's penchant for withdrawal and push the Army of Tennessee into a place where it could be destroyed. The Atlanta campaign loomed large in both

Sherman and Johnston's thinking. It was the key to success for both commanders. Johnston, for his part, had to protect the city from capture. Sherman needed to control the city to further demolish the Confederacy's capacity to fight the war. Both Sherman and Johnston expected to fight a battle for the city, but neither wanted to expose his army to an attack. Thus, the campaign resembled two wary fighters protecting themselves, but seeking an opening to deliver a devastating body blow.

## The Sherman sidestep

With its mountains and deep passes, the geography of northern Georgia (see Figure 21-2) gave the advantage to the defender. However, an aggressor with more troops can outflank a weaker opponent by using the number of passes available in the mountains. Sherman engaged the entrenched Confederate defenders only with enough force to keep them in place, while he used the rest of his army to get around and behind the entrenched troops. Sherman's approach seemed clear enough to one Union soldier: "Sherman'll never go to hell. He will flank the devil and make heaven in spite of the guards."

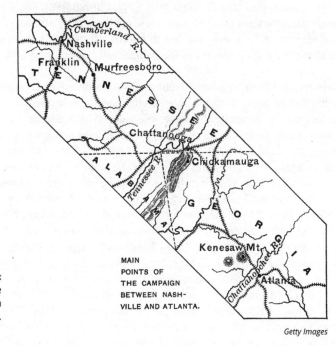

**FIGURE 21-2:** Map of the Atlanta campaign.

Getty Images

# The Johnston backtrack

Always mindful of his line of retreat, Johnston never let Sherman get fully situated before he skillfully fell back to another defensive position. Starting at Dalton, Johnston backtracked to protect his line of supply at Resaca. There, on May 14–15, Johnston fought off a Union assault and attempted his own flanking attack. He pulled back to Cassville, as Sherman slipped around Johnston's left, leaving Schofield and his men from the Army of the Ohio to face superior Confederate numbers. At Cassville, Johnston attempted to attack Schofield's isolated units, but Hood, who was to launch the attack, instead retreated, alarmed by (inaccurate) reports of Union forces threatening his rear. Johnston had no choice but to retreat to Allatoona Pass, a formidable obstacle blocking Sherman's advance.

The rail line Sherman depended on for his supplies ran through Allatoona Pass, so Johnston assumed the Yankees would fight to take the position. But Sherman fooled him. He had traveled through the area before the war and knew how difficult it would be to take. Sherman would have none of that fight; instead, he gathered all the wagons he could, stocked the troops with all the food and ammunition they could carry, and abandoned the railroad supply line to maneuver behind the Confederate defenses. Johnston had to send troops to cut off the movement, meeting the Union forces at Dallas and New Hope Church, both small towns along the Confederate defensive line. Johnston held off the enemy attacks and even initiated one of his own before Sherman began sliding off, again, to turn the Confederate right flank and regain control of the critical rail line.

At this point, Sherman played right into Johnston's hands. Hampered by rains that limited troop and wagon movement, Sherman decided to take on what he believed was a weak Confederate position at Kennesaw Mountain. Instead, Johnston's troops were in strong defenses. Sherman's assault on June 27 produced nothing, except about 3,000 casualties. A few days later, Sherman moved around Johnston again; this time Johnston fell back to the Atlanta entrenchments. It was July 10 — more than two months had gone by since the beginning of the campaign. Sherman had lost about 17,000 men (a small number by Civil War standards), but he had little to show for his efforts. Johnston had preserved his army, but he had ended up exactly where the course of the campaign dictated. The two sides faced the prospect of a long, drawn-out siege for the control of Atlanta, which threatened political disaster for President Lincoln. The siege at Petersburg was bad enough, but with two stymied Union armies merely watching entrenched and undefeated Confederate forces, a strategic stalemate such as this was too much. Johnston earned no praise for his maneuvers either. The Southern press was very critical of his constant retreats. President Davis was increasingly frustrated as well. Johnston had done nothing that he had instructed him to do at the outset of the campaign. Something had to be done in the president's mind to return the initiative to the Confederacy.

## THE BISHOP FINDS HIS REST

On June 14, 1864, in the midst of one of the small but tough fights of the campaign, Johnston, Hardee, and Polk had gathered on a hill named Pine Top to observe the approach of the Union armies. Sherman spotted the riders and suggested that a nearby Union battery take a few shots in their direction. Polk, an Episcopal bishop as well as a Confederate general, had just ridden up, intending to give his follow officers a copy of a religious pamphlet, "Balm for the Weary and Wounded," when an artillery shell hit him, killing him instantly.

**KEY PLAYERS**

Just as Johnston was preparing an attack on George H. Thomas's force while it crossed Peachtree Creek, Braxton Bragg arrived from Richmond to assess the situation (ostensibly) and relieve Johnston of his command. John B. Hood (see Figure 21-3) became the new commander of the Army of Tennessee on July 17. Hood had not been a loyal subordinate. He had played politics behind Johnston's back, criticizing him and passing back-channel messages to Richmond. The president and Bragg leaned toward believing the worst of Johnston and took the opportunity to relieve him in Atlanta. Unfortunately, Hood had not proven himself to be a competent corps commander, let alone an army commander. But the president wanted action, and Hood would do his aggressive, bull-headed best to deliver it.

**FIGURE 21-3:**
John B. Hood.

*Library of Congress Prints and Photographs Division[LC-USZ62-116391]*

# The Battle for Atlanta

The men of the Army of Tennessee had little faith in Hood; they had responded well to Johnston, and even after the retreats from north Georgia, the army was confident of success. Now that Hood was in charge, morale fell. On the other side of the line, morale went up; at least, Sherman's morale rose. Sherman had fought a cautious and careful campaign against Johnston, knowing that his opponent would give him few opportunities to strike, if any. Hood, an impetuous and often incautious man, would provide Sherman with openings that Johnston did not. Sherman did not have sufficient forces to surround the city completely. Therefore, he tried to cut off the three rail lines that fed into the city. Hood proceeded to strike out at the Union army in three battles between July 20 and 28.

Hood took on Thomas first, hoping to exploit the gap between Thomas and Schofield. Hood, perhaps, should have remembered what Thomas had done at Chickamauga. Again, Thomas was ready — this time with his troops dug in (see Figure 21-4). Hood's attack failed, costing 2,500 casualties. Hood then shifted his forces east, attacking McPherson's troops. Hood's men were outnumbered. McPherson was killed, but the Confederate attack stalled. Hood had lost another 8,000 men. Sherman shifted his forces to the west side of Atlanta, seeking to cut the southern, and last, rail line to the city. Hood attacked, once again, to stop this movement at Ezra Church. The Yankees again had entrenched and were able to stop Hood's attack. Hood lost another 2,500 men. The offensives had done nothing to alter the basic outcome of the campaign. Hood had lost about 13,000 men in confirming that fact, which the politicians in Richmond never understood. Sherman's cannons began to fire into the city.

## Sherman's supply line

For about a month, both sides settled into what everyone assumed would be a long, drawn-out contest — everyone except Sherman. To relieve the pressure on the city, Hood had sent his cavalry on a long raid to destroy the rail line Sherman depended on for supplies. Throughout the campaign, Union forces had been plagued by incessant attacks on their supply lines from Confederate cavalry leader Nathan Bedford Forrest. Sherman had established a system of repair that was so efficient that rail lines and bridges were repaired almost as fast as they were destroyed. Still, the single rail line and the awful, rutted dirt roads were vulnerabilities. It seemed as if the Confederates could interdict his supply line at will, and no matter how hard he tried, he could not put an end to Forrest. Ever restless, Sherman was not content to spend all summer watching Hood. He began to stockpile supplies, as he had done at the beginning of the campaign. His plan was to begin another maneuver around the city, once his army was free of its dependence on the rail line for supply.

**FIGURE 21-4:** Confederate fortifications outside of Atlanta.

*Barnard / The Library of Congress / Public Domain*

## Hoodwinking Hood

While Hood waited for reports of his cavalry raids, Sherman's army was quietly sidling southeast around the city, headed for Jonesboro, Georgia, a small town on the last rail line to Atlanta. With Union forces astride the railroad and essentially sitting in Hood's rear, Atlanta could no longer be defended. And so it went. What is remarkable is that Hood, now deprived of his cavalry, which were his army's eyes and ears, had convinced himself that Sherman had given up the siege and was retreating northward to protect his supply lines. He sent President Davis a message proclaiming victory and held a ball to celebrate. Reports came in that eventually convinced Hood that Sherman was now in Jonesboro with a large force. He hurriedly sent Hardee's corps to stop the Yankees on August 30, but to no avail. The Union troops were too strong, and the Confederates were too weak and too late. By September 2, with Sherman's full force astride his line of supply, Hood had to face reality — Atlanta was lost. Hood destroyed a rolling mill and 81 box-cars loaded with ammunition. The explosions signaled to everyone what had happened. To Sherman, the explosions meant only one thing, as he reported to Washington: "Atlanta is ours, and fairly won."

Hood had failed catastrophically. He had no conception of the political stakes that Atlanta represented for the survival of the Confederacy. As long as Atlanta was in Confederate control, Lincoln's political future was theoretically in peril. By gaining Atlanta when he did, Sherman undoubtedly contributed to final victory.

# Looking at the Navy's Contributions in 1864

Although the land campaigns in the Eastern and Western Theaters dominated events in 1864, the U.S. Navy made its own important strategic contributions to the crippling of the Confederacy. The blockade was slow but effective, as more and more supply ships and blockade runners were captured. But as long as the Confederacy had seaports, namely Mobile, Alabama; Charleston, South Carolina; and Wilmington, North Carolina, the blockade running would continue, and the South would continue to survive. In 1864, the navy directed its efforts against the last major seaport available to the Confederacy in the Gulf of Mexico: Mobile, Alabama.

Prior to the war, Mobile had been the main cotton-shipping port of the South. The bay had only one entrance, which was protected by Fort Gaines and Fort Morgan, and a string of 189 underwater explosive obstacles called *torpedoes* (mines). Any ship running into a torpedo would set off an explosion under her hull, sinking the ship. Not only were these defenses strong, but the Confederates also were building another ironclad, the CSS *Tennessee*, modeled on the CSS *Virginia*. This ship could serve two purposes: first, to protect Mobile Bay from attack, and second, to destroy Union wooden ships to clear the way for supply ships to enter and leave the harbor. Admiral Farragut did not want to see the *Tennessee* fully operational. He decided to take Mobile Bay by sailing his fleet directly into the harbor.

## FARRAGUT'S FIGHTING WORDS

While Farragut's order appeared to be the act of either a madman or a man with ice water in his veins, there is some background to the story. Farragut had been planning the Mobile Bay operation for nearly eight months. He was well aware of the torpedoes and spent a great deal of time in the weeks before the attack locating them. His reconnaissance discovered many of the mines, and he found that they had been in the water for so long that they were no longer functional. So Farragut's order "Damn the torpedoes, full speed ahead!" was based on a clear knowledge of the dangers and risks. This knowledge gave him the great confidence that led to victory.

On August 5, Farragut moved his fleet, a mixture of 18 monitor-type ironclads and wooden sailing ships, into battle line. Moving into the narrow channel, a Union ironclad hit a torpedo and sank; the wooden ships began shifting to avoid the torpedoes. This maneuver blocked the entrance to the harbor and left the rest of the fleet under fire from the two fort's guns. Now the ironclad CSS *Tennessee* appeared, with its captain Franklin Buchanan, who had been the captain of the CSS *Virginia*. This was the moment for decisive action.

Farragut, on his flagship USS *Hartford* (see Figure 21-5), was about the seventh ship in the line. He had tied himself to the rigging of the mainmast to get a better view above the smoke – a conspicuous target for marksmen on the *Tennessee*, who did take a few shots at the bold admiral.

Entered according to Act of Congress, November 10th, 1864, by McPherson & Oliver, in the Clerk's Office, of the District Court of the U. S., for the Eastern District of Louisiana.

**FIGURE 21-5:** USS Hartford.

*McPherson & Oliver / The Library of Congress / Public Domain*

Getting a view of the situation from his perch, Farragut decided to take the lead and bring on the engagement. As he gave the order to move forward, the USS *Tecumseh*, still in the lead, hit a torpedo, exploded, and sank in seconds. Someone warned him of the torpedoes in the channel. "Damn the torpedoes!" Farragut said, "Full speed ahead!" (His famous words have become a part of the Navy's battle heritage.) Once the *Hartford* led the Union ships past the channel, the *Tennessee* was no match for the sheer weight of numbers (see Figure 21-6). Never very seaworthy to begin with, the *Tennessee* was outmaneuvered, and her engines so damaged by cannon fire that she had to surrender. A combination of naval gunfire and ground forces maneuver led to the surrender of Fort Gaines on August 8 and Fort Morgan on August 23. The Union owned Mobile, blockading the bay and the Confederacy no longer had access to the Gulf (the city itself would not surrender until April 12, 1865). Farragut's amazing victory was welcome news to the beleaguered president.

THE GREAT NAVAL VICTORY IN MOBILE BAY, AUG 5TH 1864.

**FIGURE 21-6:**
The Battle of
Mobile Bay.

Library of Congress Prints and Photographs Division [LC-DIG-ds-04025]

# Checking on Presidential Politics of 1864

Lest we forget that war is never separated from politics, the presidential election of 1864 was a key event that ensured a Union victory. Although Lincoln is granted the stature today as one of the greatest presidents, he was not considered great in his own time. In fact, he was a very unpopular man in 1864.

People in the North were heartily tired of war by the summer of 1864. Grant had accomplished little and lost 80,000 men in the process. Sherman's progress seemed no better, with his slipping and sliding and accomplishing nothing. The human costs of the war were a heavy burden to voters of the North. In 1864, they had the opportunity to vote Abraham Lincoln out of office, the man who had got them to this point. Peace advocates became more vocal. The highly influential editor of the *New York Tribune*, Horace Greeley, told the president, "Our bleeding, bankrupt, almost dying country longs for peace." Many Northerners called for a meeting with Confederate representatives to end the war on favorable terms, leaving the issue of slavery out of the question entirely. During the summer of 1864, Lincoln was heavily pressured into opening peace talks with the Confederate government and even abandoning his abolition policy.

## The Democrats nominate McClellan

Since he had been relieved from command in 1862, McClellan had risen in the Democratic Party as a symbol of resistance to Republican policies. The anti-war Democrats (known as Copperheads) who advocated peace and reunion through a negotiated settlement controlled the party platform. The Copperheads, who disliked McClellan's pro-war stance, teamed him up with a Copperhead vice presidential candidate, Ohio Congressman George Pendleton. The Democratic platform attacked the Republicans for misusing the Constitution to suppress resistance to the war. If elected, the Democrats would call for an immediate cessation of hostilities and organize a convention of all the states to work together on a compromise to restore the Union. Of course, the Confederacy had no interest in returning to the Union; its goal was independence. However, Southerners stayed quiet, hoping to encourage the Democrats and continue the military stalemate until the November election.

No one, not even members of his own party, cleverly renamed the National Union Party, gave Lincoln a shred of chance to win the election. The party doubled down, risking everything by calling for the unconditional surrender of the Confederacy (echoing Grant's great public relations coup) and the abolition of slavery. But there were doubts that the incumbent president could carry such a platform. A movement was even afoot within the ranks to find another nominee at the convention. In late August, Lincoln wrote a memorandum acknowledging that he had virtually no chance of reelection. He pledged that it would be his duty to cooperate with the president-elect but resolved to save the Union's chances of victory, between election day and inauguration day, because, as he put it, "he cannot possibly save it afterwards." Lincoln sealed the memorandum and had each member of his cabinet sign it unviewed, committing them to support his post-election policy.

## Atlanta and the soldier vote

The fall of Atlanta changed the entire face of the election. Atlanta became a symbol of victory. Sherman's triumph at Atlanta, along with Farragut's capture of Mobile a month earlier and the good news from Sheridan in the Shenandoah Valley, made final victory seem nearer. The Democrats now appeared trapped between a pro-war stance and a policy of peace. The Republicans and other pro-Union groups rallied solidly behind Lincoln. Lincoln chose Andrew Johnson, a war Democrat and governor of Tennessee, to be his vice president to pull votes away from McClellan and demonstrate bipartisan unity. The soldiers in the field also rallied behind Lincoln, seeing a quality in him that others might have not. Thousands of soldiers cast absentee ballots from the field. In trying to lock up the vote, Lincoln, as commander-in-chief, allowed his army commanders to grant furloughs to soldiers in states where absentee ballots were not used, so that they could go home in time to vote Republican.

## The election results

McClellan carried only three states, New Jersey, Delaware, and Kentucky, with a total of 21 electoral votes. Lincoln won 212 electoral votes, carrying the rest of the North and the Border States, including the new state of West Virginia. The popular vote was solidly in Lincoln's favor as well — 2.2 million (55 percent of votes cast) to 1.8 million (45 percent of votes cast). Republicans also controlled the state legislatures and governorships in all the states, except those that voted for McClellan, as well as heavy majorities in the U.S. House and Senate. Largely, the same people who had voted for Lincoln in 1860 voted for him four years later. Lincoln also gained votes in the Border States. And the soldier vote certainly helped impress upon the North that the men who were going to do the fighting and dying were willing to keep Lincoln in office.

For the Confederacy, Lincoln's resounding reelection spelled doom for their cause. The North was united in its goal to restore the Union by force, while rejecting Confederate independence. Although the resolve of the Confederacy was unshaken, the future looked bleak, their hopes now attached to the armies of Lee and Hood to turn the tide of war miraculously.

# Sherman's March to the Sea

Sherman was faced with a choice in the fall of 1864. He could follow the instructions of General Grant, which told him to destroy Hood's army, or he could accomplish the same goal indirectly by attacking the South's ability to make war. He developed a bold plan and a truly breathtaking grand strategic movement.

Sherman took no action against Hood in the month after the fall of Atlanta. Hood decided to draw the Union army away from the lower South by moving north to threaten Sherman's 400-mile supply line. Hood assumed that if the Confederate army could pose a significant enough threat, Sherman would be compelled to follow. Of course, Nashville was vulnerable. Perhaps the Confederates could even make another invasion of Kentucky. Buoyed by this shaky logic that had plagued every commander of the Western Theater, Hood began a doomed march with the Army of Tennessee. Hood was a bold but careless thinker. If Sherman's logistical lifeline was so vulnerable, wouldn't his be equally vulnerable? Hood failed to consider this question and planned for an advance northward with no concept of how he would supply his army on the march.

Sherman did not take the bait. He reasoned that he could chase Hood all over the country and still never catch him. He decided to make Hood's threat an empty one. First, he would detach 30,000 men to defend Nashville. Thomas would take command of these troops and gather other scattered units to protect Tennessee. Thus, Sherman proposed to ignore Hood and drive through Georgia from Atlanta to Savannah, living off the land and destroying Confederate military property with the rest of his army, about 62,000 men. He would meet with supply ships in Savannah and then be prepared for any other operational movement of his army (see Figure 21-7). Starting out, his army would have no supplies except what could be carried in wagons or on the men's backs. There would be no telegraph communications with Washington. Although Lincoln and Grant were skeptical of the plan, they accepted it, trusting in Sherman's skills.

**FIGURE 21-7:** Sherman's March to the Sea.

*Library of Congress Prints and Photographs Division [LC-DIG-ppmsca-09326]*

# Beginning the march: Soldiers take all

As Sherman's collection of armies departed Atlanta, it destroyed all of the city's rail and industrial facilities and storehouses. During and after the war, Southerners would accuse the Yankees of destroying much more than military-related facilities in Atlanta. Sherman divided his forces into two wings, marching abreast and stretching 60 miles in width. They were virtually unopposed. Only 8,000 militia total were available throughout Georgia to offer any kind of resistance. Sherman's men took whatever they needed from the civilians and destroyed everything else. Although soldiers were forbidden from entering private houses, they were authorized to take any food they could find (while supposedly leaving a reasonable amount behind for the civilians). They could take horses and mules and wagons; they could destroy mills, railroads, and cotton gins; commanders were authorized to destroy any property if the population displayed hostility. The looseness of these orders gave wide latitude to commanders, and they took full advantage of the situation. The unopposed march soon became an all-day excursion for the men to grab whatever they could find, vandalizing or destroying what they didn't want. Officers turned a blind eye to most activities, especially when encountering largely abandoned plantations, which Union forces believed deserved extra-severe destruction to punish the wealthy planters for leading the South to secession and war. In their wake, they left behind women and children facing a winter of starvation and destitution. The Confederacy — in fact, all government and civil society — ceased to exist for these people. "War is cruelty," Sherman told the mayor of Atlanta, "and you cannot refine it." Thousands of Southerners now experienced that cruelty, firsthand.

Sherman's army also collected people along the route of the march. Tens of thousands of slaves — men, women with babies, even children — simply picked up whatever possessions they could carry and left to follow the Union army. The Union soldier with the blue coat and brass buttons meant freedom. Sherman himself was seen as an instrument of the Lord. Some people followed him and his army all the way to Savannah, others appeared and disappeared, and many died along the way. Slavery, as an institution, simply disappeared in this part of the South.

## THE YANKEES ON THE MOVE

At Milledgeville, the Georgia state capital as it was named then, the Union troops were like frat boys on a holiday, destroying the library, holding drunken mock sessions in the legislature, visiting the women's penitentiary, and pouring molasses into the organ of the Episcopal church. At other times, these same troops took care of orphans, protected women and children, and saved lives with unselfish acts of bravery and kindness. Neither all bad nor all good, Sherman's march continues to raise arguments, especially in the South.

## A Christmas present

Savannah was strongly defended with entrenchments and protected by a small garrison of 9,000 men under the command of Lieutenant General William Hardee. Between December 17 and 21, Sherman deployed his troops in the hope of cutting off the city and winning it a fight. Hardee refused to surrender the city and made a brave show, but he knew that he had no chance. By December 21, the Confederates had escaped, leaving the city to Sherman. After nearly a month of silence, President Lincoln received a telegram from Savannah. "I beg to present to you as a Christmas gift," it began, "the city of Savannah, with one hundred fifty heavy guns and plenty of ammunition, and about 25,000 bales of cotton."

# Assessing Sherman's Impact

In about a month, Sherman's army had marched 300 miles, hampered only by cavalry and militia, through the heartland of the Confederacy, wreaking devastation on the land and the people. He had cut off another source of supply to Lee's army and was now in a position to join forces with Grant's army. By his own count, Sherman estimated that he had destroyed 200 miles of railroad track, $20 million of property that held military value, and $100 million of other property, which he chalked up to pure waste and destruction. Most of all, Sherman had demonstrated to the Confederacy that its cause was hopeless and its destruction was imminent. It was a brutal psychological blow aimed at the will and morale of the Confederate nation.

» Winning the decision: Thomas becomes the Hammer of Nashville

» Checking on the Battle of Nashville and its repercussions

Chapter **22**

# The Destruction of Hood's Army in Tennessee, October 1864–January 1865

Lieutenant General John B. Hood, who had earned his reputation for fighting as a brigade and division commander in Lee's army, had been given command of the Army of Tennessee after President Davis relieved General Joseph E. Johnston before the beginning of the siege of Atlanta. But Hood had mismanaged the defense of Atlanta, first by wasting his men in fruitless attacks, and then by letting his army be nearly trapped inside the city when William T. Sherman's forces maneuvered south to cut off the Confederate main supply line to the city. Hood evacuated Atlanta, but he was not finished. Afterward, in excusing his failure to Richmond, he blamed everyone but himself. Worst of all, he claimed his own soldiers lacked the offensive spirit. A visit from President Davis did nothing to improve the soldiers' morale. Davis not only decided to keep Hood in command, but he also bought into Hood's completely unrealistic plan to invade Tennessee. The president placed the fate of the Confederacy in the hands of an uncertain leader. He had considered replacing Hood with General P.G.T. Beauregard but instead put Beauregard in charge of the Military Division of the West, a largely meaningless position. Outside of Hood's army, few Confederate forces were available for anything.

While Sherman struck out toward the coast on his soon-to-be famous (or infamous) march, Hood marched his 40,000-man Army of Tennessee northward, seeking to find the opportunity to change the course of the war. He had a vague notion of an invasion, seeking to win victories that would lead the Union to give up the fight and secure the Confederacy's independence. Hood, however, was neither a strategist nor a tactician. His badly managed battles at Franklin and Nashville were disasters that wasted his noble army and doomed the Confederacy. On the Union side, Major General George H. Thomas would launch one of the best-planned attacks of any officer of this war, achieving decisive results and winning the war in the Western Theater.

# Hood Moves North

**REMEMBER**

Although General Hood seemed to think that he gained the initiative from General Sherman, this was not the case. Hood's supply lines were even more difficult to support than Sherman's. Food sources were inadequate, and the rail lines that might have supported the army were damaged. Hood began his campaign with no more than a week's supply of food. Meanwhile, Union forces scattered throughout Tennessee began to concentrate with George H. Thomas in charge. Major General John M. Schofield's army of 35,000 men was detached from Sherman to support Thomas.

In moving north to join Thomas and shadowing Hood's army, Schofield moved late from his position at Columbia, Tennessee, and was almost trapped a few miles north at Spring Hill. At Spring Hill, Hood fully expected to see the Union army surrounded by his forces the next morning — but the Yankees had quietly marched northward overnight, escaping on the main road. Hood had not made his instructions clear, and his subordinate commanders lacked any coordination, or clear idea even, where the enemy was. Thus, Hood's best opportunity to gain some kind of battlefield victory slipped away.

## Running quietly: Schofield on the lam

Schofield made it safely to Franklin, but the bridges that crossed the Harpeth River were gone. He had asked Thomas for pontoons from Nashville, Tennessee, to build a bridge, but they had not arrived. Schofield was in a tight spot. His troops were very tired, having spent several days and nights in hard marching; the Confederate army was coming up fast, and he was outnumbered; and finally, his back was to a river he couldn't cross. These three things add up to a disaster of major proportions. He did the only thing he could do — offset the enemy's strength in numbers by putting his own army in entrenchments to buy time until he could cross the river safely. When Hood arrived outside of Franklin, Tennessee, on November 30, 1864, he found the enemy dug in and waiting for him.

Upon seeing the Yankee defenses, Hood ordered a frontal attack. The attack made absolutely no sense. All the troops available to him at the time were two of his three corps (about 20,000 men), and almost all of his artillery had not yet arrived on the battlefield. Thus, he was negating any advantage he had in numbers, especially against an entrenched enemy. The charge was as magnificent as any charge launched in history — but it was hopeless. Men and bayonets were no match for artillery and massed rifle fire by veterans (standing in ranks four deep in some places) protected by breastworks. One Confederate officer said later, "It seemed to me that hell itself had exploded in our faces." Nevertheless, the Confederates somehow managed to break the Union line, but they were stopped by a Union reserve force. Despite the clear failure of his attack, Hood threw part of his third corps at the Union trenches in another futile, senseless assault. The fighting didn't stop until 9 p.m. that night. The next morning, with his entire army (or what was left of it) and artillery on the field, he did what he should have done the previous day: He began a heavy bombardment of the Union entrenchments. Hood quickly discovered, however, that he was firing at empty positions. Schofield had crossed the river that night and was headed for Nashville where he linked up with Thomas, who now had 55,000 men.

## Calculating the magnitude of Hood's disaster

Franklin cost the Army of Tennessee 7,000 casualties, twice the loss of men as Pickett's Charge at Gettysburg. The army lost 53 regimental commanders. Six general officers (including the incomparable Patrick Cleburne) were killed, one was captured, and six others were wounded. Losses were heavy among the brigade and regimental commanders as well. No army can withstand such leader losses and still function. Nevertheless, Hood continued his pursuit of Schofield all the way to Nashville.

# Triumphing at Nashville: Thomas's Brilliant Plan

George H. Thomas was never a man to be hurried. He never got excited, and he never wasted men on needless attacks. But when he was ready, no one delivered combat power like the Rock of Chickamauga. So, it was at Nashville. From Thomas's perspective, Hood's army represented no major threat to him. His army was protected by the strong fortifications around the city of Nashville, and Thomas's men were well prepared to defend it. But Thomas needed time to prepare his army for offensive operations. He gave detailed instructions to his subordinate commanders, and he coordinated with the navy to secure the Cumberland River and prevent the Confederate army from crossing and bypassing Nashville. He waited for fresh horses to arrive for his cavalry. Finally, when his plan was ready, he had to postpone the attack to wait for a winter storm to pass.

Upon arriving at Nashville, Hood decided that he had learned his lesson at Franklin; he would not attack entrenched troops again. He had a novel approach as an alternative; he would set up in a defensive position with his force of about 23,000 men and wait for Thomas to attack *him.* Then Hood's army would counterattack and capture the city. It was not much of a plan, but it was about all he could do at that point. Although Richmond pressed Hood to bypass Nashville and head into Kentucky (again!) to gather recruits and supplies, Hood showed a modicum of sensibility, recognizing that his army had culminated and did not have the capability to do anything but sit in place. He therefore watched and waited for two weeks as his troops built up defenses and searched for food. Then he sent his cavalry and two infantry brigades away under cavalry commander Nathan Bedford Forrest to try and cut Thomas's supply line and harass the Union garrison at Murfreesboro. His timing could not have been worse.

Not only had Union and Confederate troops been watching each other for two weeks at Nashville, but General-in-Chief Ulysses Grant and the politicians in Washington had been watching as well. Hood's army outside of Nashville, no matter how inconsequential, was bad publicity for the administration. Grant felt pressured to prod Thomas into action, gently at first, then more insistently. He grew impatient with what he saw as Thomas's slowness. Hood was right in front of him! Why didn't he finish him off and get it over with? Thomas explained he was not ready yet and that he would deal with the Confederates when he was ready. This kind of attitude infuriated Grant. He threatened to relieve Thomas if he didn't do something fast. Facing a terrible ice storm, Thomas waited for the weather to clear. By mid-December, Grant decided enough was enough and dispatched Major General John A. Logan to replace Thomas and clear the rebels out. Grant decided that he too would follow Logan to Nashville. By the time Logan arrived, relief orders in hand, Thomas had cleared away the rebels in stunning fashion.

# The Battle of Nashville

On December 15, the weather had cleared and Thomas was ready to make his move. The attack was masterfully planned and brilliantly executed. With 55,000 men, Thomas launched a main attack on the Confederate left flank, while mounting a coordinated secondary attack on the right flank. He maintained a strong reserve to exploit success at either flank and used his cavalry on the left flank to extend his attack in depth and simultaneously threaten the enemy's rear. Hood's men, outnumbered two to one, half-starved and demoralized, were hit everywhere at once. For once, even entrenchments did not offer the defenders any advantages against the onslaught. Hood had no cavalry on the battlefield, and he had not done anything to enhance his defensive position. He had no reserve to speak of. All he could do was retreat to a secondary position two miles to the rear. The next day, Thomas's attack was so overwhelming, hitting the Confederates on three sides, that the Confederate army simply disintegrated. Thomas sent his cavalry in hot pursuit; in his plan he had envisioned the need for fresh horses to mount just such a pursuit and had been willing to wait for them. The cavalry did the trick. The Union army had lost 3,000 men but captured 4,000 Confederates. No one knows how many Confederates were killed and wounded.

# The Aftermath

Forrest's cavalry battled constantly to save what was left of the Army of Tennessee as it retreated southward. The remnants of the Confederate forces — no longer an army — assembled in Tupelo, Mississippi, on January 10, 1865. Hood was relieved at his request, and about 5,000 men, all that were left, were shifted to defend North Carolina. No significant Confederate forces existed outside Virginia and North Carolina by early spring 1865.

# Heroes and Goats

Victory usually makes heroes out of otherwise unnoticed men. Even in defeat, there are heroes, and the Confederate Army of Tennessee had many who deserved far better than they got.

# Heroes

The following are the men who served with loyalty:

>> **George H. Thomas:** Almost relieved for being thought of in Washington as too slow. A brilliant officer and superb combat leader who had often been overshadowed by others in the Union army, he never complained or felt slighted. Yet when he had his chance, he took it and in one massive, well-planned blow, shattered a Confederate army and, for all intents and purposes, ended the war in the Western Theater.

>> **Patrick Cleburne:** Died a hero's death at Franklin, leading a doomed charge against hopeless odds. One of the Confederacy's finest soldiers was sacrificed foolishly, along with his brave men.

>> **The Army of Tennessee:** Marching and fighting with only the most minimal support, they followed Hood through a disastrous campaign. Could braver or more dedicated soldiers have done what they were ordered to do at Franklin and Nashville? It is quite doubtful such soldiers have ever existed.

# Goats

Well, there is only one.

As a tactical commander early in the war, Hood had depended on courage and violent assault to overwhelm the enemy, and he was quite successful. However, he had no business commanding an army. The command responsibilities are different, and the demands of a commander at this level are greater and far more complex, requiring significant skill, such as deception, movement of forces in a campaign, coordinating the maneuver of forces to put the enemy at a disadvantage, proper use of cavalry and artillery, logistics, and the design of a campaign. Hood was simply not up to the task. His tactical ineptness, one-dimensional planning, and dull-witted reactions destroyed the Army of Tennessee more surely than Union bullets and shells did. Hood's formula for success, the spirited assault, was no longer of any use by 1864, yet he never learned. In 1865, Hood resigned from the army and returned to Texas, a man who had given the Confederacy so much — but who also took so much away.

» Seeming still dangerous: "Lee's Miserables"

» Anticipating combining the forces of Grant and Sherman to finish off Lee

» Noting the Army of the Potomac finally achieves the promise of victory

» Fighting the last battles and the great questions in the aftermath

Chapter **23**

# A Matter of Time: Petersburg to Appomattox, January–April 1865

The Confederacy was in a desperate situation in 1865. Only a few ports were open, and those were barely functioning because of the blockade. The suffering of the Southern people intensified and the armies in the field were barely holding together. But as long as General Lee and the Army of Northern Virginia existed, the Confederacy was still alive. Trapped at Petersburg, Virginia, Lee understood that little hope remained. "It is all a matter of time," he wrote.

The Union sensed victory in 1865. Lincoln had been reelected, and the armies had been victorious everywhere. It seemed as though one more coordinated push would topple the Confederacy. Lee and his army could not be allowed to escape to carry on a war that would never end; the Army of Northern Virginia had to be eliminated. With Lincoln's approval, Grant would cooperate with Sherman on a strategic plan to do just that.

# The Strategic Situation in 1865

The strategic initiative in 1865 belonged solely to Grant. In February, Lee had become Grant's counterpart, taking command of all military forces in the Confederacy. But the title was an empty one. The Confederate forces, such as they were, had no capability for any significant resistance. Grant ordered Sherman — presently in South Carolina after the March to the Sea — to head his army northward to link up with Meade's army outside of Petersburg to destroy Lee. Meanwhile, Sheridan, with his army dispatched from Grant (and reinforced by the XIX Corps from the Gulf in a remarkable movement of forces from the mouth of the Mississippi to the Potomac River), would clear Early's Confederates out of the Valley. After doing so, Sheridan would rejoin the Army of the Potomac. By applying overwhelming mass against Lee, he would be isolated and trapped. Lee's only hope was to unite all Confederate forces for a final defensive stand to save the Confederate nation. The Confederacy had only about 100 days to live.

## A CRITICAL MEETING WITH THE COMMANDER-IN-CHIEF

Grant, Sherman, and Admiral David Dixon Porter met with the president on the *River Queen* in the James River on March 27–28, 1865, to plan the final act of the war. Lincoln was worried that more blood would be shed and hoped that the war could be ended without another great battle. Grant predicted that Lee would take some action to break out before the linkup with Sherman, but he believed that Sheridan's arrival would threaten Lee's vulnerable right flank. Sherman did not see Johnston as a major obstacle but agreed that Johnston should not be allowed to move toward a junction with Lee at Petersburg. Lincoln stressed his desire that the Confederate armies be disarmed and the soldiers allowed to return to their homes. He did not seek revenge or further cruelty imposed on the people of the South, but he placed his faith in the fact that having endured such suffering during the past four years, Southerners would be willing to submit again to federal law.

# Sherman on the move in South Carolina

Sherman's troops enjoyed the role as occupiers of Savannah, Georgia, and prepared to execute Grant's grand strategic plan. The navy had not been idle. In January, it captured Fort Fisher, closing the last major Confederate port at Wilmington, North Carolina. Sherman, with 60,000 men, now moved through South Carolina, the first state to secede from the Union (and in the minds of many Union soldiers, the whole cause of the war). "I almost tremble for her fate," Sherman wrote, "but feel that she deserves all that seems to be in store for her." They indeed treated her cruelly, burning and pillaging with extra gusto. Columbia, South Carolina, was almost totally destroyed by a combination of Confederate confusion and Yankee carelessness and malice. Charleston and Fort Sumter fell in February to the navy, while Sherman's troops now in the vicinity had cut the rail line and made the city untenable. Without Fort Sumter to guard the channel into the city, the Union navy could steam right up to the docks and unload troops.

By the time the avenging army had entered North Carolina, the Confederacy had gathered the remnants of several commands to resist the enemy's progress. Lee convinced President Davis to appoint Joseph E. Johnston again as commander of this force of about 20,000 men. It contained what was left of the Army of Tennessee, as well as the various garrisons from coastal cities, now abandoned. General Johnston was confronted with a commander's nightmare — how to stop Sherman's army without risking a general engagement that clearly would mean the destruction of his own army. Johnston had little time to think. Sherman was making progress through the Carolina lowland like no one ever had. Between Savannah and Goldsboro, Sherman's men had covered 425 miles in 50 days. Through swamps, flooded bottomland, or swollen rivers, Sherman's army moved relentlessly. With discipline and organization, the army built bridges and corduroy roads over terrain thought impossible to cross in wintertime. Johnston simply could not react to his enemy's speed of movement and fell back virtually powerless.

# The Confederate strategy

Lee had devised a plan to try to keep the Confederacy alive. For the first time in the war, there would be coordinated efforts between Confederate armies. Lee ordered Johnston to delay Sherman while at the same time moving northward to Petersburg, Virginia. There the two armies would join up and with their combined force defeat Grant and Sherman in one final battle that would cause the Union to sue for peace. It was a plan that depended on nothing but hope.

# Johnston takes a stand

Johnston's army at this time almost had as many generals as privates. Among the generals were Braxton Bragg and William Hardee. The fact that very few troops were left to command in the Confederacy indicated the state of Johnston's army — an army in name only; more accurately, it was a patchwork collection of various units. Nevertheless, Johnston believed that Sherman had given him a chance to strike a blow. Sherman's army was moving in two large columns separated by several miles. It was headed for Goldsboro, North Carolina, anticipating a linkup with two corps that had been landed on the coast and were moving inland. One was Schofield's corps, which Sherman had detached to shadow Hood's ill-fated northern movement into Tennessee. The overland and sea movement of this sizeable force was a triumph of logistics and army-navy cooperation, indicating the total control Union forces now had on land and sea. If Johnston had any chance at all to prevent this linkup, he had to do something now. Johnston deployed his army to hit the one wing of Sherman's army as it marched to Goldsboro and defeat it before the other wing could come to its aid.

On March 19, Johnston sprung his trap. As the Union troops attempted to clear the Goldsboro Road of Confederate cavalry and infantry, they were struck on the flank by a heavy attack. For most of the day, the outnumbered Confederates were able to keep the enemy off balance. But by the end of the day, numbers did tell, and the Confederate attacks lost steam in the face of strong and determined resistance. Now whenever attacked, Sherman's troops began digging in. As the Confederate troops broke one line, they found themselves facing another line of entrenched soldiers with artillery. Bragg, true to his habits since Shiloh, ordered a frontal attack. The results were predictable and tragically uncalled for. By the end of the day, Johnston's men had fallen back to their original line. Meanwhile, Sherman was bringing the other wing of the army to the fight. Johnston had now dug in and was waiting for a Union attack. Sherman decided to wait and have the two corps join him so that he would have overwhelming combat power. Even while he waited, there was some heavy fighting on the Confederate left flank, as Johnston tried to prevent the Yankees from cutting off his line of retreat. After Johnston understood what Sherman intended to do, he had no choice but to retreat on March 21. The battle had cost him 2,600 casualties. Despite his advantage, Sherman took it easy after the battle. He had been hit rather hard, losing about 1,500 men, and he decided to rest and refit at Goldsboro as he had planned before moving on.

# The results in Carolina

Johnston had failed to prevent the linkup of Union forces at Goldsboro and had only given Sherman's massive army a bloody nose. There was nothing he could do to stop the enemy now. Reinforced by Schofield, Sherman now had 80,000 men and could deal with Johnston at his leisure. Still, Johnston had for once in his career stayed on a battlefield to fight rather than retreat. Even when faced with overwhelming odds, Johnston stayed, daring the Yankees to come on. But Sherman had learned his lesson at Kennesaw Mountain, just north of Atlanta. He was not about to spend lives needlessly. Johnston, for his part, showed his skill in pulling out from his defenses and escaping unscathed and technically able to fight again. As long as Johnston's army was in the field, Sherman could march all over the Confederacy and back for years, but still not win the war until it was eliminated. Johnston was at a point where his army, such as it was, could do no more.

# Lee's Fateful Dilemma: Petersburg

Lee's army had spent a summer and a winter in the trenches around Petersburg. It was not static duty. Lee was constantly shifting forces to meet threats directed at Richmond all the way to the other side of Petersburg, a distance of about 35 miles, to protect the Southside railroad, the last vital connection to the rest of the Confederacy. His 55,000 men were worn down from lack of food, disease, combat casualties, and worst of all, desertions. Lee lost 3,000 men in five weeks from desertions alone in the winter of 1864–1865. Every day the army was steadily shrinking. His appeals to the Confederate Congress for food and supplies for his men went unheeded. As state governments dissolved and supply lines broke down, the Confederate Congress had little capability to support the armies in the field.

Meanwhile, Grant's well-fed and -equipped troops, 120,000 strong, were stretching their trench lines and forts in a wider and wider arc, forcing the Confederates to extend along with them. By March, the lines were over 50 miles long. This thinned Lee's undermanned lines to an inevitable breaking point. There were simply not enough infantrymen to cover the trench line sufficiently to present an adequate defense. All it would take would be one solid thrust at the right point and the entire defensive line would collapse. Lee would have to abandon Petersburg and with it Richmond, the Confederate capital.

## Breaking out: Lee makes his move

The handwriting was on the wall. If Lee didn't do something soon, the Union army would simply out dig and outman his few defenders. Sheridan had driven Early's little force out of the Valley in March. Lee knew Grant would be calling Sheridan back to combine forces against him; Sherman was driving northward. Soon Lee would be trapped by overwhelming Union strength. Lee decided to break out of the stalemate and either regain the initiative to link up with Johnston in North Carolina or buy time for a withdrawal. His plan was to capture Fort Stedman (see Figure 23-1), the closest fort to the Confederate lines, in a dawn assault. With the fort under their control, the Confederate army could break into the lightly defended rear of the Union army and possibly escape. The attack began with Confederate troops going to the fort under the pretense of deserting (common occurrence at this stage of the game). The false deserters took out the guards and the follow-on assault succeeded in capturing the fort and about a half a mile of trenches. Before Lee could exploit his opportunity, however, Union reinforcements closed the gap and drove the attackers back to their own lines. Lee lost 5,000 men, most of them captured. Union losses amounted to 2,000. To Grant, these were negligible losses. In fact, no one in the Union army recognized this as a major attack and Lee's last attempt at offensive action. Lee's losses were devastating, leading directly to the final disaster at Petersburg.

**FIGURE 23-1:** Fort Stedman.

O'Sullivan / The Library of Congress / Public Domain

## A Crossroads: Five Forks

Five Forks was the major road intersection that led to the last rail line open to the Confederates at Petersburg. Whoever controlled this intersection controlled the railroad. Both Lee and Grant sent forces in that direction — Lee sent George Pickett (of Pickett's Charge fame; see Chapter 18) with a sizeable infantry force and Fitzhugh Lee (Lee's nephew) with the cavalry; Grant sent the aggressive Phil Sheridan with his cavalry and an army corps. This was an important development in the capability of the Army of the Potomac. For the first time large units of infantry and cavalry would combine their unique capabilities to outmaneuver and overwhelm enemy forces with firepower. Now speed and firepower were effectively combined to create a very effective combat organization. Although given strict orders from Lee to control this intersection at all costs, Pickett placed his troops poorly, and then he and Fitzhugh Lee went away to attend a shad bake (shad is a type of local fish). Sheridan's combined cavalry and infantry force ploughed into the Confederate defenses. At the shad bake, Pickett dismissed reports that his brigades were being wiped out. Only when Sheridan's cavalry troopers appeared on the scene taking prisoners did Pickett return to his command — or what was left of it. The defeated Confederates ran headlong for safety, leaving the last rail line to the Yankees, and leaving Pickett without a command. He had lost 5,000 out of the 19,000 men he had in the field (see Figure 23-2).

**FIGURE 23-2:** The Battle of Five Forks.

*Waud, Alfred R / The Library of Congress / Public Domain*

## Falling in flames: Richmond

Lee and Grant issued different sets of orders after the battle of Five Forks. Both knew the siege of Petersburg was over. Lee informed Jefferson Davis that he could no longer protect the capital of Richmond and that he was withdrawing his army west toward Amelia, about 36 miles from Richmond. Grant ordered a general assault against the Confederate line.

**TURNING POINT**

Grant's attack was overwhelming. Many parts of the Confederate line were not even manned so desperate was Lee for troops. Many units were captured in the trenches, while other units crossed the Appomattox River in fragmented groups headed for Amelia. Lieutenant General A.P. Hill was killed by Union troops advancing deep behind the Confederate lines as he tried to return to his command. On April 2, Richmond was abandoned; Confederate President Jefferson Davis and his cabinet boarded a train and moved to Danville, Virginia, which served as the last government center of the Confederacy. There, Davis issued a proclamation calling for continued resistance by the entire Southern population. As the government departed, the Confederates set fires to destroy military equipment left in the capital city. Soon the blaze raged out of control, destroying large parts of Richmond (see Figure 23-3). Mobs roamed the firelit streets that night looting and rampaging, while thousands of refugees fled the city. The following day Union troops marched into the smoldering former Confederate capital. President Lincoln himself arrived soon after for a tour of the city and sat in Jefferson Davis's office chair at the Confederate White House while an enigmatic smile crossed his face.

**FIGURE 23-3:** Richmond after its capture.

*The Library of Congress / Public Domain*

# The Last Retreat

Lee attempted to gather his scattered army together at Amelia Court House. He had ordered trainloads of food to be sent there. The troops had not eaten for several days, and they were marching hard and fast on muddy roads that brought them to the point of physical exhaustion. Nevertheless, Lee's subordinate commanders had skillfully conducted the retreat under enemy pressure. At Amelia, Lee had assembled about 30,000 men. Grant sent Sheridan south to block any possible Confederate movement in that direction to prevent a linkup with Johnston. Lee had no choice but to continue generally west, hoping to be able to turn the corner, avoid Union pursuers, and move south into North Carolina to meet Johnston (see Figure 23-4).

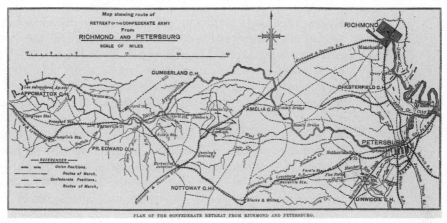

**FIGURE 23-4:** Lee's retreat from Petersburg to Appomattox.

Getty Images

But before any further plans could be made, the troops needed to be fed. At Amelia Court House the supply trains were there all right, but they were stuffed with everything from harnesses to ammunition — but not a scrap of food. Lee lost a day waiting for food that never did arrive and then resumed the retreat westward on April 6.

As Sheridan's cavalry shadowed the Confederate army's movement from the south, the Army of the Potomac was hot on the enemy's trail. The armies now marched day and night, one seeking to elude its pursuers, the other seeking to make up time. The pace of the retreat took a toll on Lee's men, and gaps began to appear in the line of march. Sheridan's cavalry took advantage, cutting off nearly half of Lee's army along with its supply wagons at Sayler's (or Sailor's) Creek. Union infantry pursuing the Confederate army caught up from behind and finished the job. Lieutenant General Richard Ewell was captured, along with about a third of Lee's army. At Farmville, just west of Sayler's Creek, the Confederate troops received their first food in nearly a week. Lee hoped to press on to Lynchburg, then swing south to meet Johnston, but the Yankees were giving the Confederates no breathing space. Sheridan sensed victory. In a telegram to Grant he reported, "If the thing is pressed, I think Lee will surrender." Lincoln received a copy of the message and passed simple instructions to his general-in-chief: "Let the *thing* be pressed!"

## Grant proposes surrender

Shortly after Lee's army had left Farmville, Grant arrived and watched what seemed like a nearly endless column of men in Union blue pass by. He sat down and wrote a message to Lee, telling him he no longer wished to spill any more blood and asked that he surrender his army. Lee was not done yet; he was headed for Appomattox Court House with the hope that there was still a chance to keep the army in the field, and with it, the existence of the Confederacy.

By the time Lee's battered army reached Appomattox, Sheridan's cavalry along with powerful infantry divisions were waiting, blocking the main road to Lynchburg and the last route southward. Lee ordered the Confederate infantry to sweep away what appeared to be a small cavalry detachment. As they advanced, the Union battle line appeared. Thousands upon thousands of infantrymen stood waiting. The Confederate troops withdrew into a defensive position. They were not strong enough to open the road, and the rest of Grant's army was closing fast behind them. Lee had run out of all options, except for the one that he hated the most. Flags of truce appeared, and Lee sent a message to Grant asking for surrender terms.

## The meeting at Appomattox

On April 9, 1865, in the little village of Appomattox Court House, Lee (resplendent in his dress uniform and sword) met with Grant (wearing a muddy private's blouse with general stars sewn on it) in the parlor of the house owned by Wilmer McLean (see Figure 23-5 for a depiction of this meeting). Lee feared the worst from Grant, though Longstreet, who had known Grant before the war, believed that Grant's surrender terms would be neither harsh nor vindictive. Longstreet was right. Certainly influenced by Lincoln's instructions at the March meeting on the *River Queen*, Grant proposed that Lee's army lay down their arms and surrender all military supplies. Officers could keep their sidearms and their horses. This stipulation prevented Lee from having to surrender to Grant the sword he was carrying. The man who became known in 1862 as "Unconditional Surrender" Grant saw no need to drive his enemy any further down by demanding Lee's dress sword. After the soldiers had been paroled, they were to be assured that the federal government would not molest them as long as they returned to peaceful pursuits. Lee asked Grant to allow soldiers who claimed horses as their own to retain possession of them. Grant, knowing how important these animals would be for spring plowing, generously agreed. Grant also ordered that 25,000 army food rations be distributed to the Confederate army. As Lee returned to his own men, Grant ordered that gunfire in celebration of the surrender be stopped. "The Rebels are our countrymen again," he told them. There was indeed a remarkable sense of camaraderie and generosity displayed by all ranks in the days that followed.

**FIGURE 23-5:**
Lee at Appomattox.

*Waud, Alfred R / The Library of Congress / Public Domain*

## THE CURIOUS STORY OF WILMER McLEAN

Wilmer McLean was an outspoken supporter of Southern independence. When the war began, McLean was living in a home near Manassas, Virginia, which just happened to be the site of the first major battle of the war. McLean's house became General Beauregard's headquarters. The house was damaged by artillery fire and occupied by Confederate troops after the battle, which ruined the house and property. McLean, a businessman who speculated (perhaps at times not altogether legally) in scarce commodities needed by the Confederate army, began looking for a quiet, out-of-the-way place where there would be no possibility of fighting. He purchased a home at Appomattox Court House. Just a few years later, however, the two armies again met near his home. Thus, in some ways, it can be said that the war began and ended at Wilmer McLean's house. Unfortunately, his house did not escape destruction a second time. Immediately after the surrender, it was nearly wrecked by Union souvenir hunters, who simply took or handed the protesting McLean money as they carted off his possessions.

# Symbolic Formalities: The Last Act

The day of the formal surrender of the Army of Northern Virginia was set for April 12. Grant, wishing to avoid the limelight, was on his way to Washington. Lee remained in his tent behind the lines. It was in a way altogether fitting that the final act between these two armies would be carried out by the subordinate commanders and enlisted men: those who had truly sustained their causes and knew intimately what the war had cost. The last great drama of the war was carried out by two of each army's best combat officers, Major General Joshua Chamberlain of the Union army, and Major General John B. Gordon of the Confederate army. Both men had fought gallantly throughout the war; both men had been badly wounded more than once, and now the two battle-hardened leaders would face each other one last time.

Gordon led the ragged but proud Confederate vanguard up the road to the formal surrender site to stack their arms and battle flags, marching silently between two solid lines of Union infantry. Chamberlain, deeply moved by the sight, gave the order for the Union troops to come to stiff attention and present their weapons in a marching salute. As Gordon recalled, it was "a token of respect from Americans to Americans." Gordon responded to the salute in a fitting act of Southern chivalry. He gracefully wheeled his horse toward Chamberlain, and as the horse dropped his head as if to bow, Gordon smartly saluted, bringing the point of his sword to his toe. He then passed orders that his own troops perform the marching salute in tribute to their former foes. All in all, over 28,000 men signed paroles and were released. Although Confederate soldiers were authorized free use of military transportation, thousands of men simply took to the roads headed for Texas, or Alabama, or Georgia, or North Carolina, or Mississippi — to go home.

## LEE MEETS MEADE

In the days following Lee's surrender, George Meade, the commander of the Union Army of the Potomac, crossed the lines to visit General Lee, whom he had known in the old army. The two exchanged pleasantries, and Lee noted the passage of time by making reference to the gray hair that now appeared on his beard since they had last seen each other. Meade conceded that it was not the passage of years that had made him gray, "but General Lee himself."

# Closing Events: The War Ends, a President Dies

Lee's surrender for all intents and purposes ended the war. But many other stories remain to tell of the last days of the Civil War. Just after the fall of Richmond, Sherman began his march northward against Johnston; his plan was to use three columns to trap the Confederate army now north of Raleigh, North Carolina. Governor Zeb Vance made contact with Sherman, pleading that the Union forces spare his state the devastation visited upon Georgia and South Carolina. He told Sherman that the Confederacy was finished. President Davis initially urged Johnston to keep fighting, but Davis was finally convinced that the only choice was an armistice to arrange terms of peace. By April 13, Johnston heard of Lee's surrender. Following Davis's instructions, he offered to meet Sherman to discuss terms of peace. A meeting was arranged for April 17.

REMEMBER

But the war claimed one more victim (see Figure 23-6), which changed the entire political landscape. Abraham Lincoln died at the hands of John Wilkes Booth, a pro-Southern actor, at Ford's theater in Washington on the morning of April 15. Sherman kept the news of Lincoln's death a secret to prevent his troops from taking revenge on the Southern populace or the Confederate army. For a man who had unhesitatingly laid the hard hand of war upon the people of the South, Sherman was eager to prevent any more destruction.

At the negotiations, Sherman revealed the secret to Johnston. Johnston turned pale and broke into a sweat, fearing the worst for the South. It was in this atmosphere of fear and uncertainty that Sherman and Johnston (along with the Confederate Secretary of War John C. Breckinridge, acting not as a Confederate cabinet officer, but as a Confederate military officer because he still held the rank of major general) negotiated a broad settlement, first as a way of gaining the surrender of all remaining Confederate forces, and second one that would establish an interim political settlement. In the document, all Confederate forces throughout the South were to surrender voluntarily. Sherman allowed the current state and Confederate governments to continue to operate and allowed Southerners to keep their property (which technically included slaves, although both generals assumed that slavery was dead) and their right to vote. This agreement was clearly far different from the instrument of surrender Lee and Grant signed. Sherman and Johnston were delving into political issues that went right to the heart of the causes of the war. The intent was to disband the Confederate armed forces peacefully and sustain the existing government structure until state officers had taken loyalty oaths to the U.S. Constitution and were accepted back into the Union by the new president. It outlined an easy transition from war to peace that in Sherman's mind reflected the goals of the late president.

**FIGURE 23-6:** Abraham Lincoln in 1865, his face clearly showing the strains of war (compare with his 1860 campaign picture in Chapter 2).

*Library of Congress Prints and Photographs Division [ LC-DIG-ppmsca-19469]*

# The politicians react

When the panicked politicians in post-assassination Washington, who were seeing conspirators around every corner and seeking scapegoats for the tragedy, received this message from Sherman, they went into fits. Although Vice President Andrew Johnson had been sworn in as the new president, the secretary of war, Edwin M. Stanton, was the de facto head of the government. Sherman was publicly censured and humiliated. He was told to negotiate Johnston's surrender based on the terms Grant had given to Lee — and nothing else. On April 26, Johnston and Sherman signed the revised agreement, and Johnston's pitiful remnants of the Army of Tennessee, not more than 25,000 men, disbanded.

## Confederate President Jefferson Davis is captured

Union cavalrymen captured Jefferson Davis and his ever-shrinking entourage near Irwinville, Georgia. Surprised at the campsite, Davis attempted to escape by running into a swamp. In the confusion, he grabbed his wife's shawl to serve as a cloak. A soldier put a bead on him and was ready to shoot, while Davis, ever the warrior, refused to stop, still attempting to make his escape. But his wife, Varina, threw herself on Davis to save him from certain death. As a final humiliation, the Yankees, seeing the shawl, later claimed that he was wearing women's clothing as a disguise. It became a very popular story in the triumphant North that dogged Davis the rest of his life. Davis ended up in chains imprisoned at Fort Monroe while the federal government pondered his fate. The other members of the Confederate government became fugitives, some even escaping to foreign countries to avoid Davis's fate.

## The last surrenders

News traveled slowly, and many Confederate units, especially cavalry, continued to fight. General Richard Taylor surrendered the last active forces east of the Mississippi on May 4, including Nathan Bedford Forrest's cavalry, defiant to the last. Nevertheless, Forrest set the example by agreeing to return home and resume a life of peace. "You have been good soldiers," he told the cavalrymen, "you can be good citizens." On May 26, General Kirby Smith surrendered all Confederate forces west of the Mississippi. This ended all organized Confederate military resistance to federal authorities.

# Victory and Uncertainty: The Reunited States

Lincoln was dead, and his desire for political reunification without animosity died with him. While the North mourned and the South stood benumbed and expectant, the radical Republicans and abolitionists stood triumphant. Without Lincoln acting as a brake on their agenda, many of them now spoke darkly of ensuring that traitors got their just desserts and that the slave owners who caused the war would burn forever in hell for their sins on the Day of Judgment. An ill political wind was beginning to blow that would soon become a raging storm.

# The last parade

Both Generals Meade and Sherman would have their day. Marching from Appomattox and Raleigh, the two armies arrived in Washington more than 220,000 strong, ready to march for a final time down Pennsylvania Avenue in a Grand Review for President Johnson and General-in-Chief Grant. Each army was showcased individually. The Army of the Potomac went first. It looked sharp, polished, and smart, in keeping with its heritage as a well-drilled and well-kept army (see Figure 23-7). Its performance was all that it was expected to be. Sherman's army — actually two armies — the Army of the Tennessee and the Army of the Cumberland, had been in the field since Chattanooga, and they looked it. Uniforms, weapons, and appearance were not up to parade ground standards. Yet when they marched, they displayed for the spectators the sublime meaning of victory perhaps more than their sister army did. They were rough and sinewy and marched with a bit of a swagger, having come here from almost half a continent away. Even the camp followers who had also become part of the army were in the parade — hundreds of freed people, men, women, children, and whole families in a motley caravan of wagons and live animals. After joining Sherman's march, they had never left the army. Now they were part of the victory as well. For over six hours the 110,000 men marched past the reviewing stand and into history.

**FIGURE 23-7:**
Army of the
Potomac II Corps
Grand Review
1865.

*Brady, Mathew B / The Library of Congress / Public Domain*

## SHERMAN'S REVENGE

Sherman had not forgotten or forgiven Stanton for his public attack for his negotiations with Johnston (see "The politicians react" earlier in this chapter). Stanton had accused him of everything from treason to presidential ambitions. Now, as his army triumphantly marched through the capital, Sherman shook hands with everyone on the reviewing stand — all except Edwin M. Stanton. As Stanton stood with his hand out, Sherman glared at him for several seconds before passing by.

## "Strike the tent"

As the nation returned to an uneasy peace brought by an ocean of blood, the former soldiers from both the North and the South found themselves in a country completely different from the one they had known. Everything had changed, and they themselves had changed most of all. A new politics was born in the aftermath of war, and as old institutions died as a result of the war, new ones would take their place. In place of a republic composed of states that held most of the power, the federal government now held power at the expense of the states. Income taxes, the draft, a national currency, federal courts, and constitutional amendments that were enforced by Congress were reflections of this new power. In 1865, the nation stood on the threshold of a transformation that would directly affect Americans for generations. Even today, we struggle with the war's meaning and how it continues to shape our understanding of who we are as Americans.

(*Note:* "Strike the tent" were reported to be the final words of Robert E. Lee, president of Washington College, when he died in Lexington, Virginia, on October 12, 1870. In a military encampment, tents are taken down, or "struck" before movement. Lee's words could have meant that the general was thinking of preparing for a final campaign, perhaps with Jackson again as his right arm. Or perhaps, he was calling an end to war and battle. The tent was no longer needed — peace had come at last.)

## A final thought

Before we leave this story, it is appropriate that we pause for just a moment to contemplate the following pictures. This first is a drawing (see Figure 23-8) of a regiment of soldiers getting ready to march. It could be either army, for the routines were the same for breaking camp, loading equipment, and assembling for the march to . . . somewhere. It could mean nothing, or it could mean everything for these men; another battle inevitably lay ahead. Yet both Union and Confederate soldiers fell into ranks and faced the dangers ahead with the same sense of duty and obligation to their comrades and to their country.

**FIGURE 23-8:** Regiment waiting to march.

*Waud, Alfred R / The Library of Congress / Public Domain*

The other four items are photos of unknown men who look at us from posterity. One is a Union soldier (see Figure 23-9) and one is a Union sailor (see Figure 23-10) One is a Confederate sailor (see Figure 23-11) and the last is a Confederate soldier (see Figure 23-12). Their youthfulness is striking; war is, after all, a young man's game. Each looks at us from across the bridge of time, asking us to remember them and to see them as they truly are: Americans.

**FIGURE 23-9:**
Unknown Union
soldier.

*The Library of Congress / Public Domain*

**FIGURE 23-10:**
Unknown Union
sailor.

*The Library of Congress / Public Domain*

**FIGURE 23-11:**
Unknown
Confederate
sailor.

The Library of Congress / Public Domain

**FIGURE 23-12:**
Unknown
Confederate
soldier.

The Library of Congress / Public Domain

# Winners and Losers: The Debate Lives On

Wars are won and lost for thousands of reasons. Civil wars, because of the bitterness and cruelty they entail, often result in long debates reflecting wounds that never fully heal. No one is ever satisfied with the answers because they hinge on so many variables. Nevertheless, several important reasons can be identified that serve as departure points for further debate and argument.

## Why the Union won

You can argue about *this* forever. There are many reasons why the Union won, but several will suffice to answer the question:

>> **The North's superior resources made the outcome inevitable.** Given all the resources the North possessed — financial, economic, industrial, manpower — it would seem inevitable that once all these resources were properly harnessed and employed, the Confederacy could not win the war.

>> **The Union had a coherent strategy (the Anaconda Plan).** From the very beginning of the war, the Union strategy was sound — blockade the South while controlling the Mississippi and drive on the Confederate capital of Richmond. Although it took four years to organize, it was the strategy that won the war.

>> **Lincoln and Grant collaborated well.** After Lincoln found a general capable of carrying out the Union's strategy, Lincoln and Grant worked closely together to ensure that the military objectives of the war corresponded with the political objectives of the war. Lincoln held a meeting with Grant and Sherman just a few weeks prior to the end of the war to outline their final strategy, including an outline of postwar intentions. Knowing the president's intentions allowed Grant and Sherman to use the military means necessary to achieve them and end the war.

>> **The moral power of fighting for human freedom.** Lincoln changed the entire nature of the war by issuing the Emancipation Proclamation. Without it, the war had no true goal. By proclaiming that the war was now one for human freedom, the Union gained a moral power that prevented European intervention on behalf of the Confederacy and sustained morale in the North.

# Why the Confederacy lost

We can argue about *this* one forever, too. There are many explanations, none of which tell the whole story, but these seem to be the most obvious reasons:

>> **The Confederacy ran out of time.** As long as the Confederacy could keep the Union at bay, either through military stalemate or a collapse of Northern national willpower, it could win the war, regardless of the North's superior resources. It was very close, but the Union stayed the course longer after the Confederacy had exhausted its resources.

>> **States' rights prevented unification of the Confederacy.** The very issue that created the Confederacy helped to destroy it. Individual state governors fought bitterly with Jefferson Davis to prevent him from consolidating power to fight the war. They withheld troops and supplies while the Confederate Congress spent its time arguing over the prerogatives of the states instead of prosecuting a war of national survival.

>> **Jefferson Davis and his generals failed to work together.** Davis wanted to be a general, not president. He never gave up trying to be a general in the area of strategy and selection of commanders to lead his armies. Davis unnecessarily interfered in issues of strategy, giving directions to his generals without ever giving them the means to accomplish his objectives. He made terrible choices for senior commanders in the Western Theater, often selecting men based on personal preference rather than qualifications. He stubbornly supported his favorites, even at the expense of overall benefits for the Confederacy.

>> **The Confederacy failed to gain the recognition of the European nations.** King Cotton diplomacy was meant to be a dagger pointed at the economic heart of Europe. Instead, it was a knife laid against the Confederacy's own throat. By purposely withholding cotton from European markets in the crucial first two years of the war, the Confederacy ruined its chances to win European support. Additionally, the Confederacy never clearly articulated its cause to Europe. Its clumsy defense of slavery, and key military defeats at the wrong time doomed all hopes of diplomatic recognition.

>> One more explanation for the Confederate defeat came from a Confederate veteran: "We just wore ourselves out whippin' Yankees!"

# 5

# Behind the Lines

**IN THIS PART . . .**

Time to go behind the lines, North and South.

Gain an appreciation for the experiences of the politicians, the common soldiers, the workers, the slaves, and women. Understand their unique contributions to the conduct and outcome of the war.

**IN THIS CHAPTER**

» **Surveying Davis as president and a government by improvisation**

» **From money to manpower to materials: Making war with almost nothing**

» **Looking at the Confederate Navy**

» **Working on foreign diplomacy**

» **Finding Confederate nationalism**

# Chapter **24**

# The Confederacy: Creating a Nation at War

With the establishment of the Confederacy in 1861, many enthusiastic Southerners made two big assumptions: The North would not fight, and the people of the South were totally united. It became obvious very quickly that the first assumption was incorrect. The second incorrect assumption revealed itself a bit less obviously but soon became an underlying theme in the story of the Confederacy.

As an anticipated short war became a long war of attrition and national survival, the Confederate government continued to expand its power in order to prosecute the war. Although the expansion of centralized power flew in the face of states' rights doctrine and was met with very bitter opposition from some state governors, the demands of war touched every home and family in the South. Everyone became a soldier in the struggle.

# Examining Jefferson Davis as President and War Leader

Jefferson Davis was born in Kentucky in 1808, a year before Lincoln, and about 100 miles from the man who would become his future opponent in war. The Davis family moved to the rich soil of Mississippi and made their fortune in cotton. Davis went to West Point, graduating in 1828.

After serving on the frontier fighting American Indians, Davis left the army to manage his Mississippi plantation and serve in Congress. He led the First Mississippi Volunteers as a colonel in the Mexican-American War and was wounded in the battle of Buena Vista. Davis became a senator on the strength of his war record, and President Franklin Pierce, a fellow war veteran and congressman, named him secretary of war in 1853. Davis proved himself an able administrator, engineering the Gadsden Purchase from Mexico to acquire land for the transcontinental railroad. From 1857 to 1860, he again served in the Senate, engaging in the fiery debates over Southern rights and slavery's expansion. Although not a secessionist, he joined his state and waited to hold some position of high rank in the army. But he soon found that he had been chosen for much different work — the presidency of a new nation.

Aristocratic and intellectual, Davis took for granted that everyone agreed with him. As a result, he had a reputation for aloofness. Although certainly disposed to a degree of coldness when dealing with people, his physical condition also contributed to his inability to build rapport. Davis was nearly blind in one eye and crippled by a series of painful illnesses throughout his adult life that made sleep almost impossible. Given the pressures of the presidency and the burdens of a desperate war, it was no wonder Davis was often out of sorts. Nevertheless, he possessed a powerful will and deep belief in the cause of independence.

From his first days in office, Davis suffered under a continuous barrage of personal attacks. One example will suffice. James L. Alcorn, a wealthy delta planter, called Davis a "miserable, stupid, one-eyed, dyspeptic, arrogant tyrant." Despite such attacks that wounded his personal pride, Davis saw the need to sustain morale by traveling the South, speaking to crowds and addressing state legislatures, always urging unity and renewing a fighting faith in the cause. He inspired the people of the Confederacy with his example. Unfortunately for a politician, Davis was extremely sensitive to public opinion and most sensitive to criticism of his choice of commanders and government officials. Although the personal attacks continued throughout the war, no one ever questioned that Davis was the best man to lead the Confederacy to independence.

## DAVIS AT WEST POINT

Jefferson Davis almost did not graduate from West Point. He had been caught at a tavern drinking liquor — a serious breach of regulations. He was tried by court martial and found guilty. Normally a cadet would have been dismissed, but his record saved him. This close shave should have kept him on the straight and narrow, but it did not. Davis risked dismissal by returning to the tavern. During one visit, he jumped over a cliff in the dark and nearly killed himself to avoid being caught by an instructor checking on wayward cadets at the tavern. He also was involved in an eggnog party that got out of hand, leading to a number of cadets being dismissed. Again, Davis was lucky; he had been put on report and confined to quarters early on and avoided being lumped in with the rest of the rowdies. He also reportedly got in a fistfight with another cadet, Joseph E. Johnston, over a girl. Johnston and Davis would have other altercations in the future.

Despite his experience as a senator and secretary of war, as president, Davis was a poor administrator who was obsessed with details and loved meetings. His cabinet meetings often lasted four to five hours, with Davis continually digressing from the main business at hand. Because the boss liked to hear himself talk, the typical result of these meetings was, in a word, nothing. As a result, many important decisions had to be readdressed repeatedly with the president.

As a war leader, Davis had a different approach than Lincoln. Davis took his constitutional role as commander-in-chief far too literally. He tried to be both a general-in-chief and a chief executive. He had proven himself a competent tactical combat leader, but he thought that experience made him a competent military strategist as well. This mindset made the temptation to meddle in military affairs irresistible. At the beginning of the war, Davis was often seen riding out toward the battlefield, trying to get a firsthand look at the action, as he did at Manassas. He often quarreled bitterly with his commanders, especially Johnston and Beauregard, over war policy and direction. He also played favorites, protecting the unpopular Bragg and the less-than-capable Hood despite evidence that neither was suited for army-level command. Lee, closest to the capital and the most visible of all Confederate commanders, masterfully dealt with the president, combining a mixture of deference and directness that made for a very good partnership. Unlike his commanders in the Western Theater, Davis left Lee alone in the Eastern Theater.

# Creating the New Confederate Government

From the very beginning of his presidency, Davis faced nearly impossible tasks. In February and March 1861, the Confederacy existed only on paper. Somehow the new government had to do everything all at once: pass laws to regulate trade and navigation, punish wrongdoers, create a workable postal system, find the money necessary to run the government, and assemble and sustain a creditable military force. The Constitution of the Confederate States of America varied more in tone than substance from the U.S. Constitution. Given the decade of wrangling (1850–1860) over the wording and intent of the constitution between the North and South, it was not surprising that the South emphasized the power of coequal states at the expense of the central government. In a reflection of the Articles of Confederation (in effect from March 1781 to 1789) that first formed the United States, the preamble to the Confederate Constitution recognized the "sovereign and independent character" of each state. While guaranteeing the inalienable right of an individual to his property, which of course, included slaves, the Confederate government also took steps to limit the future growth of slavery. At the same time, the Confederate Constitution made some variations that were intended to streamline the business of government at the federal level. Among the most important revisions were

 >> The president and vice president served a fixed six-year term. The president could not serve consecutive terms.

 >> Congress could allow cabinet officers to participate in congressional debates (but they could not vote) on any issues related to their responsibilities.

 >> The president could use the line-item veto, selectively disapproving and approving appropriations in a single bill sent to him for his signature.

 >> Congress could not fund internal improvements or provide any special protection to industry.

 >> The protection of individual property (including slaves) was recognized and guaranteed with no restrictions within the states and territories of the Confederate States of America.

 >> The expansion of slavery was intentionally limited. No new slaves from any country outside the United States could enter the Confederacy, and Congress could prohibit the importation of slaves from any state or territory not belonging to the Confederacy.

# Handling political troubles: No political parties

**REMEMBER**

At first glance, Davis seemed to have an advantage over Lincoln. He had no political parties to deal with. Lincoln was continually plagued by partisan politics between Republicans and Democrats in the North. But as strange as it may seem, Lincoln was actually better off and was able to accomplish more than Davis. Even though no political parties existed at the founding of the United States, it became clear that to conduct the business of government, political interests must unite around a specific set of principles or ideas. In the American system of government, political parties became the means by which consensus and compromise worked to accomplish the day-to-day business of the government. Without such organizations, the process of government quickly becomes every man for himself — exactly what happened in the Confederate Congress. As president, Davis had no political base of support to push his agenda through Congress and sponsor bills to become laws. With no political party identified as responsible for prosecuting the war, the president became the target for everyone's frustrations. Without political parties, pro- and anti-Davis factions emerged, especially over the centralization of power in Richmond. When not pointing fingers at Davis and his administration (or at each other), the members of the Confederate Congress wasted a great deal of time in chaos, each member shouting to be heard above the others. Needless to say, the record of the Confederate Congress is undistinguished.

## ROBERT TOOMBS (1810–1885)

Toombs is an example of the political figures Jefferson Davis had to deal with, but he was also typical of many elite Southerners — vain, proud, yet devoted to the cause of Confederate independence. Before the war, Toombs served in the Georgia state legislature and represented his state in the U.S. Senate. As Southern states began to secede, Toombs resigned from the Senate to join Georgia. He concluded his announcement by defiantly responding, "Come and do it!" to those who called for war against the South. He was named to the provisional Confederate Congress and became the first Secretary of State in 1861. Disappointed that he did not become president, he resigned after only five months and became a brigadier general. His military record was less than brilliant, except for a day of glory at Antietam, where he and three regiments spent most of the day preventing Union Major General Ambrose Burnside and his four divisions from crossing Antietam Creek. Angry over lack of promotion, he resigned and later served as state adjutant and inspector general of the Georgia militia in 1864. Toombs was always critical of Davis. (In Georgia, attacking the president was a popular political pastime.) Fearful of imprisonment, he left the country for several years at the end of the war.

# Unionist sentiment in the Confederacy

Not everybody is for war, especially when it is a civil war. Too many personal loyalties and economic ties cross sectional boundaries to achieve a total acceptance of war aims. The border states because of their unique location and the conflicting sympathies of their populations simply stood aside in the conflict, but they experienced continuous violence from armed partisans. As each Southern state voted itself out of the Union, a minority of individuals voted against secession. Most of these anti-secession or Unionist sympathizers were found in the Appalachian region of eastern Tennessee and western Virginia and the uphill country of Alabama and Arkansas. In these areas there were almost no slave owners. These anti-secessionists and Union sympathizers believed that a small wealthy elite who had nothing in common with their way of life dominated the South. They believed that secession and war was the cause of the elite, and they wanted nothing to do with the Confederacy. Although most Unionists in the South passively accepted their situation, conscription led to open resistance in many areas. In some parts of the Confederacy, anyone trying to enforce the conscription law took his life in his own hands. Many Confederate deserters headed to southwest Virginia, east Tennessee, or northeast Georgia where they formed bands of marauders, completely outside the law. In Texas, the immigrant German population was very strongly antislavery and vigorously opposed the war. The counties in the western mountains of Virginia were so strongly opposed to secession that they seceded from the seceded state of Virginia to form an entirely new state — West Virginia (actually a highly questionable legal action, especially when Northerners said that secession was unconstitutional, but this was war and allowances could be made). In areas where the Union armies occupied former Confederate territory, military authorities sought out and relied upon Southerners of Unionist sentiment to assist them in establishing a civil-military government.

# States' rights and the governors

In addition to anti-secession and pro-Union sentiment, Davis had another problem to deal with. The Confederacy had staked its destiny on the principle of states' rights. The Confederate Constitution placed the states in a position of power over the central government. The encroachments of the central government on the states had caused all the trouble in the first place and many state governors were glad to be rid of it. But the war created tensions between the Confederate government and the sovereign states. To prosecute the war, the government in Richmond imposed taxes on states and individuals, enacted conscription, and sought to expand its power by regulating the railroads and commerce to supply the armies in the field. Davis also suspended the writ of *habeas corpus*, an ancient and honored legal constraint that protected individuals against arbitrary government arrest. By suspending the writ, Davis imposed martial law wherever he considered it a military necessity. He did so in Norfolk, Virginia; Mobile, Alabama; and New Orleans,

Louisiana, at various times during the war. Generally speaking, those states that were least touched by war resisted the central government's attempts to consolidate power. The congressmen and senators who most strongly supported Davis were from states that had been occupied by Union forces.

Joseph E. Brown of Georgia and Zebulon Vance of North Carolina led the fight against the growing power of the central government and became champions of states' rights. Interestingly enough, Davis's greatest opponent was his own vice president, Alexander Stephens. Here are their issues:

>> **Joe Brown:** Brown was as loyal to the Confederate cause as anyone, but conditioned by years of opposing Yankee power, his first loyalty was to his state. Brown took the concept of states' rights to its logical extreme — he sought to create a semi-independent nation within a nation. Georgia would have its own defense force, its own defense industries, and its own financial base to support its own defense. Brown's interests were so focused on his state that he contemplated trying to negotiate a separate peace between Georgia, as a sovereign nation, and the United States when things started to go bad for the Confederacy. Throughout the war, Brown resisted the Confederacy's conscription and taxation laws. At every opportunity, Brown publicly and vocally accused Davis of trying to destroy the states and rule the Confederacy as a tyrant.

>> **Zeb Vance:** Vance, like Brown, was a strong supporter of Southern independence, but he believed that the war should be fought at the state level in order to preserve the power of the states. He was very protective of North Carolina's sovereign rights and attacked Davis unmercifully whenever he believed that the rights of North Carolina were threatened by any attempts to centralize power at the national level. Vance maintained vast warehouses of blankets, shoes, and uniforms that were never used. Intended for the use of North Carolina troops only, Vance refused on principle to release his stores to the Confederate government.

>> **Alexander Stephens:** Stephens, a tiny, frail, dyspeptic man from Georgia, believed in states' rights so much that he vigorously opposed Davis's attempts to mobilize the nation for war, fearing that the independence of the states would be compromised. He became so angry with Davis that he left Richmond to live in Georgia, where he launched an unceasing verbal and written barrage against the government. He thought the idea that independence must be assured over liberty was delusional. He seemed completely blind to the fact that unless the South won the war, all the individual liberty and states' rights talk in the world would mean nothing (see Figure 24-1).

**FIGURE 24-1:**
Alexander
Stephens.

*Library of Congress Prints and Photographs Division Washington,*
*D.C.[LC-DIG-cwpb-04947]*

# Financing the War

In 1861, like everything else, the Confederacy had to create a national finance system from nothing. The difficulties of raising money to fight the war created immediate financial problems that would soon prove to be insurmountable. The most easily negotiable means to purchase supplies was hard currency in the form of gold and silver. But hard currency was hard to come by in the Southern economy, heavily tied to agriculture. The wealth of the Confederacy was in land, slaves, and cotton, which were very hard to turn into cash money easily. People themselves had little cash on hand to provide credit to the government or pay taxes, and most of the banks in America were in the North.

Like all governments, the Confederacy had three ways to finance government expenditures: taxes, loans, and paper money — in that order. Taxation brings in hard currency that can be used immediately without incurring any debt. Loans and bonds are essentially government IOUs with the promise to pay the lender back with interest after a certain period. The least desirable way to pay for a war is to make your own money with a printing press. As long as people believe the piece of paper represents real money (hard currency), there's no problem. If too much paper money goes into circulation, people will have less faith in ever being able to exchange it for hard currency, and its value drops. Too much paper leads to rising prices and inflation, meaning it takes more paper to buy anything of value. The Confederacy, like the Union, used all three methods of war finance. But the Confederacy was forced to rely primarily on paper money to pay for the war.

## Confederate creative finance I: Bonds and taxes

Hard currency initially came from personal loans and money seized from the United States mint and customs house in New Orleans, but these reserves were quickly used up. To entice citizens to loan their hard currency to the government, Congress authorized the president to borrow $15 million in government bonds payable in 10 years at 8 percent interest. To pay the interest on the bonds, exported cotton was subject to a special tax. This bond was popular, but it dried up the last of the large cash reserves in the South. Later, Confederate bonds were sold in exchange for produce — cotton, sugar, tobacco, and rice — to support the armies. As the demands for money grew, bonds could be purchased with treasury notes, a fancy name for paper money.

The Confederate government did resort to taxation, but the results were never satisfactory. The government levied taxes on the value of slaves, luxuries, property, and merchandise. Because the real wealth of the Confederacy lay in land or slaves, the government taxes on these holdings were almost inconsequential, partially because payment of these taxes required hard currency. Later, the government would allow citizens to pay their taxes in produce, called a tax-in-kind. Taxes on imports were limited because most congressmen believed that high tariffs were characteristic of a Yankee government. Unfortunately, the Confederate government had no means to collect the taxes it levied or enforce the laws it passed to punish tax cheaters. In true states' rights fashion, the central government had to depend on the states to collect taxes that it levied. Not surprisingly, the states were less than helpful. Because of their power, state governments were allowed to pay federal taxes for its citizens, which they promptly paid with their own nearly worthless state-issued bonds or paper currency instead of hard currency. States were also borrowing money to pay federal taxes. As a result, by 1863 the tax system had pretty much broken down.

## Confederate creative finance II: Paper money

Because hard currency was so difficult to obtain, the Confederate government kept afloat on a sea of paper money, printing about $1.5 billion worth of treasury notes. These notes promised to pay the bearer hard currency two years after ratification of a peace treaty between the Confederate States and the United States. Thus, Confederate money was never considered legal tender like Union paper money was (or our own paper money is today). The value of Confederate money was backed not by gold or silver but only by an individual's faith in the future independence of the Confederacy. Whether the government liked it or not, the value of the currency was tied to its success on the battlefield. As long as the Confederacy won, the currency was solid; if the Confederacy failed, the currency lost value, and inflation was the result.

Inflation was the worst thing that could happen to a wartime economy. As prices rose and the paper money lost value, the only way the government could keep pace was to make more pretend money. With lots of paper money in circulation, both consumers and the government needed more paper to afford the same amount of goods. This led to panic purchasing — people rushed out to buy as much as they could that day because the same amount of money would buy less the next day. Such demands forced prices to rise even further and further and depressed the value of the currency. Inflation was also fueled by widespread shortages of goods. Prices rose about 10 percent a month on average during the war. Every new currency issue from the government would cause prices to rise even more rapidly. In 1863 for example, $275 bought a barrel of flour; by the end of war, flour cost $1,000 a barrel. Bad money drove out the good. Coins disappeared — they were too valuable to spend. The economy was awash with counterfeit Confederate bills and state currency. Ironically, money was so badly needed that the government considered counterfeit notes valid currency if they were turned in and stamped. The inflation rate climbed rapidly out of control: 100 percent by early 1862, 700 percent in early 1863, 4,600 percent in late 1864, and 9,000 percent in 1865. At the end of the war, Confederate notes were only worth about 1.7 cents each.

## The bottom line

As inflation drove the Southern economy into a tailspin, the armies began to feel the pinch as the government found it harder to purchase supplies. Food rations became less and less regular. Replacements for lost or worn-out equipment were no longer available. Day-to-day life behind the lines became very difficult for all but the very wealthy. Incomes could not keep pace as inflation and shortages drove prices ever higher. The Southern economy was reduced to a barter system. Union conquests of valuable farm and pastureland, wartime destruction, the widespread drought in 1862, and poor transportation led to severe food shortages throughout many sections of the South, causing enormous suffering. Hunger, and even starvation in some cases, was common in the last two years of the war. In 1863, there were food riots in Richmond led by women desperate to alleviate their hunger and no longer able to afford bread for their families. The riot was serious enough that President Jefferson Davis met the women rioters in the streets with an armed militia and announced, with watch in hand, that he would order the troops to fire if they did not disperse within three minutes. Not willing to test the president's patience, the crowd dispersed. To alleviate the suffering of the population, the Confederate government began what amounted to a social welfare system to provide public assistance to destitute widows and children. This system of welfare is another example of states' rights being challenged by the growing power of the central government in Richmond.

# Supplying Manpower for the War

Initially, both sides relied on volunteers to fill the ranks of the armies. After the first year of the war, however, the realities of soldiering and the heavy casualties tended to dampen the enthusiasm of potential new volunteers. In April 1862, the Confederacy passed the first *conscription law*, also known as the draft, extending the one-year enlistment of those volunteers already in the army and calling up Southern men between the ages of 18 and 35 for military service. The Confederate government sent agents into counties all over the states to enroll eligible men for conscription. After September 1862, the government extended the conscription age to 45; in February 1864, all men between the ages 17 and 50 were called into service.

Early in the war, there were numerous ways to avoid conscription. Those called upon to serve could hire a substitute, someone who volunteered to take the draftee's place for a certain fee. (This practice was abolished in December 1863.) Initially, schoolteachers responsible for at least 20 pupils, officers of state government, college professors, druggists, mail carriers, railroad employees, newspaper editors, workers in factories and mills, and other skilled workers involved in war production were exempt from conscription. In addition, overseers or owners of at least 20 slaves were declared exempt. Perhaps nothing the Confederate government ever did was as foolish as instituting the exemptions for slave owners and overseers, which became derisively known as the "Twenty Negro Law." The only people in the South who owned 20 or more slaves were the very wealthy. It appeared that the government was using the common Southerner's blood to save the carcass of the wealthy aristocrat. Many men refused military service, claiming it was a rich man's war but a poor man's fight. State governors only added to the general resentment and resistance to the draft by attacking it as a serious violation of states' rights. Some states had their own draft system (with their own very long list of exemptions) to supply replacements to local militia or state regiments. By February 1864 most exemptions had been abolished, and the 20-slave exemption was reduced to 15. Despite the general discontent with the system, most Southern men volunteered when faced with conscription. Conscription added as many as 300,000 men into the ranks.

# Supplying Material for the War

The Confederacy, being a newly created government, had enough trouble just getting organized let alone fighting a war. As a predominantly agricultural economy, the South produced very little for itself in mills or factories. Instead, the Southern states traded cotton and tobacco for finished products from the factories of the North and Europe, primarily Great Britain. The South's reliance on outsiders to produce everything from shoes and clothing to locomotives was a serious drawback for the Confederate war effort. The Confederacy rapidly built a centrally controlled war production organization, employing over 70,000 people. One of the most fascinating and least-told stories of the Civil War is how the Confederacy equipped and supplied the hundreds of thousands of men who fought in the armies.

## Josiah Gorgas and his miracle

**KEY PLAYERS**

The Confederate chief of ordinance, the man responsible for outfitting armies with all their weapons and equipment, was from Pennsylvania. Josiah Gorgas had the unenviable task of providing arms, equipment, and ammunition to the widely scattered armies throughout the South. He proved to be a genius at creating an industrial base capable of supporting a nation at war out of almost nothing. Until the Confederacy established its own war industries, blockade running and Union arms and equipment captured on the battlefield provided the initial supplies. At the onset of the war, Caleb Huse and Edward Anderson were sent to Great Britain as purchasing agents for the Confederate government. Using cotton to secure credit, they acquired 350,000 Enfield rifles. Purchasing agents from several Confederate states procured another 150,000 Enfields.

However, the war could not be fought with purchased and captured supplies alone. Gorgas established arsenals in Richmond, Fayetteville, Augusta, Charleston, Columbia, Macon, Atlanta, and Selma to manufacture weapons. A U.S. arsenal seized in South Carolina produced 16,000 artillery shells, 3 million rifle cartridges, and 10,000 weapons. Foundries at Macon, Columbus, and Augusta made cannons. Augusta also had a powder mill. Tredegar Iron Works, a private factory in Richmond under government contract, made torpedoes, propeller shafts, plates for ironclads, cannons, naval guns, and machine parts. Building a weapons industry overnight was not Gorgas's only challenge. There were no factories in the Confederacy capable of producing either clothing or shoes. Government factories in Richmond, Augusta, Columbus, Selma, and Atlanta were set up to meet the demand. Because of a shortage of leather, shoes were made of canvas with wooden soles. Gorgas also had to supply horses and mules for the army, but with the loss of Kentucky and Tennessee early in the war, horses and mules were increasingly hard to come by. By late 1864, about a quarter of all cavalrymen in the Confederate army were without horses, and there were no animals available to pull wagons and artillery. Nevertheless, Gorgas had established the means that allowed the Confederacy to be nearly self-sufficient in war production, despite the blockade. His contribution to the Confederate war effort was inestimable.

## Getting food to the soldiers

If it is true that an army travels on its stomach, then the most hated man in the ever-hungry Confederate armies had to be Lucius Northrop, the commissary, who had the thankless job of supplying food for the troops. Northrop was, indeed, the most hated man in the entire Confederate government. Personally difficult to deal with, Northrop enhanced his rancid reputation with his approach to an admittedly Herculean task. No one liked to deal with him; every army commander declared him incompetent, and the newspapers delighted in raking him over the coals. As inflation destroyed the purchasing power of Confederate money, Northrop ordered his purchasing agents to seize food. The outcry against Northrop's high-handed and sometimes brutal methods was universal, but Jefferson Davis refused to dismiss him. Davis and Northrop had been friends before the war, and despite all evidence to the contrary, Davis stood by him.

Sadly, for the men in the field, plenty of food was available, but transportation was completely inadequate. A combination of great distances, poor roads, inadequate rail lines, and insufficient rolling stock prevented regular deliveries to the troops in the field. When rations did arrive, the food was often spoiled because there were no means to preserve it. States' rights also served to cripple supply efforts. Rail movement, so critical to the conduct of this war, was never coordinated on national scale. State and local rail companies refused to allow the Confederate government priority to move troops or supplies in their areas. This situation, plus the lack of replacements for rails, engines, and rolling stock worn out, damaged, or destroyed during the war, led to a near breakdown of the transportation system. Even critical war production suffered from the lack of raw material deliveries. The Tredegar Ironworks, for example, had a yearly capacity of 24,000 tons of finished goods but never reached far beyond a third of its capacity because of insufficient deliveries of iron. The secretary of war was not given control of the movement of all troops and war supplies within the Confederacy until February 1865. By then it was far too late. When the armies of Lee and Johnston finally surrendered, their soldiers had plenty of ammunition with them — but they hadn't eaten a decent meal in months.

## HOW THE CONFEDERACY MADE DO

Common salt and sugar became a luxury in the South after 1863. Sweet potatoes, rye, corn, and even acorns were parched and roasted to serve as a coffee substitute. With flour so expensive, acorns were ground into meal. The lack of cloth caused problems for everyone. Scarlett O'Hara's use of draperies to make a dress in *Gone With the Wind* is not an exaggeration — even carpets were made into clothing. Because the Confederate government could not afford to clothe its soldiers in regulation uniforms, the troops most often wore homespun pants and a jacket dyed with juice from walnut or butternut hulls, creating a brownish-gray color known as butternut. Buttons were made of wood, horn, or bone. Wooden-soled shoes with leather or cloth uppers were common among those who preferred wearing them. Most went barefoot all summer. Dogwood or sweet gum twigs were used instead of toothbrushes. As paper became scarcer, newspapers were published on a paper substitute made of straw and cotton. Sometimes even wallpaper was used as newsprint.

# Detailing the Confederate Naval War

The Confederacy had to trade to survive. Confederate naval strategy centered on keeping the great ports of commerce open to commercial shipping. These ports included Norfolk, Virginia; Wilmington, North Carolina; Charleston, South Carolina; Savannah, Georgia; Pensacola, Florida; Mobile, Alabama; New Orleans, Louisiana; and Galveston, Texas. The strategy was sound, but the Confederacy was at a serious disadvantage at the beginning of the war — it had no navy. But it did have a secretary of the navy, Stephen R. Mallory, who wrung everything he could out of the Confederacy's capabilities to produce a significant, even sophisticated, naval force.

## Struggling to build a navy

In the decade before the war, the South built about 20 percent of all U.S. ships. Most were built at Norfolk, Charleston, Savannah, New Orleans, and Mobile. Outside of the Norfolk naval yard, though, few Southern shipyards were very large, and the South lacked the foundries, rolling mills, machinery, and skilled workers to manufacture steam engines and armor. Ordinance was another limiting factor; only Tredegar Ironworks could cast guns for warships. Although other foundries and ordnance centers were established, manpower shortages and the lack of iron limited production. The loss of Norfolk and New Orleans in 1862 was a crippling blow. As the naval war became more of a river war after 1862, the Confederacy's naval production yards were located in the interior of the South. The ironclad *Arkansas* was put together along the Yazoo River; another ironclad, the *Albemarle*, was built in a Georgia cornfield. These facilities also turned out small, well-armed, shallow-draft ships built of wood and protected with sheets of iron armor (thus, the term *ironclad*), whenever it was available. Transportation and supply problems continually hampered construction. Late in the war, as iron plate became almost nonexistent, some Confederate ships became "cottonclads," using cotton bales to provide protection for the crew that was more psychological than anything else. The shortage of iron plate for armor combined with the importance of controlling the rivers against incursions by the U.S. Navy led to the invention of underwater mines, which the Confederates called torpedoes. Torpedoes could cover stretches of water where there were no shore batteries, or could be placed at difficult passages of the river. The half-submerged mines would detonate when struck hard enough. Like modern mines, they were designed to explode below the unarmored waterline of ships. Some of these torpedoes were so sophisticated that they could be detonated electrically.

## CONFEDERATE SEA RAIDERS

Liverpool, England — not the Confederate states — became the birthplace of the seagoing Confederate navy. British shipbuilders in cooperation with Confederate agents in England constructed warships disguised as merchant ships. The *Florida*, along with the *Shenandoah*, the *Tallahassee*, and the *Georgia*, all contributed to the destruction of the Union merchant fleet that was so complete that the fleet did not recover fully until World War I. But the most famous Confederate ship was the *Alabama* (see the following image); her captain, Raphael Semmes, became the Confederacy's naval hero. For two years, Semmes and his mostly European crew tracked down Yankee ships all over the world. In June 1864, he met a Union warship, the *Kearsarge*, outside of Cherbourg harbor and lost his only naval engagement. A friendly British yacht rescued most of the *Alabama*'s crew, including Semmes, and sailed to England.

*(continued)*

*(continued)*

The *Florida* was intercepted by accident off the coast of Brazil by the *Wachussett*, which rammed the Confederate raider in port on October 7, 1864, and towed her off as a prize, much to the dismay of the captain (First Lieutenant Charles Morris) and some of his officers, who were ashore at the time (see the following image). Arriving in triumph at Hampton Roads with the prize, the Union captain, Commander Napoleon Collins, faced an international incident. He had violated Brazilian neutrality, and the Brazilian government demanded that the ship be returned along with an official apology. The Navy claimed the *Florida* was accidently sunk in port, but an official apology was on the way. Commander Collins faced a court martial and was discharged in 1865. After the heat died down, Collins was quietly reinstated to his former rank, eventually becoming an admiral.

THE CAPTURED REBEL PRIVATEER "FLORIDA" AND THE UNITED STATES STEAMER "WACHUSETT."—[SEE PAGE 707.]

The last Confederate flag to be lowered was on the *Shenandoah*, a raider that had been in action since 1864. On the last days of the war the *Shenandoah* was operating in the Bering Sea capturing U.S. whaling ships. Notified by a passing British ship in August that the war was over, Lieutenant Waddell sailed his ship to Liverpool to end his war, arriving in November 1865.

## Blockade running

To those observing the war from afar, the Confederacy represented a bonanza for the daring investor. After 1861, the South's tobacco and turpentine became scare commodities in Europe. As a result of the Union blockade and the rate of return for bringing such goods to the markets in Europe, an individual could become rich overnight. The law of supply and demand gave birth to a fleet of mostly British blockade runners with captains and crews who would have made Sir Francis Drake proud. The Bahamas, Bermuda, and Havana became the haunts of these ships, which used stealth, speed, and deception to slip past the Union ships on patrol. Bold captains used weather and light conditions to mask their movements, used false lantern signals, flew other national flags (including the U.S. flag), and changed the nameplates of their ships to fool the Union naval patrols. They became the lifeline of the Confederacy, exchanging weapons, material, medicines, and luxury goods for raw materials. Even though the volume of supplies never was enough to meet the demand, especially as the war went on, the blockade runners provided critical support to the war effort.

# Struggling with Diplomacy: European Recognition

The war forced the United States to deal carefully with the two dominant powers of Europe, England and France. Both the Union and the Confederacy knew that the war could be won in Europe. The name of the game was simple — recognition. In the business of international diplomacy, sovereign states recognized the legal status of other states. The Confederate States of America sought to prove to the sovereign nations of the world that it had a right to exist as an independent state. At the same time, the United States of America sought to prove to the sovereign nations of the world that the Confederacy had no right to exist. Intervention — European nations providing military support to the Confederacy to ensure its independence through force of arms — could come with recognition. Either one spelled defeat for the Union. To make matters worse, it was clear that the Confederacy had strong supporters in the ruling classes in both countries. Their influence at the centers of power made the threat of European intervention very real. For their part, the European governments were uninterested in the survival of the Union. The growing power of the Unites States in the Western hemisphere was troubling. If the United States became two nations, the rulers of Europe's two largest empires certainly would gain some long-term advantages. The one potential stumbling block to recognition was the Confederacy's support of slavery, a very unpopular notion among the European working classes. Likewise, France and

Britain had outlawed slavery in their empires. Despite its unpopularity, slavery, at first, was not an issue in the war. As the war began, President Lincoln had explicitly declared that his goal was to save the Union. This gave the Europeans something of a diplomatic fig leaf, allowing them to ignore the domestically unpopular slavery issue and still support the Confederacy.

## The blockade

Part of the diplomatic wrangle over recognition involved the legal status of the Union blockade of the ports from Virginia to the Gulf of Mexico, which President Lincoln had declared in 1861. International law only recognized effective blockades, meaning that the president could not just declare a blockade without having the actual military means to enforce it. After the blockade declaration, both Britain and France declared neutrality but at the same time allowed the Confederacy access to their ports. This gave the South the international legal status of a belligerent, indicating that the Confederacy had a legitimate cause to engage in war. Using this status, the Confederacy pressed the blockade issue hard. It was only a paper blockade they argued, and no nation should respect it. This meant that if U.S. warships stopped British or French ships from entering Confederate ports, they were guilty of a hostile act that could lead to war. Of course, war between the United States and any European power ensured the independence of the Confederacy.

Jefferson Davis appointed two distinguished Southerners, James M. Mason of Virginia and John Slidell of Louisiana, as commissioners to court the French and British. In October 1861, the two men left from Charleston on a blockade runner headed for Havana, Cuba, where they boarded the British mail steamer *Trent* preparing to depart for England. Upon arrival in England, Mason would take up his duties there, while Slidell continued on to France.

The USS *San Jacinto*, commanded by Captain Charles Wilkes, arrived in Cuba looking for Confederate raiders when Wilkes heard that Mason and Slidell were preparing to leave. He intercepted the *Trent*, fired warning shots, boarded her, and took the Confederate commissioners prisoner. Wilkes brought them back to the United States, where they were held in a fort in Boston harbor. His act of derring-do made Wilkes a national hero. But no one in Great Britain was amused. Wilkes had violated just about every rule of international law and insulted the British flag. No one treated the world's only superpower that way — the United States had to be put in its place. The British fleet was made ready for war, and a message was dispatched to the United States demanding an apology and the release of Mason and Slidell. To make sure the Lincoln administration got the point, 11,000 British regulars were sent en route to Canada.

## THE SHOE ON THE OTHER FOOT

In the case of the *Trent,* the British government was quite angry that a U.S. warship had stopped a neutral vessel and seized passengers, in direct violation of international law. But just 50 years earlier, British warships had stopped neutral American ships to seize passengers believed to be British citizens. These insulting and illegal acts led the new United States government to declare war on Britain, resulting in the War of 1812. Now in 1861, the tables were turned, and the British got a taste of their own medicine from Captain Wilkes. They didn't like it any more than the Americans had. The British and Americans thus switched roles from the 1812 crisis — nothing unusual in the game of diplomacy.

The British demands inflamed Northern public opinion in favor of war. The two imprisoned Confederate commissioners were prizes not to be given up easily. Besides, if there was one group that some Yankees hated more than rebellious Southerners, it was the British. But Lincoln had no interest in fighting two wars at once. Mason and Slidell were released along with the necessary apology. The American minister in London, Charles Francis Adams, and the British minister in Washington, Lord Lyons, worked to keep the *Trent* affair from becoming the cause of a war by ensuring that both sides could retreat with honor intact.

## The decisive year for recognition: 1862

**TURNING POINT**

Applying the King Cotton strategy, the South sought to force the issue of recognition by enacting a self-imposed voluntary embargo on cotton exported to Europe. The goal was to starve the French and British economies of the precious raw material that drove their major industries to the point that they had to recognize the Confederacy or face economic collapse. This approach left thousands of English textile workers unemployed and, along with the series of Confederate battlefield victories throughout the summer of 1862, provided the British with an incentive to end the war. The British government contemplated extending an offer to mediate the conflict to end the hostilities. If the Union refused to accept mediation, Britain would recognize the Confederacy. Napoleon III, emperor of France, talked with Slidell about having France, Great Britain, and Russia cooperate to halt the war for six months. Again, if the North rejected the idea, the European powers could recognize the Confederacy or intervene militarily on her behalf. All that was necessary was a decisive Confederate victory on Union territory. With Lee in Maryland and Bragg in Kentucky, that victory seemed very close. But the battles of Perryville and Antietam, though indecisive, resulted in the withdrawal of the invading Confederate forces. The various mediation and recognition proposals vanished overnight. Of far greater significance for the Confederacy's future was the issuance of the Emancipation Proclamation. After

January 1, 1863, all slaves held in a state or a part of a state that was in rebellion were declared free. More a statement of intent than a legal order, the proclamation served its purpose. It changed the strategic direction and purpose of the war and eliminated the fig leaf the Europeans had been hiding behind. The United States was fighting now for both union and human freedom. Intervention in favor of the Confederacy would mean fighting against these ideals — something no government could afford to do.

## Diplomatic highlights with Britain, France, and Russia

Although official recognition was not forthcoming, the British government turned a blind eye to clear violations of neutrality by allowing ships intended for the Confederate navy to be built in British shipyards. These ships included fast cruisers to attack Union merchant ships on the open seas and ironclad rams, intended to destroy the blockade, secretly paid for by the Confederate government. The legal argument was that the cruisers, like the famous *Alabama*, were merchant ships, even though they were built for speed and maneuverability like a warship. The ships ran up the Confederate flag and mounted cannons only after they entered international waters. The British government, therefore, had no legal ground to prevent their construction and delivery. The rams were clearly warships, but the British explained that they were being built for the French. It was no secret, however, that they would be delivered to the Confederacy. Under heavy Union diplomatic pressure in 1863, the British government finally made sure that the rams would join the British, not the Confederate, navy.

Napoleon III's government was actually more sympathetic to the Confederacy than were the British. An independent Confederate States of America would further his ambitions for France, but he was reluctant to take any action without British support, which was not forthcoming after 1862. Taking advantage of the war's distraction for the United States, Napoleon flaunted the Monroe Doctrine (this document, issued by President Monroe in 1823, warned European powers not to interfere with countries in the Western Hemisphere) and created a French dominated client state in Mexico. The French never had complete control in Mexico, and this prevented Napoleon from providing direct assistance to the Confederacy through Texas and Louisiana. Confederate diplomatic attempts to influence the French-supplied Emperor Maximilian in Mexico to aid them in gaining French recognition of the Confederacy failed. In June 1863, Confederate supporters in Britain, with the strong backing of the French emperor, openly debated the issue of recognition in Parliament, but the twin Union victories at Vicksburg and Gettysburg gave the opponents to recognition the ammunition they needed to table the proposal. In 1865, the Confederacy sent Mason and Slidell out for one last meeting with the French and British, offering emancipation of all slaves in the Confederacy in return for recognition and survival. By this time, the war was all but over; the South's last card had been played too late.

Interestingly enough, the one nation that wholly supported the Union was the one that had just freed an entire class of people from bondage. In 1861, the Russian tsar, Alexander II, granted freedom to millions of peasants (called serfs), who had been bound to the land and owned by the nobility for centuries. In the fall of 1863, two Russian fleets entered New York and San Francisco harbors to spend the winter. Although the Northern press made much of the visit as a counterbalance to the pro-Confederate leanings of the British and French, and the Republican administration welcomed the fleet as a powerful expression of support, the Russian government had other objectives. Russia feared the possibility of war with Britain and France, and as a precautionary measure, needed warm-water winter ports to ensure that the fleets were available for offensive action if war did break out.

## Assessing Confederate diplomacy

The Confederacy displayed a stunning naïveté when preparing their diplomatic strategy. Assuming that the world could not live without Southern cotton, the Confederacy wasted valuable time waiting for the world to come to them. They made a serious, and fatal, miscalculation. Great Britain, the target of this King Cotton diplomacy, had nearly two years of raw cotton stored in warehouses before the war began. The economy was not significantly affected until 1862 — only after the Confederacy had decided to abandon its cotton embargo strategy in order to purchase supplies and obtain hard currency through cotton sales. But by that time the blockade had tightened, limiting how much cotton could reach Europe. Increased cotton imports from Egypt and India eased shortages and decreased Britain's reliance on Southern cotton. In addition, Britain was reaping enormous profits by supplying both the North and South. Another unforeseen economic factor shaped the diplomatic battle. Europe had experienced several years of poor grain harvests, which the great farms of the North easily made up. Thousands of tons of grain were exported to Great Britain alone. This had an important effect on diplomacy. Simply put, Great Britain needed Northern wheat more than Southern cotton. Thus, her neutrality was ensured by the need to maintain a steady supply of food. Over time, Union military power became a serious instrument of diplomacy, and with Canada vulnerable to a possible U.S. invasion, Britain was careful not to push the United States too far.

REMEMBER

In the end, the Confederacy's attempts to gain full recognition were crippled by its shortsighted and unrealistic reliance on the King Cotton strategy and the failure to recognize, until too late, the burden that slavery placed on its claim as a great nation. Northern diplomatic efforts were highly effective in redefining the Union's strategic goals and using the moral power of freedom to assure European neutrality. In addition, the Union used its burgeoning economic and military power to keep the ambitious European powers at bay and ensure their support of U.S. diplomatic objectives. The often-overlooked diplomats representing the United States and the Confederacy decisively shaped the direction of the war. Their successes, as well as their failures, ensured that only Americans themselves would determine the final outcome of the American Civil War.

# Creating a Nation: Confederate Nationalism

Despite the daunting challenges, those who chose to create a new nation had succeeded. The leaders of the Confederate government believed that they had perfected the old Constitution, making it more closely reflect the original intent of the Founding Fathers, even harkening back to the original Confederation (the source of the name of the new country). Even by 1862, the Confederate States of America had become recognizable as a new nation; it had, it seemed, a sense of destiny within itself. In Great Britain, the future prime minister William E. Gladstone made a speech in 1862 in which he remarked that despite its attachment to slavery, "there is no doubt that Jefferson Davis and other leaders of the South have made an army; they are making, it appears, a navy; and they have made what is more than either — they have made a nation." Creating a nation, especially in war, requires sacrifice; and Southerners, undoubtedly, did sacrifice. Throughout the war, they displayed patriotism and selflessness that transcended social class, and maintained faith in a cause that they believed God had blessed and ordained. Even in the midst of total destruction and defeat, the Southerners did not give up easily or willingly. Despite defeat, this sense of Confederate national identity did not disappear. Although initially willing to accommodate to the Union victory, Confederate nationalism remained a potent source of mobilization and resistance in the troubled postwar period as former Confederates were excluded from participating in the restoration of their states as equal citizens.

In the end, independence became more important to Southerners than the Southern way of life defined by slavery. By 1865, the Confederacy had sacrificed both the sacred cows of states' rights and slavery for national survival. Ironically, the central cause of the war in the first place was willingly destroyed by both the Union and the Confederacy in the crucible of war. That such an outcome came through the deaths and suffering of untold hundreds of thousands of soldiers and civilians, rather than through peaceful compromise and political accommodation, makes the war an even greater tragedy.

# Chapter **25**

# The Union at War: Creating a New Republican Future for America

Unlike the states of the Confederacy, the states of the Union were largely untouched by the hand of war. The Union was also able to bear the economic burden of the war more easily. But President Lincoln faced problems similar to those of President Davis in conducting the war.

The Union army and navy were completely unprepared for war and had to be built from scratch; the war consumed money at a previously unimaginable rate, creating the need for astronomical sums to flow through the treasury. The war also consumed men at astronomical rates; the struggle to keep the ranks filled and meet the huge manpower requirements of a two-theater war was unremitting. Lincoln, like Davis, had to contend with a fractious congress. Moreover, Lincoln had the problem of maintaining a weak political coalition, while fending off increasingly strong anti-war efforts.

In the end, Lincoln and the Republican Party maintained the political coalition and marshaled resources far better than the Confederacy. But in all the hoopla over winning the war, the Northern public forgot that while the war was going on, the Republican Congress had been busy passing legislation that would have far-reaching effects on the future of the nation. Even in the midst of a war, the country was experiencing rapid change that reflected the Republican Party's vision for a new America.

# Looking at Abraham Lincoln as President and War Leader

One of Lincoln's great challenges as president was to glue together a coalition of political groups ranging from old Whigs and Know-Nothings to suspicious conservative Northern Democrats and radical abolitionist Republicans. Fragile political alliances in the Border States also had to be maintained. To add to his trouble, he had to convince these groups that his war policy was the right one and that his strategy for winning the war was sound. The military defeats in the troubled years of 1861–1862 pushed Lincoln toward emancipation as an essential element in the strategy for winning the war. Emancipation angered everyone: The radicals wanted to go further, and the conservatives wanted to slow down. Even in the last brutal years of 1863–1865, Lincoln held the coalition together. It is a tribute to his political skills that he was able to accomplish this feat.

**REMEMBER**

Lincoln by all appearances was unimpressive. Tall and awkward, wearing rumpled clothing, he had big hands and feet and a homely face that gave him a rough look that sophisticates in Washington found amusing. He told people who asked about his policies that his policy was to have no policy. He never seemed to tire of telling jokes and stories, often at inappropriate times. But Lincoln possessed a shrewdness for politics that few understood or appreciated. Lincoln could make even the most insufferable glad-hander believe that he had bested the president, when just the opposite had occurred. This was one reason why his cabinet, filled with egoists, cranks, and hardheads, worked so well and accomplished so much. Lincoln also exhibited a mastery of the English language that has rarely been equaled. He put the power of words into the equation of war, making clear for everyone what the war meant and why it was worth the cost.

# Financing the War

Like the Confederacy, the Union had no preparation for financing the war. But the North had significant financial resources at hand. These resources, though initially unresponsive to the demands of the war, were quickly retooled and modernized to form the basis for what has become the nation's current financial and banking system.

## Borrowing money: Loans and bonds

At first, the government financed the war as it had always financed its wars — by borrowing money. Just like any other borrower, the government went to the banks. Government borrowing amounted to a little over a billion dollars. But loans were insufficient, and the government had to seek other sources of income. During the war, about $1.5 billion worth of bonds were issued, promising to pay 6 percent interest redeemable after 5 years, and for a period of up to 20 years. Nearly one million people in the North bought these bonds as an expression of patriotism and support for the war. These bond campaigns, heavily publicized and marketed, became the model for the great war bond drives of World War I and II.

## Taking money: Taxation

In 1861, Congress passed an income tax on incomes over $800. A year later, Congress got the hang of the taxation process and began putting taxes on everything imaginable, creating a Bureau of Internal Revenue to help collect the money. Income tax brackets were set up, with ever-lower incomes feeling some tax bite and upper-income brackets getting hit the hardest. Eventually, incomes of $10,000 and above were subject to a tax of 10 percent. Excise taxes were imposed on nearly every consumer item, especially tobacco and liquor (both still favorites of the government today). Taxes were imposed on nearly every product or service. These taxed items included luxuries, raw materials, manufactured items, corporate dividends, and federal employees' salaries. There were taxes on licenses and even newspaper advertisements. The tariff was increased, not only to protect domestic manufacturers, but also to squeeze additional revenue from the cheaper foreign imports. Taxes brought in about $600 million over the course of the war.

## COMPARING THE EFFECT

The result of the North's heavy emphasis on taxation over issuing paper money to finance the war is seen in comparing the inflation rates of the Union and Confederacy during the four years of war. In the North, the inflation rate ran about 80 percent. Very high, but manageable, when compared to the Confederate inflation rate of 9,000 percent.

## Making money: Greenbacks

The pressure for funds grew so rapidly that the Union government had to turn to printing paper money. In 1862, Congress passed the Legal Tender Act. The name of the law is important because unlike Confederate paper money, greenbacks (as they were called) were considered money, equal to gold or silver. This status, plus the public's confidence in the worth of this paper, prevented inflation from getting out of hand. The $450 million in greenbacks issued throughout the war represented only about 16 percent of the total debt, but the widespread use of greenbacks helped to create a national currency. The National Banking Act, passed in 1863, showed the growing financial strength of the federal government. This act was intended to replace the prewar, chaotic, state banking system and currency with a national currency and federally chartered banks.

# Running the War: Congress and the President

The struggle over who ran the war continued until the war was over. Lincoln used his constitutionally ill-defined powers as commander-in-chief to issue orders and directives to military commanders and issue the Emancipation Proclamation. Congress, on the other hand, believed its constitutional responsibility to provide for the army and the navy and appropriate funds gave it the power to run the war. While Lincoln still held most of the cards, Congress made sure that someone was watching over his shoulder. This ever-present watcher took the form of the Joint Committee on the Conduct of the War. The committee was dominated by radical Republicans, Thaddeus Stevens from the House and Charles Sumner from the Senate, whose agenda was to abolish slavery using the war powers of Congress. None of the radical Republicans had any military experience, yet impatient with the pace of the war, they spent a great deal of time investigating senior officers in the Army of the Potomac, most of whom happened to be Democrats. The committee had broad subpoena powers and, therefore, was a force to be reckoned with. While often creating a painful spectacle to watch, as the committee members dissected battlefield decisions and second-guessed generals, they also did some good, tracking down corrupt contractors and identifying egregious wastes and inefficiencies in the use of government funds.

## Non-Wartime legislation

The war was a boon for the Republicans. For years, the slavery controversy had prevented regional political alliances from dealing with legislation intended to support westward expansion and settlement. The Southern congressmen had always opposed every internal improvement measure, mostly because they felt that the South would not see any measurable benefit from it. Now without a Southern voting bloc in opposition, the Republican-dominated Congress could enact legislation at will with the goal of transforming the country in the image of the states of New England and the Midwest, while also creating in the process a permanent Republican dominated government. To meet these goals, Congress passed higher tariffs (which the South had always opposed) to protect and encourage domestic manufacturing. It passed legislation for the construction of a transcontinental railroad (which the South wanted to go through the Southwest) to benefit markets in the eastern and midwestern states. It also passed the Homestead Act in 1862. This act, reflecting the Free Soil ideology at the heart of the Republican Party, allowed anyone who occupied 160 acres of western government land for five years and paid a nominal fee to then obtain outright ownership of it. To encourage western growth, Congress passed the Morrill Land Grant Act, which authorized federal land grants to states to establish agricultural and mechanical colleges, with the purpose of developing an agricultural-industrial economy like that in the Republican dominated eastern United States (and whose graduates would in the future vote Republican as well). All modern fans of the big college football and basketball powers out West and Midwest owe thanks to the 37th Congress of 1862.

## Opposing and disloyal: The peace democrats

Northern Democrats were critical to the success of the war effort. Lincoln needed their cooperation and support to win the war. The Democrats were split into three groups. The *War Democrats* were strong supporters of Lincoln's policies. The *Conservative Democrats* mistrusted Lincoln's war aims and were uncomfortable with emancipation. This group hoped to see the Union restored as it was before the war. The third group was the *Peace Democrats.* This group was small but very vocal, with a power base among urban Catholic immigrants and within the Midwest states of Ohio, Indiana, and Illinois, where Southern sympathies were strong. The Peace Democrats opposed the war and advocated negotiation and compromise. As Union fortunes on the battlefield shifted, the Peace Democrats became stronger. The Republican press called them Copperheads, implying their opposition to the war was as dangerous as the copperhead snake. The Peace Democrats wore this label as a badge of honor. It is said that some even took to wearing Liberty Head copper pennies on their lapels to identify themselves. To head off the opposition, Lincoln, using his role of commander-in-chief as justification, suspended the writ of *habeas corpus*, authorizing summary arrests to stop anyone from disrupting the war effort or acting disloyally. Individuals were subject to arrest and trial by military court. In 1863, Congress gave the president formal power to suspend the writ but allowed the accused to be brought before a grand jury to determine whether an indictment should be issued. Throughout the war years, about 14,000 Americans were arrested and held for disloyalty or suspicion of being disloyal.

## CLEMENT L. VALLANDIGHAM

Ohio congressman Clement L. Vallandigham was the descendent of a Virginia family and was married to the daughter of a Maryland planter. Probably the most prominent Copperhead, he was an open opponent of Republican war policies and simply wanted to see the Union restored to "prewar conditions," by which he meant the state of the Union in 1820, before the slavery issue had been raised. On May 1, 1863, the Ohio Democrat made a public speech decrying Republican policies and calling for a negotiated settlement of the war, using France as an intermediary. He told the crowd that the war was not for the restoration of the Union, but for radical abolitionist goals. He was promptly arrested for disloyalty by General Ambrose Burnside, the recent commander of the Army of the Potomac who now was hidden away, tending to administrative duties in Ohio. The hapless Burnside thought that he had done a sterling service for the country, but as usual, he had badly miscalculated. Vallandigham was tried by military court, found guilty of treasonous acts, and imprisoned in Cincinnati. Vallandigham used his imprisonment to grandstand and badger the Republican administration: "I am a Democrat — for the Constitution, for law, for the Union, for liberty — this was my only crime." Burnside's blunder embarrassed the government enough that Lincoln commuted Vallandigham's sentence and banished him to Confederate territory. Not finding the Confederacy to his liking, Vallandigham ran the blockade and went to Canada. Despite facing the penalty of imprisonment if he returned from exile, Vallandigham disguised himself with a pillow in his shirt and a false mustache and returned to the United States in time to denounce Lincoln publicly in the 1864 presidential election. This time, Lincoln wisely ignored him.

# Fighting the War

With their large industrial and commercial base, the states of the North made the transition to war production with relative ease. In fact, the economy grew and expanded during the war. The mechanization of farm production — a trend that has continued until our own time — took hold, allowing men to join the army and have the wife and children *still* plant and harvest a bountiful crop. Shipbuilding grew enormously to meet the needs of the navy and internal transportation. Railroads expanded as well, under the necessity of providing military transportation. In factories throughout the North, machines took over for people to meet the demands of the armies. The North was on its way to becoming the dominant economic powerhouse of the country.

## Drafting soldiers

After the first enthusiastic response to Lincoln's call for 75,000 three-month volunteers in April 1861, the number of volunteers dwindled, especially after the Union defeats in Virginia. To avoid political fallout, Lincoln arranged in July 1862 to have the state governors politely request that the president call for 300,000 more volunteers to serve three years. This quota was much harder to fill. To meet the demands for manpower, the federal government began calling state militia units into service for nine months. Congress did not pass a national conscription law until March 1863. This law made men between the ages of 20 and 45 eligible for three years of military service. A drafted man, however, did not have to serve. He could hire a substitute to serve in his place, or the draftee could buy his way out of service by paying $300. Because this was equal to half a year's pay for the average laborer, only about 86,000 men took advantage of this option before it was ended in 1864. The draft brought in 46,000 men, with another 118,000 serving as substitutes. Needless to say, draftees and substitutes were not given a warm welcome in veteran combat units made up of three-year volunteers. Like the draft in the South, the Northern draft laws were intended to stimulate volunteering, rather than serve as the main pipeline for replacements.

To further stimulate volunteering, recruits received a cash bounty from the federal government. In 1861, the bounty offered was $100; in 1864, it was increased to $300. A veteran who reenlisted received an extra $100. Additional bounties were frequently offered by localities to meet draft quotas. Depending on the cash inducements a state also offered, a volunteer could make big money. This practice encouraged fraud in the form of *bounty jumping* — a soldier would enlist in one place, get his cash bounty, promptly desert, enlist in another place with a false name, and start all over again, usually deserting for good when the scam had run its course. After milking the system, some Union deserters formed bandit gangs in western Pennsylvania, robbing and plundering.

## SHODDY

"Shoddy" is a term invented in the Civil War for Union uniforms made by unscrupulous contractors who took sweepings, scraps of cloth, and lint, and then glued and pressed the materials together to make a uniform jacket. Although the jacket looked serviceable, it immediately fell apart when worn, usually when the material became damp with sweat or rain.

## Resisting the draft

No federal law comes without some sort of bureaucracy to enforce it. The draft law was no different. As the war moved into its third and fourth years, federal officers enforcing the draft were met with obstruction and disaffection, violence and threats. The Democrats were especially vocal in their opposition to the draft law and its enforcement. At times, federal troops or state militia units had to be called out to quell disturbances. One of these disturbances became the greatest riot in U.S. history. Horatio Seymour, governor of New York, was as hostile to Lincoln as some Southern governors were to Davis. Many New York City residents had strong Southern sympathies because of trade and commercial ties and an equally strong animosity toward the Lincoln administration. Irish immigrants were especially opposed to both abolition and emancipation.

In July 1863, just two weeks after the battle of Gettysburg, Irish mobs opposing the draft fought police for three days, lynched any Black man they saw, whom they blamed for starting the war in the first place, and burned down a Black orphan asylum. On the fourth day of the violence, Union troops arrived in the city fresh from Gettysburg and in no mood to put up with such violence from people not in uniform. They shot enough of the rioters to calm things down quickly and allow the police to restore order.

## Building a navy

The U.S. Navy had 1,457 officers, 7,500 men, and 90 vessels ostensibly in service when the war began. Only half of these ships were in actual serviceable condition. Of those serviceable, only fourteen vessels were available for duty against the Confederacy. To meet the requirements of the Anaconda Plan, which called for a naval blockade of the Confederacy's 3,500 miles of coastline, bays, and rivers from Virginia to Mexico, the government had to put ships afloat, and support and repair them for as long as was necessary. Diplomatically, ships afloat also put teeth into Lincoln's declaration of a blockade, even though the blockade itself was a legal recognition of the Confederate States of America as a belligerent — in other words, a separate government. To meet these demands, the navy took just about anything that could float; steamboats, ferryboats, fishing boats, river boats, yachts, tugs, and even barges were converted into warships, mostly in name only. To give them a military look, army cannons were anchored to the decks and sheets of iron or tin were nailed onto their sides (see Figure 25-1). Within eight months, the U.S. Navy had 264 vessels floating at sea. By 1862, the number had nearly doubled.

**FIGURE 25-1:**
Union sailors
abord the USS
New Hampshire.

*The Library of Congress / Public Domain*

In the meantime, the navy sought to recruit new sailors, and the vast resources of the North were put to work producing fast, agile, and powerful warships capable of running down the sleek blockade runners, as well as the shallow draft gunboats and ironclad warships capable of operating along rivers and bays. By the end of the war, the navy had 6,000 officers and 45,000 men serving on more than 600 ships, most of which were steam-powered, including 60 ironclads. As the blockade became more efficient, it became clear that the final outcome of the war would be determined not only on land, but also at sea, as the Union navy took the offensive in 1864 and 1865 to close the last ports available to the Confederacy.

# Building an Economy: Northern Industrial Production

Northern industry experienced a general downturn after secession, primarily because its major market, the Southern states, had left the Union. The government's demand for uniforms, shoes, iron, copper, coal, leather, weapons, wagons, and machinery soon made up for the loss of the Southern market. Northern industry not only expanded during the war, but production technology expanded also, making factories more efficient, and therefore more profitable. Wartime labor shortages were filled with women and children. Northern industry not only produced war goods, but it was also able to produce consumer goods. In effect, the North's economy, without the Southern states, was producing enough to support Northern consumer demand and fight a major war lasting four years. It was a startling achievement that foreshadowed the vast war-making power of the U.S. economy in two world wars.

Chapter **26**

# Wartime in America: Its Effect on the People

The lot of the common soldier in the Civil War was very similar whether the man wore blue or gray. Although the Union soldier was generally better fed and clothed than his Confederate counterpart, the soldiers experienced the same boring routines, endured the same exhausting marches, griped the same gripes about their officers, and faced the same fears in battle. At times, this common experience drew them close together in comradeship, but also made them fierce opponents on the battlefield.

The women of the Union and Confederacy took part in the war in many ways, serving as nurses, factory workers, farmhands, or spies. Likewise, African Americans played important roles in both armies. As a people, African Americans were transformed by the war in a way that no one had thought possible four years earlier. In addition, American Indians during the war had to make difficult choices to preserve their interests. For soldiers, women, American Indians, and former slaves alike, the experience of the war not only brought about changes that affected them for the rest of their lives, but also brought about changes that have affected the lives of people in the United States ever since.

# Meeting the Common Soldier: Everyman

The soldier of the Civil War, most typically in his early 20s, was a highly independent character. Almost half of the men who served had been farmers or worked on a farm before the war. About a third were skilled and unskilled laborers, and one-tenth held white-collar or professional jobs. Although he showed respect for authority and submitted to the logic of military drill and discipline, he maintained his individuality, usually displayed by the slouch he adopted in ranks. Soldiers respected good officers and they responded willingly to their orders, but they also displayed open contempt for poor or incompetent leaders. Privates displayed little or no respect for rank, often addressing a general in the field as he would another private. Because furloughs (an approved leave of absence from the army) were rare, soldiers often decided on their own when their services were required. Desertions, which the men called taking "French leave," were common, especially in the Confederate armies. Most went home to take care of their families and returned to their units in the spring, but as the war went on and the plight of women and children became more desperate, larger numbers of soldiers did not return. The bright faces of youth in carefully kept uniforms became veterans' faces, now browned by exposure, their bodies tough and lean, careless of appearance, carrying only the essentials, and capable of enduring tremendous hardships. In the process, Johnny Reb and Billy Yank became some of the best fighting men in the world. For his service, a Union soldier was paid $11 (increased to $16 in 1864) a month; the Confederate soldier was paid $13.

## Eating what the army gave you

Soldiers throughout the centuries have always been concerned with the quality and quantity of their food. Fresh food was (and still is) always preferred over preserved rations, but it was (and is) often hard to come by. Although Union troops usually could expect to see rations of fresh bread and meat, and a regular coffee ration, Confederate soldiers saw less and less of such items as the war went on. The Confederate soldier's diet was usually a whipsaw of feast or famine. When fresh food was not available, both sides shared the same basic diet of *hardtack* (a dry flour cracker so hard that it often had to be broken with a rifle butt) and salt pork (or "sowbelly" or "salt horse" as the soldiers called it). As time went on, even these rations became hard to come by in the Confederate army. For example, in the winter of 1863, the Confederate soldier's ration consisted of 18 ounces of flour and four ounces of bacon (a generous term for it, according to those who received it). Rice, sugar, and molasses would arrive infrequently to supplement the ration.

# Living the life of a soldier

Unlike the often-romanticized stories of a comfortable outdoor life, in reality heat, dirt, long marches, thirst, freezing cold, lice and disease were the soldier's constant companions. The long winters in camp were numbingly boring for the men of both armies. They whiled away the hours and days waiting for the next meal or playing card games. When things were quiet, an informal truce would be called at points in the line where opposing units were close. The Yankees would trade coffee, an item almost nonexistent in the South, for tobacco, something hard to come by in the North. The men would also trade newspapers, talk quietly (and disparagingly) about the war and their officers, then head back to their own lines. Often just before an attack, the pickets (soldiers on guard) would call out to their counterparts to warn them. After the men were on the march again, all the good relations with the enemy were just a memory. Soldiers also got rid of packs of cards or sets of dice on the march. Cards and gambling were considered a sinful pastime in 19th-century America, and soldiers did not want to have such symbols of depravity on their bodies if they were killed. If they survived, of course, soldiers bought or made another deck as soon as they could and returned to their old habits.

# Wearing the blue or the gray

By 1863, soldiers of both armies had learned what was useful and what was not. The Union soldier wore a blue wool blouse over a flannel shirt, and light blue wool trousers held up by suspenders. In the Army of the Potomac, he wore a kepi, a cap with a short visor; in the west, Union troops often wore slouch hats. He sometimes exchanged the uncomfortable regulation knapsack for a rolled blanket, which he slept on at night. He put this over his left shoulder and tied the ends on his right hip (see Figure 26-1). The blanket bedroll usually had in it extra clothing, personal items, and a waterproof sheet. In addition to his blanket bedroll, he carried a cartridge box on a long strap, which hung across his body in the same manner as the blanket bedroll. He usually carried his canteen the same way. The cartridge box carried 40 rounds of ammunition. If there was time before a battle, soldiers were issued extra ammo, which they usually put in their pockets. On his leather belt, he carried a leather pouch containing percussion caps, which ignited the powder charge loaded in his rifle, and a bayonet.

As a means of unit identification adopted during the war, Union soldiers in the Army of the Potomac wore colored symbols on the tops of their kepis. Each corps in the army had a symbol, such as a Maltese cross, a circle, or a diamond. Each division in that corps had a different color assigned to the corps symbol: red for the first division, white for the second, and blue for the third. Often a brass letter designating the company would be added below the symbol. When several corps were transferred from the Eastern Theater to the Western Theater, the westerners in some cases copied the symbology in their own units. These symbols became highly prized and were the forerunners of the unit patches worn on U.S. military uniforms today.

**FIGURE 26-1:** Two soldiers show how they carried their supplies.

*Waud, Alfred R / The Library of Congress / Public Domain*

The Confederate soldier's uniform usually was hardly a uniform at all. He wore whatever he could, often captured from Union supply wagons, obtained from home, or stripped from the dead. He usually wore a wool hat, with the front brim often pushed up. He wore a short gray jacket over a homespun cotton shirt. His trousers were held up with a leather belt, which held the percussion cap box and the bayonet. Sometimes a Confederate soldier would obtain a Union belt with its large oval brass plate marked "US" in raised letters and almost always wore it with the "US" upside down. He carried his blanket bedroll, cartridge box, haversack, and canteen in the same manner as his Union counterpart. (See Figure 26-1.) In combat, he usually pushed the blanket bedroll further behind his back and shifted the cartridge box to the front of his body for easier loading and firing of his rifle. If he had shoes, they were in bad shape, as were his socks, if he had those. It was not unusual to see a Confederate soldier carrying a frying pan slung over his back. Both in camp and on the march, frying pans were invaluable for cooking rations.

Also slung over the Confederate soldier's left shoulder and hanging on his right hip were a tin cup and canteen and sometimes a canvas haversack containing the day's rations. The bayonet for soldiers of both armies was an all-purpose tool — used for digging, for spitting meat over a fire, as an expedient candle stand, and very rarely, as a weapon when things got really serious. Bayonets mounted on the weapon interfered with loading, so soldiers only attached them (*fixed* is the military term) when close combat was imminent.

Officers were generally dressed better than enlisted men, although as the war progressed, many took on a much more casual form of dress (see Figure 26-2). By the end of the war, even General Grant adopted a more comfortable uniform, wearing a private's blouse with his lieutenant general's rank sewn on.

**FIGURE 26-2:** Typical officer's uniform.

Waud, Alfred R / The Library of Congress / Public Domain

# Fighting illness in the ranks

One of the great tragedies of the Civil War is that even though the number of killed and wounded in battle was terribly high, more soldiers died from disease than from combat wounds. Of all the Union soldiers who died in the war, nearly three out of every five died as a result of disease. Of Confederate soldiers who died, the number was nearly two of every three who fell victim to disease.

The majority of deaths due to illness during the war were from typhoid fever, pneumonia, and dysentery. The remainder died from diarrhea, malaria, and tuberculosis. Early in the war, recruits came from all over the country with no medical examinations and congregated in unsanitary camps. The measles, mumps, chicken pox, whooping cough, and a host of other contagious diseases swept through the troops. Without any immunity to these diseases, many soldiers were incapacitated for weeks; hundreds of others died. With no knowledge of bacteria or viruses, soldiers drank contaminated water, ate food that was often spoiled, and served as hosts for a variety of insect pests, particularly lice, that carried disease. Their poor diets and constant exposure to the elements made soldiers more susceptible to disease. Once stricken, a sick soldier often got worse; colds rapidly turned into pneumonia. The state of medical knowledge at this time had no treatment for most of these diseases, and a soldier either recovered on his own or died. Illnesses in the ranks depleted the strength of both armies and had a terrible effect on morale.

## Caring for the wounded

During the war, approximately 110,000 Union and 94,000 Confederate soldiers died of combat wounds. If wounded, a soldier who could still walk made his way to the rear to the field hospitals, usually a barn or large shed. Often even a slightly wounded man was assisted to the rear by several of his "friends," who were looking for an excuse to avoid the front lines. Musicians, cooks, and skulkers rounded up from their hiding places carried the more seriously wounded to the rear on stretchers. Ambulance units that located and transported casualties later replaced these often-unreliable angels of mercy. The field hospital surgeons tried to stop bleeding and treated only the wounds they best knew how to deal with. Often this procedure meant, quite simply, amputation. The Minié ball, the most common rifle projectile in the war, was a large, slow-moving missile that caused a rather large wound. A wound anywhere other than in an arm or leg was almost always fatal because the Civil War physician had neither the medical knowledge nor the capability to treat such wounds.

At the field hospital (see Figure 26-3), the injured soldier was dosed with chloroform and put on an elevated flat surface, usually a door or table from a nearby farmhouse. The surgeons and their assistants could perform amputations quickly, piling the limbs into a ghastly heap nearby. (In fact, that was how many knew where to look for the field hospital — by the pile of arms and legs outside the building.) Wherever possible after surgery, the wounded were moved into houses, put on porches, or even laid out in backyards to await transportation (often nothing more than carts or wagons) to a hospital. Many men died of either shock or infection after an amputation because doctors had no knowledge of the germ theory of disease and had no concept of even the most rudimentary rules of hygiene (such as washing one's hands and instruments before and after surgery). Bacterial infection was thus passed from one patient to another as the doctor treated them. Amazingly, a wounded soldier who had received an amputation still had a 75 percent chance of survival.

**FIGURE 26-3:** Confederate hospital in Richmond.

*Russell, Andrew J / The Library of Congress / Public Domain*

# Taking in prisoners of war

Early in the war, soldiers captured in battle were paroled or exchanged. A prisoner who was paroled pledged not to fight again and was released to go home, usually carrying a piece of paper that reflected his status. After 1863, prisoners were held until an exchange could be arranged, usually a one-for-one arrangement. After 1864, no more exchanges were made, primarily because the Union discovered that exchanges served only to replenish the ranks of the Confederate army. The Union, with sufficient manpower to draw on, benefited little from exchanges. Therefore, the iron logic of war condemned thousands of Union and Confederate soldiers to a sad fate. The North had 220,000 Confederate prisoners; over 26,000 died. The South had 127,000 Union prisoners; 22,000 died. Tragically, many Northerners died of neglect, mismanagement, and ignorance at Confederate prisons such as Andersonville, Libby Prison, and Belle Isle; many Southerners died at Johnson's Island, Camp Douglas, and Rock Island for the same reasons.

# Changing Women's Roles in the Civil War

The primary domain of women in the years prior to the war remained in the home. Family and home and demonstrating a steadfast loyalty to the fighting men and their cause were the hallmarks of women's role during the war. Although vitally important to the morale of the soldiers in the armies, this was not enough. Women voluntarily took on nontraditional tasks to support the war effort. The war transformed the perceptions of women in American life.

One of the first activities of women to do more to participate led to the establishment of ladies' aid societies. These organizations sprang up as women in both the North and the South took the initiative to do more on their own to support the soldiers, providing clothing and medical supplies and also raising funds for the war effort. The overwhelming number of casualties produced by the great battles of the war, as well as disease from crowded and unhealthy camp conditions, offered an opportunity for women to assist in helping return the sick and wounded back to active service. Far from their families and their communities, the sick and wounded faced a terrible burden. Women volunteered at all levels, responding to the overwhelming need. Dorothea Dix, a nurse and activist, was appointed to establish a federal nursing program. Between 15,000 and 20,000 women in the North served as nurses. Catholic nuns also came to the aid of suffering Union and Confederate soldiers.

Northern women supported the war effort through the U.S. Sanitary Commission, which distributed food, clothing, and medicine to wounded soldiers. Men and women of the commission visited army camps to instruct in the proper methods of disposing of waste and protecting sources of drinking water.

Women, both Black and white, could be found serving in various ways in Confederate hospitals. In 1862, the Confederate government began hiring nurses. In Richmond, which held the largest and greatest number of hospitals in the Confederacy, women filled most of the nurse and administrator positions because of the shortage of men outside the army. Two hospitals — Chimborazo (8,000 beds) and Jackson (6,000 beds) — were perhaps the largest facilities of their kind in North America. Shortages of food and medicine also hampered efforts and made patients' recovery even more difficult. In hospitals or makeshift collection points of wounded men, women did whatever they could. Often kindness was all they could offer. In the hospitals, women cooked food, washed clothing and linen, wrote letters for patients, sang, decorated the wards, and comforted the dying. Although the names of most of these women have been lost to history, there are a few who are famous. Kate Cunningham, a 27-year-old woman, traveled from Mobile to Corinth to help wounded Confederate soldiers after the Battle of Shiloh. Mary Ann Bickerdyke, known as "Mother Bickerdyke" to Union soldiers, became a famous army nurse and hospital administrator as well as a favorite of General Sherman. Clara Barton, founder of the American Red Cross, was the most famous nurse of the war. She worked at many hospitals bringing medicines and supplies. She actually helped recover casualties from the Antietam battlefield during the fight, and President Lincoln later appointed her to assist in identifying missing Union soldiers in the South. See Figure 26-4 for an example of a nurse during the Civil War.

**FIGURE 26-4:**
Nurse Ann Burtis Hampton, Virginia 1864.

*Liljenquist Family collection / The Library of Congress / Public Domain*

## An essential workforce

For both the Union and the Confederate war effort, the demand for production of war material and the expansion of the government bureaucracy to manage the war led to the addition of women to the workforce. Women worked in government offices and entered into factory jobs to replace men filling the ranks of the armies. Women in both the North and the South worked to produce ammunition, tents, clothing, shoes (there never seemed to be enough of these), and other articles.

## The cost of war: Refugees and starvation

Because nearly all men were in the army, Southern women took on the responsibilities of not only maintaining the farms and plantations, but also maintaining the national morale. Women were often the most vocal patriots and stirred religious efforts to purify Southern culture of its vices through prayer and fasting so that victory for the Confederacy would be assured. Women in Virginia, Mississippi, Tennessee, Alabama, South Carolina, and Louisiana found themselves under Union military occupation and martial law, where they often became a thorn in the sides of the Yankees, who endured countless insults and acts of open defiance.

As the war went on, many Southern families became refugees. As many as 200,000 women and children moved across the South seeking safety, usually arriving in cities when they had no place else to go. As Union troops approached, slaves often left the farms to seek freedom or to search for relatives. Food shortages and impossibly high prices led to sickness, despair, hunger, and a great weariness. By 1865, the women who had sustained the troops in the field for so long and maintained the nation's morale and hope now were writing letters to their men that described their destitute situations, their starvation, and their sickness, and that asked them to come home. Soldiers left the army by the thousands in those final months, leading directly to the Confederacy's rapid defeat in the first months of 1865. In one month in the winter of 1864, for example, Lee lost 8 percent of his army's strength due to desertion. A woman living in Virginia's Shenandoah Valley recalled how, in 1863, two of her runaway slaves returned with Union cavalry to free another slave woman and her children still on the farm. The Yankees told the slave that she could take anything from the farm with her. The only possession she wanted to take away with her, the newly liberated woman said to the soldiers, was herself.

## Spying for the North and South

Women served important roles as collectors of valuable intelligence information for both armies. As noncombatants, they were free to travel between the lines, making observations and reporting to military officers. Many Southern women traveled between the lines smuggling medicine, gold, and food under their clothing or in false-bottomed suitcases. Many became famous for their exploits. Here are some stories from three of the most well-known spies of the Civil War:

>> **Mary Elizabeth Bowser:** Mary Elizabeth Bowser was a former slave educated in Philadelphia before the war at the insistence of her former master's abolitionist daughter, Elizabeth Van Lew. Van Lew remained in Richmond during the war and passed information to Union spies. Late in the war, she recruited Bowser to help her by having her obtain a job as a servant in President Davis's residence, known as the Confederate White House. She reported to Van Lew what she had overheard in meetings or read from dispatches at the president's desk. (He never thought to hide these papers because slaves were not supposed to be able to read or write.) This information ended up in the hands of General Grant. Although he was aware that the Union army seemed to know what he was thinking, Jefferson Davis never discovered the spy in his own house.

>> **Belle Boyd:** Belle Boyd spied for the Confederacy in the Shenandoah Valley, passing important information on enemy troop movements to Stonewall Jackson during his Valley Campaign. Both in 1862 and in 1863, she was arrested for carrying letters and papers of value to the Confederacy across enemy lines, spending time in a Union prison after each arrest. Exiled by the Union government, she fled to England.

>> **Rose O'Neal Greenhow:** Rose O'Neal Greenhow, a society girl from Maryland, was well known in Washington before the war. During the war, she used her Washington connections to collect valuable information that she passed to General Beauregard just before the first battle of Bull Run. Imprisoned twice for her activities, Greenhow continued to smuggle information out of Washington. She was exiled to the Confederacy in 1863 after her second prison term. Shortly thereafter, she appeared in Great Britain and France to seek support for Confederate independence. In 1864, she attempted to return to the Confederacy on a British blockade runner. Chased by a Union gunboat as they approached Wilmington, North Carolina, the blockade runner struck a shoal. Fearing capture, Greenhow attempted to reach land in a small boat. The boat capsized in rough seas and she was drowned. Her body was recovered, and she was buried with full military honors in Wilmington.

# Taking Note of the African American Contribution

Frederick Douglass, a former slave who became one of the most eloquent spokesmen for African Americans, once said that after a Black man wore the uniform of his country, no power on earth could deny his right to citizenship. Many African Americans found the war to be their ticket to freedom. Former slaves who had abandoned their masters enlisted in the Union army to earn their citizenship and prove their worth. Likewise, slaves in the South served many critical roles in supporting the war effort. Of course, as an inherent part of the Southern population, they endured privations and suffering as the war progressed, and became part of the growing refugee problem in the last year of the Confederacy. Some served willingly, others did not, but their efforts kept the Confederacy alive for four years.

## Union: The U.S. Colored Troops

After the Emancipation Proclamation was issued, Congress authorized African Americans to enlist in the army (see Figure 26-5). Part of the reason for this was to offset Union losses in the battles of 1862. In addition, as Union forces moved deeper into the Confederacy, many slaves were employed to support the army by digging entrenchments, hauling supplies, and burying the dead. Over 160 units were formed, and about 180,000 African Americans served in the Union army during the war, a number representing nearly 10 percent of the entire Union army's strength. About 20,000 African Americans also served in the U.S. Navy.

**FIGURE 26-5:** Teamsters, Army of the James, 1864.

*Library of Congress Prints and Photographs Division [LC-DIG-cwpb-02004]*

The enlistees were segregated from white troops, and white officers led the units (although by the end of the war there were some Black officers in the units). Until 1864, Black soldiers were paid less than white troops. There was widespread prejudice against Black people in general and especially in the ability of African American soldiers to fight. As a result, many units were shipped off to relatively quiet areas. But in numerous small battles in Missouri, Louisiana, and Oklahoma, between 1862 and 1863, the newly raised regiments proved their worth in battle, gaining a reputation for determination and courage.

At Milliken's Bend, Louisiana, U.S. Colored Troops (see Figure 26-6) performed admirably in repulsing a Confederate attack. The 54th Massachusetts is probably the best-known African American unit. Its participation in the attack on Fort Wagner, South Carolina, in 1863 has become legendary. Although the attack failed, and the 54th lost nearly half its men, the unit's heroic assault attracted widespread admiration in the North. In the last two years of the war, African American units became more visible and fought with distinction in Grant's Virginia campaign, especially at New Market Heights outside of Richmond. They also participated in the initial assault on Petersburg, capturing a key fort and several cannons, and fought in the Battle of the Crater. U.S. Colored Troops served as the occupation force after the fall of Richmond. As a testimony to their important contribution on the battlefield, 16 African Americans won the Medal of Honor. Because they were often given the toughest assignments in battle, their casualties were heavy. About 32,000 African Americans enrolled in the army died in combat or from disease.

**FIGURE 26-6:** A unit of U.S. Colored Troops.

Smith, William Morris / The Library of Congress / Public Domain

## African Americans in the Confederacy

Estimates state that between 60,000 and 90,000 African Americans served with the Confederacy in various capacities. The contributions of African Americans to the Confederacy's war effort were inestimable. Over 90 percent of the coal miners in Virginia were African American; Tredegar Iron Works in Richmond, one of the most important arms-producing factories in the Confederacy, employed 1,200 African American laborers, representing over half its work force. These were skilled laborers who were deemed so valuable to the war effort that they had special privileges equal to whites. Thousands of African Americans also built fortifications, served as teamsters, grew crops, and worked in factories. Slaves were quick to recognize that the war was changing everything, and that life would never return to what it had been before the war. As a result, slaves became more independent minded and less accepting of the system of bondage that they recognized was growing weaker every month. Slavery as an institution was dying under the blast of war and African Americans began changing their circumstances accordingly. Although white Southerners reacted with shock and sadness to these changing circumstances, they, too recognized that there was no returning to prewar conditions.

In 1864, General Patrick Cleburne and other Confederate officers proposed the once impossible idea of enlisting slaves to serve in the Confederate army. Those slaves who volunteered would win their freedom at the end of their enlistment. By 1865, with defeat all but a reality, and willing to undergo a revolutionary way of thinking about slavery itself, the Confederate Congress in 1865 passed a measure authorizing the formation of African American units to fight as free men for the Confederacy. By the time President Davis signed the measure into law in March, the few African American companies that were raised never saw battle — the war ended in April.

# Discovering the American Indians

The Cherokee tribe prior to the Civil War was considered to be a separate nation within the United States. Like other parts of the nation, it too displayed divided loyalties. American Indians (including Stand Watie) owned slaves for the same reasons white Southerners did, although the status of slaves in the Indian territories was different than in the Southern states; usually a slave and an American Indian master enjoyed a more equal social relationship. Many American Indians feared U.S. government policies toward them and turned to the Confederacy as a means to protect their land and property. Others resisted Confederate entreaties and supported the Union occupation of much of Indian Territory (present-day Oklahoma). There were three regiments of infantry to defend the territory against Confederate incursions. They fought in several small engagements in Missouri and Arkansas.

Stand Watie was a Cherokee Indian and a member of the tribal council. When the war began, he joined the Confederacy and became a colonel. He raised a cavalry regiment of 3,000 other Cherokees. At the battle of Pea Ridge in Arkansas,

March 7–8, 1862, Watie's unit captured a Union artillery battery. Throughout the war Watie's unit, composed of Cherokees, Osage, Seminoles, and Creeks, played constant havoc with Union supply lines. He was promoted to brigadier general in 1864 and was the last Confederate officer to surrender, on June 23, 1865. Other American Indian tribes, including the Choctaw and Chickasaw, joined mounted units. Altogether, American Indians contributed 11 regiments and 8 battalions of cavalry to the Confederacy.

Ely Parker was an Iroquois leader (see Figure 26-7), a member of the New York state militia, and he supervised government construction projects throughout the Midwest. In 1860, he met Ulysses Grant, who became a lifelong friend. When the war began, he volunteered to raise a regiment of Iroquois to fight for the Union. New York's governor rejected his offer. Attempting to join the army, he finally succeeded when Grant stood before Vicksburg. Grant needed engineering expertise and sought out his friend. His engineering skills brought him acclaim, and in 1864 he became a member of Grant's personal staff. When Lee and Grant met at Appomattox, Grant selected Parker to draft the surrender papers because of his penmanship and his elegant writing style. He served on Grant's staff until 1869, achieving the rank of brigadier general. When Grant became president, he served as the head of the Bureau of Indian Affairs.

**FIGURE 26-7:** Ely Parker (shown on the left).

Henszey & Co / The Library of Congress / Public Domain

# 6

# The Civil War Tourist

**IN THIS PART . . .**

Get some tips on visiting and appreciating Civil War battlefields.

Explore opportunities to deepen your appreciation of the Civil War and its meaning for you.

# Chapter 27

# Getting Ready to Travel

A s indicated in the introduction, the Civil War is a very important part of American history. One of the purposes of this book is to give the reader just enough information to get interested in getting up and going out to a battlefield. Part of the thrill of learning history is that you can often visit the places where the great events of the past actually happened. There is a special attraction to these places because they hold truths and understanding that go far beyond what you have read in a book or heard about. It is an opportunity to connect with the past and rekindle in your imagination what it must have been like. Sometimes the feeling is truly overwhelming.

Many Civil War battlefields have been preserved for visitors. These places allow you to gain a deeper appreciation of the events and their greater meaning to our history as a whole. Visiting Civil War sites brings the war and all its tragedy and glory to life. You can walk the ground of Pickett's Charge or stand at the Bloody Angle at Spotsylvania. You can gaze over the fields at the fortifications protecting Vicksburg; you can walk over Snodgrass Hill, or climb Lookout Mountain, or stand on Burnside's Bridge and walk along Bloody Lane. You can stand behind the stone wall at Fredericksburg or stand at the Crater, still a giant scar on the land after 150 years. You can walk with the spirits of those Union and Confederate soldiers who still seem to haunt the woods in the Wilderness and Chancellorsville. You can sense the chaos in the woods and groves of Shiloh, feel the thrill of fear and anticipation with the boy soldiers at New Market, and even get the same red dust on your shoes that thousands of Confederate soldiers kicked up while walking up the road to surrender at Appomattox. History does not have to be dull and empty — it is vibrant with meaning. Simply put, battlefields allow you to touch the past.

# Planning Your Trip

Depending on your motivation, you can take on a battlefield any way you want. For most Civil War fanatics, this is not a problem. However, if you are not a fanatic and are a little confused or intimidated at the prospect of visiting a battlefield, fear not. People's interest in the Civil War varies. Some like the in-the-dirt minuscule details, others like only the big picture, and still others are completely without any bearings at all and simply want to explore and be exposed to it. There are all types in between, as you probably know. With a more than casual interest in the Civil War and a little planning, you can make a visit to a battlefield or a historical site both worthwhile and uplifting.

Like anything else, setting realistic goals is important. Deciding exactly what you want to do will determine how much time you spend at the battlefield or historical site. The following are some examples of ways you can set your goals:

>> Often a book you have read, a newspaper article, or a television show has sparked your interest or curiosity about an event in the war. Use that as the basis for a trip to go and explore that question or see that site to gain a greater appreciation.

>> Getting a general overview of the events is easy to do by simply driving or walking around at random. Often something of interest appears during these ramblings that leads to further exploration.

>> Another approach is to select a specific unit, perhaps the one a relative served in, or a famous regiment of one of the armies, and follow it through a battle (or even a campaign). A visit to a battlefield in this way can deepen one's appreciation for the experience of the common soldier and can allow you to share in a unit's heritage.

>> If you admire a certain Civil War general (or generals), visiting a battlefield to follow in his footsteps, so to speak, is always fun. Here you can survey the terrain he saw and evaluate the decisions he made. This approach allows you to know the man and the soldier better.

>> Those who are more ambitious can follow an army's entire campaign, driving down roads the army marched on and stopping at sites along the way. Although this can involve some good map-reading skills and usually a thorough understanding of strategy, tactics, logistics, and command, it is not necessary. Sometimes taking to the back roads with a purpose in mind is an adventure in itself.

>> If you like, you can go to a battlefield and cover the events hour by hour, and regiment by regiment, spending hours (even days) on just one section of the battlefield. Clearly this demands the most preparation and research and is reserved for only the most dedicated Civil War enthusiasts.

As these examples suggest, setting goals becomes important, depending on your level of interest and purpose for visiting. Knowing what you want to do and how much detail you want to delve into will determine how much time you should set aside for a visit. Some people employ all these methods over the years. Starting with a general orientation, they revisit the battlefields year after year as their interest grows, adding another layer of detail and understanding. So, as your interests change, so do your goals and the time you will invest in your visit.

# Using Your Time Wisely

With all the conflicting priorities in people's lives today, defining what time they will spend on the things they value is more important than ever. Therefore, to avoid wasting time, a visit to a battlefield must involve an assessment of how much time you want to invest. This includes not only the time it takes to get to the battlefield, but also how much time to spend at the site. The goals you set for your visit will determine the time you should spend. Here are some examples:

>> If your goal is a short orientation visit or an examination of a specific portion of the battlefield, plan to spend at least one hour but no more than three, including stops (markers, museums, visitor center).

>> If your goal is to follow a specific unit or commander, plan to spend four to eight hours, depending on your level of interest and the amount of detail you want to delve into.

>> If your goal is to follow a campaign, a car trip can take anywhere from four hours to several days, depending on the campaign and the amount of detail you want to pursue. You can also break the campaign into several smaller chunks or the most important portion that allows you to make the best use of your time.

>> If your goal is a thorough study of an aspect of a battle or an in-depth examination of a battle, one day is never enough. Again, depending on your energy, bank balance, and level of interest, this can go on for a while. Leave a forwarding address and pack clean underwear before you leave.

# Taking Three Methods on a Battlefield

After you have determined your goals and the time you want to spend, you must decide on the best method to visit the battlefield. If you do not take the time to look at the best method that suits your level of interest, odds are you will be disappointed with your experience at the battlefield. Therefore, I suggest three possible approaches.

# Mounted

This is travel by vehicle through the battlefield without getting out of your car. Most battlefields administered by the National Park Service are set up to allow you to stop at specific sites and read markers from your vehicle. This method involves the following considerations:

>> **Advantage:** This method will give you a general overview and an appreciation for the scope of the battlefield. You get through at your own pace and stop where and when you want. If the weather is bad, this may be the only way to see the battlefield.

>> **Disadvantage:** You pretty much see only what you can from the road. Distances can be distorted, and the markers tell only the briefest part of the story of the battle. Vehicle travel can tend to fragment the battlefield as you go from one stop to another.

# Mounted/dismounted

With this approach, you still spend most of your time in the vehicle, but you get out and walk around at the places you want.

>> **Advantage:** This is good for those who are interested in a specific place or event on the battlefield. You can combine the general orientation with a point of interest on which you want to spend more time. You can also combine several points of interest and spend time where you want. If you have done a thorough study of the battle and the terrain, this is an excellent approach to examining key events. This also works well for a campaign tour.

>> **Disadvantage:** Sometimes this method allows you to be too ambitious, trying to stop and see everything. It can be done, but it tends to reinforce the short attention span. Stop here, take a look, run to the next stop. This method requires some self-discipline and preplanning so you don't get off track.

# Terrain walk

This approach puts you at the soldier or leader level and places you in their footsteps. You discover how high the hill is, how deep the creek is, what you can see from what point. It is the ultimate battlefield experience for these reasons:

>> **Advantage:** This method puts you in the middle of the action and allows you to notice things that soldiers themselves encountered.

>> **Disadvantage:** You need to be in reasonable physical shape and highly motivated. This type of tour will take a long time. Those who take this approach are usually well prepared with maps, books about the battle, and good shoes. Such a trip can be very frustrating if you are not thoroughly prepared. But if you are prepared, it is extremely rewarding.

These are general guidelines, of course. But for those new to the world of Civil War battlefield exploration, these methods are a good way to match goals with time. As you become more comfortable and confident, a visitor can improve their visit by an imaginative combination of the three basic methods.

# Chapter **28**

# Visiting a Civil War Battlefield

The previous chapter helps you to establish goals for visiting Civil War battlefields, to look at the time you want to spend on your trip, and to decide upon a method to take on the battlefield — 90 percent of the solution. This chapter helps you to complete your plans and get the most out of the experience while you're at the battlefield.

## Fine-Tuning Your Trip

When planning a trip to a Civil War site, an important step is to decide who's going on your trip. Although it may sound a bit silly, this is actually a significant consideration in your planning. Trips must be geared and designed with the toleration limits of other visitors in mind. In other words, do not plan a full-scale campaign trip followed by all-day terrain walks if no one else wants to delve into that much detail. Otherwise, the trip will quickly be ruined for everyone. Gauge the interest level and enthusiasm of your companions and lay out the trip accordingly. (To find out more about the three approaches to visiting a battlefield — mounted, mounted/dismounted, and terrain walk methods — see Chapter 27.)

## Getting an enthusiast

Another approach is to invite a knowledgeable authority to travel with you and act as an informal guide. Many Civil War enthusiasts are more than willing to take people on tours of their favorite battlefield. They always have interesting stories to tell and provide a valuable perspective on the events that occurred there. Often, bringing along an enthusiast is a good way to get family participation and a satisfying introduction to a battlefield. You can also go alone with an enthusiast, get a good feel for the battlefield, use the approach you like best, then act as your own guide for others who are interested in exploring the battlefield with you. Your local Civil War Round Table or the park service can connect you with an enthusiast (the author is also available if you are really up for it).

## Checking the Internet

Any book written at the opening of the 21st century would be terribly remiss if it did not mention the Internet as a resource in preparing for a battlefield visit. Some Civil War Internet stuff is top-notch; other stuff is, well, unsatisfactory. The National Park Service (NPS) is the best place to start. Visiting a specific battlefield website offers helpful information, including virtual tours of some battlefields online. You can also find many websites that allow you to download just about any kind of map you want — from topographical to aerial and period maps. Photos of battlefields can give you a feel for the terrain, and guidebooks, unit histories, and battlefield descriptions are also available. The American Battlefield Trust (https://www.battlefields.org) works to preserve Civil War (and other) battlefields. It is also an excellent site that provides detailed battle maps and a wealth of excellent Civil War information. Any battlefield visitor will profit from a visit to this website and may be inspired to support its charitable work in purchasing and preserving land associated with Civil War battles.

## Bringing the right stuff

What you bring depends on your level of enthusiasm and interest. A first-time visitor may only want to obtain a park brochure and take a driving tour, also known as the mounted approach to touring a battlefield. You don't need to prepare for this type of visit. Sometimes bringing along a history of the campaign or battle adds to the appreciation and becomes a ready reference when using the mounted/dismounted method. Some people like to spend a few days before a battlefield visit exploring the library for accounts of the battle to get a firm understanding of events and to identify locations that they may want to visit. Still others purchase terrain maps and photocopy pages of texts. These people may bring along a chest or a backpack of books — all marked and available for immediate reference — and look for exact locations of units at key times during the battle.

These are the people who enjoy the terrain walk method. Generally speaking, here are some things to think about bringing on your visit:

>> **Binoculars:** Civil War generals used them extensively to survey terrain and troop movements. You can do the same. Binoculars give you a better appreciation of distance, and key terrain will stand out as you examine the battlefield from different perspectives. For example, you can examine a particular spot from the point of view of the defender, then move and look at it from the point of view of the attacker. What you see (or don't see) will surprise you.

>> **Maps:** The term *maps* here includes everything from the basic visitor center brochure and guide (which are almost always excellent) to highly detailed terrain maps. You can find a map to fit any level of interest. Regardless of complexity, a map gives you the basic information you need to understand the events that took place. A map also gets you properly oriented and allows you to locate the most important points of interest to guide you there.

>> **Books:** Depending on your level of interest and enthusiasm, books can be very helpful in pointing out details of events that are often overlooked. Sometimes it can be very rewarding to stand on the ground and read a famous historian's narrative of the event or read the firsthand account of a soldier who fought on the ground you are standing on. Combining a written narrative with a visual survey of the battlefield certainly can help deepen your appreciation and understanding.

>> **Food and water and restrooms:** Having adequate supplies is important and will help maximize the time you spend on the battlefield. Make sure to have something to drink in your car or backpack. On summer days in Virginia, Mississippi, or Tennessee it gets pretty hot, so plan ahead. Snacks are always a good idea, depending on how much time you plan to spend. You usually have to trek back to the visitor center to use a restroom, so it pays in more ways than one to plan ahead.

>> **Rain gear, hats, sunscreen, bug spray:** If you like to get out of the car and explore, or are planning a terrain walk, don't forget to be ready. Make sure you are prepared for the hot sun and annoying bloodsucking insects in summer. Sometimes the best time to visit a battlefield is in the late fall or winter, when the trees are bare and more of the terrain is visible. The weather can often be unpredictable, so planning ahead is important.

>> **Money:** Some Civil War battlefields require an entrance fee, which you pay at the visitor center. Here you will usually find a gift shop that has books, maps, and trinkets that may attract your eye. You can also pick up your battlefield guide and map brochure here. Other opportunities for siphoning money out of your pocket usually abound in places near the battlefields.

# Getting Oriented: The Visitor Center

It is not a good idea to drive out to a battlefield and start looking at markers and terrain without having some idea of where you are on the battlefield. If the battlefield you're visiting is operated by the National Parks Service (NPS), you'll find that a stop at the visitor center is always worth your time. A quick Internet query will take you to the NPS site for the particular battlefield you're interested in. You'll find many useful resources there to prepare you for your visit. At the visitor center, you can find free information, brochures with maps, and knowledgeable people who will answer questions. Sometimes the visitor center has a theater or an electric map that gives an overview of the battle. Often they also contain a display of artifacts from the battle. You can get oriented at the visitor center and plan where you want to go and what you want to see. Make sure you know your location on the map you have, and make sure you know where the places you want to see are also identified on the map. Always keep yourself oriented to where the forces were at the sites you want to look at. This will prevent you from getting lost or looking in the wrong direction when you get to the place you want to see. Try to picture in your mind what units were located where, both while you're driving around and also when you stop somewhere. At the battlefields that are operated by state park commissions or private groups, you may not find a visitor center. In that case, go to the most prominent or well-known site on the battlefield and orient yourself to the terrain and identify the locations you want to stop and visit. You can then backtrack to where you want to start.

## Asking the right questions

Visitors to battlefields are sometimes afraid to ask questions because they think that asking questions makes them appear dumb. Whether you're talking to a park ranger or touring the battlefield with a knowledgeable expert, phrasing a question that can be answered succinctly and still give you the information you want is difficult. Battles revolve around four factors: terrain (the lay of the land), leadership (the actions of the army, corps, or division commanders), firepower (the employment and effects of various weapons on the battlefield), and logistics (the support and supply of the armies in the field). Thus, you can always base a question on any of these four factors and get a satisfactory answer. Here are some sample questions that are common to all battlefield studies that will give you instant credibility:

>> **For terrain:** What is the most important piece of ground on this battlefield? Why? How did the terrain affect the placement of soldiers and weapons on the battlefield? Did this make a difference in the outcome of the battle? Why did this particular area become a battlefield?

- » **For leadership:** Which commander had a better idea of what was happening on the battlefield? Why? What was the most important decision each commander made in this battle? What happened as a result? What caused this general to win (or lose) this battle?

- » **For firepower:** Did artillery play a significant role in this battle? Why or why not? Did the troops dig entrenchments? Why? Where did firepower play the biggest role in this battle? What was the result?

- » **For logistics:** What supply problems did the armies have? Did they affect planning in any way? How did the armies deal with casualties? How did they get food and ammunition to the front lines? What critical areas did the army have to protect to prevent it from being cut off from its source of supply?

## Finding the best monuments and markers

Some battlefields are loaded with monuments and markers — so many that getting to every one would take days. Some visitors feel that they must look at every statue and every sign to understand the battle. This is not true. In fact, the people who do this often walk away bewildered and frustrated, rather than informed. Avoid this problem by knowing your goals, having a method, and orienting yourself upon arrival at the battlefield.

Veterans of the war often raised the monuments on battlefields to commemorate both the deeds of their unit on the field and their fallen comrades. The passage of time has often obscured those individual unit contributions (unless you happen to have an in-depth knowledge of specific units, then the location of these monuments is significant). Some monuments on certain battlefields that should not be missed. Asking about the best monuments at the visitor center is always worthwhile.

In addition, markers on the battlefield are sometimes confusing. There are many markers that locate where a specific unit was during a specific period in the battle. If you are not visiting a battlefield to examine events at such a level of detail, don't be distracted. Instead, look for those markers that identify significant events on the battlefield. The NPS is good at placing descriptive markers at the important sites. Look for these during your visit. Often states will have a marker along a main road indicating an important event related to a battle or a maneuver. When traveling in your car near a battlefield, be alert for these markers. They will help orient you. Pulling off the road to read these markers is always best; whizzing by at 50 miles an hour puts a dent in your reading comprehension, and those 180-degree high-speed turns you make when you realize you have passed a marker tend to make other drivers nervous. Be careful!

# Appreciating the Terrain

If you have no information on a particular battle, a visit to the battlefield can still be useful by taking time to observe the lay of the land. This is called *terrain appreciation*. Hills, woods, valleys, creeks, rivers, bridges, railroads, main roads (especially intersections of main roads), and ridges all are significant to military operations. Look for these features at the battlefield and you will most likely find some marker or monument indicating that something important happened there. These terrain features dictated how and where a commander placed his units, either to protect them from enemy fire, screen them from the enemy's view, or protect a critical area and prevent the enemy from capturing it. The good thing about the lay of the land is that while everything else changes, the land usually does not. The same terrain the Civil War armies encountered is often still there for you to see just as they did. Often Civil War battles were focused on the control of a single important piece of ground, and if you go to that piece of ground, you can understand the entire flow of the battle. Always keep the importance of terrain in mind when visiting a battlefield.

# Studying, Stories, and Reflection

Battlefields lend themselves to study and storytelling. Some people like to spend a great deal of time reading everything they can about a battle before visiting the ground. Certainly, studying the aspects of the battle can raise your understanding and appreciation of the events that took place on the battlefield. But study is not necessary for appreciation. One interesting thing about battlefields is that a visitor always comes away with some kind of story about what happened. It could be the historical facts; it could be an anecdote; it could be a tale of mystery, heroism, or tragedy. It could be all three. What is important is that these places allow you to take something away with you.

Battlefields are repositories of memory; they speak to visitors in many ways. There are places on certain Civil War battlefields that rise to the level of consecrated ground, places of courage and sacrifice so great that the echoes of those acts still linger in the air. You can stand literally where great men stood and see the fields they saw and try to imagine what they were thinking. But you must take the time to listen. No matter how much time you spend on a battlefield, take the time, even if just a minute or two, to let those memories speak.

# 7

# The Part of Tens

**IN THIS PART . . .**

Gain an opportunity to argue with the author — agree or disagree with the worst generals, biggest "firsts," and biggest "what-ifs" lists.

Find the best battlefields and how to navigate them.

» Noting the oblivious strategists and planners

» Uncovering the poorest combat officers

» Looking at the generals who were in way over their heads

Chapter **29**

# The Ten Worst Generals of the Civil War

Some officers appear born to lead men, while others — well, they succeed in accomplishing nothing except large casualty lists. I'm not saying that poor generals are necessarily men of bad character or have evil intent. They are just unfortunate enough to be put in places of great authority and responsibility and do not have the abilities to do what needs to be done. The bad generals of good character usually know they are in over their heads and have the good sense to remove themselves from command. The truly bad generals are those whose egos are so great that their careers are more important than anything else. They will persist in bumbling around and getting men killed for nothing. They are still around, folks — to the eternal regret of good soldiers everywhere.

Appearance is no indicator of a good general — even though most of the guys on this list more often than not *looked* like generals. On the other hand, Grant and Sherman hardly looked like generals, but they performed far beyond what most people believed they could do. The selections here are based on continuous bad leadership, a conspicuous display of ineptitude in war, and the amount of ill will they inspired among their troops and subordinates. The following generals, who often made the "Goats" lists in this book's battle reports, are listed in no particular order. I leave it to the reader to rank them.

# Braxton Bragg (1817–1876)

Bragg's greatest failure as a commander was his personality. He was a very good organizer, and a man of excellent character. But he was a harsh disciplinarian, and his plans usually had no purpose, because he had no concept of campaigning, especially in knowing to what strategic purpose his battles were leading. Usually, Bragg lost his focus either just before or just after a battle, leaving his subordinates to decide for themselves what they were supposed to do.

This problem was compounded by Bragg's inability to deal with others. His subordinate commanders loathed him. As a result, he found that his orders were almost never carried out properly. He had almost no friends — none except the one who counted most — President Jefferson Davis. When everyone else had lost patience with the argumentative and carping Bragg, Davis always sided with his friend. Bragg, therefore, could continue in his ways. In combat, this often meant frontal assaults on strongly defended positions and a dogmatic attachment to a plan already rendered useless by changing events.

# Nathaniel P. Banks (1816–1894)

Banks fought the entire war without contributing much to the Union cause. A member of Congress, former governor of Massachusetts, and president of the Illinois Central Railroad before the war, Banks was an essential player on the Republican team. This translated into a general's commission and command. He was beaten in the Shenandoah Valley repeatedly in 1862, becoming the negative example of what not to do as a general. Confederate troops dubbed him "Commissary Banks" for his army's habit of leaving behind its supply trains and depots when beaten. Jackson seemed to have had Banks's number. At Cedar Mountain, Jackson again took him to task. This ended Banks's contribution to the Union cause in the Eastern Theater.

After a short stint guarding Washington, Banks went south to Louisiana to clear Port Hudson in support of Grant's move against Vicksburg. Banks made such a mess of this maneuver that he was all but useless. In 1864, Banks was selected to move against General Kirby Smith's forces in the Trans-Mississippi up the Red River. With a formidable army supported by a strong naval force, Banks made a haphazard and slow movement up the river where his army was defeated at Sabine Cross Roads, losing more than 2,500 men. The campaign was a fiasco from beginning to end — he could not coordinate with the navy or other army commanders. At the end of the campaign, Congress conducted an investigation of the mess. After the war, Banks returned to Congress, where perhaps his skills were better appreciated.

# Ambrose E. Burnside (1824–1881)

Burnside — he of the luxurious sideburns and whiskers — stood six feet tall and was an imposing figure in his uniform, sash, and sword. Alas, the handsome general was a better recruiting poster than he was a commander. Burnside had the good fortune to experience modest success when all other Union generals were falling on their faces. In 1862, he had captured some sand on the coast of North Carolina. While the troops remained behind to battle sand fleas and mosquitoes, Burnside joined his friend Major General George McClellan with the Army of the Potomac. At Antietam (see Chapter 14), Burnside, with nearly a third of the entire army available to him, was unable to solve the basic tactical problem of crossing a bridge under fire. It took him nearly all day, and when he was within striking distance of victory, his attack fell apart when General A.P. Hill arrived to drive him off.

In the aftermath of the Antietam mess, Lincoln selected Burnside for command of the army. To his credit, Burnside pleaded with the president to select someone else. He was not up to the job, he told Lincoln. But he took it anyway, and he led the army to its greatest defeat, at Fredericksburg in December 1862. About a month later, Burnside attempted a flanking march around Lee's army that quickly bogged down in the winter rains to the point that Burnside had to call off the operation and return the men to winter quarters. From then on it was known as the "Mud March," and it marked the all-time low point of the army's morale. Burnside soon disappeared into the bowels of Ohio, commanding a military department that would cause no one harm. But Burnside found a way, harassing the obnoxious anti-war politician Clement Vallandigham and causing the Lincoln administration endless headaches. He was competent at Knoxville, defending fortifications against a poorly conducted attack by Longstreet.

Burnside returned to the Army of the Potomac in 1864 and took command of a corps that included several regiments of U.S. Colored Troops. He squandered many of these troops in the disaster at the Crater in the summer of 1864. From then on, Grant was careful to keep Burnside as far away from the important action as possible. Burnside was a poor planner, an inept commander, and unimaginative in the application of the military art. Yet he looked good in uniform, had a pleasant personality, and wore a winning smile. He translated all of this into a brilliant postwar political career, serving as governor and then senator of the state of Rhode Island.

# John B. Hood (1831–1879)

Hood actually doesn't belong in this chapter completely. Up until 1864, Hood was one of the Confederacy's best division commanders. As a combat leader, he was superb and his reputation as a fighter only grew as time went on. His Texas

Brigade was one of Lee's elite fighting units, and Hood was always personally leading his men in the most brutal fighting of the early years of the war. He was such an inspiring leader that the men would chant his name as they advanced into battle. Hood soon became a division commander in General Longstreet's I Corps. As a division commander, he still displayed the fire and aggressiveness that had made him a great combat leader. His troops spearheaded the attack on the second day at Gettysburg (see Chapter 18). There he was wounded in the arm, losing the use of the limb. But that did not stop him. He was soon back in action and led Longstreet's attack at Chickamauga (see Chapter 19). He was wounded in the leg and had the limb amputated. Even this did not slow him down. He served poorly as a corps commander under Johnston in the operations in north Georgia, never able to think at the level required to employ a large unit in combat. Regardless, he was promoted to lieutenant general, and took command of the Army of Tennessee in 1864.

Then the tide turned to Hood as one of the worst generals of the Civil War. Hood was a brilliant officer at the brigade and division levels, but he had no business commanding either a corps or an army. The command responsibilities at these levels are different, and the intellectual demands are greater. Throughout the war Hood had depended on courage and violent assault to overwhelm the enemy. While that tactic can work well at the regiment or brigade level, it is much less effective at the division, corps, and army levels. Success at the regiment and brigade level in this war depended on personal courage and direct assaults to capture small pieces of terrain. At the division, corps, and army levels, war is much more complex and requires attention to more sophisticated skills, such as deception, maneuvers, proper use of cavalry and artillery, and the design of a campaign. Hood's scope of vision was far too narrow, and above brigade level his battle management skills were terrible. Hood could only use his army as a giant brigade. He never overcame his limitations.

Hood also dabbled in political backdoor deals. He influenced President Davis — who greatly admired Hood's courage and battlefield leadership — to select him as the new commander of the Army of Tennessee, where Hood was an unmitigated disaster. He could only display tactical ineptness, one-dimensional planning, and dull-witted reactions when the situation called for operational finesse and adept maneuver. Hood made costly frontal assaults that wasted his army's strength and sapped its morale. He battered himself into impotence outside of Atlanta and ignored his enemy's capabilities at the most crucial time in the Confederacy's life, when the nation's fate lay in the hands of Northern votes who would reject Lincoln and the war and sue for peace. Instead, Sherman was able to take the city just in time to make a decisive turn in the Republican party's political fortunes. Hood then destroyed his army in a series of bizarre and foolish frontal assaults on well-entrenched Union troops at Franklin and Nashville. Hood is a fine example of an officer promoted beyond his skill level. Just because you are a good tactical commander doesn't mean you should be promoted to command at a higher level. Recent history abounds with rapidly promoted but out-of-depth generals who deliver similar outcomes.

# John B. Floyd (1806–1863)

Floyd served as James Buchanan's secretary of war and became a brigadier general after joining the Confederacy. Accused of some sneaky tactics as secretary of war (such as fraud and stockpiling weapons in federal arsenals in the South just before secession), Floyd displayed similar double-dealing in his one and only moment of importance. Floyd played an important role in allowing McClellan to become the Young Napoleon when Floyd mismanaged the defense of western Virginia (now West Virginia).

Transferred to Kentucky, he was later assigned as commander of Fort Donelson in Tennessee. Floyd so mismanaged the garrison and its defense that he all but allowed Grant to capture it without a fight. Floyd was no general; he was, in fact, a coward. Essentially giving the order of every man for himself, he escaped from the fort. The fall of Donelson was a significant strategic blow to the Confederacy in the Western Theater and set Grant on the path to military glory. Davis wisely relieved him from any command responsibilities and placed him in a position in Virginia where he would do no harm. Floyd's death in 1863 passed largely unnoticed.

# Benjamin F. Butler (1818–1893)

Men such as Butler, a Massachusetts Democrat who supported the war, were crucial to Lincoln's war coalition. Butler was a prominent member of the state government and was appointed a brigadier general of volunteers. In 1861, his unit opened the rail lines to the capital through Baltimore that Southern sympathizers had blocked and destroyed, and as a result he earned a major general's appointment from the president. Butler went on to have a more disproportionate influence on the war than anyone intended. He was an ineffective troop commander. When faced with anything more than token opposition, he always lost the battle. Butler's modest advance up the Virginia peninsula from Fort Monroe in 1861 was sharply turned back, but he did gain some undeserved notoriety as a competent commander for capturing Hatteras Inlet in North Carolina. Butler is credited with giving the title of "contraband" to runaway slaves who entered Union lines. Butler reasoned that because they were still property under the Constitution, he could legally refer to them as captured war material, or contraband, applying the legal term for such items.

By May 1862, Butler served as the military governor of New Orleans after its capture by the Union navy. Butler governed the city competently, but at the same time ensured that he, his political cronies, and his family benefited handsomely. Southerners called him "Spoons" Butler for allegedly stealing the silver from the house he had taken over as his headquarters. He made himself thoroughly unpopular and was recalled in December 1862 (Nathaniel Banks, who, as we have seen, was not much better, replaced him).

In 1863, Butler became commander of the Army of the James and was included in Grant's overall strategy for conquering Virginia in 1864. Butler performed so ineptly that he maneuvered his two corps into a neck of land on the James River that allowed the Confederates to entrench across and sew him up as tight as a hatband. Butler's troops were useless to Grant for much of the campaign. Butler also mismanaged attacks at Petersburg and Fort Fisher, but his political influence was such that Grant could not get rid of him until Lincoln's reelection was secured. Grant promptly sent him home to await orders (which, of course, never came). Butler became a member of Congress in 1866, serving more than a decade. He later became governor of Massachusetts and ran unsuccessfully for president in 1884.

# Leonidas (Bishop) Polk (1806–1864)

Polk was another of Jefferson Davis's favorites and a man who achieved high rank quickly without demonstrating competence. An Episcopal bishop before the war, Polk gave up his position to become first a major general in 1861, then lieutenant general in 1862. Polk had the air of a man who always knew better than his commanding officer. By 1862, Polk had responsibility for the defense of a large part of the Western Theater. He was a fair to good organizer, but unimaginative and, perhaps, a bit lazy. He made the undoubtedly fatal error of violating Kentucky's neutrality, which led directly to the Union taking control of the upper Mississippi and western Tennessee.

As a high-ranking general, Polk had to be given significant command. Usually, the command was far too great a responsibility for his capabilities. Although a man of great physical courage — he led four assaults against Union defenses at Shiloh (see Chapter 9) — Polk was beyond his depth as a corps commander, and it showed in his often flawed battle performances at Perryville, Murfreesboro, and Chickamauga (see Chapters 15, 16, and 19). In each case, he interpreted his orders broadly as he saw fit, moved too slowly, or squandered opportunities. He also spent time helping Davis play the commander roulette game in the Western Theater, providing advice on the men he thought were best suited to take over the Army of Tennessee.

When an artillery shell killed Polk during the 1864 Atlanta Campaign (one of the most improbable cannon shots in the war), Jefferson Davis called it the Confederacy's greatest loss since Stonewall Jackson. In reality, Polk was mourned more for his qualities as a man than as a soldier.

# Joseph Hooker (1814–1879)

No one thought higher of himself as a combat commander than Joe Hooker. And no one displayed less ability. He seemed to have hit his peak as a captain, earning a reputation for bravery and personal leadership during the Mexican-American War. In 1862, Hooker emerged from civilian obscurity to gain a brigadier general's commission. (West Point graduates were especially valued early in the war and given high ranks to entice them back into the service.) He gained political support within the Lincoln cabinet from Salmon P. Chase and became a standout in the highly politicized Army of the Potomac. But he had some serious negatives — he was known as a heavy drinker and a womanizer; he also had something of a mean streak when dealing with higher-ranking officers.

Hooker led a division and then a corps competently during some of the Army of the Potomac's most terrible battles in 1862 and used his modest success as a battlefield commander (the newspapers erroneously called him "Fighting Joe" Hooker) to lobby against Ambrose Burnside remaining in command after the debacle at Fredericksburg. Given a chance to take command of the Army of the Potomac, he did this with relish and aplomb. The army benefitted from his organizational skills. His headquarters, however, was known to be a rather wide-open place where a lot more than military planning went on. His campaign plan against Richmond in the spring of 1863 was sound on paper, but what would make it work would be the skill of the commander, not empty boasts. The army's defeat at Chancellorsville cemented the reputations of Lee and Jackson as great combat leaders; it ruined Hooker's. He was completely ineffective in command and lost his nerve. As Lee moved north, Hooker seemed bewildered and slow to react.

Lincoln removed him from command before he could do more harm. He was transferred to the Western Theater along with the XI and XII Corps to support Grant. Hooker took command of the two corps, now combined and renamed the XX Corps. He and his troops performed adequately at Chattanooga, and his command did well during the Atlanta Campaign, but he quarreled with Sherman over who would take command of the Army of the Tennessee after McPherson's death in 1864. Hooker fully expected to be named the commander because he was next in line in seniority. Sherman would have nothing of seniority and selected a more able subordinate. Hooker asked to be relieved, and Sherman quickly acceded to his request. Hooker spent the rest of war in anonymity, retiring from the army in 1868.

# John Pope (1822–1892)

Like many other officers in the Union army in the Eastern Theater, John Pope was given one chance to be a great general. Like some others, his flaws in combat leadership and inability to command at higher levels doomed him to failure when he was counted on the most to succeed. Pope had the good fortune to begin the Civil War as a captain and a relative to President Lincoln's wife. He found himself a brigadier general very quickly and demonstrated some competence in the Western Theater, capturing key Confederate redoubts on the Mississippi River in 1862. He was promoted to major general and became part of Halleck's tortoise-slow approach to Corinth after Shiloh (see Chapter 9).

Pope got his chance for greatness when he was moved to the Eastern Theater to take command of a new army, the Army of Virginia, being formed to defend Washington in the wake of McClellan's disappointing Peninsula Campaign. Early on, Pope deluded himself into believing he understood the strategic and tactical situation better than anyone else did. He made bombastic statements and grandiose declarations about how he was going to change things in Virginia. These statements were so obnoxious that he earned the disdain of enemies *and* friends. Pope prompted additional ire by deciding to make war on civilians, a shocking concept at the time, but one that became the centerpiece of Grant's grand strategy of 1864–1865.

As a field commander, Pope made the fatal error of believing his concept of the situation was perfect. Every commander must make certain assumptions about the enemy to plan his campaign. The best generals are always willing to change their assumptions based on subsequent information they receive. Regardless of any other information that discounted his original assessment, Pope believed only what he wanted to believe. For Pope, facing Lee and Jackson, this was a fatal blunder. He was fortunate his army was not entirely destroyed at Second Manassas (see Chapter 13). Pope was hastily transferred to the northwest, where he operated against the Sioux for the rest of the war. He stayed in the army and was able to retire as a major general in 1886.

# P.G.T. Beauregard (1818–1893)

Pierre G.T. Beauregard was a general who would come to know well that all glory is fleeting. A West Point graduate, he won honors during the Mexican-American War, where he was wounded twice in battle. He was one of the first officers to join the new Confederacy, and he found himself commanding South Carolina troops in Charleston Harbor. There he won a deceptively easy victory at Fort Sumter (see Chapter 3) and became the first hero of the new nation. Nicknamed "The Little Napoleon" and "The Little Creole," Beauregard appeared to be destined for great things.

He took command of Confederate forces at Manassas (see Chapter 8) and, after being reinforced by Joseph E. Johnston and his Army of the Valley, won a victory in 1861 in the first major battle of the war. Beauregard displayed limited abilities as a battlefield commander, but shared the spotlight with Johnston, who took overall command of the action. Beauregard soon ran into trouble with Confederate President Jefferson Davis, who disliked the Louisianan's prideful, confident manner. Davis sent him away to the Western Theater as a full general to serve as Albert Sidney Johnston's second-in-command. At Shiloh (see Chapter 9), Beauregard again displayed his limitations as an army commander when he took over for Johnston and made some seriously flawed decisions that led directly to the Confederate army being driven from the field on the second day. After the battle he went on sick leave without Davis's permission. The president took advantage of this minor breach to relieve Beauregard of command in an act of spite that still makes little sense.

Until 1864, Beauregard was the commander of Confederate forces guarding the coastline from South Carolina to Florida. He oversaw the defense of Charleston against Union naval and infantry attacks. Later, he took command of Confederate forces protecting Lee's vulnerable right flank and the strategic supply lines to Richmond and the Army of Northern Virginia. Beauregard did get the best of Ben Butler, trapping his army at Bermuda Hundred (see Chapter 20) after defeating him at Drewry's Bluff (a victory, but no one would ever claim Ben Butler was much of an opponent). With a very limited force, Beauregard managed to contain the initial Union attacks on Petersburg until Lee could reposition his army. It was a brilliant effort and certainly Beauregard's finest moment as a commander. After Lee arrived in Petersburg, Beauregard found himself without a job. He ended up as the commander of the Western Theater, but after Hood's spectacular failure, he essentially had no troops to command. He then served as Joseph E. Johnston's second-in-command in North Carolina until the end of the war. After the war, he gained infamy as the Louisiana lottery supervisor.

# George B. McClellan (1826–1885): Honorable Mention

George B. McClellan was, undoubtedly, the best organizer and manager of military operations in the American army until World War II. But as a battlefield commander, McClellan was completely ineffective. McClellan also had a very high regard for his own destiny and often saw field command as something he had to do to fulfill a greater calling. After winning some minor but highly publicized engagements in western Virginia, he became convinced that he was the man to save the Republic, a notion he never let go of throughout the war. He became known as "The Young Napoleon," and displayed a masterful understanding of politics in Washington.

McClellan almost single-handedly created the Army of the Potomac and then defied anyone to force him into using it for anything other than parades and drills. He was much loved by the soldiers, who called him "Little Mac."

McClellan always had good plans; he just did not have the will or the ability to direct them. Essentially, he hated to see his soldiers killed or hurt. He could not stand to see his beautiful instrument tarnished. He shrunk from battle and physically withdrew from the fields where his men were fighting. Partly because of his reluctance to fight, he tended to believe reports that he was outnumbered. This created a sense of caution that was nearly paralytic. Inevitably, when his plans went poorly, he blamed everyone — the War Department, Lincoln, and Stanton, the secretary of war. During the Antietam campaign (see Chapter 14), he had the opportunity to end the war in the Eastern Theater, but could not overcome his reluctance to bring the army to battle. In the attack, McClellan lacked resolve; in the defense, McClellan looked only for escape. Lee built his reputation on the irresolution of George McClellan.

The man of destiny was relieved from command after Antietam, and he returned to New Jersey, expecting a call to return to command that never came. But a different kind of call came via the Democratic Party in 1864. He became its presidential candidate but had trouble reconciling his desire for victory with the party's plank calling for an end to the war. Despite this, he might have won if not for key Union victories, especially Atlanta, that gave the North hope that the war could be won. He continued to be active in politics, serving as governor of New Jersey from 1878 to 1881.

# Chapter **30**

# The Ten Biggest "Firsts" of the Civil War

The Civil War produced an amazing number of changes in warfare. New weapons and strategy that first appeared during this war are still used by modern armies today. Technology had a great effect on the conduct of the Civil War, and so it still does today. Ever since the Civil War, technology continues to shape the modern battlefield. People think that developments such as hand grenades, land mines, torpedoes, rotating armored gun turrets on ships, submarines, booby traps, and railroad-mounted artillery are relatively recent because they all have been common elements of 20th-century warfare, but they originated in the Civil War. Likewise, amphibious assaults, naval camouflage, repeating rifles, trench warfare, and aerial observation, which are still commonplace on the modern battlefield, first made their appearance on Civil War battlefields.

Given all these developments and many more that occurred during the Civil War, narrowing the list to the ten most important "firsts" is difficult. I apply some criteria to help narrow the focus:

» First, the development must be easily recognizable.

» Second, it must have had a significant effect on the development of warfare in the modern world.

» Third, it must have had a significant effect on the conduct of the Civil War itself.

Based on these three criteria, the following most important "firsts" stand out. They appear in no particular order; they are presented simply for the sake of consideration and discussion.

# The Growing Dominance of the Defense

The *Minié ball*, the conical bullet fired from a rifled musket, was a new innovation on Civil War battlefields. The rifle bullet changed tactics on the battlefield forever. This caused units to seek to build entrenchments and earthworks to protect themselves against rifle fire. As we saw in the campaigns in both the Eastern and Western Theaters in 1864, entrenchments were employed routinely whenever units halted. Attacks against these entrenchments became extremely costly (Spotsylvania, Cold Harbor, Kennesaw Mountain), requiring army commanders to use movement to bypass these defenses. When they could not be bypassed, a siege had to be conducted (Vicksburg, Petersburg, Atlanta). As infantry weapons (and artillery) became even more effective between 1870 and 1914, movement, firepower, and maneuver were decisive. But without movement or maneuver, firepower ruled the battlefield, forcing units to dig earthworks. The French, British, Russian, Austrian-Hungarian, and German troops in 1914 quickly learned the same lessons that Sherman's, Johnston's, Lee's, and Grant's troops learned in 1864.

# Minesweeping: Naval Mines

Known as *torpedoes* during the Civil War, thousands of these new inventions were placed in the channels and waterways of the South's main ports for defense against Union warships. In fact, most of the losses the Union navy experienced in the war were a result of a ship striking one of these torpedoes. This caused the Union navy to develop its own countermeasures to protect its ships from torpedoes. One of the countermeasures that it developed was the *minesweeper* — a ship specifically designed to detect and to neutralize underwater mines. Mining and countermining warfare have been a central part of naval operations ever since.

# Starting Undersea Warfare: The Submarine

The CSS *Hunley* was the first submarine to sink a warship. Little more than an iron boiler about 30 feet long, it was more of a danger to her crew than to the enemy. Eight crewmen powered it by turning a hand crank that rotated the propeller. It floated just below the surface with an officer sticking his head out of an open hatch that stood above the water to guide the vessel. It was intended to tow a mine under the hull of a Union ship guarding Charleston Harbor. The mine would strike the hull and sink the ship. In tests, though, the *Hunley* sank three times, killing most or everyone aboard each time. But the idea of being able to break the Union naval blockade of Charleston was too compelling and too important to abandon. On February 17, 1864, the *Hunley* set out to attack the USS *Housatonic*. Although what exactly happened is still a mystery, the fact remains that the *Hunley* sank the *Housatonic* and the concept of undersea warfare became a critical part of modern naval strategy. Restoration work continues on the submarine at the *Hunley* museum in Charleston.

# Changing Tactics and Moving Quickly: The Railroad

One could argue that the Union won the Civil War because it had better and more efficient rail lines than the Confederacy. Very early in the war, it became obvious that large armies operating across a continent could not be supported or supplied by road only. Railroads could move tons of food, fodder, ammunition, and supplies over long distances, efficiently and quickly. Grant and Sherman in the Western Theater were tied to their lines of supply for most of the war, dependent upon the railroad to sustain their forces. Nathan Bedford Forrest made his name by destroying railroads as fast as the Yankees could repair them. Lee's last retreat was along a rail line — he moved to Appomattox Station in the hopes of receiving food supplies from rail cars he had dispatched earlier. After Sheridan had cut that rail supply line, Lee had no other option but to surrender.

The railroads changed strategy. Troops now could be moved from one theater of war to another rapidly, allowing generals to mass their forces for a decisive blow against the enemy. At Manassas, at Chickamauga, and at Chattanooga, the tide of battle was turned because of the use of rail transportation to bring additional troops to the battlefield. From the Civil War on, no staff ever planned a campaign without studying the rail network of friendly and enemy forces.

# Battling without Bullets: Psychological Warfare

In their famous March to the Sea from Atlanta to Savannah in 1864, the Union armies of William T. Sherman hardly saw an enemy soldier, let alone engaged in any battles. Yet Sherman's campaign is considered one of the decisive events of the Civil War. Why? Modern warfare shows that often you do not need to defeat an enemy army on the battlefield. You can still cripple that army's ability to fight by striking at its will to face you in battle. Today this is called psychological warfare, and it is an important part of any modern general's war plans. Few practiced psychological warfare better than Sherman. He went after the Southern people and their morale. Defenseless against Sherman's troops, Southerners watched as tens of thousands of well-equipped and well-fed, blue-clad soldiers marched across a 60-mile front. Such a sight of raw unrestrained military power was depressing enough, but the people also suffered the cruelty of war directly, losing their homes and property to the invaders. Another equally important psychological effect was on the slaves who witnessed or heard of the mighty army of bluecoats coming to set them free. Slaves declared themselves free with their feet, following the army in a massive throng. The combination of physical destruction, destitution, and collapse of the social and political order was a deathblow to the Confederacy. After civilian morale was crushed, the Confederate army's morale followed, as soldiers deserted in droves to return home and take care of their families. Thus, the Army of Northern Virginia grew steadily smaller, just as if it had been suffering combat losses every day, yet no bullets had been fired and no battles had been fought. The Union victory demonstrated the importance of national will and civilian morale in sustaining a national war effort. From that point on, no general would neglect protecting the home front, while seeking to undermine the morale of his enemy's civilian population.

# Using Air-to-Ground Communication

Today, armies can observe troop movements from hundreds of miles in space. That technology, as breathtaking as it may be, had its origins in the simple act of Union inventors in 1861. Using a balloon, observers were able to ascend several hundred feet into the air to count Confederate troops and locate their disposition. The Union army made use of balloon observation throughout the war. To make reporting easier, a telegraph wire was attached to the basket holding the observer. Thus, a double first: the first aerial observation and the first air-to-ground communication. Although of limited use during the Civil War, the concept of aerial observation in support of military operations was never questioned; it only awaited technology to catch up to make it more useful to the battlefield commander. Now, military aircraft and space platforms provide nations with strategic and tactical military information on potential enemies every day.

# Dominating the Seas: The Ironclad Warship

All modern navies trace their origins to the Civil War ironclad. The battle between the *Monitor* and the *Virginia* in 1862 marked a dramatic end to the age of sail and initiated new navies molded by the twin giants of the industrial age — steam and steel. The U.S. Navy built a number of ironclads to patrol the coast of the Confederacy. Although cramped and overheated, the basic design of the *Monitor*-type ironclad was sound and became the prototype for other armored ships. Soon, all the major powers of Europe were putting armor plate on steamships made of steel. As technology improved, the small ironclads of the Civil War grew, becoming the Dreadnought and the modern battleships of the twentieth century. These ships, employing the rotating steel turret containing large guns first seen on the *Monitor*, would rule the seas until World War II.

# Talking over Wires: The Telegraph

Just before the onset of the war, Congress created the U.S. Army Signal Corps. Initially, both sides employed signal flags and mirrors to relay information to commanders. But this was limited by line of sight and the danger of intercepted messages (both sides used the same signal system, all having been trained in the army prior to the war). But the telegraph quickly came to be the dominant form of communication for the armies. Presidents Lincoln and Davis received the latest news over the telegraph.

By the end of the war, the telegraph had become an indispensable means of communication. General Grant, as commander of all Union armies, used the telegraph to send orders to General Sherman, 800 miles away, while he traveled with the Army of the Potomac. As this army moved, the signal troops laid 200 miles of wire a day to meet the needs of the commanders in the field. Telegraph lines were the primary targets of cavalry raiders of both sides, and Sherman purposely cut off his reliance on telegraph communications to undertake the march to the sea. Today, instantaneous communications including voice and video are an essential part of military operations. Although the technology is more advanced, the principles and process behind today's military communications technology would be familiar to Lee, Grant, or Sherman.

# Increasing Firepower: The Repeating Rifle

Although the dominant weapon of the war was the rifled musket firing the Minié ball, about 400,000 repeating rifles were issued to Civil War units, primarily to Union cavalry units. These weapons had a distinct advantage over muzzle-loading weapons, because they employed a metal cartridge rather than a paper cartridge that essentially had to be disassembled and then reassembled manually by the soldier. The process of loading and firing the rifled musket was time-consuming and often clumsy, requiring extensive drills to get the process down correctly in the stress of battle. But the metal cartridge could be inserted directly into the chamber of the weapon and fired. The spent cartridge was ejected by opening the breech so that the weapon could be reloaded. Some models enabled the soldier to load several cartridges at once and, by use of a lever-cocking mechanism, eliminated manual loading. Soldiers needed little training to master this process, and the repeating rifle gave the individual soldier a significant increase in firepower over an enemy using muzzleloaders.

At Chickamauga, for example, the Union forces of Wilder's "Lightning Brigade," equipped with the seven-shot Spencer repeating rifle, effectively delayed the first Confederate advance because of the volume of fire that a relatively small number of men could direct against infantry units. The 21st Ohio infantry, equipped with a five-shot Colt revolving rifle, helped stop the Confederate assault on Snodgrass Hill. As a regiment, the 21st maintained a volume of fire equal to a division, expending over 43,000 rounds – an astronomical number for any combat unit. This unit's contribution allowed General Thomas to guard the Union retreat, preventing the army's annihilation. Muzzleloaders went away quickly after the Civil War; they were replaced by a variety of rifle designs all employing metal cartridges and rapid-firing reloading mechanisms. Today, all modern armies are equipped with rifles and pistols whose designs directly relate back to the repeating weapons employed in the Civil War.

# Born in the Civil War: The Machine Gun

Both the Union and Confederate armies experimented with primitive *machine guns*, a weapon designed to produce a high volume of fire against attacking infantry. Most of these guns saw only limited service and none of these weapons had any effect on the war itself, but the concept and design came to be perfected late in the war with a weapon known as the *Gatling gun*. The Gatling gun used rifle barrels mounted on a rotating cylinder. As a hand crank rotated the cylinder, the barrels fired and were reloaded sequentially. For the next 40 years, armies all over the world employed the Gatling gun. By the time of the Great War (World War I), lighter, more accurate, and effective machine guns were deployed in all the armies of Europe. The machine gun changed warfare forever as it dominated the terrible battlefields of the Western Front. Indispensable in modern tactical combat, the machine gun had its birth in the Civil War.

# Chapter **31**

# The Ten Biggest "What Ifs" of the Civil War

No one who studies the Civil War or visits a battlefield can help but think "What if?" The question is a valid one to ask, because the Union victory in the Civil War was not a sure thing by any means. To win the war, the Confederacy had to be both lucky and good. Thus, many of these "what ifs" are related to events and outcomes that hurt the Confederate cause. The fate of much of the world's future history was balanced on chance, luck (both good and bad), and circumstance. By taking a look at some of these "what if" scenarios, you can always get a discussion (or even more) started by simply opening a conversation about the Civil War with the question "What if . . ."

The following are topics intended to stimulate discussion, debate, or dispute, depending on your mood. Sometimes it is nice to ask the question and then stand back to watch the fireworks as people get wrapped up in the endless possibilities of what the world would be like if certain events had come out differently than they did.

# What If the Confederates Had Pursued After Manassas (Bull Run)?

The First Battle of Bull Run in July 1861 ended with the defeated Union army falling back in disorder toward the safety of Washington. As officers lost control of their units, the army's retreat turned into a rout (this is a military term for the disintegration of a military organization — every man for himself, in other words). What would have happened if generals Johnston or Beauregard, or later Jefferson Davis when he arrived on the battlefield, had decided to order a general pursuit of the enemy? A good number of Confederate units had not been engaged, and cavalry and artillery were available to chase the enemy into Washington itself. Would the war have ended? Would the Union government have abandoned Washington? Would the Lincoln government sue for peace after such a debacle? Would a Confederate pursuit of the defeated Union army have led to any decisive long-term results? Would the total defeat of the Union army have affected Northern resolve to continue the war?

# What If Grant Had Been Killed at Shiloh?

While rallying his defeated troops during the battle, Grant was nearly seriously wounded or killed by a shell fragment. In 1862, he was a relatively unknown officer. Shiloh almost ended his military career anyway. But what would have happened if Grant had been killed or cashiered from the army in disgrace after Shiloh? Could the Union have won the war without him? Was his strategic brilliance and instinctive grasp of the link between strategy and campaigns essential to victory? Who could have taken his place? Could any other general in the Union army been able to orchestrate the Vicksburg Campaign or the 1864–1865 cross-theater approach to conduct simultaneous campaigns to crush the Confederacy?

# What If Fort Sumter Had Not Been Fired On?

What if Davis had decided that building the Confederacy's military strength and winning friends in Europe were more important than national honor? What if he had called Lincoln's bluff and allowed the Sumter garrison to be resupplied without taking any military action? Sumter would have had little military effect on activities in Charleston anyway. What would Lincoln have done? As a new president, how would he be able to deal with the political fallout? If the U.S. flag had not been fired upon, could Lincoln have relied upon the state governors to supply troops? Would he have had to use force against the Confederate states to coerce them back into the Union — and therefore become the aggressor?

# What If McClellan Had Not Found Lee's Lost Orders?

During the Confederate invasion of Maryland in 1862, Lee's entire campaign plan fell into McClellan's hands by a stroke of incredible luck. The result was the battle of Antietam, where Lee was able to hold on by a combination of heroic acts by his soldiers and the overcaution of McClellan. Nonetheless, the battle was decisive strategically because it allowed Lincoln to issue the Emancipation Proclamation. What would have happened if McClellan had never known of Lee's intentions in this campaign? McClellan was an inept commander who would have given Lee every opportunity to fight the kind of battle he wanted, placing McClellan and the Army of the Potomac in a position where Lee could have gained a decisive victory — and independence? What would the destiny of North America have been if a decisive battlefield victory had led to Confederate independence?

# What If McClellan Had Won Decisively at Antietam?

Technically, McClellan did win the battle at Antietam, but he allowed Lee's army to slip away to fight again. What if McClellan had suddenly realized what was actually happening on the battlefield and ordered a general advance through the center of Lee's lines after the Union breakthrough at Bloody Lane? Would Lee's army have been destroyed in this battle? Would this defeat have ended the war? What kind of peace potentially would have followed in 1862? Would McClellan have become the savior of the republic that he always believed himself to be? What kind of political fortunes would McClellan have reaped as a result of the destruction of the Army of Northern Virginia and Union victory over the Confederacy? Would peace and reunion actually have been easier, and the issue of slavery and its demise been more of a political process of negotiation after the terrible bloodshed of Shiloh, the Seven Days, Second Manassas, and Antietam?

# What If Johnston Had Not Been Wounded at Seven Pines?

The loss of Joseph E. Johnston at the battle of Seven Pines in 1862 forced Confederate President Jefferson Davis to turn to his military advisor, General Robert E. Lee, to take command during this great crisis. McClellan and the Union army were standing before Richmond, the Confederate capital. Lee was known only as the general who had lost western Virginia to the Confederacy a few months earlier. But Lee took command, and the rest is history, as they say. What if Johnston had not been wounded? With Lee relegated to serving in a relatively minor advisory position, what would the Confederate army under Johnston have accomplished? Would Johnston have defended the capital, defeated McClellan, and saved Richmond from capture? What would Johnston have done with Jackson's command? Would McClellan have overwhelmed Johnston's army and taken Richmond, thus ending the war? This, of course, opens the questions we just addressed about a decisive Union victory at Antietam.

# What If Davis Had Adopted a Different Strategy in the West?

Confederate President Jefferson Davis's strategic decision to defend everywhere at once in the Western Theater had disastrous consequences. What if Davis had decided on a more flexible strategy to defend key points vital to the Confederate war effort? What if he had adopted a strategy of an active defense in the west, trading space for time and seeking a decisive battle when Union armies were vulnerable with their long and vulnerable supply lines? What if Confederate strategy in the Western Theater focused on naval power dominating the Mississippi, Cumberland, and Tennessee Rivers to deny Union access to the interior of the South?

# What If Lee Had Won at Gettysburg?

This battle is considered the decisive battle in the Eastern Theater. What if Lee had won this battle on Northern soil? Would Lincoln have appointed a new commander to replace Meade? Where would the Confederate army have gone next? Would the victory at Gettysburg have been too costly for Lee's army to exploit? Would the Lincoln government have been able to survive politically after this defeat? Would this victory have made the difference for the Confederate strategic goal of

European recognition? How would Northern morale have been affected? Could the Confederacy have gained anything from a victory at Gettysburg after experiencing a simultaneous defeat at Vicksburg?

# What If Davis Had Relieved Bragg Earlier in the War?

General Braxton Bragg was a loyal friend of Jefferson Davis. Because of this friendship and because of his antipathy toward Joseph E. Johnston, Davis kept Bragg in command of the Army of Tennessee long after he ceased to be effective. What if Davis had swallowed his pride a bit and put Johnston in charge earlier than he finally did? Could Johnston have turned the fortunes of the army around if he had taken command in 1862 or 1863? Could Johnston have carried out Davis's grand strategic designs for the Western Theater? What if Robert E. Lee had taken command of the Western Theater after the death of Albert Sidney Johnston or after Bragg was relieved of command?

# What If Jackson Had Not Been Lost to Lee and the Army of Northern Virginia?

The team of Robert E. Lee and Thomas Jackson is legendary in American history. Few American military commanders have had such compatibility and innate understanding of each other's intentions and abilities. Lee and Jackson were spectacular. What if Jackson had not been wounded at Chancellorsville? Would the Army of Northern Virginia have been truly unbeatable? Would the outcome of Gettysburg have been different if Jackson had led his corps? Would Lee's battle plans have been different in the 1864 campaign if Jackson had lived? Could Grant have defeated the team of Lee and Jackson? What would Jackson have done after the war — win or lose?

» **Exploring a battlefield to get the most out of your visit**

» **Keeping the proper perspective**

# Chapter **32**

# The Ten+ Best Battlefields of the Civil War and How to Visit Them

The following list of battlefields is not all-inclusive. You can visit literally hundreds more by using any of the methods recommended in Chapter 27. This chapter includes only the major battle sites discussed in this book. Although the battlefields have been categorized by method, this does not imply that you can only see these battlefields via the method recommended. These are simply recommendations — by all means, visit any and all of them by any means you want or can! This chapter is simply a way of acquainting you with various battlefields and offering some suggestions for visiting them according to the methods offered in this book.

It would not be fair to leave you high and dry without some additional guidance and direction on what Civil War battlefields best lend themselves to each method discussed. While every battlefield can be successfully approached using any of the three methods described, this section matches the best method to a major battle-field you may want to visit.

# Best Battlefields by the Mounted Method

Here are the battlefields that you may want to consider seeing using the mounted method:

>> **Gettysburg:** The park's layout enables you to visit without ever leaving your car. The routes are clearly marked, and you can easily drive around the battlefield and see the major sites. You can get a general appreciation for the key events of the three-day battle.

>> **Antietam:** This small battlefield is well laid out for the driver. It is easy to examine key points from the car and get a good appreciation of the flow of the battle. From the car you can gain an appreciation for Lee's dilemma in defending his position.

>> **Chattanooga:** The key points of the Chattanooga siege and the site of Grant's breakout are easily accessed, and a short drive will give the visitor an appreciation for the strength of the Confederate defenses as well as the daunting problems the Union army faced in breaking the siege. A short drive will take you to the Chickamauga battlefield.

>> **Chickamauga:** At one of the first battlefields preserved for visitors, you can drive along the Union defensive line and observe where Longstreet's corps broke through. You can also drive around Snodgrass Hill where George H. Thomas won the name "Rock of Chickamauga."

>> **Murfreesboro:** The battlefield park itself is small, covering the final Union main defensive line, and therefore easy to drive through. You can drive other routes that generally follow Bragg's initial attack and the site of Sheridan's counterattack.

>> **Vicksburg:** A quick drive to this city and its importance to the Confederacy will become immediately apparent. A road follows the main Confederate defensive line around the city. You can examine the earthworks and consider the problems facing the Union in attempting to take the city by storm. Another road follows the Union line to the national cemetery where over 16,000 Union soldiers are buried. A stop at USS *Cairo* is essential.

>> **Petersburg:** Like Vicksburg, the park roads at Petersburg follow a 23-mile route that parallels the siege line with stops at Fort Stedman and the Crater.

>> **Valley Battlefields, 1862 and/or 1864:** You can easily travel the Shenandoah Valley, which features numerous stops at the sites of many battlefields (many of which are not preserved) from both Jackson's campaign of 1862 and Early's campaign of 1864.

# Best Battlefields by the Mounted/Dismounted Method

Following are some battlefields that may lend themselves to either the mounted or dismounted method:

>> **Manassas (First and Second):** Nearly swallowed by development, these two battlefields are best seen through a combination of riding and walking. First Manassas battlefield has several sites to which you can drive. You can easily walk the main battlefield. Second Manassas requires a bit more perseverance, but will reward the visitor with a better appreciation for Jackson's defensive stand and Longstreet's attack.

>> **Fredericksburg:** This site provides a good combination of driving along the Confederate defensive line to view key points and stops to walk over the terrain where thousands of Union soldiers fell in the face of massed Confederate rifle and artillery fire.

>> **Seven Days Battles (1862) and the Campaign of 1864:** If you have your chronology straight, the tour of the Seven Days battlefields and battlefields of 1864 can be very rewarding. The park service has an excellent map that will enable you to travel to the various sites. Some sites are only marked and cannot be visited, but others (such as Cold Harbor, Gaines's Mill, Fort Harrison, Malvern Hill, Drewry's Bluff, and others) are very good for short tours.

>> **Shiloh:** This battlefield, which looks much as it did in 1862, features a good network of roads (most of them coinciding with the original roads), which enable the visitor to stop at the important sites to get a general understanding of the battle. However, to appreciate this battlefield fully, you must walk the fields to understand what fighting in these woods must have been like for the untried, untrained soldiers on both sides.

>> **Bentonville:** This large battlefield site enables a good tour by car and stops for exploration of the well-preserved trench lines. One can readily appreciate Johnston's sound decision for choosing this position to fight.

- » **Chancellorsville:** Another battlefield that enables the visitor to drive through easily, this one begs closer examination by walking and exploring. You can best appreciate the true meaning of the command-and-control problems as well as the difficulties of fighting and maneuvering in these woods by actually walking the trails.

- » **Fort Sumter:** This is the only battle site that you can see solely by the mounted/dismounted method because you must take a boat out to the fort. After you dismount, you can explore the ruins of the fort and get a sense for what Major Anderson felt when he withstood the bombardment. You can also fully appreciate the amazing effort it took for Confederate soldiers and sailors to hold the fort throughout the years of intense bombardment they withstood.

- » **Cedar Creek:** This easily accessible battlefield park provides visitors with a good overview of the 1864 battle and an appreciation for why Early won the first phase of the battle and why he lost the second phase.

# Best Battlefields by the Terrain Walk Method

Any battlefield will reward the dedicated terrain walker. Even the smallest fields reveal much to those who take the time to study the ground in detail. A full day often is not enough for the enthusiast.

- » **Gettysburg:** This is the terrain walker's ultimate effort. There are three days of battle to cover all in one place. Gettysburg has all kinds of hills, valleys, woods, rocks, and open fields to explore — all of them significant. It can take days, even weeks, of walking about to examine every site.

- » **Spotsylvania:** Although you can cover the area in a car, this site is best appreciated at the soldier's level. You must walk the Confederate defensive lines to appreciate their complexity and soundness. You must also view the lines from the Union side and appreciate the courage involved in attacking those defenses during those terrible days in May 1864.

- » **Wilderness:** This is another site where a car will get you to the high points, but until you attempt to explore the Wilderness, you haven't really been on a terrain walk. You will need a topographical map, a compass, and some real cross-country navigation skills. After you are in the woods, you are on your own. You can get lost easily, just as thousands of men did during this confused and brutal battle.

>> **North Anna:** This site provides a rewarding visit for those who want to do some thorough research and map study before they head out. Little is marked, and you have to ask permission from landowners to visit some places, but there is much to see for the trained eye and willing explorer.

>> **New Market:** Probably the best battlefield for the beginner to test out a terrain walk, this is the site of the 1864 battle that ended one part of Grant's three-part strategic offensive against Lee in 1864. It is small and easily accessible. The visitor can walk the field where the Virginia Military Institute cadets charged and examine how well placed the Union defensive position was. You can also get a good appreciation for the importance of artillery placement on a Civil War battlefield.

>> **Sailor's Creek (also known as Sayler's Creek):** This site is a bit out of the way, but it's a good battlefield for the dedicated terrain walker. The battlefield requires some background study, but you get a good appreciation for the power of the Union army at this time and the weakness of the Confederates.

>> **Perryville:** This site is another out-of-the-way battlefield that rewards the dedicated terrain walker. Time spent in preparation for a visit here will pay big dividends. It's a good site to walk to understand the Confederate attack and the Union predicament. Sheridan's often-unappreciated role here is better understood when you are actually walking the ground.

>> **Appomattox:** This site is meant to be walked and appreciated for its symbolism and its larger meaning for the nation. The small village retains its 19th-century character and encourages exploration.

>> **Chickamauga:** Some wonderful opportunities are here to follow specific units across the battlefield or to trace Longstreet's attack to get the Confederate perspective of attacking Snodgrass Hill. The area is very much as it was in 1863, so you can get an appreciation for how difficult command and control was for both Union and Confederate commanders.

>> **Gaines's Mill:** A well-preserved Seven Days battlefield that can be explored easily from the Union and Confederate perspectives. Additional land has recently been acquired that has expanded access to conduct more detailed exploration.

# Index

# X

# Y

# About the Author

**Keith D. Dickson** is Professor Emeritus of Military Studies, National Defense University. Dr. Dickson earned his Ph.D. in American history at the University of Virginia and taught at the Virginia Military Institute. He is a retired Army Special Forces officer. He and his wife Karen live in Virginia Beach, Virginia.

# Dedication

This book is dedicated to my grandfather, Robert E. Dickson. He instilled in me his love for, and interest in, the great saga of the Civil War. This effort is a slight attempt to honor him and to show my thanks for the gift he gave me that has shaped my life.

# Author's Acknowledgements

I acknowledge with great affection and respect the students of the Joint and Advanced War Fighting School who accompanied me on the numerous battlefields we visited. To share my great passion for learning from the past and to touch history with all of you was a great privilege and one of the high points of my professional career.

I also thank my director, Captain Miguel "Boo" Peko, USN (Ret.), for giving me the opportunity to lead these excursions and allowing me free rein to wax both poetic and philosophic as we stood together on hallowed ground.

The Wiley team could not have been more supportive or helpful. It was a very satisfying experience, and I am very grateful for having the opportunity to work on this new edition. My special thanks to Linda Brandon for all her hard work and personal dedication to my success.

## Publisher's Acknowledgments

**Acquisitions Editor:** Elizabeth Stilwell

**Managing Editor:** Michelle Hacker

**Development Editor:** Linda Brandon

**Copy Editor:** Amy Handy

**Technical Editor:** Troy Guthrie

**Production Editor:** Tamilmani Varadharaj

**Cover Image:** © Peter Newark Military Pictures/ Bridgeman Images

# Take dummies with you everywhere you go!

Whether you are excited about e-books, want more from the web, must have your mobile apps, or are swept up in social media, dummies makes everything easier.

**Find us online!**

# Leverage the power

**Dummies** is the global leader in the reference category and one of the most trusted and highly regarded brands in the world. No longer just focused on books, customers now have access to the dummies content they need in the format they want. Together we'll craft a solution that engages your customers, stands out from the competition, and helps you meet your goals.

## Advertising & Sponsorships

Connect with an engaged audience on a powerful multimedia site, and position your message alongside expert how-to content. Dummies.com is a one-stop shop for free, online information and know-how curated by a team of experts.

- Targeted ads
- Video
- Email Marketing
- Microsites
- Sweepstakes sponsorship

**20 MILLION** PAGE VIEWS **EVERY SINGLE MONTH**

**15 MILLION** UNIQUE VISITORS PER MONTH

**43%** OF ALL VISITORS ACCESS THE SITE **VIA THEIR MOBILE DEVICES**

**700,000** NEWSLETTER SUBSCRIPTIONS TO THE INBOXES OF **300,000** UNIQUE INDIVIDUALS EVERY WEEK

# of dummies

## Custom Publishing

Reach a global audience in any language by creating a solution that will differentiate you from competitors, amplify your message, and encourage customers to make a buying decision.

- Apps
- Books
- eBooks
- Video
- Audio
- Webinars

## Brand Licensing & Content

Leverage the strength of the world's most popular reference brand to reach new audiences and channels of distribution.

## For more information, visit dummies.com/biz

# PERSONAL ENRICHMENT

| | | | | | |
|---|---|---|---|---|---|
| **Staying Sharp** | **Facebook** | **Guitar** | **Investing** | **Beekeeping** | **Digital Photography** |
| 9781119187790 | 9781119179030 | 9781119293354 | 9781119293347 | 9781119310068 | 9781119235606 |
| USA $26.00 | USA $21.99 | USA $24.99 | USA $22.99 | USA $22.99 | USA $24.99 |
| CAN $31.99 | CAN $25.99 | CAN $29.99 | CAN $27.99 | CAN $27.99 | CAN $29.99 |
| UK £19.99 | UK £16.99 | UK £17.99 | UK £16.99 | UK £16.99 | UK £17.99 |

| | | | | | |
|---|---|---|---|---|---|
| **Meditation** | **Pregnancy** | **Samsung Galaxy S7** | **iPhone** | **Crocheting** | **Nutrition** |
| 9781119251163 | 9781119235491 | 9781119279952 | 9781119283133 | 9781119287117 | 9781119130246 |
| USA $24.99 | USA $26.99 | USA $24.99 | USA $24.99 | USA $24.99 | USA $22.99 |
| CAN $29.99 | CAN $31.99 | CAN $29.99 | CAN $29.99 | CAN $29.99 | CAN $27.99 |
| UK £17.99 | UK £19.99 | UK £17.99 | UK £17.99 | UK £16.99 | UK £16.99 |

# PROFESSIONAL DEVELOPMENT

| | | | | | | |
|---|---|---|---|---|---|---|
| **Windows 10** | **AutoCAD** | **Excel 2016** | **QuickBooks 2017** | **macOS Sierra** | **LinkedIn** | **Windows 10** |
| 9781119311041 | 9781119255796 | 9781119293439 | 9781119281467 | 9781119280651 | 9781119251132 | 9781119310563 |
| USA $24.99 | USA $39.99 | USA $26.99 | USA $26.99 | USA $29.99 | USA $24.99 | USA $34.00 |
| CAN $29.99 | CAN $47.99 | CAN $31.99 | CAN $31.99 | CAN $35.99 | CAN $29.99 | CAN $41.99 |
| UK £17.99 | UK £27.99 | UK £19.99 | UK £19.99 | UK £21.99 | UK £17.99 | UK £24.99 |

| | | | | | | |
|---|---|---|---|---|---|---|
| **SharePoint 2016** | **Fundamental Analysis** | **Networking** | **Office 2016** | **Office 365** | **Salesforce.com** | **Coding** |
| 9781119181705 | 9781119263593 | 9781119257769 | 9781119293477 | 9781119265313 | 9781119239314 | 9781119293323 |
| USA $29.99 | USA $26.99 | USA $29.99 | USA $26.99 | USA $24.99 | USA $29.99 | USA $29.99 |
| CAN $35.99 | CAN $31.99 | CAN $35.99 | CAN $31.99 | CAN $29.99 | CAN $35.99 | CAN $35.99 |
| UK £21.99 | UK £19.99 | UK £21.99 | UK £19.99 | UK £17.99 | UK £21.99 | UK £21.99 |

**dummies.com**

**dummies®**
A Wiley Brand

# Learning Made Easy

## ACADEMIC

9781119293576
USA $19.99
CAN $23.99
UK £15.99

9781119293637
USA $19.99
CAN $23.99
UK £15.99

9781119293491
USA $19.99
CAN $23.99
UK £15.99

9781119293460
USA $19.99
CAN $23.99
UK £15.99

9781119293590
USA $19.99
CAN $23.99
UK £15.99

9781119215844
USA $26.99
CAN $31.99
UK £19.99

9781119293378
USA $22.99
CAN $27.99
UK £16.99

9781119293521
USA $19.99
CAN $23.99
UK £15.99

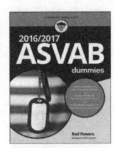

9781119239178
USA $18.99
CAN $22.99
UK £14.99

9781119263883
USA $26.99
CAN $31.99
UK £19.99

## Available Everywhere Books Are Sold

**dummies.com**

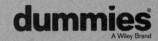

**dummies®**
A Wiley Brand

# Small books for big imaginations

### GETTING STARTED WITH Coding
Get Creative with Code!

Camille McCue, PhD

9781119177173
USA $9.99
CAN $9.99
UK £8.99

### MODDING Minecraft™
Build Your Own Minecraft Mods!

Sarah Guthals, PhD
Stephen Foster, PhD
Lindsay Handley, PhD

9781119177272
USA $9.99
CAN $9.99
UK £8.99

### MAKING YouTube® VIDEOS
Star in Your Own Video!

Nick Willoughby

9781119177241
USA $9.99
CAN $9.99
UK £8.99

### DESIGNING Digital Games
Create Games with Scratch™!

Derek Breen

9781119177210
USA $9.99
CAN $9.99
UK £8.99

### GETTING STARTED WITH Raspberry Pi®
Program Your Raspberry Pi!

Richard Wentk

9781119262657
USA $9.99
CAN $9.99
UK £6.99

### EXPERIMENTING WITH Science
Think, Test, and Learn!

9781119291336
USA $9.99
CAN $9.99
UK £6.99

### CREATING Digital Animations
Animate Stories with Scratch™!

Derek Breen

9781119233527
USA $9.99
CAN $9.99
UK £6.99

### GETTING STARTED WITH Engineering
Think Like an Engineer!

9781119291220
USA $9.99
CAN $9.99
UK £6.99

### WRITING Computer Code
Learn the Language of Computers!

Chris Minnick and Eva Holland

9781119177302
USA $9.99
CAN $9.99
UK £8.99

## Unleash Their Creativity

**dummies.com**

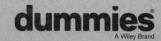

dummies®
A Wiley Brand